Cut Loose

Cut Loose

Jobless and Hopeless in an Unfair Economy

Victor Tan Chen

UNIVERSITY OF CALIFORNIA PRESS

University of California Press, one of the most
distinguished university presses in the United States,
enriches lives around the world by advancing scholarship
in the humanities, social sciences, and natural sciences. Its
activities are supported by the UC Press Foundation and
by philanthropic contributions from individuals and
institutions. For more information, visit www.ucpress.edu.

University of California Press
Oakland, California

Library of Congress Cataloging-in-Publication Data

Chen, Victor Tan, 1976- author.
  Cut loose : jobless and hopeless in an unfair economy /
Victor Tan Chen.
    pages cm
  Includes bibliographical references and index.
  ISBN 978-0-520-28300-8 (cloth : alk. paper) — ISBN
0-520-28300-7 (cloth : alk. paper) — ISBN 978-0-520-
28301-5 (pbk. : alk. paper) — ISBN 0-520-28301-5
(pbk. : alk. paper) — ISBN 978-0-520-95885-2 (ebook)
— ISBN 0-520-95885-3 (ebook)
    1. Unemployed—United States.   2. Unemployed—
Canada.   3. Automobile industry workers—United
States—Case studies.   4. Automobile industry
workers—Canada—Case studies.   5. United States—
Economic conditions.   6. Canada—Economic
conditions.   7. United States—Social conditions.
8. Canada—Social conditions.   I. Title.
  HD5724.C4896   2015
  331.13′70973—dc23

                                        2014047160

24   23   22   21   20   19   18   17   16   15
10   9   8   7   6   5   4   3   2   1

For Elijah and Micah.
May you know a world of grace.

THE SCHOFIELD KID. Yeah, well, I guess they had it coming.

WILL MUNNY. We all have it coming, kid.

—*Unforgiven* (1992)

Contents

Acknowledgments

This book would not have been possible without the cooperation of the former autoworkers I interviewed. I greatly appreciate the thoughtfulness of their perspectives and the kindness with which they welcomed me into their homes and lives.

Reading the work of William Julius Wilson convinced me to become a sociologist. His constant encouragement helped me pull through my fallow periods. The idea for the book emerged out of my conversations with Katherine Newman. Her eloquent and engaged scholarship was the model for the kind of book I sought to write here. Neil Fligstein humbled me with his kindness throughout, and I am grateful to him and Heather Haveman for their wonderful feedback and support. Bruce Western provided spot-on critiques and suggestions, besides lifting my spirits with his cheerful and down-to-earth attitude.

I will always be grateful to Naomi Schneider for believing in this book. Her advice has made it much better. I am indebted to Howard Kimeldorf, Vicki Smith, Jennifer Lee, and the anonymous reviewer at the University of California Press, who provided all I could ask for in terms of insightful, constructive, and encouraging feedback, and pushed me collegially to think of my work in new and important ways. Ally Power was remarkably helpful throughout the editorial process. Roy Sablosky did a superlative job copyediting the manuscript. My thanks as well for the exceptional assistance of Leslie Davisson, Francisco Reinking, and Christopher Lura.

I owe a special debt to the innovative scholarship of Dan Zuberi. He and my other teachers, Gwendolyn Dordick and Martin Whyte, provided terrific advice. I also want to thank Lisa Adams, Paul Attewell, Steven Attewell, Keith Banting, Elaine Bernard, James Biles, Ramón Castellblanch, Jennifer Choo, Julia Chuang, Matt Desmond, Cyrus Dioun, Joshua Freeman, Eric Giannella, Pat Hastings, Jim Lincoln, Helen Marrow, John Levi Martin, Keith Neuman, Paul Osterman, Leslie Paik, Megan Peppel, Maritsa Poros, James Quane, Danny Schneider, Jeremy Schulz, Ofer Sharone, Debbie Siegelbaum, Susan Silbey, Sandra Smith, Pamela Smock, Margaret Somers, George Steinmetz, Reed Stevens, Louis Uchitelle, Andrew Valls, Natasha Warikoo, Frederick Wherry, Yu Xie, and Alford Young for their thoughtful suggestions.

This book would not exist without the support of the American Sociological Association and the National Science Foundation. I am grateful for their postdoctoral fellowship. My deepest thanks go to the Harvard Joblessness and Urban Poverty Research Program, whose generous grant made my fieldwork possible. I greatly appreciate the resources provided by, at Harvard, the Weatherhead Center for International Affairs, Multidisciplinary Program in Inequality and Social Policy (funded by NSF Integrative Graduate Education and Research Traineeship grant no. 9870661), and Graduate Society; and, at Berkeley, the Institute for Research on Labor and Employment (IRLE), the Center for Culture, Organizations, and Politics, and the Canadian Studies Program. I would like to personally thank Patricia White at the National Science Foundation; Sally Hillsman and Jean Shin at the American Sociological Association; Pamela Metz, Jessica Matteson, Kathryn Edin, and Katrin Kriz at Harvard Sociology and Social Policy; Berkeley Sociology, especially Tamar Young; Hadidjah Rivera, Myra Armstrong, and Margaret Olney at the IRLE; and Irene Bloemraad and Rita Ross at the Berkeley Canadian Studies Program. At Virginia Commonwealth University, my new academic home, a number of people—Jennifer Johnson, Julie Honnold, David Croteau, Jim Coleman, Alison Baski, Rob Tombes, and my other amazing colleagues in the sociology department—gave me a final push of encouragement and resources to finish the book. I also want to thank the folks at *In The Fray* magazine, my journalistic home, especially fellow veterans Aimee Walker and Liz Yuan.

In Michigan and Ontario, several people were amazingly generous in helping get my project off the ground: Linda Ewing, Rick Isaascson, John Byers, Bob Mitchell, and Frank Grace Jr. of the UAW; and Sanja Maric, Tammy Anger, Candy Eagen, Tim Stewart, Tony Masciotra, and

Kimberly Arquette of the CAW. I also would like to thank the many individuals who shared their insights with me or helped in other ways, including Rich Boyer, Amy Bromsen, Ray Cassabon, Bill Costie, Dave Crosswell, Maureen Curtis, Richard Feldman, Amanda Good, Harvey Hawkins Jr., General Holiefield, Al Iacobelli, Grace Lee Boggs, Lon Lleshaj, Minsu Longiaru, Daniel Luria, Darlene Malcolm, Rick McHugh, Nate Martin, Keith Mickens, Lynn Minick, Marion Overholt, Bill Parker, Joseph Peters, Michael Pizzimenti, Vince Precopio, Laurell Ritchie, Carol Roy, Dimitrios Sabalis, Diane Soucie, John Stallings, Jim Stanford, Cary Stewart, Mark Van, Mike Vince, LaChandra White, Michael Wilson, and Sheila Wisdom. My thanks as well to Lourens Broersma, Dorothy Sue Cobble, Barry Eidlin, Brian Halpin, Mark Granovetter, Dwaine Plaza, and Cristobal Young.

During the writing of this book, Katherine Chen, Sally Cheriel, Angie Chuang, Liu-hsiung and Pat Chuang, David Fisher, Mallory Floyd, Royce Hall, David Harding, John Ho, Yul Kang, Bob Keeler, Randy Klein, Ellen Lee, Ken Lee, Tom Lee, Frank McNamara, Darius Mehri, Hannah Mowat, Steve Newey, Alexander Nguyen, DooJin Paik, Nicole Phillips, Víctor Ramos, Wendy Roth, Keith Rushing, Jordan Schreiber, Rose Tantraphol, Audrey Thomas, Van Tran, Honza Vihan, Eddie Walker, and Gwen Young were especially strong sources of moral and practical support, and I can't fully express how grateful I am to them. Tony Sipp, once my teacher and now my friend, was big-hearted in his encouragement and feedback, as usual. Thanks as well to Jack Womack for helping me think through my ideas over drinks at Charlie's Kitchen. Finally and most importantly, I would like to thank my family for their unwavering love and support. My parents, Chu-Chen and Larry, and my brother, Vincent, lovingly taught me the ideals central to this book: merit and equality, fraternity and grace. My wonderful wife Emi and my two sons Elijah and Micah have given me a reason do this work, and to be hopeful about what lies ahead.

CHAPTER I

They Had It Coming

"You all remember," said the Controller, in his strong deep
voice, "you all remember, I suppose, that beautiful and
inspired saying of Our Ford's: History is bunk. History," he
repeated slowly, "is bunk."

—Aldous Huxley, *Brave New World*

John Hope lost his job in 2009. For fourteen years he had worked at a
car plant near Detroit, heaving truck bumpers onto the practiced balance of his lean, muscled arms and machine-polishing away the wounds
in the rough steel, readying them for immersion in a chemical bath that
would gild each piece with a thin layer of luminous chrome. It was a
work of magic, conjured up in a foul, fume-drenched cavern, an industrial alchemy that transformed masses of cheap base metals into things
of beauty and value.

John, fifty-five, excelled at the work. Every day on the job meant
handling metal and machinery that could, with a moment's indecision,
crush or maim him. He took pride in the strength required to hold the
bumpers without tipping over, and the skill needed to buff each piece
precisely, so that every hairline nick or abrasion disappeared, the chemical sheen wrapped perfectly across the smooth steel, and the bumpers
arrived at the end of the line looking like lustrous silver jewelry. "If I
ain't doing it good, you're going to lose the money," notes John in his
Alabama drawl.

His Southern roots linger in that whirling, excitable, workingman's
voice, but his job—and the pride, status, and paycheck that came with
it—long ago separated him from a personal history of vicious rural poverty. Deserted by young parents when he was just a baby, raised by a
grandmother who had to abandon him about a decade later when she
went blind, John learned to fend for himself. For a time he and his older

brother slept in vacant houses and cast-aside cars, on porches and forest floors.

As a teen John headed down to Florida and laid pipe. Then the lure of Detroit's auto plants, with their union-won wages, took hold of his imagination. John followed a cousin up there in the seventies, as the industry was marching unwittingly into the decade's oil shocks and a first brush with foreign-made, fuel-efficient cars.

After a stint doing construction, John worked in the chrome-plating industry. For a time John made good money doing piecework, but soon the factories started installing huge machines to polish their bumpers, relegating humans to the leftover work of burnishing imperfections. "A man might run one hundred bumpers a day, but this automatic did a thousand or so a day," John notes. "Automatic takes all the money out." At least for the workers, it did; the company slipped the money saved into its pockets—before competition drove those profits lower, too. That was the way the market worked.

John took a job at a plant in Highland Park, a small municipality surrounded on all sides by Detroit. The United Auto Workers, the feared union that Walter Reuther had built into a fortress of labor in the early half of the twentieth century, represented the workers there. For over a decade John saw his income rise steadily—to $50,000 a year, overtime included, for forty-five to fifty hours of work a week. It was enough to support his family of four, enough to buy a red-brick ranch house in the city, enough to give his daughter and son video games, clothes, and other trappings of a middle-class American childhood. It was enough for John to look back and feel pride in what he—an abandoned child, a once-homeless boy, son of the dirt-poor South—had accomplished.

Then the Great Recession hit. On Wall Street, years of heedless risk-taking wreaked collateral damage on industries and households suddenly cut off from credit and income. Governments bailed out banks and other financial giants. In Detroit, years of neglect of quality and product lines brought about a similar reckoning for General Motors, Ford, and Chrysler. Sales of their gas-guzzling cars dropped to record lows, forcing two of the once–Big Three to come begging for government help, too, and all three to shed workers and plants. As America's automakers fell, the damage spread to the feeder plants that supplied them—and that, thanks to now well-developed processes of outsourcing, actually employed twice as many people.[1]

The economic ripples sank many feeder plants, including John's. First, production stalled. John was laid off for the summer. His family's water heater died around then, too, so for a time they boiled water for baths, as John didn't have cash on hand for a replacement. Eventually he was called back. But shortly afterward, his company decided to ship all the work to one of its larger factories, to cut costs. More than a hundred workers were terminated, John included.

Perhaps he should have seen the end coming. For years now, the economy had moved away from chrome, away from factory jobs, away from the manual labor he knew. Polishing, too, had been dying the death of so many proud crafts, the victim of a mercurial consumer market that, for better or worse, fancied cheap, easy-to-replace plastic. But John knew he was a good worker. "By God, I never was a problem for nobody," he says. "I treat everybody nice and I work hard. I never had a criminal record. I never been in trouble. . . . That makes me a better man." With his work ethic and skill, John thought there would be a place for him in a big company. He was wrong.

Now it is the middle of winter, and John is feeling the loss of income hard. He draws $774 every other week from unemployment, but his partner Christina is a stay-at-home mom, so those checks alone must support both of them and their two kids. Having already been sucker-punched by last year's layoff, they have used up their savings and are now three months behind on their mortgage. When I visit them on a frigid day in January, two stove burners have been left fired up, providing heat. The furnace is shut off because John doesn't have $1,000 to repair it.

But his family is not on food stamps or welfare, he points out. They have never gone bankrupt—yet. If he could just find a job, everything would turn out all right, John declares. All these problems would retreat like bad dreams. "You're used to working, and getting what you want," he says. "When you're not working, it's like being in jail, but you have to get your own food." He slaps his knee and shrieks with laughter. It is the way he deals with adversity—with a smile and a devil-may-care quip. Ask him how he copes, and he will flash a wide grin. "I feel good. I got a great sense of humor." Ask him about his job search and he'll say things will work out. "As long as you believe, you're going to be all right," John says, with his idiosyncratic penchant for referring to himself—whenever his frame of mind turns serious—in the second person. "You got to believe. You got to be happy."

To a point, this works for John. But as the conversation goes on, the certainty starts to unravel, the defensive smiles recede. "I'll be back to work soon," he insists—but then adds, after a pause: "It can be stressful."

He scours the Sunday paper for job listings. He calls around and visits factories but has yet to find a promising lead.

John starts to talk about the last vacation he took, seven years ago. He went down to Birmingham to see his mother for the first time since he was eleven months old. John stayed with her for a week. He has not seen her since. "I ain't used to her," he says. As for the grandmother who raised him, she died a decade ago. His father died five years ago. All his good friends worked at the plant—and now that job is gone, too. "When you work fourteen years, them are all the friends you got. A bunch of guys with nowhere else to go."

The job was more than a job. "To me it's real bad," he says slowly, forcing out each syllable, "because the thing about my job—man, it makes me think—my job was like my mother and father to me." Quietly, John starts to sob. He wipes the tears on the denim collar of his button-down shirt, rubs his eyes gently with his fingers. "It's all I had, you know," he goes on. "I worked hard because I had no mother and father. I was cut loose. I hate to think about them. . . . When you growing up young, your mother and father, they take care of you. And I ain't never had that. . . . All my life I depended on my job as my mother and father. If I could only make it every day, I know I'm all right."

As hard as he worked, as loyal as he was to his corporate parent, John was still let go. "When you used to working at a place, you thinking you got you a job," he says. But times have changed. For workers like him, there is no more security, no more loyalty—no more forgiveness of error. "You can't make no mistakes," he says. "You got to do everything perfect. You can't get into trouble. You can't do nothing. You got nobody to run to."

His employer's betrayal has wounded him, though John tries not to show it. He blames himself for not working harder. He blames the union for not caring enough for merit and diligence. But he never really blames the company. They were just doing what made business sense, and what would be the use of anger or regret? "You move from that day on to the next day. I can't look back at how much money I made, or what I did, or what jobs I had. I got to thank God I'm alive." After all, he did well, for a time. He supported a family and bought a home on those factory wages. Now he needs to look to the next destination, holding fast to the commonsense creed that has kept him going all these years: *Stay happy. Keep a smile on your face. Keep your head up.* The words are his Hail Mary, a Panglossian prayer to push down deep the motley anxieties and stresses of his new, uncertain life. "That's just the thing that makes to kill you inside—the worry. I had fun, I made money, and like I say I'm going to look for me another good job."

He pauses, lost in thought. "I'm an old man now," he adds, softly.

. . .

When the world's financial markets collapsed in 2008, millions of workers lost their jobs. In the months that followed, the unemployment rate hit peaks of 10 percent in the United States and 8.7 percent in Canada. In Michigan, the rustiest link of America's long-battered Rust Belt, unemployment rose to over 13 percent, the highest in the country. At the height of the economic crisis, fifteen million Americans and 1.5 million Canadians were out of work. Four in ten Americans experienced long-term unemployment—a spell of joblessness longer than six months.[2] That figure was double the share in previous modern U.S. recessions. So many people were out of work for so long that government bureaucrats had to bump up the maximum length of unemployment that job seekers could disclose on surveys—from two years to five.

As devastating as it was, the recession only accelerated long-standing trends. The past four decades have seen the erosion of key institutions—ranging from labor unions to the two-parent family—that have historically helped many households prosper, especially the less than well-to-do.[3] While ordinary families have struggled, inequality has climbed—in America, to heights not seen at least since the early part of the last century, with the top 10 percent of earners taking in half the country's income, and the wealthiest 10 percent owning three-quarters of its wealth.[4] Even though the economy has grown, middle-class households still have less income than they did at the turn of the century. Though significantly lower, income inequality in Canada has also increased. The gap between the pay of CEOs and their workers narrowed temporarily during the recession, but it has steadily risen in both countries over the years—in the United States, from a 20-to-1 ratio in 1965 to just shy of a 300-to-1 ratio in 2013.[5]

At the same time, the job market has become more uncertain, for office workers as well as factory workers. Just as they have invested incessantly in manufacturing plants, office machines, and other forms of physical capital, companies have increasingly sought out workers with the kinds of human capital—skill, intelligence, flexibility, creativity, initiative—that contribute noticeably to the firm's bottom line. Less fortunate workers now scramble to get hours on the clock or to turn their temp jobs into permanent ones. Technological progress and cross-border competition have wiped out many of the good jobs they once held. Expectations have, in turn, changed profoundly: from how long employees stay with one firm, to how much their retirement depends on rolling the dice in the stock market. These changes have rewarded those able to deal gracefully with greater risk. Yet, they have also opened wide the divide that already existed between more and less advantaged workers.[6]

When the economy was doing well, the consequences of these trends were not obvious. The last recession, in 2001, was mild and short. Then came the worst economic dislocation since the Great Depression. Families suddenly found themselves vulnerable, cut off from the credit that had masked their feeble growth of income. Workers who lost good jobs struggled to find new ones, lacking the skills and experience now in demand in a trimmed-down economy that had quickly learned to do more with less.

Years after the recession officially ended, the American economy continues its slow-burn recovery. While GM and Chrysler have paid back their government loans and started making money again, the auto industry and the broader manufacturing sector continue to employ hundreds of thousands fewer people than they did before the recession.[7] Nationally, the unemployment rate has slid downward and the labor market has added jobs, but some of those laid off have simply stopped looking for work. Even though a third of the country's nine million unemployed have been out of work for six months or more, federal and state governments have already rolled back the time limits for unemployment benefits. In Canada as well, the amount of time that workers there are typically out of work remains high.[8]

In this book, I argue that unemployment has become a more dangerous proposition for working families, thanks to rising inequality and uncertainty and a harsh culture of judgment. I study the long-term unemployed, the forgotten stepchildren of a market economy that has, over several decades, transformed the world in many ways for the better. I compare America and Canada, two sibling countries that help us understand the ways that small but significant differences in policies and culture matter for those out of work. I focus on well-off blue-collar workers, who today straddle the divide between a faltering middle class and an impoverished working class, exemplifying some of the trends that affect them both. And I profile former autoworkers at plants in the heart of North America's auto industry, a group that perhaps more than any other symbolized the economic might and egalitarian prosperity of the world's postwar industrial workshop.

Major studies written about the changing character of the working class have drawn a rich portrait across the decades: their advances and setbacks, their pride and prejudices.[9] My book sets itself apart in several ways. To put it simply, I focus on today's long-term unemployed, giving us a window into the lives of these luckless men and women amid a major economic crisis that led to massive layoffs and, at one point, faced the world with the possibility of utter market collapse. In a comprehensive and detailed fashion, this book also describes the impact of national policies and a host of other factors—institutions like the labor market and family, identities like gender and race—on the well-being and prospects of ordinary workers running to keep up with a quickly changing world.

More specifically, this book makes five contributions to our understanding of unemployment, inequality, and social policies. First, I argue that long-standing economic, political, and technological trends have transformed the labor market in ways that have devastated the job prospects and security of ordinary workers. For this group, getting a *good* job with decent pay, benefits, and working conditions increasingly requires education and other markers of human capital, as well as the cultivation of certain social skills that fall under the category of cultural capital.[10] Amid rapid technological change and an accelerating capital race, hard work—the key to the American Dream—is no longer enough to secure a good job, as the struggles of my workers show. The expanding and tightening criteria for success demand both a strong work ethic *and* proven ability, making the job prospects of the long-term unemployed much worse. At the same time, today's labor market is not a true meritocracy—that is, a system in which people advance based solely on their ability and achievement. It is what I call a *stunted meritocracy*. At the labor market's topmost tiers, as other scholars have noted, elite workers continue to band together to block off their professions from competition, win tax breaks and favorable regulations, pass down advantages to their families, and find other ways to manipulate the market and thus keep themselves, and their children, employed and well compensated.[11]

Second, my research teases out how and why social policies matter to the unemployed, in part by comparing the impact of policies on either side of the U.S.–Canadian border. The common perception—in America at least—is that Canada is a socialist paradise/hell, the country where hippies go when they're fed up with hegemony, a land of unrepentant liberalism that boasts universal health care and "conservative" politicians who behave more like the left-of-center Democrats south-side. In his classic comparative study of the two countries, sociologist Seymour Martin Lipset described a "continental divide" of culture and policy, with America a bastion of individualism and libertarian policy, and Canada decidedly less so.[12] Among other things, Canadians have long favored a greater role for government in regulating the economy and tamping down inequalities. The United States has historically been less generous in helping its less advantaged workers and families, most obviously in its unwillingness to adopt Canada's model of universal health coverage, where the government pays the costs of care. While the American labor movement once had more reach than its Canadian counterpart, the situation reversed in the 1960s with the rise of an influential political organization, the New Democratic Party, that championed the interests of Canada's workers. In spite of all the ground it has lost in recent years, organized labor there remains relatively stronger, thanks in part to government policies that make it much easier to form a union and get it recognized.

Beyond the simple stereotype, of course, in other ways the two countries are quite alike. Canada, for instance, stands closer to America than to Europe in the scope of its social safety net and the workings of its economy. However, recent scholarship continues to emphasize key differences between the two countries and how they matter in real and profound ways. For instance, pioneering research by sociologist Dan Zuberi on the working poor in the United States and Canada (which inspired this book) suggests that policy continues to play a significant role in ameliorating inequalities up north, even in the face of seemingly inexorable forces like globalization.[13]

In line with this view, I started my research believing that the historically stronger social safety net in Canada would ease the hardship of the unemployed in a much more vigorous way, as it did for the working-poor families Zuberi studied. Surprisingly, the results were mixed. Because the Canadian government has pulled back its worker-friendly policies in recent years, even as America offered emergency help to the recession's unemployed millions, the expected Canadian policy advantage did not appear in all areas, and certainly not to the extent I had expected. I explain in concrete terms why this is so. That said, one key way that Canada's social safety net did give substantial help to my workers there was by lifting the incomes of lone-parent families. Of all the families I got to know, on both sides of the border, unemployment hit the single parents the hardest, a hint of the confluence of disruptive trends washing over much of society—and yet swamping the working class. Declining rates of marriage and rising numbers of children born out of wedlock, alongside growing risk and a dwindling selection of good jobs, meant that these vulnerable workers swiftly fell into desperate circumstances once they lost their jobs. Targeted policies in Canada, though, helped ease that suffering.

Nonetheless, the third point that this book makes is that crafting good policies is not enough. They also need to be skillfully implemented. Throughout the book, I describe the experiences of the long-term unemployed across a wide range of interacting settings: within their families and relationships, in their dealings with social service agencies and hospitals and schools, and in their searches for good jobs to replace those they had lost. This more complete picture of the lives of my workers allows me to show in concrete detail how policies are experienced on the ground. Benefit levels and eligibility thresholds are not the only things that matter, as their stories make clear. Sluggish, impersonal, and inaccessible bureaucracies weakened the effectiveness of various kinds of assistance in important ways. More broadly, I find that institutions of government, unions, and corporations failed workers on both sides of the border, providing little but bandages for the intractable problems they faced. Whenever unemployment checks got delayed and training programs ran out of funds, bureaucratic inaction became real to my workers in painful ways. Yet their hapless situation also suggests that inadequate implementation matters in our daily lives in ways that we, the gainfully employed, may seldom consider: in the audit we may or may not get during tax time, in the long lines to get our cars titled or benefits secured, in the fine print we may sign without a clue, in the union dues we pay with little apparent return—or in the union we never get to join, because of the toothless enforcement of government regulations.

Fourth, the book gets into the heads of the long-term unemployed, giving them the chance to talk honestly and openly about how they make sense of their new circumstances. As a sociologist, I focus on the *social* effects of the economic downturn, the ways that unemployment affects individuals not just in terms of the sizes of their bank accounts and mortgages but also in their day-to-day lives—as members of households and communities, as individuals with a sense of their own identity and self-worth. As they struggled to piece together new careers, my workers dealt with the anxiety of an uncertain and viciously competitive job market, the hurt of relationships tested—and sometimes broken—by crisis, and the shame of an unemployed and unengaged life that, in their desperation, might not seem worth living. Some of my men, once proud of their contributions to a shared bank account, saw their relationships unravel after they lost their jobs. For their partners, romance without finance quickly became a nuisance.[14] That said, in spite of all the rhetoric about the economic chasm yawning before today's male workers, the quarter of my respondents who were women also coped badly with long-term unemployment.[15] Among other things, single women hustling to survive felt the need to turn to less-than-desirable men in order to slow down their economic free fall.

More broadly, society's attitudes about success and fairness shaped the sense of worth and deservingness that my workers clung to, in fear of what was to come. Building on seminal work by other scholars, I examine how the dominant culture of individualism, self-reliance, and critical judgment influences even unionized blue-collar workers—a group that has long championed collective strategies and egalitarian ends. Especially in the United States, my autoworkers responded to long-term unemployment in an individualistic fashion. As their unemployment deepened, they came to the pragmatic and rational view that they needed to rely on themselves. This outlook was, in turn, reinforced by what I call *meritocratic morality*—an up-by-the-bootstraps philosophy long linked to the American Dream but now quite prevalent elsewhere as well. With its belief that anyone can succeed based on their own efforts and abilities, meritocratic morality channels the anger and disenchantment of the unemployed into a particular narrative, one that deepens feelings of shame, criticizes government and unions for their alleged inefficiency and unfairness, and defends corporations as creators of growth and jobs. While this attitude remains stronger among other classes of workers, some of the former autoworkers I talked to had adopted portions of it to explain what happened to them, and most felt the need to defend themselves against its wounding judgments.[16]

Many of us take for granted that meritocracy is a good thing. And certainly it has very positive consequences for both individuals and society. But when taken to an extreme, I argue, it leads to the judgment of less successful people as lazy, uneducated, and incompetent.[17] For the jobless, it also feeds a poisonous self-blame.

The book's final contribution is to point us toward one possible, if partial, solution to this problem. At the end of this book I make an original case for not just the social policies to improve the prospects of ordinary workers, but also a kind of political organizing devoted to bringing about a less judgmental and materialistic ethos in society. My argument is that efforts to level the playing field or even reduce inequality more directly can only go so far, because egalitarianism ultimately embraces many of the same tenets of materialism and economic conflict that meritocracy does. It, too, is limited by a fundamentally zero-sum viewpoint, which believes that society's scarce resources must be apportioned according to an arbitrary measure of social justice—as opposed to an arbitrary measure of merit. I argue that we must go beyond these two narrow moral understandings and rethink how our society views and treats the people whom the labor market inevitably, and perhaps increasingly, will discard. What I call a *morality of grace* is an attempt, both pragmatic and idealistic, to ease some of the sting of failure and yet also prevent the kind of class warfare that leaves all bloodied and embittered.[18]

. . .

I began planning my research in the early days of the recession, when financial institutions were toppling and markets roiling, caught in a downward spiral of unbounded panic and uncertainty. With so many out of work, I wanted to look across the Detroit River to see how policy differences mattered for the long-term unemployed. To do this, I took unemployed autoworkers who did the same job at similar plants—with the chief difference being the country they lived in—and compared how they and their families fared during the crisis years of 2009 and 2010. My workers lived in the Detroit and Windsor metro areas, on the two sides of the U.S.–Canadian border. They came from the Chrysler engine plants in Detroit and Trenton, Michigan, paired with the Ford engine plants in Windsor; and the Chrome Craft plating plants in Highland Park, Michigan, paired with the Chromeshield plating plants in Windsor. All were minutes from Detroit, and the plating plants were all owned by Flex-N-Gate, an American firm that supplies the Big Three (and whose owner, Shahid Khan, also owns the Jacksonville Jaguars NFL football team). When they worked, the Americans were members of the UAW, and the Canadians were members of the Canadian Auto Workers, which had been part of the UAW until it split off in 1984.

All in all, I interviewed seventy-one recently or currently unemployed workers. Half of my interviewees were jobless and looking for work. A quarter had gone back to school, and a half-dozen had left the labor market for other reasons. Several had found full-time work—though all of them in positions that paid much less than the ones they had left— and several had part-time jobs but were looking for something better. In addition to interviewing these workers, I observed their families and communities, talked with local experts, and analyzed union and company documents, assembling a detailed portrait of unemployment and economic distress during the Great Recession.

Some readers may wonder why I chose to focus on autoworkers. First, more than perhaps any other group, the autoworker symbolizes an egalitarian past that has largely disappeared. The consequences of that loss are, I argue in this book, profound. In the boom years that followed World War II, an era of powerful unions and gated economies, autoworkers led the way in winning good wages for ordinary workers. Indeed, the rapid growth of standards of living across the last century arguably had its roots in the car industry, from Henry Ford's heralded decision to pay his laborers $5 a day—doubling the wage of the average worker—to the legendary sit-down strike at GM's Flint complex that launched the UAW (and the militant wing of the broader labor movement) to national power.[19] Most of those working the assembly lines never went to college, yet with generous overtime, cost-of-living adjustments, and pensions underwritten (at growing expense) by individual companies, they could toil their way into middle-class neighborhoods, middle-class retirements, and middle-class dreams of stability and success. In turn, the remarkable contracts that the UAW's leaders negotiated inspired other unions to copy its strategies. Nonunion companies competing for labor and fearful of organizing drives were forced to match surging wages elsewhere.[20]

Then the Detroit automakers and the UAW began their long decline. The blows came, one after another. Amid an oil crisis and economic stagnation in the seventies, consumers embraced cheap, fuel-efficient cars built overseas. In America, when politicians threatened to stanch the flow of imports, foreign automakers began to open up factories in the South, where right-to-work laws made organizing harder. Later, as governments loosened trade restrictions, the Big Three shut plants and moved some of their operations to Mexico and elsewhere. Many of the factory jobs that had sustained urban neighborhoods and company towns vanished, hollowing out once-vibrant communities.[21]

The wild popularity of the SUV energized the industry during the nineties, but it was only a brief respite: the union rolls continued to shrink, and the Big Three continued to bleed market share. In 2007, the companies demanded their own pound of flesh from the UAW: a two-tier system, with new hires brought aboard at half the wages of veterans. The union agreed, trading a measure of solidarity for a promise of security.

As bad as things got in these years, those plants that were still left continued to provide good livelihoods. Getting that job offer from Chrysler or Ford, my workers said, was like winning the lottery: unexpected, and perhaps undeserved, but life-changing all the same. It allowed them to provide amply for their families, enjoy a standard of living better than their parents, and entertain the hope that, with a solid upbringing, their own children would someday do better.

Then, in 2008, the auto industry imploded. Confronted with the worst car market in decades, the major automakers responded with a wave of cost-cutting. Tens of thousands of Big Three workers were ushered out the factory doors with buyouts and early retirement. GM alone scrapped thousands of dealers, shuttered more than a dozen plants, shelved three car brands, and cut a third of its hourly workforce. Reliant on the Big Three, parts suppliers—which did not offer their employees nearly as much in the way of job protections—were wiped out. A third of their U.S. workforce disappeared over the course of the recession.[22] Meanwhile, the UAW agreed to humbling concessions, including the end of a provision that paid laid-off Big Three workers close to their full wages—a remarkable benefit that had stood for a quarter of a century as the epitome of job security, or union overreach, depending on your perspective.

My autoworkers were once some of the luckiest people in the labor force: well paid thanks to their years of seniority, looking forward to hefty pensions upon retirement, sheltered by a stalwart and respected labor movement. But for them, and for many other working men and women today, things have fallen apart. Having lost those good jobs, they are now some of the unluckiest workers to be found: their skills outdated, their retirements uncertain, their unions in retreat, and their future employment doubtful.[23]

A second reason that I find autoworkers interesting to study is that they put in sharp relief many of the trends that have shaped, and continue to shape, the labor market for blue-collar and white-collar workers alike. Arguably, as a class of unionized plant workers, autoworkers represent the prototypical core of the traditional working class, and not the middle class. However, much as the sociologist David Halle described the subjects of his classic study as "working men"—factory workers whose experiences on the shop floor made them class-conscious, but whose consumer lifestyle at home made them middle-class—I see my autoworkers as a hybrid class.[24] On the one hand, they are working-class in terms of the labor they did and the cultural perspective they have, a sensibility imprinted by their education, occupation, and family background. On the other hand, their income and job security (thanks to union-won contracts) and consumption (housing, cars, consumer technology, and so on) make them more like the white-collar middle class.[25] My workers tended to have relatively high wages, with annual incomes in the range of $50,000 to $90,000 for the Big Three workers on either side of the border, and $30,000 to $50,000 for the parts workers—not including what their spouses or partners made. In other words, they were solidly middle-class blue-collar workers—the backbone of the postwar middle class, and a sizeable portion of the labor force even today, but a group under-studied because of the popular focus on the college-educated or the poor.[26] Here, it should be emphasized that while the ranks of the college-educated have grown, they are still not a majority of the adult population, and a fifth of America's workers continue to clock in at blue-collar jobs.[27] It is vital to understand what is happening to this significant segment of the labor force as the economic waters rise around them. And since it can be argued that no class of blue-collar workers built itself as high a perch as the American and Canadian autoworker, it is especially instructive to examine how this once-favored group is dealing with the long-term unemployment that has already affected, or awaits, multitudes of today's less advantaged workers. If they can't make it, after all, who can?

As I've mentioned, the market machine has threshed a much broader swath of the workforce than those toiling in factories and construction sites. In our postindustrial age, workers throughout the middle and bottom tiers of the labor market—white-collar and blue-collar—have seen their good jobs steadily winnowed away, replaced by other jobs that tend to pay well for those at the top, and less well for those below. My unemployed autoworkers provide one useful way to understand this transformation, standing as they do in an uncomfortable space between the older economy's entrenched industry and the newer economy's rootless individualists—between the stable if monotonous employment of postwar society, and the frenetic free agency of today.[28] Indeed, they have arguably experienced a wider range of the ongoing changes in the economy and society than many workers immediately above or below them in the pecking order.

For example, my workers are finally encountering market trends that began to affect white-collar managers and professionals years ago. Especially now that they have lost their jobs, the logic of "career management" has percolated into the thinking of even former unionized autoworkers, who are expected to network, train, and search, with ever-greater sophistication and never-ending persistence, so that they will continue to be employable. While today's start-up culture of "personal brands" and entrepreneurial initiative does not influence these workers as much as it does their more privileged counterparts, they, too, are starting to have to play that game if they want good jobs.[29] At a time when cars are run by computers, factories are manned by robots, and supply chains spread across the world, education and certification in key industrial trades are vital on many shop floors. Less obvious competencies increasingly matter, too: computer literacy, soft skills of communication and teamwork, and hard skills of math, reading, and problem solving.[30]

At the same time, unemployed autoworkers have long endured the kinds of trends that are now spreading to white-collar workers with middle-of-the-road college educations. Sophisticated machinery and off-shoring wiped out factory jobs in rich countries years ago. Nowadays, complex and powerful computing is doing the same in the office, leaving fewer good jobs and more competition for them. My blue-collar workers also demonstrate changes in the family—growing single-parenthood and fewer, more fragile marriages—that have hit less educated households the hardest, but have transformed the entire society. As the educational speedup that I describe in this book erodes the value of the skills that even more educated workers possess, and as family structures increasingly stray from the income security and stability of the two-parent, married model, working people at every level may find themselves beleaguered and left behind.

THE RISE OF THE STUNTED MERITOCRACY

The economy's stunted meritocracy and society's culture of judgment are two of the defining challenges of our time, I argue in this book. As a prelude to the discussion in the chapters that follow, let me say more about them, and how they help us to understand the challenges faced by many of today's workers.

At its best, the corporation has historically been a "mother and father" to American workers. There was less assistance for those out of a job, but the dynamic U.S. economy held out a promise that those who *did* find work would be cared for. Protected by tariffs, red tape, and the lackadaisical pace of communication and commerce, some corporations stepped up. In the early twentieth century, chocolate magnate Milton Hershey and shipping tycoon Henry Kaiser built first-rate schools, libraries, and hospitals for their laborers. Perhaps the most potent motivation for such enlightened self-interest, of course, was the specter of picketing workers. As labor unions gained power, they, in turn, pushed for policies favorable to workers. During the early postwar period epitomized by the "Treaty of Detroit"—a landmark agreement between the UAW and General Motors—strong unions, progressive taxes, a high minimum wage, and other worker-friendly policies and institutions broadly distributed the gains from growth.[31]

Scholars have argued that this postwar period was an aberration. Amid the rise of a serious economic and ideological challenge to capitalism, societies everywhere were forced to dwell more on the well-being of their workers, in hopes of keeping communism at bay. Two world wars and high inflation devastated the accumulated fortunes of the rich, dramatically pushing down inequality. As a result, even "laissez-faire" America saw the emergence of a virtuous circle of egalitarianism: an economics of government intervention, a politics of collective action and shared prosperity, and a culture of solidarity—of course, all relative to what had existed before.[32]

In recent decades, however, trade barriers have fallen, engaging the world in a fierce competition over cutting costs, seeking talent, and building brands. New technologies have exploded, eliminating certain jobs, creating others, and raising the value of highly skilled workers.[33] Unions and governments have loosened their hold on the market, their attempts to intervene quashed not just by economic pressures but also by interest groups hostile to corporate oversight and the tax-reliant welfare state. The financial sector has racked up greater power, infusing its favored ventures with capital even as it bends the management of corporations and the governance of nations in line with its interests.[34]

These trends of globalization, innovation, and deregulation have shattered the barriers faced by certain groups and multiplied opportunities for those with ability and drive.[35] For elite workers, the corporate parent is alive and well: high-flying tech companies boast twenty-first-century versions of the company town, with free international cuisine and coffee shops, massages and spas, games and athletic facilities, day care and doctors, and other in-house amenities for a workaholic staff. At the same time, the transformation of the labor market has raised the stakes of the economic game—and placed ordinary workers in a precarious position. For them, success and failure increasingly depend on the individual alone, unshielded by the unions and government policies that once reduced both rewards and risks. Meanwhile, social safety nets that depended on employers to fill in their gaps are coming under intense strain, as government budgets grow tighter and these corporate "mothers and fathers" demand more from ordinary workers—the surplus children still under their care.

One of the narratives that the Great Recession helped popularize was that a college degree is no longer sufficient—a lesson that a generation of graduates swiftly absorbed as they tossed their commencement robes aside only to find themselves unemployable. Clearly, degrees in certain fields have become much stronger magnets for today's employers. As computers take over the routine tasks being done in the office cubicle as well as on the factory floor, the labor market is becoming more polarized, with the rapid growth of a service sector that still employs unskilled workers—though largely in poor jobs with low wages—and the hollowing out of the middle. Unemployment has risen even among the college-educated since the turn of the century.[36] Technological progress creates new jobs, but the good jobs are scant and harder to qualify for—epitomized to an extreme degree today by tech startups that sell for billions of dollars but employ only dozens of well-vetted workers. It may be that the pace of progress, as the economist John Maynard Keynes once predicted, is outrunning the pace at which society can find new jobs for its workers—or, I might add, train them for those jobs. Meanwhile, research finds that those laid-off workers who do find employment see their wages drop substantially, with the effects persisting for decades.[37]

And yet, as grim as the prospects currently are for those graduates whose office tasks have been outsourced or automated, they are altogether frightening for workers who never went to college to begin with. The recession may have pushed many of them directly into unemployment, but it was just one sharp drop in a long downhill march. Today, college graduates in America are unemployed at about half the rate of high school graduates. (For the young, the college advantage is even starker.) A similar, if slightly smaller, gap exists in Canada.[38] While these differences have fluctuated in size over the years, the edge in earnings and employment that the more educated enjoy is dramatically higher today than it was in the seventies. Likewise, research by Harry Holzer and his collaborators concludes that education has become more decisive in getting good jobs.[39] With this reality in mind, we can talk about a "meritocratic" labor market for ordinary workers—even if it is also important to note that the situation has gotten worse for the relatively better-off segment of this group, the white-collar workforce.[40]

Faced with already swollen ranks of more advantaged competitors, the less educated struggle to catch up in the quickening race for credentials and to win the few good jobs that remain. Older workers, the hardest hit by long-term unemployment, fall into an ersatz early retirement, spending their remaining decades in economic limbo—unable to find decent work but lacking pensions sufficient to pay the bills. Justified or not, some of those with chronic health conditions give up on the labor market altogether and start collecting disability payments, lowering the measured unemployment rate but merely shifting the social problem to other policy arenas.[41]

. . .

A careful look at today's labor market reveals at least three tensions inherent in meritocracy—both in theory and in practice. Even in a society with competitive markets and equal chances for all to succeed, society moves toward a stark inequality. This is the dystopian image of meritocracy that sociologist Michael Young had in mind when he coined the term in his 1958 book, *The Rise of the Meritocracy*. In the fictional society of the novel, equal opportunity and meritocracy triumph over egalitarianism. People are repeatedly and perfectly sorted by their intelligence and effort, with the talented and hard-working rising to the top, and the untalented and indolent falling to the bottom. The gulf between them widens further as the talented children are nurtured and the untalented ignored, the elites put in power and democracy gutted.[42] True equality of opportunity and true meritocracy, Young argues, lead to an aristocracy of the talented to replace hereditary aristocracy. They also lead to the poverty and self-hatred of the untalented, who no longer can argue that they were not given a decent break.[43]

Young offers a sociological understanding of the way that a perfect meritocracy leads to rising inequality. His perspective complements recent work that offers an *economic* understanding of the way that a perfect *market economy* leads to rising inequality. Analyzing historical data from countries throughout the world, economist Thomas Piketty concludes that, in the absence of countervailing forces like wealth-destroying war and aggressive government intervention, the growth in the return on capital typically exceeds the overall economy's growth rate. In short, it is normal for the rich to get richer, while everyone else struggles futilely to catch up. Inequality is baked into capitalism's pie.[44]

Meritocracy is the human face of the inequality-generating market machine. Within a meritocracy, those with ability and drive rise to the top, thanks to the impartial ways that the invisible hand distributes its rewards. The quest for greater profits should naturally weed out inefficiencies, pushing employers to seek out those meritorious individuals who are more productive. If those inefficiencies include well-paid jobs for individuals with ordinary skills—the historical basis of the middle class—so be it. After all, much good comes from a focus on merit alone. Profit-seeking companies have incentives to care primarily about a worker's ability to do the job, and not aspects of her background she can't control—gender, race, sexual orientation, and so on. Therefore, talented individuals from whatever marginalized group can succeed.

Young and Piketty argue that inequality is the inescapable outcome of even the ideal manifestation of a meritocratic market. Whether or not you agree, meritocracy as practiced in the real world is not ideal. For as much as society idolizes meritocracy in theory, elites continually game the system to preserve their privilege. They do this in two ways: by manipulating markets (market advantage) and by passing down educational and cultural advantages to their children (family advantage). By pursuing family advantage, elites subvert equal opportunity.[45] By going after market advantage, they sabotage meritocracy itself.

Let me point out more plainly here that *meritocracy* and *equal opportunity* are distinct, if often confused, concepts.[46] The first is a system that sorts by ability and achievement. The second is a system that offers equivalent opportunities to attain that merit. A society where a fair combat determines status can remain meritocratic in principle, even if the children of warriors always end up on top thanks to their parents' mentoring and resources. Indeed, this is why a meritocracy that is supposed to focus on individual merit actually tolerates certain forms of discrimination. The fact that certain groups do not have equal opportunities to develop their talents gives the employer a troubling rationale for "statistical" discrimination against members of those groups who, according to data or opinion, are less productive or costlier to employ.[47]

In today's integrated global economy, we see plenty of examples of extraordinarily talented individuals—from pop musicians to business leaders—who have ridden admiring markets into superstardom, their rare and world-class ability speaking to the justice of the overall system. But it is important to remember that they are not the norm. As a whole, those at the bottom have a worse shot at success—especially in America, where they now have a much harder time rising up the income ladder than is the case in Canada.[48] As research shows, how much schooling people wind up getting has a great deal to do with socioeconomic class and the educational resources that parents can thereby muster.[49] The children of less educated workers are largely at a disadvantage here, with parents who have not gone to college themselves lacking the finances or cultural refinement to pave a sure path to higher education. Indeed, as early as age three, huge gaps exist between the test scores of the children of college graduates and those of the children of high school graduates. This inequality persists into high school, along with gaps in soft skills that also shape later success: motivation, self-control, self-esteem, the ability to work with others.[50] Throughout their lives, the children of elite workers can also use their multitude of advantages to pull ahead in terms of the quality, and not just the quantity, of their education (a point I will return to later in the book). That leads to an even starker inequality between the career trajectories of those lucky enough to be born well-to-do and those of everyone else. Here, I do not wish to overstate the decisiveness of a comfortable upbringing. Clearly, family advantage is just one of many factors that determine a person's success, and luck and other traits that have little to do with merit can also be key—as research has found, even individuals raised in the same family experience a wide range of outcomes.[51] Nevertheless, it is an important advantage, and one crucial to the stunted meritocracy that has emerged.

Political scientist James Fishkin has put forward a useful theory to explain how family advantage makes equal opportunity impossible. Society, he writes, distributes wealth and status on three grounds. According to the principle of merit, qualifications for positions should be evaluated fairly. According to the principle of equal life chances, the likelihood of a child's later success should not depend on arbitrary traits like gender, race, and family background. According to the principle of family autonomy, parents should be free to shape their children's development. The problem, Fishkin argues, is that these three principles are in constant tension: choosing any two of them rules out the third.[52] If we want equal life chances for all, we have to prevent parents early on from giving their children a leg up in the race, or otherwise impose remedies later in life, such as various forms of redistribution and affirmative action, that will weaken the link between a person's merit and her reward. Likewise, if we want meritocracy, we have to find ways to diminish family advantage, or otherwise accept the fact that opportunities will not be equal. Obviously, in real life the tradeoffs are less stark, a matter of degrees rather than black-and-white conditions, but they are meaningful nonetheless.

It is perfectly understandable that parents want to do everything they can to give their children the best possible opportunities for success in life. Unfortunately, elite workers can prepare their children for the labor market in superior ways, and this presents problems for the children of ordinary workers trying to compete for the economy's limited number of good jobs. Furthermore, family advantage is not the only way that elites wield outsized influence in the labor market.

In their pursuit of market advantage within the world of work, those already at the top game the meritocratic system, ensuring that those who rise to join them are not necessarily the most deserving. Even as some of these elites trumpet the virtues of the free market, they engage in practices that economists call rent-seeking, suppressing competition and twisting the rules in their favor. For example, many of the highly paid professional classes—from doctors to lawyers to university professors—have successfully walled off their fields of specialty through licensing, certification, and other forms of social closure that prevent talented newcomers from making inroads.[53] The true victors in the deregulated marketplace, however, are high-level managers and financial workers—increasingly the same class. Without strong unions or social movements to counterbalance their sway, corporate managers have gained ever-larger shares of the economy's bounty. They have also coopted government. On the one hand, they have weakened it by gutting rules and dispensing with oversight. On the other hand, corporations have actually *grown* government by weaving a tangled web of legislation that has furthered their specific interests, from targeted tax breaks to competition-killing patents. Dominated by corporate executives, the richest 1 percent have made out handsomely in recent years, even as the wages of other workers have not kept pace with their growing productivity.[54]

To be sure, elites are not the only people who employ these tactics. From public-school teachers to nurses, from UPS drivers to police officers, workers across the social spectrum continue to throw around their aggregate weight. Licensing laws protect heating technicians, hair stylists, and interior decorators. But these are the lucky (and besieged) few, however much they make the news with every strike, pension disagreement, and new licensing rule. The great mass of other working people have lost the postwar protections of strong labor unions and activist government policies to create and protect jobs. With the withering away of these institutions, and with the large numbers of individuals seeking out the dwindling number of jobs not automated or outsourced, the sorting by markers of merit has quickened in the lower and middle tiers of the labor market, the ordinary market. Workers there now find themselves in a survival-of-the-fittest reality, where continued employ-ment depends on each person's ability to climb up the ladder quickly—and where those on the bottom rungs have little hope of catching up.

In other words, my argument is a *relative* one, describing a shift in the ordinary market toward perceived individual merit and away from collective solutions. Because elite workers remain able and willing to assert their own power, what has emerged is a stunted meritocracy. It tolerates anticompetitive machinations and cronyism in the elite mar-ket, even while demanding individual responsibility and proven skill from other workers, who no longer wield as much strategic power to defend their interests as the elites do—in a collective fashion.

. . .

Combined, the three tensions I described above reveal the fundamental paradox of meritocracy. Even in its ideal form, meritocracy would lead to inequality. In its stunted, real form, elites find ways to fence off their higher ground. They band together in the marketplace to neutralize meritocracy. Their families pass down advantages to preserve their place in the social order—at the expense of equal opportunity. In these ways, market advantage and family advantage contradict the very ide-als of meritocracy and equal opportunity. In the next section, I will discuss how this behavior by elites is an example of the group-centric perspective I call *fraternalism*, one of several ways that society distrib-utes its opportunities and rewards.

MERITOCRATIC MORALIZING

For workers across the labor market—factory workers and office work-ers, low-wage laborers and well-paid professionals—long-term unem-ployment is a psychologically painful experience. However, there is at least one difference in the way it affects workers like mine. For many of them, not having enough education and other proofs of merit becomes yet another source of self-blame. Their dim self-appraisal was summed up by a word that some of them used to describe themselves: *loser*. After all, society sends them the message—even in union towns like Detroit and Windsor—that less educated people should not be paid well. "They just see us as money-grubbing slobs," said one of my Cana-dian workers. Particularly during the recession, the public raged against unionized autoworkers in newspapers and radio and online forums.

They were finally getting their due reward for demanding too much in wages and benefits—more than the market should ever have allowed.

Even in better economic times, however, there are few left today who bemoan the demise of the high-wage, low-skill jobs that once sustained a strong and broad middle class. In her study of the shuttering of a Midwestern Chrysler plant in the late eighties, anthropologist Kathryn Dudley talked to middle-class professionals who felt that the layoffs were a "justly deserved fall from grace." Thanks to labor unions, they said, uneducated workers were paid much more than they deserved. Organized labor's "artificial" interventions disrupted the natural workings of the market, where wages depend on your value added: what you know, rather than whom you know.[55]

Sociologist Katherine Newman has dubbed this perspective *meritocratic individualism.* "At the center of this doctrine is the notion that individuals are responsible for their own destinies," she writes. One's career is a narrow path of rectitude, and hard work and sacrifice will prove one worthy of the destination. "Cast this way," Newman adds, "success is not a matter of luck, good contacts, credentials, or technical skill, but is a measure of one's moral worth, one's willingness and ability to drive beyond the limitations of self-indulgence and sloth."

This is our modern-day, secular version of the Protestant ethic, but even more uncompromising in its vision, having rid itself of the softening hues of civic virtue in which the Puritans dutifully wrapped their dogma. Even industrial workers, the heart of the downtrodden proletariat that Marx believed would one day lead his communist revolution, cannot ignore it. If some of them at first view their layoffs as a collective tragedy—the grim harvest of what corporations, unions, and governments had sown—with time they come to see their protracted joblessness as an individual, moral failing: a deserved comeuppance from the foolish decisions they made, sometimes decades ago.[56]

In this book, I examine some possible ways that the culture of meritocracy has changed, thanks in part to society's shifting understandings of what merit is. I define this perspective, meritocratic morality, in opposition to three other kinds of moral thinking regarding advancement in society and the distribution of economic rewards: *egalitarian morality, fraternal morality,* and *grace morality.* The figure shown here, "Morality and reality," describes these four ideologies, or systems of belief. As the reader will note, I have adapted three of them from the theories of James Fishkin.[57]

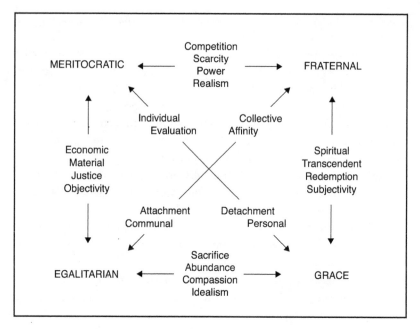

Morality and reality. Four opposing perspectives determine opportunities and outcomes within society. These moral viewpoints can exist purely as ideology (culture), or they can reflect the reality of how society is organized (social structure).

These moral principles can be put into practice in the real world, creating the corresponding social systems of meritocracy, egalitarianism, fraternalism, and grace. The distinction between the individually held ideology and the socially enacted reality is an important one, which I will return to later. But let me focus first on the culture, the shared modes of thinking and behavior that my unemployed workers use to make sense of their situations.

Meritocratic morality follows market logic. The market demands certain skills, and individuals need to get the education and experience to supply them. The focus here is on economic concerns: the constant measurement of every increment or decrement of power and status. Yet meritocratic morality is also a *moral* belief system, based on two principles, equal opportunity and individual responsibility. An individual suffers an injustice whenever she is denied the right to compete with others on a level playing field. But when the rules are fair, whatever happens ultimately depends on the individual's perseverance. Success, therefore, is a sign of moral virtue—and inequality is all in the game. You succeeded because you did what you were supposed to do. You failed because you did not plan ahead and work hard. In this way, meritocratic morality justifies the ways of the market to ordinary men and women.[58]

Of course, even adherents of meritocratic morality do not believe that society is utterly fair in its distribution of rewards. They recognize that they live in an imperfect world where the rules can often be twisted in favor of certain interests. Meritocratic morality can tolerate a degree of dissonance between the ideals of merit and the reality of corruption because the ideology provides self-justification and hope to its true believers. Yul Kane, a forty-two-year-old Canadian who used to work at Ford, exemplifies this attitude. Faced with the infuriating outcome of the recession's bailouts—"they pay these multimillion-dollar payouts to these people who screwed things up"—Yul has not had his faith in meritocracy shaken one bit. Children today may be spoiled, with everything "handed to them"; teenagers working at McDonald's may drive Mustangs because "banks will give anyone a loan"; company executives may "fuck up" and still get golden parachutes. But Yul is better than that. "I'm the type of person that if I say I'm going to do something, and I shake your hand, then that's the way I am," he says. The meritocratic ideology stresses the individual's dignity amid the teeming, undeserving masses, in this way defending the market economy from popular discontent and alternative ways of viewing the world.

One of those alternatives is egalitarian morality. This is a moral perspective that seeks economic justice for the *collective*. It desires a leveling of inequalities so that all individuals share equal life chances—a fair shot at improving their lives. At its most extreme, it is also about achieving equal life *outcomes*: alleviating the suffering of the world's dispossessed majority by radically redistributing the spoils of·economic activity. Today's "egalitarians" in Europe and North America tend to be much more moderate, seeking a combination of meritocratic and egalitarian aims revolving around equal opportunity. And yet, just like meritocrats or communists, they behold the world with an economic lens focused on each gain or loss. Precise measurement is necessary in order to transfer the appropriate amount of wealth and power to the poor and weak.

Historically, fraternal morality has been the most prevalent and powerful code of conduct: the morality of the tribe, the rudimentary beginnings of society. It understands humans as social creatures, living within groups and attempting to advance their interests. The fraternal perspective is moral in the sense that it creates bonds of obligation to the group. It restrains the behavior of the individual, prioritizing the interests of the collective rather than his own. The family is the archetype for all forms of fraternity, which have become ever more complex as society has evolved, from yesterday's tribes, clans, and castes to today's corporations, platoons, and unions. In the competition among these groups, there are no universal ethics, only the furtherance of the group's aims. Might makes right. Yet, in identifying with that group, the individual does not merely satisfy her desires for power and prestige. She also finds spiritual gain: the transcendent joy and dignity of joining a larger whole. The word "fraternal" refers to masculine brotherhood, and that is something I want to emphasize, for there is also a dark side to fraternalism: its exclusion, its homogeneity, its chauvinism.

The fourth kind of moral code is what I call the morality of grace. Grace is a concept from Christian theology, and refers to the favor of God, offered to chosen individuals as a gift of salvation—undeserved and unmerited. As someone who is not religious, I hesitate to use a term with such historical baggage, but I feel it best captures the antithesis of the meritocratic ideology: a spiritual perspective of nonjudgment and abundance; a foil to an economic perspective of measurement and scarcity. It is worth emphasizing that grace morality is not synonymous with religion, which often veers in the direction of temporal values of might and merit.[59] The viewpoint I have described can be seen in certain Christian traditions, but it is evident in many other belief systems, and can be secular as well.

Like egalitarian morality, grace morality offers a compassionate perspective, offering help to the "undeserving." But unlike egalitarian morality, grace rejects the categories of right and wrong. It is in fact antithetical to justice, in that it offers neither retribution nor restitution, but forgiveness. It also downplays the importance of material circumstances. Under grace morality, individuals give up their wealth and power—not for the sake of redistribution per se but because these possessions and positions are not significant when viewed from the broad vantage point of life, the universe, and everything. Earlier interpretations of grace often argued that only certain individuals were chosen by God to be saved, but here I conceive of grace as universal. Redemption is not based on deservingness. It is available to all.

Even in libertarian America, we can look back through history and see all four moralities wrestling for dominance. The early Puritans championed the view that salvation occurred through God's grace alone.[60] Today's politicians tend to use meritocratic and egalitarian rhetoric on the stump. If our culture celebrates these diverse values, however, the social structure of fraternalism often prevails in reality. Even avowedly meritocratic or egalitarian institutions channel the economic rewards of competition or redistribution to certain favored groups. Parents pass down advantages to their children, and elite workers bar entry to their professions. Labor unions favor the interests of their members and leaders over those of the entire working class. Venal governments sermonize about free markets or populist redistribution while growing rich from the schemes of crony capitalism. Political parties, the avatars of modern democracy, encourage a tribal sort of partisanship, where the enemy is always wrong.

Meritocratic morality deserves special attention in this book, however, because of the ways it seemed to influence my unemployed workers when they doled out blame for their predicament. Obviously, the men and women profiled in this book are not saints. Some were skilled caretakers of their households amid hard times, but others succumbed to debt and wastefulness, frivolity and despair. Yet their failings reinforce a key point: *individual* morality runs deep in society, even as the social apparatus that shapes and constrains the individual's free will grows larger and stronger, even as discerning the behaviors that constitute the "good" becomes a harder, murkier enterprise.[61] Personal responsibility is crucial, but so are the realities that impinge on a person's ability to choose well: the personal temperament and talents he is born with, the education and experiences that shape the preferences and predilections she calls her own.

Another fundamental tension in the meritocratic ideology is its premise that all can reach the capitalist nirvana. As political scientist Jennifer Hochschild notes, "Everyone cannot simultaneously attain more than absolute success. Capitalist markets require some firms to fail; elections require some candidates and policy preferences to lose; status hierarchies must have a bottom in order to have a top." The institutions of society, Hochschild continues, "are designed to ensure that some fail, at least relatively."[62]

In the meritocratic perspective, however, we tend to ignore the fact that deprivation is not just absolute. What results is a kind of material myopia. We seek ever-more affluence and believe ourselves better off with every new bit of economic value added to the national statistics. But after society reaches a threshold of prosperity that countries like the United States and Canada long ago surpassed, the link between happiness and income is not so straightforward, research shows.[63] Further improvements increasingly depend on our ability to improve our *relative* status—for example, moving to an upscale neighborhood, or moving up within the corporate hierarchy at work. Yet, obtaining these so-called positional goods is by definition a zero-sum game. One person's gain is another's loss. This may explain the fierce economic competition between the top income earners and top wealth holders, an endless race for (happiness-producing) bragging rights to the largest bank accounts and estates. This tug-of-war is played out in the lower tiers of the labor market as well, as workers like mine try to catch up with those higher up in the hierarchy.[64]

As I describe in chapter 2, however, there are not enough decent jobs for everyone, not even all the deserving, and the situation may worsen in the future, if technological progress over the long run turns out to be job-killing rather than job-creating, or if education fails to keep up with the economy's needs. The meritless masses who fail to achieve a respected livelihood suffer for it, lacking the status equivalent of the linen shirt that Adam Smith famously described as a luxury for the ancient Greeks and Romans but a "necessary of life" for the contemporary European day-laborer. For today's low-wage worker, relative deprivation means not just lower status but also, as Smith observed, the shame that comes with it.[65]

Decades after abandoned factories first started to litter the landscape, the shock has dissipated. The factory workers now being cut loose are well aware that they are obsolete—and for that reason, they berate themselves all the more for their failure to adapt. Of course, the belief that they can adapt is itself an extension of this idealistic mindset, which affirms that everything will work itself out, with dedication and patience and "a smile on your face." This idealism extends, too, to society as a whole—not just in the great faith it places in the proposition that laid-off workers can be retrained, but also in the Darwinian morality it attaches to the outcome.[66] Those who are hungry enough for success do well. The rest suffer—and rightly so.

. . .

In the chapters that follow, I describe the experiences of the long-term unemployed in three areas: their individual efforts to ascend the meritocratic ladder, the social policies that are designed to keep their unemployment from spiraling into poverty, and the family life that urges them onward—or pulls them down. (Loosely, these themes match

James Fishkin's principles of merit, equal life chances, and family autonomy, which themselves mirror the three republican ideals: *liberté, egal-
ité, fraternité.*) I then build upon this work by examining the institutions and cultures that surround the unemployed and mold their
views.

In chapter 2, I examine the prospects of autoworkers who have lost
their jobs and now seek to retool themselves for an evolving labor market.
At every level, governments in both countries express great enthusiasm
for retraining. Yet the task is daunting for many former factory workers,
who by their own confession are not well suited for booming industries
that demand higher education or compliant customer service. In general,
Canada's retraining system improved the opportunities and outlook of
my workers there to a greater degree, thanks in part to action centers:
support centers funded by government and staffed by their former coworkers, who tailored help to their specific needs and guided them through
poorly managed and underfunded government bureaucracies.

Yet the larger problem—one that the social safety net does not adequately address—centers on the relative lack of skill that hinders workers like mine. The race for greater amounts of education and skill means
that the bar keeps rising and the contest speeds up. Expectations rise
about what is acceptable in terms of education, experience, and personality. The job-application process becomes more professionalized,
bureaucratized, and complex. Yet my workers lacked the pedigree and
resources to fare well in this competition, where finding *good* jobs or
schools means going up against younger, more tech-savvy rivals without
the baggage of failed careers and work-years wasted on the pursuit of
antiquated skills. The lingering effects of the economic crisis have made
their odds even worse. If retraining for the new economy was the man-
tra of the Clinton years, the massive levels of long-term unemployment
unleashed in recent years challenge the hopeful expectations of economists that, with the right policies, no worker will be left behind.

Chapter 3 describes the economic, social, and psychological blows
that unemployment delivers to laid-off workers, and the ways that policies soften them. Lack of health insurance on the U.S. side was a major
challenge for workers already struggling with their job search, who
now found themselves fighting a second front against physical and
mental illness—often aggravated by the stress of their predicament—
and the steep medical bills that followed. With their single-payer health
care system, Canadians experienced fewer problems affording care.
Prescription-drug costs and other gaps in public coverage did cause

hardship, but action centers filled in some of those gaps, connecting my autoworkers to other sources of help or negotiating with companies on their behalf. In terms of unemployment benefits, however, the policy differences were not so clear-cut. America's benefits actually lasted longer, thanks to temporary policies. Their shorter window of assistance meant that Canadians who could not find new jobs fell sooner into the stigmatized welfare system, with ruinous consequences for their psychological well-being.

In one particular area, however, Canada's income supports were clearly superior: assistance to single-parent households. Chapter 4 focuses on these targeted policies and their consequences for families. More so than their college-educated counterparts, less educated workers have moved away from marriage and toward single-parenthood. When they lose their jobs, then, the economic repercussions are all the more vicious, compounding the disadvantages already faced by these workers. In Canada, single-earner families with children—both single parents and married households with just one, now unemployed, worker—receive heftier benefits, compensating for their fragile finances. This key policy difference may help shape attitudes toward the importance of the bread-winner in both countries.

One issue that complicates my comparison of the United States and Canada is race. My American autoworkers were mostly black, and my Canadians were mostly white, a result of how I went about finding my interviewees as well as the distinct demographics of the communities I studied.[67] As historian Thomas Sugrue has argued, racial segregation and discrimination in Detroit and other major cities dramatically worsened opportunities for black workers and their families, as whites left them behind in tottering, tax-starved neighborhoods and blocked their entry into well-paid occupations that could replace the factory jobs decimated by disruptive economic trends. As a result, unemployment and poverty have historically hit these households the hardest.[68] When I examine the effects of social policies, the racial differences among my workers become a limitation, as race also plays a role in the worse outcomes observed among my African American workers.

Race is central to my analysis in this book, and I discuss its role extensively in chapter 3, exploiting my study's racial differences to hone in on the mechanisms by which race blunts the impact of social policies. In addition to the lingering discrimination my black workers continue to face in the job market, the dearth of resources in their social networks, I argue, made it harder to turn to family and friends for loans, gifts, and job leads, which my white workers, on the other hand, often relied on. There are some additional factors affecting the link between race and unemployment that are worth noting at the outset. In regard to the growing numbers of households headed by single parents, recent research has found that this trend has deeply affected the white working class as well.[69] Also, as I will describe, the Canadian system did provide either more funding or better policy implementation in terms of its family supports, universal health care, and retraining policies, and in these areas, white Canadian autoworkers also fared better compared to their white American counterparts, with a connection to specific policies up north.

Indeed, what became striking in my analysis of the policies available to my jobless workers was the serious problem of implementation. Funding was inadequate, and my workers encountered numerous bureaucratic barriers. (On the Canadian side, the situation was somewhat better for those who made use of the action centers.) In chapter 5, I explore how their encounters with failing institutions prompted Americans and Canadians alike to take a dismal view of the prospects for government and labor unions in a transformed economy. The disenchantment they felt tended to go hand in hand with a realistic recognition that what they really had to do was pull themselves out of their situation—by the bootstraps. The sentiments that my autoworkers expressed, however, sometimes went beyond their personal experiences and their avowed realism. Perhaps to a greater degree than was the case for blue-collar workers in earlier, more halcyon times for organized labor, some of my workers voiced fervent support for the meritocratic ideology. Many others felt the need to defend themselves, more or less dexterously, against its strident claims—that the better educated should be rewarded more in the labor market, and that unions protect the lazy and irresponsible. Meanwhile, prolonged unemployment in a market that idolizes the successful and talented chipped away at their sense of decency and self-respect, as I describe in chapter 6. In this particular comparison, the racial mix of my workers is less of a hindrance, because the national pattern I observe—that Americans experience more self-blame and are more opposed to labor unions than Canadians are—pushes in the opposite direction, reducing some of the impact of the racial differences that past research has discerned. (This body of work—most notably the work of sociologist Michèle Lamont—finds that black workers are more collectively oriented than whites are.[70])

In chapter 7, I conclude by discussing possible responses to the high levels of long-term unemployment and inequality that today's stunted meritocracy and culture of judgment strengthen and make harder to bear. A sturdy safety net can greatly alleviate the hardships endured by workers who lose their jobs, but it is important to focus not just on the quantity of benefits but also on the quality of the bureaucracies that provide them. More broadly, however, these policies reach a point of diminishing returns, thanks to the economic and political pressures that confront a large, expensive welfare state, and the difficulties that conventional unemployment policies confront in addressing the predicament of the long-term jobless in any meaningful way. The loss of these workers' well-being stems from more than the drop in their incomes, and their ability to find good jobs en masse depends on more than just grabbing credentials. New Deal–style interventions to create jobs and dampen inequality, as well as legislation and organizing to promote unions and other worker-friendly institutions, might go further. But the politics of the moment in many countries do not adequately support this turn to activist government policies, and in any case what may come with the egalitarian dream must give us pause. I argue that political attempts to organize and advocate on behalf of ordinary workers and families could benefit from explicit efforts to temper the popular appeal of meritocratic morality, especially among elites. I propose a new politics that might succeed in balancing the goals of liberty, equality, and fraternity, allowing for a measure of grace in a labor market characterized by the relentless conditionality of merit and advancement.

Throughout this book, I use the experiences and perspectives of individuals to show the real-life consequences of the trends and patterns I highlight in my research. For the most part, I chose to focus on selected individuals so that I would not lose readers in a flurry of quotes and personalities. I use my other interviews as needed to flesh out certain points, and summarize the views of my interviewees when it is important, but my hope is that readers will come away from this book truly understanding the people profiled in its pages.

My other hope is that the perspective I present in this book is not caricatured as anti-market. That is not my position. The market economy is one of humanity's greatest achievements, a powerful tool that—under the right conditions—can allocate resources efficiently and spur innovation and economic growth. In recent decades, properly fettered market forces have helped millions in the world's poorest regions climb out of poverty, develop their talents, and share in the culture and wealth of an integrated global society. Furthermore, the postwar period was no utopia. We cannot ignore the prejudices that choked off career possibilities for many individuals, especially women and minorities, or romanticize the brutal, monotonous, and authoritarian conditions that factory workers endured. Indeed, with its focus on human capital, the market economy over the long term has been a liberating force for many workers, replacing drudgery with more creative and stimulating work and helping push aside certain forms of discrimination as harmful to businesses who want to cultivate talent—in whatever individual it may reside.[71]

Yet, for all its inefficiencies and constraints, the postwar economy did lead to a broadly shared prosperity. After all, one person's inefficiency is another person's good job: when ordinary factory workers secured wages far greater than their education would otherwise permit, it gave them dignity and helped build a strong middle class. It moved society in the direction of income equality. As factories began opening their doors more widely in the decades that followed, the good jobs that remained became engines of upward mobility even for the most disadvantaged groups.[72] As I will explain, my black workers in particular rose up from poor neighborhoods, pulling up their extended families along the way. For women, too, these jobs could be paths out of painful circumstances. Several of the women I interviewed confided to me that they had suffered domestic abuse in past relationships. Getting a well-paid factory job, they said, had helped them escape the violence and fear at home.

Over the decades, the anomalies of the old economy have been smoothed away, with each profit-boosting closure and concession. Today, with the loss of their high-paying, low-skill jobs, my once-envied workers have suddenly been transformed into the economy's undereducated and unproductive "losers." Having chosen unwisely (it seems in hindsight), they find themselves defective parts on a quickening assembly line, too riddled with the scrapes and notches of their personal histories to be plated with the slick gloss of education and skill. Their radically different circumstances are a sign of how just how profoundly the labor market has changed, for better and for worse.

While some degree of inequality is necessary for the market economy to operate the way it should, I worry that we have gone too far in that direction. Democracy is not sustainable with a widening gulf of income and understanding between those with advantages and those without—a concern, I should add, that some conservative thinkers share.[73] Writing during the Second World War, economist Karl Polanyi made this very point: the laissez-faire capitalism that triumphed in the nineteenth century ultimately unleashed social pressures that led to the undoing of the global economy and the rise of the extremist causes of fascism and communism.[74] After Europe lay in ruins, political movements in many countries sought to soften the sharp edges of the market without turning to the utopian thinking of any of those three distinct systems—in a sense, fraternal, egalitarian, and meritocratic dreams that inevitably faded into nightmares. But in the late twentieth century, that history was forgotten. Free-market economic idealism rose from history's ashbin.

Even beyond the moral outrage and social discontent it stokes, there is troubling evidence that inequality harms the well-being of individuals caught in its ambit. These include lowered levels of health and happiness, especially for those at the bottom, but for those higher up as well. As I described above, in a modern industrialized society our well-being increasingly depends on positional goods of zero-sum status and exclusive possessions, so the commonplace argument that we can just grow the economy's pie and thereby help the least well-off runs into problems.[75] Once past the threshold of absolute affluence necessary for happiness, those lower down in the economy—even a booming economy—experience their low status in a most tangible way: as a blow to their dignity. And whether we cheer or jeer the mammoth gains of elites in recent years, the vexing reality that many hard-working men and women can no longer make a decent living is another reason to reconsider our society's current priorities.

Finally, the trade-off between efficiency and egalitarianism should not be overstated. There is evidence that income equality is good for economic growth. Even in highly competitive industries some profitable companies take the "high road" of a well-paid, well-treated, even unionized workforce, betting on the gains to be had from higher productivity and morale and lower turnover.[76] In turn, we have to ask what the costs are of discarding so many workers in the name of a dynamic and flexible economy—social costs that are not always tallied in the standard metrics of economic success. As the stories of my workers suggest, the toll of long-term unemployment on families and communities is immense. It brings into question the very idea of economic efficiency, and whether the gains of consumers and companies are worth all the suffering. There is a difference, in short, between unemployment in the abstract—unemployment as a "fresh start," a "shrewd" business move, a market "imperative"—and unemployment as it is lived and endured.

. . .

It is no longer enough to be a hard worker, John Hope has learned. He played by the rules, but the rules of the game have changed. The livelihood he tried to build over a half-lifetime of work now has little value in the eyes of others. Suddenly he is supposed to be a different person. He should have known, when he was parentless and homeless, to stick with school. He should have known, when he was driving trucks and building freeways, to attend college. He should have known, when he was building a life for his kids with his factory wages, to train for a new career. Instead, he stuck with the principle he had learned young: an honest day's work with his hands would get him by.

Back then, school was the furthest thing from his mind. "I couldn't wait to get old and get a real job," he says, laughing. He took off after eleventh grade, believing, as many did, that he could do better. Decades later, John dismisses the idea of returning to school so that he can compete with twenty-year-olds. "I'm about fifty-five years old . . . not much you can do now. Don't too many people want you when you get that old. I tried to be smart, but what can you do?"

John has started going to food pantries. For Christmas, a local children's hospital gave his kids clothes and gift cards. That saved the holiday. But now it's a new year, and the bills keep piling up. If he can't rework the terms of his mortgage, he will have to declare bankruptcy, he says.

John remains hopeful that things will, in time, work out. "You don't know what the next day brings. Sometimes it's a good day, sometimes it ain't. But you got to make them all be the same." God will take care of him, he says. "I feel I ain't got what I used to have. But I know I got God on my side. And maybe the stuff ain't meant for me. God may not [have] meant that for me. You accept whatever you got coming. . . . Some people think somebody owe you something. I don't think like that. I thank God for what I have and that's it."

In his darker moments, though, John will admit to being troubled by what happened. "You work so long and then you find a good-paying job and then. . . . You don't know what to think." Weren't he and his coworkers doing good work all those years? His bosses thought so at first, but then new management came around and thought differently. "You might see it one way, another person see it another way. But that's how it goes. I guess that's the chance you take, working. You don't know what nobody is gonna do no more these days, you know what I mean?"

Trust and goodwill turn out to be, like so much else in the modern marketplace, ephemeral and conditional. Having liquidated its stores of tradition and obligation, the market has little willingness anymore to indulge ordinary workers like John. It has little patience for inefficiency and naive notions of loyalty and propriety. It has little respect for history—beyond the sharply delimited history of a résumé.[77]

But the immaterial qualities of life—affection, trust, faith—depend mightily on a past of shared experience. Without this grounding, the ability to connect deeply, to feel more than just fleeting impulses of admiration, pleasure, and lust, never takes root. For John, the loss of his job—the loss of the one "parent" he could depend on—has left him with a hole inside. These days, he finds himself dwelling on the family he lost years ago. He remembers when he was a boy, and wanted desperately to see his father, an itinerant truck driver. That's why he headed to Florida when he was a teen—relatives told him his father might be there. John never found him.

In his forties, John learned his grandmother was dying. He went home to Alabama to see her one last time. "I was her baby," he says. "My daddy . . . he didn't come back. She took me and loved me like she would do him." Word had been sent to the son, too, but he never showed. "He could have been back," John muses. "He didn't come back. I didn't get to see him."

Years later, relatives sent him a photo of his father, with the news that he had died of a heart attack. "I wait all these years to see my dad alive, and he come back dead." John did not attend the funeral. He had never had a connection to the man in that box.

"I didn't know him," John says. "All I know is I tried to take care of myself."

CHAPTER 2

All This Garbage from Life

Education and the Capital Speedup

Some animals were meant to carry each other, to live
symbiotically for a lifetime—star-crossed lovers, monoga-
mous swans. We are not those animals. The slower we move,
the faster we die. We are not swans. We're sharks.

—George Clooney as Ryan Bingham in *Up in the Air* (2009)

When Hannah Frey first started working for Chrysler, in the mid-nineties, the company had lost its legendary CEO, Lee Iacocca, and was
scraping the bottom of car quality lists. The automaker that had once
brazenly dared in commercials, "If you find a better car, buy it," was
now seeing its reputation smeared by scandal and poor reviews. In the
plants, workers say, the incentives favored quantity over quality—how
many engines could be shipped out the door to meet quotas and win
plaudits for managers, with less regard for catching defects in the ever-
more complex machines underneath every hood.

Hannah was on the front lines of that battle, auditing the engines that
made it off the lines at Detroit's Mack Avenue Engine Complex. She
would go over every inch of the engine, making sure the cam covers were
sealed down, the oil levels were just right, the throttle bodies were not
sticking, the dipsticks were in place, the bolts were all screwed on—tight.
Once, the foreman ordered a forklift driver to cart away a rack of three
engines that Hannah hadn't had time to check yet. Hannah stopped the
driver. They bickered. Finally, Hannah sat on an engine, straddling it like
a horse. "They're not going nowhere until I look at them," she barked.

Hannah had her way.

In five years of auditing hundreds of engines a day, she missed defects
in just six engines. "I was praised for that," says Hannah, fifty-four. She

had always been a hard worker. When she was ten she sold bread at a bakery for fifty cents an hour, to help out her mom, a Detroit single parent and bartender who survived alternately on tips and welfare checks.

As a young teen, Hannah left home because her stepfather, she says, was sexually abusing her. When she was eighteen she moved back to Detroit. She ended up spending two months in a homeless shelter—"eating cheese sandwiches and grateful for it." About a year later, she pulled herself up with the help of a man she later married, her first husband. He was a former marine, and he ran their home like a boot camp—with him the drill sergeant. One day he came home from work in a foul mood. "So what the hell did you do all day?" he snapped.

Hannah was exhausted from taking care of their baby. For the first time in their marriage, she talked back. "I just don't want to take any of your shit right now," she told him.

He grabbed her, slammed her against a wall, and started choking her. Hannah reached out for a pan she had on the counter and started pummeling him in the head. He let go.

Hannah divorced her husband. Waiting tables to support herself, she eventually got certified as a medical assistant. The pay, however, was not enough to survive on, she says. She later found a job at a private investigations firm that paid twice as much—$14 an hour—but after six years they let her go.

Then, in 1995, she got the job at Chrysler.

For the first time in her life, Hannah felt she was doing a job that truly mattered. "It gave me such a feeling of pride, such a feeling of worth, that I was there. And I was going to do the best damn job that I could do." When she was poring over transmission flexplates and engine belts, she imagined a woman like herself, with two kids, stuck on a desolate road somewhere because of a broken-down engine—because she had missed something. "So I was always very . . . almost to the point of tedious, to make sure that everything was right when it went out that door," she says. By then, Hannah had remarried. Things were looking up.

Several years later, Hannah was inspecting a transmission. She bent over and twisted her body around, a flashlight in hand, to get a look at the flywheels. Suddenly, she heard something behind her crack.

She had herniated a disc in her lower back. Years of climbing up and down and bending over and around engine blocks had finally caught up with her. She needed surgery. When she returned to work, the pain lingered. "I never was the same after that." Management noticed. Their attitude toward her cooled.

When car production cratered during the recession, Hannah and some of her coworkers were reassigned to another plant. Workers there had seen their friends laid off to make way for the Detroit people with higher seniority. "You shouldn't be here," they threatened. "Watch your back."

It was a constant mental fight to stay calm amid all the harassment, Hannah says. It was not that she was unaccustomed to the tribal mentality of plant life. Once a quiet and timid person, Hannah had long ago learned to put on her "Chrysler face" whenever she drove into the parking lot: the hard-boiled, don't-mess-with-me attitude of a factory worker. "If you show any weaknesses, you'll get eaten alive," she says. "You have to walk in there with 'I'll kick your fucking ass' attitude—excuse my language."

She is not an imposing woman. At a first glance, Hannah seems almost delicate: pale skin wrapped in a blue-green tracery of veins, soft hazel eyes staring out from wire eyeglass frames that look more librarian than factory worker. But then you see the bulging flesh along her wrist bones, swollen from carpal tunnel syndrome—another mark of her years at the plant.

When she was transferred, Hannah started working on the line again: flipping cams on top of cylinder heads, lining up rocker arms, bolting down the parts. To reduce costs, management had consolidated jobs and sped up the line. Each engine had to be done in twelve seconds. With the pain in her wrists and her lower back, Hannah could not keep up. Her foreman had no sympathy. "You should take the buyout and get out of here," he snapped.

So she did. In the fall of 2009 Hannah left Chrysler. The severance package would provide her and her second husband with enough of a financial cushion while she looked for a new job, Hannah thought. But then her marriage fell apart. She struggled to pay the mortgage on her suburban home by herself. Eventually, she moved into a friend's place in a seedy neighborhood outside Detroit. Unable to tap unemployment insurance because of her buyout, she saw her savings dwindle away as the months dragged on.

Meanwhile, Hannah was running into bureaucratic roadblocks getting government help with her job search. She filled out an application at a state job center, but no one called back. She visited their office two times to follow up. "We don't take walk-ins," she was told.

Hannah told the caseworker that she was supposed to be eligible for government-paid retraining, but had no idea how to access it. "I'm here asking for help, but I'm not getting any help," she insisted. "I'm slipping through the cracks."

"The person you need to talk to isn't here," the representative replied.

Hannah asked about scheduling an appointment. "We don't have anything available right now," she was told. "Too many people are off work." (By March 2010, the wait lists for retraining had grown to over 20,000, as demand grew but federal funding dropped.)

Hannah says she understands. "They are overworked. They don't have time for somebody who is just walking in off the street, I guess." Yet the cat-and-mouse game of agency appointments and applications is another headache she doesn't need. She is already anxious about her chances in today's job market. Like the assembly line at her plant, the competition has sped up, and she doesn't have the college degree that employers want, Hannah says. What she learned in her decades-old training as a medical assistant is now forgotten or outdated, and in any case the questionable school she attended—which somehow crammed a two-year program into nine months—went out of business years ago.

The stress has reached a point where Hannah needs to take anti-anxiety medication every night to soothe her to sleep. No one will hire her, at her age, with her various ailments, with her lack of education—and she knows it. "You got a lot of kids that are coming out of college," she says. "They don't have health issues behind them. They don't have all this garbage from life."

Now that she realizes how tough the job market has become for someone like her, Hannah regrets her decision to take the buyout. "What a stupid thing to do," she says, sobbing. "Because I would still be working and I would still have insurance and it was a stupid thing to do."

Her position at Chrysler, she now realizes, was a "dream job." Yes, it was tedious and dreary and even, at the end, dangerous. But the wages and benefits? A daughter of a single mom on welfare, a homeless teen, an abuse survivor—Hannah had gone through "hell," as she puts it. But when she started working at the plant, she told herself she had finally made it. "Everything was a fight, but when I got the job at Chrysler, it was like, 'Okay . . . I can take care of me.'"

Now, she tells herself, "Here I am again." As a kid, all Hannah wanted to do was leave her poor neighborhood. But she has landed right back—in another zip code, but with the same corners manned by the same drug pushers and alcoholics. "I'm just feeling kind of hopeless," she says. "I tried to get help and I'm just being pushed aside." She just wants a job, she insists. She doesn't want welfare. "I'm so scared that's where it's headed. I would be some lonely old woman sitting in an indigent housing [project] somewhere and lucky to get her cheese and her milk for a month."

Part of her thinks she would have wound up beaten up in a parking lot if she had tried to stick it out among her enraged coworkers at the plant. Still, she says with a wry laugh, maybe that wouldn't have been so bad.

"I would have at least had insurance to pay for the injury."

. . .

Unemployed workers like Hannah soon realize they are weighed down by the "baggage" of their past years. In a flexible economy geared toward customer service, they are burdened by the swaggering machismo they learned on the shop floor, as well as the scarlet letter of their past union membership. Even though many of them established a track record of hard work in their previous careers, they lack the abilities that employers desire when handing out today's good jobs—abilities that are often signaled by a college diploma in a relevant field.

For workers like mine, acquiring skills in high demand can set them on the path to promising and well-paid careers—especially when tuition help is coupled with in-person advising and cash transfers to families. However, it is unclear whether retraining can really work for this group as a whole. Under the speedup I describe in this chapter, those who start at the bottom of the hierarchy of human and cultural capital struggle to catch up amid a rising standard in the quantity and quality of the expected educational credentials, and in the savviness and sophistication of the expected job-search strategies. What has made this meritocratic treadmill possible, and propelled it forward, is the progress of markets and metrics. Galloping technological change outruns the training that workers have obtained so far, pushing them to enhance and refocus their expertise. Better methods of evaluation—what I call the new technology of meritocracy—multiply the traits that separate the good worker from the bad. The economy's sought-after jobs go to individuals with more privileged backgrounds, who have the resources and pedigree to pursue the more refined search strategies and attend the better schools. Even when they make great efforts to retrain, workers like mine often find themselves overwhelmed by more advantaged competitors and more advanced technologies.

DAMAGED GOODS

José Santos remembers what it was like at the plating plant years ago, before the owner got bought out. In the morning, there would be fruit and bagels with cream cheese laid out. The workers could help themselves. At the end of the month, the old man might hand out checks for fifty or a hundred dollars. "My sales were good today," he'd say.

Funny thing was, José recalls, some of the workers didn't appreciate the generosity. "What a cheap guy," they'd grumble. "He's sending us leftovers while he eats good." "He's giving us pennies." At least he's giving us something, José would reply.

That became clearer when the corporation took over. The new managers struck a different tone. "They'd walk by you, they didn't even say hi," José says. Business was business, and when business was no longer good, they cut José loose.

He's a stocky man with a broad face and crew-cut black hair, the skin under his brown eyes creased with lines. While we talk, he stands up every once in a while and places his hands on the edge of a couch for support. He has a bad back, he says, the result of several spills he took on the plant floor. The pain is so intense he can't sleep at night without prescription sleeping pills.

Now thirty-eight years old, José immigrated to Chicago from El Salvador when he was a teen. Within a few days he got beaten up in high school. He hated it there. Luckily, his family eventually moved to Canada. His single mother worked long hours as a nanny and maid for rich families, and left José in the care of his aunt, who raised him.

Right out of high school, José started studying construction engineering at a local college. But then he got the job at Chromeshield. "Working midnight shift every day and going to school—it was very hard," he says. It was hard on his ego as well as his body. His coworkers called him a "spic." They taunted the immigrants mercilessly. In a way, José understood why. "If you're a white person, and you're working in a factory next to another immigrant that just came—well, you had the opportunity of going to school and doing something better for yourself, and you didn't take it," he says. "You have a little anger, and you're showing it by picking on people."

Not long after he started working at the plant, José's HR manager pulled him aside. Because of his classes he was missing work, she said, and he'd have to choose one or the other. He chose work. When he dropped out of college, his mother became bitter. "She brought me here to be somebody," José says. "By me not fulfilling her desires, I let her down." They don't talk much anymore, he adds.

Now that he's lost his job, José realizes just how big a mistake he made all those years back, when he was a dumb teenager. "I could have had better choices," he says. "I could have made something better out of my life. . . . I have experience doing my job, but I don't have a diploma that backs me up—to say, 'Okay, this is what you are.'"

Recently, he got accepted into a plumbing training program at the same college he used to attend. But faced with surging demand, the government started targeting its retraining funds more narrowly, and José was left out. He says he couldn't afford to pay for the program by himself, so he had to give up his spot. It irks him that he had spent weeks calling and driving around to research the job market for his intended profession—a requirement to get the government's retraining help—and all that effort was for naught. "You get demoralized," he says. For the last three months José has worked a part-time job sweeping and mopping the floors at another car plant, but he gets few hours— two or three Saturdays a month at best—and no possibility of getting hired full-time by the cleaning company, which has taken over the plant's outsourced janitorial work.

After more than a year unemployed, José has blown through his savings. "They say that you should be able to save for about five months [in case] you lose your job," he says. "But hardly anybody can save that, with what you make here." He and his wife have been living in the limbo of bank overdraft for many months now. They can't afford medication for a pinched nerve that Aimee, who works in a nursing home, is suffering from, so they've gone without. They owe about $24,000 on their credit cards and a line of credit, and if things don't improve within the year, he says, they'll have to declare bankruptcy.

Some of José's coworkers have their hopes pinned on the possibility that the plant will reopen. He has no such illusions. He still talks to a former supervisor who moved to Indiana to work for one of the company's plants there. His friend worked there for over a year, clocking in fifteen to twenty hours a week in (unpaid) overtime every week. It was too much, and he quit.

Don't get your hopes up about another good job in this industry, his friend told José. "Over there, they're paying nine, ten dollars an hour, to little Mexicans that don't have their papers."

. . .

Since the labor market bottomed out in 2010, the economy's new jobs have tended to be in service industries with low wages. Over four years, manufacturing accounted for 7 percent of job growth, but the typical new job in that sector paid less than the national average.[1] Charlie

Calhoun, forty-nine, says that the factory jobs available now are nothing like the ones he and his coworkers lost. "They wanna pay you a McDonald's wage," says the American former parts worker, who is married and cares for his granddaughter. "And they're doing you a big favor, then. . . . If somebody could tell me how you could raise or run a household on $250 a week, I'll be glad." It's not even worth it to go off unemployment benefits for a low-wage job with no promise of even forty hours a week, says Ray Chong, thirty-nine, another parts worker. "Go work yourself to death, and then get laid off again? . . . You're gonna use gas money, then do an $8.50 job? Come on now."

Looking farther down the horizon, government reports predict that the jobs of the future will be concentrated in health care, computer systems design, business consulting, education, and "green" industries—building wind turbines and other renewable energy sources. But these flourishing industries generally need many fewer workers—and better-educated ones—than the car plants once did.[2] As for the auto industry, industry observers believe that the good jobs there will look something like those at Chrysler's Global Engine Manufacturing Alliance plant in Dundee, Michigan. There, sophisticated machinery restricts the need for manual labor, and getting a job requires a two-year technical degree or comparable experience. At the time of that plant's founding, the chairman of an influential industry think tank noted that education requirements were becoming the norm even in car factories: "The idea that you could be a third-grade dropout and earn a salary in manufacturing is no more."[3]

Ray Chong wasn't a particularly good student. After he graduated from high school, his immigrant parents wanted him to go to college. But Ray liked working with his hands, and he didn't want to spend years in school before he started making money. After a stint in the U.S. Navy, he got a job at the plating plant, where he spent almost two decades. Then the plant shut down. It was inevitable, says Ray. The downsizing had been going on for years, and given how much less-educated workers like him were being paid at the end, companies came to a simple conclusion: "You made too much. We don't need you." He doesn't really blame them. The owner must be making the right decisions, he concludes, because his company is expanding.

It's a tougher world out there, Ray points out. "You're paying more on your insurance, and they're paying you less money." Meanwhile, on the job market you need to have skills in order to compete—"be multipurpose," as he puts it. "That's just the bottom line of every job. You got to be able to do more than one or two jobs." You can't expect to have any job forever, he adds, and you can't expect to be trained on the job—employers want the complete package, up front. "They want somebody certified and got experience on what they're doing. Ain't no more off the street, 'Watch what I do, and do it.'"

For workers like Ray, without college degrees, the available jobs tend to be concentrated in two sectors. The first is white-collar clerical work. But those jobs demand communication and computer skills, and technology and outsourcing have taken over many routine tasks in the office, too, pushing even college-educated workers into redundancy.[4] The other alternative is, of course, the McJobs and Wal-careers of the burgeoning service sector, those restaurant and retail jobs that require a physical presence and cannot be outsourced. A few prominent firms in these sectors continue to follow the old corporate playbook of Henry Ford, who paid well to reduce attrition and to ensure that his workers could afford to buy the cars they made. But these companies are exceptions, and they appear to be swimming against the economic tide.[5] The demand for service workers has grown enormously, but on the lower tiers of this sector, the supply of workers has grown even more, as other industries downsize and as more women and immigrants compete for the available work. As a result, the jobs that less educated workers can actually obtain tend to pay dismal wages that often must be subsidized by government tax credits, food stamps, and health insurance for the poor.[6] Furthermore, a number of studies have found that few of those toiling on these bottom rungs of the labor market are able to move on up to better-paid work. The new economy's dreary underbelly of low-wage work illustrates what I would call the "Walmart theory of economic trade-offs": everyday low prices that are good for the individual customer are bad for the workforce that must survive on everyday low wages, and bad for the community that must tolerate an everyday low tax base.[7]

The rise of temporary and part-time workers makes employment in the service sector even more uncertain.[8] Three years after losing his job at Ford, Sal Cheriel has finally settled for working at a janitorial service—cleaning the very plants where he used to work—for $15 an hour, less than half his autoworker wage. Sal insists he isn't ashamed of his new occupation, but some of his old Ford factory mates gossip at his expense. "I hear from somebody else that they're talking about me cleaning washrooms," says Sal, a forty-seven-year-old Canadian. "It's none of their business, but it bothers me." He remembers how he used to talk down his racist coworkers—the ones who taunted him with the words *terrorist* and *Taliban*—by telling them, self-righteously, that native-born people like them should be doctors or lawyers, not factory workers. "You shouldn't be working in this place because you've got all the benefits that this country can give you," he would needle them after one of their occasional shop-floor tirades. "But you chose to work in this factory, so that's your problem. . . . People like you wouldn't even get a peon job in my country." That shut them up.

But even his meager janitor's paycheck will soon be out of Sal's grasp. After 89 days, just before his probationary period ends, Sal will be terminated—his boss has told him so. The company is firing another three full-time workers, so temporary workers like him have no chance at employment. It's wrong, Sal says, that companies can get away with stringing along workers like him for 89 days and then letting them go. He needs a job, even a low-wage job, to keep paying his bills, which includes college tuition for his two older sons. (His wife P.J. works at a Tim Hortons coffee shop, but the family can't make it just on her low wages.) "You work so hard in your life, you build up equity, and now you're going to lose it because nobody will hire you," Sal says.

At establishments from Jamba Juice to Target, managers use new technologies of just-in-time scheduling to determine exactly when and where to deploy their labor, throwing low-wage employees into a competition for hours. Sometimes, the metrics they use to dole out hours to perennial part-timers are painfully clear. Scott Shipman, formerly at Chrysler, has found a part-time job at a department store, but management gives him hardly any hours. Some weeks he isn't scheduled to work at all. His manager has told him up front that if he gets more of his customers to sign up for store credit cards when he is manning the cash register, he'll get more time on the clock. (In ways like this one, the performance criteria for keeping even a cashier job have grown.) "It's kinda like an unwritten rule," Scott says. "And that's why maybe I'm on a 'vacation' as far as all this coming week." He laughs, but without hours, he can't pay his bills. After his unemployment dragged on for months, Scott could not keep up with the $900-a-month payments on his subprime home mortgage. He went through a foreclosure, wound up in a one-bedroom apartment, and then—when his savings dried up—moved in with his parents.

As they look to start new careers amid the twin pitfalls of bad jobs and few hours (often in the very same position), the situation of these workers brings to mind the joke about the two elderly women at the

Catskill mountain resort. One of them said, "Boy, the food at this place is really terrible!" The other said, "I know—and such small portions!"

. . .

Within today's more uncertain and polarized labor market, my workers suffer from several traits that put them at risk of entrenched unemployment. They are older and less educated. Their experience is outdated and was acquired at unionized workplaces. And the factory culture they are used to puts them out of sync with the chief commandment of today's consumer culture of entitlement: servile customer service.

My workers came from an industry that had experienced waves of downsizing in the decades prior to the Great Recession. Thanks to union rules, those with the least seniority had gone out the door first. Thanks to union-won wages and benefits, turnover had been minimal. This meant that those who remained in the plants tended to be older. (The median age of my workers was forty-three.) Not surprisingly, the long-term unemployed in general tend to be older workers like the ones I got to know. Employers generally see them as poor investments. They assume that older workers cannot adapt to new times, new practices, and new technologies as quickly as their younger counterparts—a not unrealistic assumption, which my workers brought up time and time again in explaining their own failures in the labor market.[9]

Among my older workers, the decision to head into the factories had seemed, at the time, quite rational. In Detroit and Windsor, the incentives had been clear: factory jobs were the golden ticket to a middle-class lifestyle. But now, with hindsight, my workers see those decisions as bad ones. D.J. Packer, a sixty-year-old Canadian worker let go from his parts plant, went to school in the mid-eighties with the goal of becoming a counselor. A college adviser talked him out of it. There wasn't a big demand for that profession, he said. D.J. would have better luck in the auto industry. Four decades later, D.J. is in school again, studying to become an addictions counselor—again. Hard-hit Windsor needs social workers, he says. "I think back now and I'm saying, 'I should have taken that [course].'"

In both countries, most of my workers confessed to having had little interest or success in school back when they were young. They talked about how they enjoyed working with their hands and liked the idea of bringing something tangible and useful into the world. A few, however, had sought out higher education before the car plants lured them away. In this sense, the existence of high-paying, low-skill jobs unprofitably persuaded talented individuals to leave their natural abilities fallow. David Vihan, a forty-five-year-old ex-Ford worker, had been an A student in high school. "If I applied myself schooling-wise, who knows what I would have ended up doing?" he says. Instead, he drank heavily in his brief and underachieving college career—his "six-month bender." After a series of low-wage positions got him nowhere, David managed to get a job at Ford. Over the years, he grew comfortable in the factory, a secure retirement assured. "I thought I was a lifer," he says. But David was laid off in 2008, and found himself unexpectedly back in school, studying medical accounting. His life has come "full circle," he points out, now that he is back on the white-collar career track. "I wanted that one year to party and it's taken—what?—thirty years." (And yet, starting over after Ford has been a painful, disorienting experience, David adds: "I'd go back in a heartbeat.")

Beyond their lack of youth and education, my workers also face a political disadvantage: they are marked as former union members.[10] Judging from comments they hear from employers, Americans and Canadians alike believe that companies look down on former autoworkers as lazy or only willing to work for unrealistic wages. One American parts worker says he can't tell employers that he took a college course on labor law. "You tell them that, you never will get hired." Employers don't "come right out and say it," he adds, "but that's what's going on." In fact, representatives from the state job center bluntly advised him and his coworkers not to disclose their union histories. "That's just like putting a red flag saying, 'Don't hire me,'" an official told them.

In one sense, workers like mine would seem ideal job candidates. It was quite common for them to put in twelve-hour days and six-day weeks when production ramped up. Mitch Beerman, thirty-three, often worked seventy-hour weeks at his Canadian parts plant. (The years of intense labor destroyed his body, he notes: his knees have no cartilage left because of "all the walking and banging into the line with my knees.") Mitch took vacation only three times over thirteen years there, and would volunteer to do maintenance even during plant shutdowns. "Instead of just sitting at home all day," he says, "I'd rather be going to work and do something." Nevertheless, Mitch's record of hard work has translated into little reward on his recently updated résumé. He can't find a job after more than a year out of work.

Since the beginning of the Great Recession, there has been a vigorous debate among economists about whether today's unemployment is structural or cyclical. One group believes that unemployed workers are failing to find jobs because they do not have the specific skills that today's employers want—a mismatch that has been underway for decades, but that the economic crisis made glaring. The other group argues that a simple lack of demand means businesses are not expanding and hiring, and once spending takes off again—perhaps with the government's help—strong growth will return.[11] Regardless of whether the so-called skills mismatch is a good explanation for what happened after the recession, it is something much on the minds of my workers.

In earlier times, they say, they possessed the kinds of merit that the market wanted. But now it demands more. "It used to be you come up and say, 'Okay, I've got a strong back,' and all that," says Charlie Calhoun, the American parts worker. "Strong back don't mean shit. You gotta have dedication and you've gotta have some kind of smartness, or something." At the plant, there were workers who couldn't read or write, says Randy Simpson, another parts worker. "But them days are over with. They don't want no dummies working for them. You've got to have something. You've got to know something."

In today's competitive job market, hard and hungry workers abound, while the truly skilled man or woman is hard to hire. Economic trends have raised the market value of workers with a wide range of traits: intelligence, creativity, self-reliance, sociability, ambition, entrepreneurialism. What is valued now, especially to get in the door at a company, is not just effort but ability. This idea of talent matters differently at different points in the labor market.[12] As Richard Sennett argues, among upper-to-middle-level managers, merit means being flexible above all: not mastering a skill or having experience (in fact, too much experience at one firm makes the worker seem "too ingrown") but having the "potential" to be good at many things, and thus adaptable to the needs of an ever-evolving market.[13] To find a job, blue-collar job seekers may need to conform less to particular cultural sensibilities than their white-collar counterparts do, as I will discuss later in this chapter. But the bar for workers like mine has been raised, too, especially in the search for good jobs that pay well. Certainly more so than it was in the postwar period—and perhaps more so than it is for today's white-collar workers—human capital is decisive for workers at these lower levels of the labor market, with a diploma as its most convenient proxy.

Hard work is still important, my workers said. Nevertheless, what they called "smart work" matters more—having both the discipline and the intellectual ability to learn a complex skill. In other words, it is about attaining the ideal of "craftsmanship" that is disappearing within the higher tiers of the labor market: blue-collar workers are moving in the direction of the "old-fashioned notions of merit" of white-collar workers, who are already moving on to new talents.[14] Because skill, and not hard work, is decisive, bad decisions made years ago not to acquire those skills now come back to haunt my workers. James Channing, a former parts worker who grew up in Windsor, dropped out of school after the ninth grade because he was always getting in trouble. He went to work at a bowling alley, running the pin machine in back for $3.25 an hour. "I wish I'd have stayed in school," he laments. "It's just kind of embarrassing for me. . . . I'm used to working. I'm used to holding my own." But it is tougher for workers like James to make it on their own. He has applied to dozens of positions, mostly at factories and stores—"I don't have the education for anything else"—but has yet to get his first interview after fourteen months of trying.

Granted, James could spread his net even more widely, but at age forty-three he refuses. "I don't want to work at McDonald's or something like that, you know? I don't want to throw on a goofy hat." For the good jobs still out there for less educated workers, the competition is astonishing, James says. Companies advertise to fill a few dozen spots and get deluged with thousands of applications. It's hard not to get discouraged. Again and again, he circles back to the humiliating fact that he is a dropout. "So what do I gotta do? Go back to school for four years?"

Past research suggests that the path that factory workers took to advance within the plant has long been evolving. "The traditional prerequisites for getting on in the world—perseverance, determination, ambition, resourcefulness—were *in* the individual," wrote the sociologist Eli Chinoy in his classic study of autoworkers. By the postwar decades, however, his autoworkers had to learn to "get along" with associates and managers in order to rise up the career ladder. The focus on hard work had shifted somewhat to personality. Nevertheless, thanks to the seniority system imposed by unions, Chinoy adds, advancement was also "increasingly collective in character."[15] Nowadays, merit as measured by education matters more in getting a good job than was the case in Chinoy's time, when union jobs—and the nonunion jobs competing with them—were still relatively widespread. What is also different is that workers no longer have any hope of spending decades in one job. "People gave their all to these companies, and in the end, the company is still there and you're gone," says Ziggy Dordick, forty, a former Ford worker. And the companies themselves get bought up and reorganized, he points out. Family, he says, is the only constant—and yet that, too, as I will describe in chapter 4, is up for debate.

Being a worker in demand today is not just about having cognitive ability or even soft skills of playing well with others. It also includes cultural skills not often taught in factories. In this sense, the idea of a skills mismatch is somewhat narrow, focused as it tends to be on technical competencies. In the professional world, sociologist Ofer Sharone argues, American employers look for a personal "chemistry" between the job candidate and her potential coworkers. In other words, they are looking for the right amount of cultural capital—the refined personality and appearance that mark a candidate as a worthy member of a team. The working class, Sharone points out, do not necessarily need to cultivate such chemistry. Yet, even former autoworkers are learning how crucial the presentation of self is in the segments of the economy that are actually hiring.[16] Offices are looking for white-collar mannerisms and gray-cubicle blandness. In a factory, Ziggy points out, you just have to "do your job." "But then when you get out, you find [out] the real world is, you have to really work it. You have to find ways, you know. If you never golfed, you golf now, 'cause that's what the guys do on the weekends." Ziggy remembers how union officials would lecture the workers on how, in the old days, workers had to bring bottles of wine to the foreman to get a job. Now those days are returning, he says—he sees his fellow job seekers bringing doughnuts and coffee to woo potential employers. "That's how you're going to get hired," he says.

A comfort with customer service is also key. In this "the customer is God" era, restaurants and retail outlets need workers who can throw on a cheery, grin-and-bear-it demeanor like a suit. To find jobs at these places, my workers need to shed the tough exterior they developed in a male-dominated, hard-drinking workplace. (Alcoholism and drug use are still rampant in the plants, many of my workers say.) Also, the sometimes profanity-laced, politically incorrect language that is common on the plant floor has no place in the workplaces now hiring. American Mal Stephen, fifty-one, points out that the Chrysler plant was "liberating" because you "didn't have to wear a tie, didn't have to shave, didn't have to wear matching socks." Yet these are the very preferences that make former factory workers unsuitable for certain service jobs, which require careful attention to the appearance and personality that workers project when dealing with customers.

Gender plays a conspicuous role here. Pundits called the Great Recession a "mancession" because its impact was felt disproportionately by men. In 2009, the gap between male and female unemployment rates was the highest since World War II.[17] (That divide has narrowed since then.) Women were a quarter of the workers I interviewed, but their experiences were more mixed than the term "mancession" might suggest. The married women I talked to tended to cope better with unemployment, but the single women did not (as I will discuss in chapter 4). At the same time, my male workers faced unique challenges of their own. The factory floor where they had spent their formative years is a world apart, culturally speaking, from the offices and hospital wards and nurseries and classrooms where the jobs of the future are materializing. Health care, education, and other booming sectors are skill-intensive fields where women have traditionally predominated, at least in the lower and middle tiers.

Yul Kane, a forty-two-year-old former Ford worker, served abroad in the military. He remembers applying for clerical jobs after he came back to Windsor. The director of one personnel agency told him that he normally would be an ideal fit—"good background and has dealings internationally"—but he just didn't have the "look" employers wanted. They preferred that a woman provide the "frontline service," she said. Yul ended up getting some interviews, but none panned out. "It'd always get down to the final interview and then the one who always ended up getting hired was the busty blonde or another redhead," says Yul, who went on to a career in the Windsor auto industry—a place where such politically incorrect language was better tolerated, too.

Beyond their perceived surfeit of testosterone, factory veterans may also be hindered in getting service-sector jobs by a lack of modern-day sensitivity about race. Sarmad Dakka, thirty-one, is a second-generation immigrant. He says that coworkers at his plating plant would taunt him occasionally. Things reached a head when Chad, a coworker he had once been friendly with, started joining in. "Hey, Paki, Canadian winters are cold," he'd say. The rest of the guys would laugh. Chad was trying to show off to them. After one incident, Sarmad, who isn't Pakistani, told his former friend nicely that he needed to stop. Chad kept it up.

Chad is the taller of the two. Sarmad is "on the short side," he admits, though his well-built frame is visible even underneath a thick winter fleece. In any case, Sarmad knew he couldn't just let the insult go. He didn't care about what Chad thought; he cared about the rest of the crew. "These guys would have thought every day they could come in there and just call me a Paki," he says.

"Listen," he told Chad, "if you call me a Paki one more time, you're going to get it." The second he finished that sentence, Chad repeated the slur.

Sarmad slugged him.

His supervisor was there, as well as the union's vice chair and a shop steward. The plant manager was down the hall. No one reprimanded him. His foreman later said he was glad that Sarmad had stood up for himself. "That guy's got such a big mouth."

If he had been working in an office, Sarmad could have lost his job. With a violent crime on his record, he probably wouldn't have been able to find a new job, he points out. But in the plant, his willingness to fight won him respect.

. . .

As tough as factory life could be, it is important to remember that the industry's high wages and benefits made the choice to enter the factory gates quite prudent at the time many of my workers started their careers. Likewise, something not at all under their control—the recession—had much to do with the situation my workers later found themselves in. Laid off in the downturn and unable to find new jobs as the economy slowly recovered, they racked up months of unemployment that made them seem damaged goods.

In this way, the long-term unemployed suffer from a temporal mismatch as well. Employers look at the gaps in their résumés and are loath to take a chance. A study of the long-term unemployed in America found that only a third of those jobless since the beginning of the recession had found a job after an extended period of time—half of what a standard economic model would predict.[18] Joblessness begets joblessness.

SECOND CHANCES

Yul Kane joined the Canadian Army in 1989, and rose quickly through the ranks. But after several years of intense service—including a year in the Balkan war zone—he was worn down. He was recommended for officer training at the Royal Military College of Canada, but he turned it down. His then girlfriend Sara and her young son had just followed him to his posting in Ottawa. He couldn't leave them again for two years at the academy. "For a change I wanted family first, rather than career," he says.

It had taken him just six years to reach the rank of master corporal, but now he was having second thoughts about devoting his life to the military. His career manager flew into town with a new request: "I want you to go back overseas for another year."

"I haven't been back for two years," Yul said. He was burnt out, he added, after his tour of duty in the former Yugoslavia.

"If you don't go, then I'll basically halt your rank," the manager said.

"You know what? I'll halt it for you." Yul decided to resign.

Back in Windsor, he eventually landed a job at Ford, with the help of an uncle who worked there. At the time, Yul was already working as a data-entry clerk at a government agency. The office job paid $11 an hour; Ford paid $19. Yul decided to keep both jobs. Many people new to Ford got cut before their 90-day probation ended. So, for 66 days, Yul worked nonstop: a twelve-hour midnight shift at the Windsor factory, on top of an eight-hour workday at the office. "I was kind of used to it from the military. I'd grab a shower right at the plant, and I'd have a big lunch pail over in my car with ice packs and all that." After his shower he would head over to his office job. He would change his clothes in his car—a pair of Dockers khakis, a dress shirt—and gulp down a coffee from the closest Tim Hortons. When his workday was finally done, Yul would head home, grab three hours of shuteye, and then head back to the plant. He used the weekends to catch up on sleep ("eight hours sleep each day—it felt like you're getting twenty"), while continuing to plow through Saturday and Sunday twelve-hour shifts for Ford.

On the 67th day, Yul was laid off. But he was one of the fortunate ones: Ford called him back a year later. He continued to work twelve-hour shifts regularly—pulling in $100,000 a year, on average, with all the overtime. "I liked working hard," he says. "And my wife used to give me shit—that I'd go home and I'd be so exhausted." He'd want to sit down and "decompress," but his stepson, Nick, would want to play. "You've got to give me a half hour," he'd tell Nick. Like many parents, Yul was torn between the responsibilities at the two ends of his daily commute. But Ford was paying him a good wage to do a good job, he points out. "Every job I ever had, that's what was expected of me," he says. "So that's what I did." It was a work ethic he learned from his own mother, a divorced single mother who raised Yul and his two sisters while running her own health club six days a week, sixty-eight hours a week.

Yul ended up spending a decade in the auto industry. One day at the plant, a lift truck turned a corner too quickly and crashed into the guardrail in front of him. The force wrenched the rail out of the floor and whipped it into his back, sending him flying several feet forward. After the initial pain subsided, Yul counted himself lucky and went back to work. But a few hours later his back stiffened up like wood. He headed to a medical center. The injury turned out to be a bulging disc in his spine. Yul took the rest of the day off, but came back the next day. "I went to work—popping Tylenol 3s like they're M&M's." The pain was unrelenting at first, but he ignored it ("I'm a little bit screwy in the head at times"). He ended up having to wait almost two years to see a neurosurgeon about his problem, but he learned to exercise regularly to control the pain.

Throughout 2007, rumors circulated in the plant that more layoffs were coming. This time, they turned out to be true. Yul's last day was a few weeks before Christmas. That day, Yul worked his full eight hours, as diligently as he normally did—to the puzzlement of some coworkers. "Why the hell are you doing that?" they asked him.

"I've got a job to do," he said.

Yul found it hard to cope with life after Ford. He had memories of growing up in Windsor's public housing after his parents divorced. And now he, who used to work in the government office that handled unemployment insurance, was on those benefits himself—though he told himself that he wasn't one of those welfare recipients "milking the system." He was using it temporarily to get out of "this rut," he says. Still, it hurt his pride to depend on anyone's help. He fought with his wife about finances. "I was probably on edge more, probably drank a little bit more."

In the first months after his layoff, Yul applied for dozens of jobs— from assembly-line work, to sales positions, to security details. Some managers said he was underqualified. Others said he was overqualified. "They want someone that they think is going to be younger, quicker, stronger," he says. Yul also ran into employers who felt—as he puts it—that "people who worked at the Big Three don't want to work."

"I'm sorry," a factory manager once told him, "but we can't pay you what the Big Three pays."

"Well, did I say I wanted what the Big Three paid?" Yul asked. "I'm just saying give me a shot." Yet the company wasn't willing.

Eventually, Yul got fed up with the constant rejections and decided to go back to school. A high school graduate, Yul tapped Ontario's

Second Career program, which offered up to $22,000 (U.S. dollars) in financial help to retrain. The former military man is now studying to become a nurse. As a man, Yul thinks there may be more opportunities for him there. In this he is not unlike many of today's job seekers, who are reconsidering gender roles more intently as the job market becomes more cutthroat.[19]

Yul says he doesn't see nursing as unmanly. In fact, he sees similarities between serving in an infantry unit and serving in a hospital ward: "It's all about teamwork." And he likes taking care of people. "If someone walks in here and starts ripping you," he says, "I'd probably be the one in front of you, saying, 'I'm going to back your ass up.'"

But it was tough convincing Sara that he should go back to school. She had recently had surgery for a back injury and was still on unpaid leave from her factory job. The couple had spent the last several months watching their years of savings evaporate. Even after he won over his wife and started his classes, Yul found himself wondering if he had made the right decision. It had been two decades since he'd been in school, and he'd never been a great student to begin with, he says. He had trouble retaining anything from his lectures and textbooks in his forty-something brain. He would find himself locked in a room upstairs, trying to plod through his homework, while Nick was tearing around the house. Yul's temper would get the better of him, and the yelling would ensue.

But now that he is in his second year, Yul is learning to balance school and family obligations better—as is his son. "Dad, you got homework?" he'll ask Yul when he gets home. "Okay, I won't bother you." In turn, Sara has come to accept her husband's decision to return to school. She points out that she wouldn't be able to do that at their age. ("You'd better not say that," Yul tells her, "because you may have to one day, too.")

Studying for a degree has given Yul a sense of purpose that he had been missing ever since he lost his job. "I always worked. If I'm not working, I'm going a little bit nuts," he says. "I don't necessarily like the schooling process, but I like having a place to be."

Ontario's retraining program gave Yul the wherewithal to consider another shot at school. "That's a one-time opportunity," he notes. "So I want to make sure that I get this in. That's very important." He hopes that, with the proper training, he'll be able to find a job in the Windsor area. He can't uproot his family again. And he can't return to his nomadic military life, when he was away for long stretches of time. Ten-year-old

Nick has not seen his biological dad since he was a toddler. Yul calls the boy his son. "I'm the only dad he knows. I don't want him thinking his dad walked out on him again."

If he had stayed in the service, Yul points out, he would have become an officer and would probably be retired by now. "But that's not what we're all about, right? I came back to Windsor because my family is here, everyone's getting older, and I just wanted to come back. I wanted to carve out my little niche in society and coach hockey and be with the woman I love and my kids. And that's what I'm doing."

. . .

Retraining policies on both sides of the border are explicitly designed to push workers away from declining industries and toward the hi-tech, high-skill occupations of the economy's dynamic sectors. During the time of my fieldwork, Michigan's No Worker Left Behind program paid up to $10,000 over two years to cover the expenses of those seeking degrees or certificates in "high-demand" fields.[20] Ontario's retraining program, Second Career, also provided two years of paid training, but offered a more generous and more extensive array of supports: more than twice as much money to pay for tuition, books, transportation, and living allowances.[21] What is more, my choice to study Michigan makes the American retraining system look better in my analysis than it actually is. Cobbled together from a variety of funding sources, Michigan's retraining program was particularly innovative and exceptional compared to what was offered in other states, and it also ended quickly, in 2010. Now that the program is gone, a Michigan worker can get, at best, a few thousand dollars to cover any tuition costs for retraining, as is more typical under America's grossly underfunded workforce development system.[22]

That said, the retraining support provided to a *particular* group of American manufacturing workers was the most munificent of all the programs I studied. Devised by the Kennedy administration as a way to mollify labor groups upset over trade agreements, the federal Trade Adjustment Assistance program places a well-reinforced safety net under manufacturing workers laid off because of foreign competition. These fortunate workers receive longer unemployment benefits—discussed in the next chapter—and a more plentiful retraining fund. (Thanks to emergency legislation, during the recession, service-sector workers could temporarily apply for these benefits, too.) At the time of my study, Michigan routinely covered tuition costs of up to $15,000 a year for up to two years. Because of this program's narrow focus, America has a lopsided approach to retraining. It is by far the most generous to a small group of manufacturing workers who can claim they've been harmed by foreign imports.[23]

These important details—the exceptional and temporary nature of the Michigan retraining program and the access that my particular autoworkers had to a more generous federal program—exaggerate the strength of America's retraining policies. My workers enjoyed key protections that weren't available to most of the country's unemployed.[24] However, it is important to note that the generous assistance provided in theory did not always work out so well in practice. The plants I studied were all certified for trade-adjustment benefits, with the UAW shepherding the petitions through the complex process, but the parts plant was not until 2010—a year after the layoffs.[25] Due to the delay, my parts workers did not see any of the federal program's benefits until after my fieldwork was completed.

In fact, out of all the American workers I interviewed, only one—an ex-Chrysler worker—was going to school with the program's help. Others said they planned to make use of it in the future, but a third of my Chrysler workers claimed they had run into problems accessing it.[26] One worker told me he wasn't even aware that he, as a buyout taker, could apply when he left Chrysler. Another failed to enroll at her community college within a year of her layoff, and was told she was therefore ineligible. A third found a program in Georgia to train him to become an electrical lineman because he couldn't find a similar course in Michigan. Even though the retraining funds are federal, the state-administered program refused to pay for the out-of-state program. A fourth took courses at a culinary school but ended up paying his tuition out of pocket. He was waitlisted for required courses offered only at certain times of the year, he says, and the program wouldn't permit a long pause between classes.

Rose Scott, thirty-eight, went to the state job center near her home in Pontiac looking for advice about these kinds of retraining options. She came to the point of tears because no one was helping her. "You're on your own," she says, describing what it's like at the center. "'Okay, here's the computer,' and that's that." A former Chrysler worker, she asked about applying for the trade-adjustment program. "I don't know anything about that, but I'll put your name on the list," the representative said. She asked about No Worker Left Behind. The next open informational session was months away, he told her. "We'll put your name on the list."

Eventually, Rose was able to find more knowledgeable guidance through a state job center set up, in a special partnership, right in one of the UAW's training buildings. But she is still anxious about what is going to happen next. She plows through job applications, trying to keep herself from getting too depressed. She continues to wait for the government funding to come through so that she can go back to school. "As long as I get the schooling . . . I'll find me a job, because there's something out there. But you just need the education, you know?" In her view, retraining offers a hope of something better, and in spite of all her frustrations so far, Rose Scott is clinging tenaciously to that hope.

The kinds of bureaucratic problems that Rose and others ran into mattered, because who received what kinds of benefits tended to predict the trajectories of my workers. Darius Harding, thirty-seven, was the one American able to tap the federal program, which paid his $31,000 tuition for a twenty-month aircraft-mechanic course. "I would feel shame if I wasn't in school," he says. "I couldn't see myself as a man just sitting around doing nothing." But because he is a full-time student and feels challenged by his studies, being unemployed "doesn't bother me a bit." Taking classes, he adds, is "a job in itself."

Workers who had to rely on the stingier, oversubscribed state program, No Worker Left Behind, tended to be less happy. Its funding dried up as the federal contribution declined, and in 2010, the state decided to stop adding people to its waitlist, which had climbed into the tens of thousands. One of my parts workers told me he wanted to use the state money to study computer repair. He was told that the program wasn't accepting new applicants, but to call back later. Three months later, he was still waiting.

Like Michigan, Ontario found it hard to sustain its retraining schemes amid surging demand. In just sixteen months, its Second Career program surpassed a three-year goal of helping 20,000 people. Low on funding, it began prioritizing the long-term unemployed, the less educated, and those with lengthy work histories. Even then, there was no guarantee. James Channing, the former parts worker, asked a nonprofit about tapping Second Career; they told him it was too late. The program was out of money and not accepting new applicants—even high school dropouts like him. "If they're not gonna pay, I can't afford it," James says. "I don't have a cent. I don't even have money for the bus."[27]

Liz Jung, a forty-six-year-old former Ford worker, was shut out even before the reforms: she is studying for a university degree, and Second Career won't fund that. She no longer receives unemployment benefits, either, because she is a full-time student. (Fortunately, her partner's income is enough to cover her tuition.) Liz admits she was a hard partier when she was in college decades ago, but these days her professor calls her "neurotic" because she is so fixated on doing well in her classes. Liz's three daughters, her son-in-law, and her two grandkids now live at home, she points out. Two daughters are finishing up school, and the oldest, Irene, recently lost a contract job as a medical assistant—ironically, she was let go a week before she had to take time off for major surgery. ("You would think in a hospital, they'd be a little bit more understanding, right?") For Liz, completing her education—quick—is imperative. "This is your last kick at the can," she says. "I've got to make this work, because now, you've got a family to provide for." It frustrates Liz that she can't get more in the way of help.

In general, though, my Canadian trainees fared better than their American counterparts. For one thing, tuition supports in Canada go further because tuition there is generally lower.[28] The infrastructure of schools to retrain unemployed workers also tends to be better funded there. The United States spends more than any other nation on higher education, but this is largely due to the huge amount of money it pours into private institutions. Its expenditures on public institutions, which include its overwhelmingly public system of junior and community colleges—where much of the retraining dollars go—fall sharply below Canada's.[29]

Not surprisingly, my Canadian workers were much more pleased with the quality of the education they were receiving. The superior funding for training made a difference for them—as did a special set of advocates working on their behalf, as I'll discuss next.

. . .

When a large layoff occurs in Ontario, government officials are required to respond immediately—within twenty-four hours of hearing the news. They contact the company and its workers and help them get access to various services. With the province's help, the employer and employees may also decide to set up an action center. Action centers assist laid-off workers with their job searches and serve as clearinghouses for information about training, benefits, charities, and the like.[30] Companies frequently chip in some of the funding, though other times—particularly when a firm goes bankrupt—the province pays for everything.

Much more targeted than the generic career centers on both sides of the border, each action center usually focuses on workers let go by a single employer. Importantly, they are often staffed by some of the very people who were laid off.[31] These "peer helpers" receive one or two days of training. At the center, they give in-depth advice on applications for government assistance, making sure their fellow unemployed workers avoid bureaucratic pitfalls. They help with résumés and discuss job openings and training opportunities. They advocate on behalf of individual workers, making phone calls, writing letters, and even acting as interpreters. (In the next chapter I'll have more to say about their role in helping workers cope with unemployment.)

More broadly, the action centers provide an approach tailored to the needs of their clientele. At times they arrange for their own classes, to fill in gaps they see in their workers' educations. For example, one action center for parts workers near Toronto (many of them immigrants) had an instructor from the local school district come regularly to the center to teach its workers basic reading and math. In a comfortable environment where they know many people and their peers expect them to show up, older workers can ease themselves back into a classroom setting after decades away.[32] When workers want to take classes elsewhere, the centers will often coordinate workshops for skills training and sign up workers in-house. One unemployed worker I talked to took a course to renew his forklift license through his center, which paid the fee, too. "You just sign for it, and it's paid for"—it's that simple, he says. At their most involved, centers use their bulk buying power to negotiate special courses, push down tuition rates, and arrange internships. For instance, Ford's center in Windsor found a way to enroll its workers in an oversubscribed nursing program by convincing the college to set up a new course just for them—starting at a time of the year that fit with their pressing need to find work, rather than the school's calendar.

Yul Kane, the ex-Ford worker, says that taking classes with his former coworkers has taken away some of the anxiety of returning to school in his forties. They study together and provide each other with a support system. He is especially close to a classmate who used to work at his plant. "When I have questions I call him up and he helps me out a lot," he says. He wonders if his friend truly knows how much he helps—not just with homework, but also with processing everything that's happened since he left Ford.

In all these ways, action centers bring together former coworkers and forge new ties between older, nontraditional students who share the experience of losing their jobs. That makes the centers more effective as job-search resources and places for informal counseling. In other words, they are generators of what sociologists call social capital, the more and less tangible benefits of personal relationships, cooperation, and community.[33] Like all forms of social capital, however, the strength of these ties can also have a less positive side. One of my workers complained that the action center was cliquish, leaving workers like him—those who didn't pal around with the peer helpers—out of the loop of information about job openings. "They help the little group that is close to them," he said.

The government representatives who oversee the centers tend to take a hands-off approach, giving the centers the freedom to spend their money and concentrate their efforts on the kinds of activities that they think will best help their workers (including, at times, political protests). "When you start to dictate to people how things are going to be done, you've lost what the process is all about," says Mark Van, a twenty-year veteran of advising adjustment programs in Ontario. In his line of work, he says, the key thing is flexibility: letting the workers figure out what they really need and not imposing a cookie-cutter approach. In this way, the province's approach to adjustment departs from the stereotype of government as a rule-bound bureaucracy.[34]

On the American side, there have been peer programs for unemployed workers in several states. But they have not been nearly as well used or widespread as the Canadian programs (which inspired them) have been, and they have depended heavily on the involvement of labor unions willing to push the idea. Furthermore, almost all of these programs have shut down or scaled back their work in recent years, due to budget cuts and the hostility of anti-union governors.[35] As for my workers, a few of the former Chrysler employees went to the in-house state job center I mentioned earlier, which offered help better tailored to their backgrounds. But none of my American workers had access to any peer program. While my Canadians could turn to their union brothers and sisters for support at the action centers, my Americans told me it was up to the local leadership to intervene on behalf of the people they liked. "The union chief don't tell you what's going on," complains one worker.

Lynn Minick, a workforce development specialist for the National Employment Law Project, has helped set up a variety of peer programs—everything from sending out roving peers to bowling alleys and other places where their unemployed coworkers hang out, to establishing fully staffed centers right across from plants being closed. He wonders why the Department of Labor doesn't use this approach more when large layoffs strike. "I think people who serve dislocated workers can tell you that where they've had the use of peers, those have been the most successful dislocation events," he says. (One study of peer programs found that they significantly increase how many workers end up using various government services.[36]) Given America's excessively decentralized approach to workforce development in general, Minick says, most states face little in the way of pressure to make contact with companies and workers going through a layoff, much less deploy peer counselors to help them. Instead, they tend to respond to layoffs in a half-hearted fashion, at most sending out their representatives to give the affected employees a one- or two-hour orientation session about government services—at a time when the workers are just coming to grips with the loss of their jobs. "You're losing 80 to 90 percent of people right there," Minick says. (My American workers attended these orientations, they said, but the spotty knowledge they had about retraining programs suggests they weren't really listening, either.)

While some self-starters will always get by on their own, other people benefit from training and advice to help them become productively employed again. With the support of their peer helpers and a generous government retraining program, my Canadians tended to be more optimistic about their chances in the labor market, better able to direct their financial aid toward ambitious goals (for example, nursing and accounting rather than truck driving and culinary arts), and less troubled by financial problems.

One factor that may have improved their outlook was the fact that two-thirds of the Ford Canada workers had *not* taken a company buyout, which meant that in theory they could have been called back to their old jobs. My Ford workers could hold out the hope, then, that their unemployment would be temporary, even if they'd had no luck so far getting a new job. That said, a third of these workers *had* taken the buyout and thus could not be recalled. None of my other workers—American Chrysler workers, American and Canadian parts workers—had this option, either. My study did not follow these workers over the long term, but a union-sponsored study of similar groups of unemployed autoworkers near Toronto—Chrysler workers and parts workers—found that a third of all workers went back to school and ended up getting a job related to their training.[37]

THE SPEEDUP

Mal Stephen was one of the lucky few to make it through the factory gates before they shut. Born in Detroit, he was raised by his mother and grandmother. He called both Mom. His father, who sold heroin, was never around. As a young man, Mal enlisted in the Navy to leave Detroit and its factories. But after coming home and plodding through a series of low-paid temp jobs, Mal realized that the auto industry was the only game in town. That was the only career path that offered someone like him the pay a college graduate might receive. When he landed the job at Chrysler, he worked hundred-hour weeks at the plant when he could, easily supporting his wife and two children with the prodigious amounts of overtime. And with every contract, his wages went up. "I went to $30 an hour, plus all the benefits in the world," Mal says. "Nothing compares to that. I mean, that I could get—that's gone now. You can't make a hundred thousand dollars a year without a college degree now."

After Mal was laid off from his job at Chrysler for a long stretch in 2007, he took a buyout. At first there were little jobs, here and there, but the downturn made people reluctant to part with their dollars, and the work petered out. A year after he left Chrysler, his wife left him, taking the kids with her. Mal sank into a depression. To take his mind off his troubles, he fished off a pier along the Detroit River, catching bass, muskie, pike, and walleye. "If it wasn't for fishing I probably would have killed somebody," he says.

As his finances continued to deteriorate, Mal turned to his mother, a recovering alcoholic, for support. Their bond is tight. When her drinking problem was at its worst, he had been the one to take her to the hospital. The staff had strapped her to a gurney and sent her to rehab. She has not had a drink since 1999. Now that her son is the one in need, she has ponied up thousands of dollars. "She's my savior," Mal says.

But as supportive as his mom has been, her generosity cannot give Mal what he really needs: a job. He knows he needs to reinvent himself to compete in today's job market, but how? He went to community college years ago, but dropped out. Later, he studied computers at a career institute and received a certificate, but that knowledge is useless—back then "there was no PowerPoint," he points out.

With no good job prospects, Mal decided to try the education route one more time. He signed up for computer and business math classes at a private training center, which claimed to be able to condense two years of curriculum into sixteen weeks. Michigan's retraining program footed the $4,200 tuition, and at the end, Mal received a certificate. But now, Mal insists he barely learned anything. Even his instructor admitted the pace was impossible, he says. Mal and his classmates went through the fiction of learning, so that they could put it on their résumés and the state could write them off as retrained.

The way Mal looks at it, the quality of that training was so poor that there is no way he can compete with college graduates heading into the labor market after childhoods suckled on the latest technology. "I still haven't got a job in my skill," he says, a year after his coursework. Government-funded retraining, Mal has concluded, is a joke. "That's just a way for these people in these little cheap schools to make money," he says. "Everybody's scamming the money. Ain't nobody serious about anything."

. . .

Evaluations of retraining programs tend to show few, if any, benefits. A year or more of community college is linked to increased earnings, but only if the training is targeted at particular fields where workers are in demand, such as business and health.[38] One evaluation of Michigan's No Worker Left Behind program found that two-thirds of participants who completed their training found work. However, a more rigorous evaluation of Trade Adjustment Assistance—using a statistically matched comparison group—found mixed results for that much more generous federal retraining program. On the whole, participants garnered *less* income over a four-year time period than the control group. (Some workers, particularly younger ones, had caught up and seemed on an upward trajectory by the study's end, however.)[39]

As any TV commercial for online learning will tell you, many unemployed workers—even high school dropouts—do end up finding good jobs after going back to school. Pursuing education is certainly an admirable and rational strategy of self-improvement for any laid-off worker. However, we have to ask how realistic the odds are for the overall population of less advantaged job seekers. Even if every one of these workers could get a degree from, say, a community college, there are not enough good jobs out there for them, at least in the short-to-medium run. A surge in education across the board won't make all the low-wage jobs cleaning hotel rooms and bussing tables disappear, and it is unlikely to make those jobs much better. As Paul Osterman and Beth Shulman note, "In the very long run, the general increase in education might encourage employers in other [higher-paying] sectors of the economy to invest in technologies that make use of new skills." But this gradual transformation, they add, won't be of much help to today's low-wage workers, and perhaps even their children. The same could be said for my unemployed workers, who are unlikely to gain as large a benefit from education as their better-positioned rivals in the job market do.[40]

Indeed, individual success stories may also distract us from the larger picture of growing inequality in the educational system. First, the quantity of the schooling required to get and stay employed at a *decent* job has risen.[41] If they don't want to "throw on a goofy hat," my workers need to vie with the legions of younger workers seeking out the few good jobs left in the part of the labor market reserved for mere mortals. In the competition for credentials to distinguish themselves, they are running to stand still in an economy where the more advantaged workers tend to stay one step ahead. Second, the relatively poor education that these workers receive at their lower-tier schools and training centers degrades the value of whatever academic successes they can achieve.

An analogy from the factory floor is useful here. Workers on the assembly line know that it does no good to work faster on the line, because once one person quickens her pace to impress the boss, management wants everyone to do it. The line gets sped up. The harder you work, the harder you'll be worked. Any individual advantage eventually disappears, and the group suffers from a more demanding work environment.

This "speedup" applies far beyond the factory, to various other segments of capitalism's production line. Financial markets grow, generating new assets to accumulate. Consumer markets expand, creating new products to buy. And labor markets evolve, cultivating new skills to sell. Throughout these domains, elites lead the way, with their trickle-down culture of ever-shifting desires and ideals. Opportunities and varieties multiply, and quality and productivity improve, in the market's unending competition. And notably, the winners tend to take all—leading to the concentration of capital, the centralization of production, and the stunting of meritocracy.[42] (These trends have implications for how workers and consumers alike view their choices in the market, as I will discuss in chapter 6.)

How does this process play out in today's labor market? Individuals are seeking a limited number of good jobs and jockeying for relative position. They gain relative position by accruing more education or using increasingly sophisticated strategies in their job hunt, thereby broadening their options and enhancing their perceived quality as candidates. However, as everyone adopts these search strategies and improves upon their education, the threshold required to get a good job rises. The result is a competition that constantly ratchets up—an arms race played out across résumés.

For this intensifying competition I use the term *capital speedup*. It is relevant to everything from the physical capital of the assembly line, to the human capital of the educational arena, to the cultural capital of the white-collar workplace. It derives from, and reinforces, economic inequality.

Sociologist Randall Collins has described a similar process. What he calls *credential inflation* involves a "spiral of competition for education" and "rising credential requirements for jobs" across all sectors of society. In 1910, Collins points out, less than 10 percent of Americans obtained a high school degree; now, the vast majority do, and the degree has become "little more than a ticket to a lottery in which one can buy a chance at a college degree—which itself is becoming a ticket to a yet higher-stakes lottery." In Collins's view, academic degrees are continually becoming more valuable not because of stronger demand for a better-educated labor force but because of the expansion of schooling itself, which plays a useful social role in doling out jobs within the educational sector and "warehousing" people of working age—thus holding down unemployment. Collins goes so far as to argue that schools add little or no value to workers' skill sets, which are developed on the job. "Compare the financial success of the youthful founders of Apple or Microsoft, some of them college dropouts, with the more modest careers of graduates of computer schools," he writes.[43] This pessimistic view of education squares with research that finds that "limited or no learning" occurs in American colleges, with a third of students making no significant improvements in analytical reasoning, critical thinking, and written communication skills over four years.[44]

The possession of credentials, then, reflects not ability but merely one's relative position in an increasingly stratified hierarchy that, like an accordion, is being pulled from both ends. When those at the bottom obtain college degrees, those in the middle will respond by securing more advanced degrees—thereby transforming even master's programs into the twenty-first-century equivalents of trade schools. The relative positions of the two groups in the eyes of employers will not change overall, even if isolated individuals move up or down. What ultimately results is not unlike the constant and fruitless competition described in the classic Dr. Seuss story, "The Sneetches," in which the eponymous avian creatures are divided into a favored group born with stars on their bellies and an outcast group of their hapless, starless peers. Despairing of their lowly status, the plain-bellied Sneetches pay money to have stars stamped on their bellies. The star-bellied Sneetches retaliate by having their stars removed, prompting the plain-bellied ones to efface their new ones, prodding the star-bellied ones to inscribe them again . . . and so it goes.[45]

In a similar fashion, the theory of credential inflation suggests that schooling itself does nothing. Attending classes is the equivalent of adding a star to one's belly—it's cosmetic. Ability, not education, determines later earnings, and any apparent connection between the two arises because individuals with higher ability tend to receive more schooling *and* more income. On the other hand, the sheepskin that schooling ultimately confers means a great deal. It is a signal (however arbitrary) that tells other people a particular individual is worthy.

However, studies conducted using natural experiments and other innovative approaches to isolate the effects of ability and education suggest that this theory may go too far in dismissing the link between education and income.[46] An alternative interpretation is that schooling does make a difference—but the effect diminishes as other individuals also acquire that level of education, necessitating further investments. Evolutionary biologist Leigh Van Valen put forward a theory—the Red Queen hypothesis—which is relevant here. Van Valen conceived of evolution as an arms race between competing species, whereby a species must continually evolve and improve its fitness in order to keep pace with predators or parasites that might otherwise overrun it. This constant competition is necessary to maintain a species' niche in the ecosystem.[47] (The name of the theory is taken from another children's story—Lewis Carroll's *Through the Looking-Glass*—in which the Red Queen says, "Now, *here*, you see, it takes all the running *you* can do, to keep in the same place. If you want to get somewhere else, you must run at least twice as fast as that!") Under the logic of the Red Queen effect, as workers at the bottom seek out training and credentials, they do acquire more in the way of skill and cognitive abilities. Yet, those higher up respond to their diluted market power by getting even more education. This back-and-forth dance leads to a struggle between individuals, but stasis overall. Running faster, but staying in place. Ever-increasing competition, yet with a surprising consistency of inequality.[48] While the Sneetch effect implies that there is no difference in the qualities of the two groups—the existence of a mere star, a mere credential, is the basis of segregation—the Red Queen effect suggests that real improvements are made during the struggle, yet the relative distance between the two groups does not change.

Both of these theories have something to say about the realities my workers face in today's labor market. While the Red Queen effect captures the upward-ratcheting rivalry over the prudent amount of schooling to acquire, the Sneetch effect better describes the zero-sum contest over often more or less meaningless distinctions of educational quality.[49]

. . .

Unemployed workers are not blind to the escalating competition that surrounds them. Though she already has a GED, Audrey Calvin, a forty-four-year-old Canadian, has gone back to school to get a "real" high school degree in a special program. The former parts worker paid for the six-month course because she believes that employers look askance at GEDs—a hunch that research bears out.[50] The amount of education required to get a good job keeps rising, she points out. "Even to pick up a bag of garbage off the corner, throw it in the back of the truck—as a garbage man you need a [high school degree]." Employers are pickier about a job candidate's education in other ways, she adds. "You can't even go to an interview and show a diploma—diploma's not acceptable anymore. They want your transcripts from the school because it's too easy to get diplomas off the Internet now and just change the names."

A small minority of my workers, Americans mostly, questioned whether they really were learning something in their training, or just gathering up pieces of paper to prove something to employers. But most of my workers believed in the value of their second-chance education. An epileptic, Audrey foundered in special education as a child, and remembers vividly "how much I used to cut myself down, and get cut down, for the work I did." Finally, she is learning what she didn't learn before. As a worker, she is improving her store of human capital.

The problem is, like Alice chasing the Red Queen, she is gaining ground in the meritocratic race only to lose it. Even when she gets her diploma, Audrey points out, her chances will be slim in today's labor market. The quantity of training that workers like her can afford, the lack of relevant experience they currently have, their advanced age—all these things relegate their résumé to the bottom of the stack, even in the sectors that are hiring.

Out of convention and convenience, we often gauge the economic impact of schooling by looking at how many degrees a person has. But not all education is equal. When more people start getting the same kind of credentials, employers search more assiduously for other signals—including *where* they went to school—to differentiate the better candidates from the worse.[51] In other words, the speedup occurring in the educational sector may be a matter of not only the higher quantity of schooling but also its refined quality or selectivity.

To the extent that higher quality makes a difference, job seekers from elite schools learned more there than those who graduated elsewhere. To the extent that a school's selectiveness is important, employers believe that these elite graduates know more based on the institution's prestige. Taking this latter argument to an extreme, venture capitalist Peter Thiel has made the case that higher education is fundamentally about exclusion rather than real learning. "It's something about the scarcity and the status," Thiel says. "In education your value depends on other people failing."[52] Just as more credentials may not mean more skill, the prestigious name of a school may simply signal a Sneetch-like distinction between the anointed and everyone else, won through zero-sum competition.

Studies on how college quality affects earnings find that the alumni of more selective schools make more money than their peers from less selective ones. There is also evidence that this advantage has grown over time. Perhaps either a Red Queen effect (from the better quality of selective schools) or a Sneetch effect (from their higher prestige alone) is at work here. But another possibility is that these exclusive schools make no difference either way. They are just good at getting already talented individuals to join their student bodies. They don't improve a person's natural talent, and talent alone is what matters to employers. Research that attempts to sort through these possible explanations finds that, overall, graduates of more selective schools went on to make the same amount of money as students of similar ability who attended less selective schools.[53] This line of research implies that what really matters in the labor market is ability, period. However, in that same study, among students from low-income families, the ones who graduated from more selective schools *did* earn more. For those with less advantaged backgrounds, a Sneetch or Red Queen effect may therefore operate, with prestige or educational quality, and not ability, linked to greater earnings.[54]

As is the case for the inequalities of skill I discussed earlier, the educational gap between the best and the rest is primarily an issue for white-collar workers to deal with.[55] And for most people *retraining* for jobs, the differences in quality among the various training centers and community colleges are not so stark. That said, these distinctions do exist, as my workers were well aware. They commented on the poor training and job-search advice available to them, especially at the for-profit schools that aggressively go after state-funded trainees. An

American former parts worker called them "little rip-off schools." "They're milking the government for money," said an ex-Ford worker, who visited a hole-in-the-wall academy in Windsor that misrepresented its services just to get him in the door. Nevertheless, a growing number of students are plowing government grants and loans into these training institutes.[56] (The union-sponsored study mentioned earlier found that 40 percent of laid-off Canadian autoworkers who went back to school attended private training centers, and their criticisms of retraining tended to focus on the second-rate education they received there.[57]) In the Detroit area, one former Chrysler worker notes, new schools of dubious quality are sprouting like mushrooms to rush newly laid-off workers—including a few of his friends—through training for in-demand fields like nursing. Meanwhile, other friends of his are racking up student debt to take classes at Internet-age correspondence schools like the University of Phoenix. "That ain't nothing," he says.

In their race for credentials, less educated workers are hobbled by their meager savings and limited government tuition checks, along with their lack of academic aptitude and relevant experience. Not as well versed in the worlds of self-directed learning outside high school—yet another dimension of cultural capital—they find it harder to identify the better schools and to navigate the educational bureaucracy. As a result, they are more likely to settle, or to have to settle, for underfunded community colleges or mediocre for-profit schools intent on getting them in and out the door as quickly as possible. These are cheap, if government-subsidized, solutions to the problems facing these workers, and like with most cheap solutions, they get what they pay for.

As I will discuss further in chapter 6, the creeping inequality of educational merit also matters to my blue-collar workers in the ways that it cements their inadequacy. As they race to catch up with the rest of the labor market, the explosion of new criteria for educational success allows their more advantaged competitors to continue to proclaim their superiority across multiple dimensions: number of diplomas, quality of education, prestige of school. More belly stars, and snazzier ones to boot.

THE MEASURE OF ALL THINGS

The market-driven need for continual improvement multiplies the methods of evaluation in every domain, intensifying competition and allowing the advance of meritocratic measurement over the whole surface of society. From power to industriousness to skill, everything can be reduced to dollar amounts of costs and benefits, even factors seemingly outside the ken of economic analysis: the value of the world's rainforests, the value of a human life. The impact of this growing capacity to quantify has been profound. In recent decades, new and improved financial metrics have made it easier for shareholders to track the performance of companies, placing further pressures on them to perform and making it harder to retain inefficient workers.[58] While money is perhaps the most-used measuring stick, it is not the only one. New regimes of standardized testing, for example, have transformed the classroom, prodding not just students but also teachers and administrators to perform based on quantifiable, if controversial, measures of ability.

What I call the new technology of meritocracy has also transformed the labor market. Just as scientific management made the use of time on the job measurable and thus more ruthlessly efficient, processes of rationalization have occurred in the evaluation of job candidates. The speedup of required skills has intensified now that more information exists by which to evaluate a worker's relative superiority or inferiority, pushing that worker to excel according each new metric. In turn, companies facing determined rivals need to find ever-new criteria by which to sift the very best wheat from the chaff.

As a result, the rising competition that today's workers face goes beyond the amassing of desirable skills. It extends to the hiring process itself, as the selection of candidates for jobs across the occupational strata has steadily become more professionalized, meticulous, and bureaucratic—in crucial ways favoring the well-educated and cultured.[59] Firms and industries have developed scientific, quantitative approaches to evaluate education levels, economic activity, psychological well-being, and other factors relevant to employers making decisions among pools of job applicants. Nowadays job seekers are supposed to "sculpt" their résumés, "hone" their pitches to prospective employers, and "grow" their professional networks.[60] It is about building a superior job-candidate package, what management gurus like to call your "personal brand," which encompasses all aspects of your life, each one measured and evaluated. Meanwhile, employers are adopting new strategies for finding and vetting employees, such as doing targeted searches on social networking sites. Unsurprisingly, the less savvy fall behind.

Earlier in this chapter I suggested that the expanding definition of merit and the widening gaps in educational quality have become critical concerns not just for professionals but also—to a lesser, but still noteworthy, extent—for their working-class counterparts. The same class difference applies to the job search itself. According to the research by Ofer Sharone mentioned previously, white-collar workers need to step into an interview not just with the right credentials on their résumés but also with the right presentation of their personalities and personability.[61] In ways like this, the criteria for job-search sophistication are more exacting for professionals. But more is being demanded of job seekers like mine, too. Rather than showing up at the job site and buttonholing the boss, they need to go on the Internet. Rather than just having the requisite experience, they need a "snazzy" résumé and a cheerful demeanor. Rather than just showing their competence on the job, they need to pass skills tests, drug tests, personality tests, "integrity" tests, and criminal background checks. These new requirements erect new hurdles of bureaucracy that block workers with less cultural capital at their disposal—a shrewdness acquired in their families, neighborhoods, and schools.[62]

Perhaps because it has its roots in the kinds of economic and technological innovations that are diffusing everywhere, the capital speedup does not appear to be much different on the two sides of the border (though, for what it is worth, my Canadians were more confident in catching up to those ahead of them). My workers in both countries commented on how much the job search had changed since their last forays into the market, decades ago. You had to do little to get a job at the plant, they said—just fill out a simple application. The orientation process, too, was hardly onerous. "I filled out the application Wednesday, took my physical Thursday, and I was working there Monday," says an American who started working at a feeder plant in the eighties. "Back then, you didn't have to do all that junk you have to do now." A Canadian remembers how his father worked sporadic shifts at a Chrysler plant in Windsor a generation ago. "Back in them days," he says, "you could work at Chrysler's, save up a little bit of money, quit, and go and try and find something else. If you didn't find nothing, you could go back." There were plenty of jobs out there, says an American former parts worker, and getting fired didn't matter so much. But employers do things differently nowadays, even for factory jobs. "At first you go fill out your application . . . then get screened again for a job interview, then you go to a hands-on training. They want to pick the cream of the crop out there. The one that's gonna really add something to the company—bring something to the table."

The frenzied competition of today's labor market makes the old days in the factories seem almost bucolic. Mal Stephen, the former Chrysler worker, points to the futility of job fairs, which have become popular ways for employers to spread their net wide for job candidates, but entail another layer of interviewing and formality that weeds out the uninitiated and unsophisticated. "I dressed the part and talked to everyone, and you know, blah blah blah," he says. "Nothing ever happened from a job fair. Not for me. Matter of fact, for nobody I know." With huge crowds and just five minutes to talk to an interviewer, there is such a low signal-to-noise ratio that the exertions seem almost pointless.

Interestingly, the cultural capital that less educated workers must exhibit in the job interview includes not just flashy ability but also the right degree of understated subservience.[63] Sal Cheriel, the Canadian ex-Ford worker, says he has applied for numerous customer-service jobs in the Windsor area. Years ago, he managed a luxury hotel and did a stint running a clothing store, both of them abroad. But so far, no one at the casinos and hotels and banks he has applied to has offered him an interview. Sal remembers applying for a job at the Gap and going to a group interview at a hotel. (Group interviews are another new gauntlet that workers like mine find themselves hustled through.) "I sat in a semicircle of people—all white people, and all young people," he says. He had run a clothing store before, and he knew all the answers to the questions the two hiring managers raised—after all, he had once sat on the other side of the table. Fully engaged, Sal posed his own questions and offered suggestions, amply demonstrating his knowledge of the business. He thought he did well. But afterward, nothing happened. It savaged Sal's pride that he—a former manager with years of experience—never heard back from the Gap. In thinking back on the interview, Sal wonders if he came on too strong. "They don't like that. Because they see you're smarter." Even when looking for today's low-wage jobs, workers have to tiptoe across a cultural line, one that in their case may require a degree of servility as well as skill.

In these lower tiers of the labor market, the winnowing of job candidates can be unforgiving, blowing away any inconsistencies and nonconformities through the rigor of multiple interviews, batteries of testing, background checks that flag even violations without criminal charges, and zero tolerance for substance abuse and other failings. In particular, run-ins with the law—not unheard of among the factory population—have become devastating for a job seeker's prospects in an era of instantaneous online information and never-forgotten (and thus never-forgiven) records of past behavior. For example, one of my ex-Chrysler workers has a felony conviction for selling marijuana, which she admits prevents her from pursuing her childhood dream of becoming a nurse. Health care and education, the economy's booming sectors, also happen to be the least willing to overlook criminal transgressions.[64]

By shining a light on the widening divide not just in education but in the job search as well, capital speedup extends our theoretical understanding of the labor market's ever-quickening race. With their growing criteria for merit, and their improved ability to evaluate it, companies have forced job applicants to become more sophisticated in their searches, putting those with less finesse at a marked disadvantage. Beyond their wrangling over educational credentials, workers, in turn, seek out an edge in other arenas of their fight over good jobs. The thread connecting these various contexts is the endless process of differentiation from an initial state of inequality. This inequality is itself a cause of the poor outcomes that less educated workers experience on their career paths, and efforts to improve their situation without first addressing the underlying imbalance of power, I will argue at the end of this book, can only go so far.[65]

LIBERTY IN THE LABOR MARKET

Psychologist E. L. Thorndike once observed that there is nothing wrong with being average.[66] Yet, in a fiercely competitive culture where respect is based on ability and achievement, the underlying message is that everyone must be, like the children of Lake Wobegon, above average. Our innovation-hungry society admires those risk-takers who ride out on the edge of each new wave, and disdains those laggards who fail to prepare for what is coming. It is a somewhat peculiar moral calculus, given that many of my unemployed workers were nothing like Aesop's grasshopper, singing the summers away in idleness. They worked hard for years, breaking down their bodies in dirty, dangerous labor. But, as I've described, their years of experience in the hard-nosed, hypermasculine environment of the plant floor, with its inattention to physical appearance, social graces, or customer relations, do not translate well to the service-sector jobs that now abound. Their long-term unemployment and their suspect history at unionized plants keep employers at bay. But as the broader culture of judgment makes clear to them, their real failing lies elsewhere: they were not prescient enough to recognize the changes taking place. Before the shift toward the high-stakes capitalism of the late twentieth century, lifetime employment was more common, and merit was more commonly understood at its most basic, egalitarian level: as effort. Today merit is a matter of not just your dedication (which is a given) but also the talents that allow you to contribute meaningfully to the company's profits. For those with both the will and the ability to seize the market's newfound liberties, there is no limit to success. But most ordinary workers have no such luck. And my workers—many of whom are long past their sell-by dates—have a particularly hard time convincing employers to take a chance. In ways like these, a modern economy shorn of countervailing institutions—such as the unions and activist governments that once tempered management's power—leaves many workers exposed to a stunted meritocracy that sees them as valueless and superfluous.

In general, the retraining and career counseling to be had on the U.S. side was more impersonal, bureaucratic, and difficult to access. Thanks to a combination of generous support and personal intervention, the Canadians tended to make the move from the shop floor to classrooms with greater ease and optimism, a continuity of relationships and assistance smoothing over the rough patches of their transition. Although more resources were theoretically available to them, my American workers—because of ignorance, program inflexibility, or simple lack of interest—did not use them. They generally fared worse, with fewer of them in schooling and more of them uncertain and anxious about their employment prospects. It is worth repeating that my Americans were from that lucky group of workers who lived in a state that for a time invested heavily in retraining. They were also from that lucky group of unionized manufacturing workers who could tap substantial federal grants for retraining. The situation would likely be much worse for unemployed workers hailing from areas of the country that provide even less in the way of policy, or areas of the economy that historically have not had strong unions or the strong protections they have won.

Even for those autoworkers persistent and fortunate enough to find training opportunities, their chances in a second (or third or fourth) career are bleak. I have used the term *capital speedup* to describe a constant competition over human capital and cultural capital that maintains the overall condition of inequality. Workers like mine struggle just to preserve their current position in a labor market that demands greater credentials and also greater selectivity in those credentials, greater efforts in the job search and also greater sophistication in that search. Meanwhile, technological progress allows merit to be measured and evaluated ever more precisely, further multiplying the criteria by which workers are judged and sorted. This not only adds to the pressures already pushing down on them within the stunted meritocracy, but also helps further meritocratic morality's narrative that they are unworthy across a growing number of measures.

My workers do not have the more privileged kind of pedigree—one that combines education, social class, and cultural refinement—to position themselves well in this transformed market. As employers pay more for human capital, the quantity and quality of the education that people receive continues to depend mightily on the good fortune to have grown up in an environment that fostered learning. In a job-search process that requires increasing sophistication to find good jobs, these individuals find themselves with an acute deficiency of the appropriate social skills as well. As a result, they start out behind everyone else in the race for good jobs: with a chance to succeed, yes, but not one worth betting on. In the years ahead, as inequality grows, ordinary families struggle to keep up, and automation further raises the bar of skill required for good jobs, the broader majority of working men and women may also find themselves in similar straits.

I need to reiterate that for *individuals* it makes perfect sense to pursue further education and job-search assistance. Barring some sort of collective action to change the overall system, there is no alternative but to make oneself as competitive as possible. Not surprisingly for an academic, I also share the widespread belief that education is worthwhile in ways that have little to do with a person's position in the social order. Beyond being morally good in and of itself, it benefits society in a multitude of ways, from increasing productivity to bringing about a more politically engaged citizenry. For all these reasons, retraining throughout a person's life should be promoted. My point in this chapter is to question whether education and job-search assistance have been oversold as a solution to the woes that workers are experiencing in today's labor market.[67] From the viewpoint of society, what is best for the individual is not necessarily best for the entire class of less advantaged workers who will, on average, lose out in the contest for good jobs.

For the problems posed by their relative lack of skill, unemployed workers in the laissez-faire U.S. economy might be expected to fare better, at least according to neoclassical economic theories that promote free markets. In time, an unleashed private sector would generate new jobs, and even less-educated workers would ride the tide to employment, as employers become less selective in their hiring and return to their earlier strategies of cultivating labor over the long term. However, the high levels of unemployment brought about by the Great Recession undermine this assumption. In addition, any skills mismatch that exists in today's labor market would also undermine the benefits of America's dynamic engine of job creation, since the companies that are hiring workers need those of a particular, advanced skill set. Workers like mine must retrain for a growing industry first—and be fortunate enough to bet on the right one—before they can seek out the available jobs. Once they do, though, they may still find themselves at a persistent disadvantage in the intensifying meritocratic struggle.

In the farther future, technological change may also hinder our ability to educate our way into broadly shared prosperity. In the past, the advent of new technologies eliminated some jobs but always created new ones to replace them, as technology made possible the creation and fulfillment of new consumer desires—luxuries that eventually become necessities. Nevertheless, there is reason to believe that this time will be different. Automation in the past freed a broad swath of the middle class from manual labor, so that they could train themselves to do mental tasks in comfortable offices. But those mental tasks are now being automated, too. In recent years, a number of commentators have offered breathless predictions of a brave new world where elite workers run the robots that do everything—except, perhaps, the work of an obsequious servant class that caters to the elite's whims.[68] That vision of the future may never occur, or it might take much longer than these experts prophesize, like the flying cars and robot housekeepers that we've long been waiting for. Yet, it is a serious possibility, one that has troubling implications for ordinary workers struggling to find a foothold in the rapidly moving market.

. . .

Audrey Calvin is learning how far behind she is in the race. When she started working at Chromeshield in 1998, Audrey never sat down for an interview with the boss. A friend who worked there passed along her résumé. She got a phone call, went in for orientation, and did a four-hour trial on the line. "Come back in two days and you'll be working," she was told. That was it. "I've never had an interview in my life for a job," Audrey says.

Now that she is back on the job market, Audrey is figuring out how a professional hiring process is supposed to work. She went to a course on how to interview for a job and participated in a role-playing session.

"What do you like to do?" the mock interviewer asked.

"Well, I like to play poker," Audrey began. " . . . and I like to go to Windsor Spitfires [games] and—"

"That's not what they're asking you," the interviewer interrupted.

"What do you mean? That's what I like to do."

"No, they want to know what you like within that type of work."

She confesses that she is still figuring out all the proper answers to the proper questions, including what her new career should be. "I truly don't know what the hell I want to do," she says. "I have to do some soul-searching. Do I have time to soul-search? No. I have to get on this next week." It's been more than a year since she lost her job at the feeder plant. Her savings are already plumbed, her credit cards maxed out. For the time being she is working part-time—$174 for twelve hours a week— at her plant's action center, which is scheduled to shut down in a few months. The center has given her a constructive outlet for her energy and frustration, and she has poured herself into the work on behalf of her former coworkers. She knows their pain. Audrey says she "cried a lot" after she was laid off, and has since been in "constant depression" about her financial situation—though most days she is in denial. "It's easier to put the bills off to the side than to deal with it because you know once you turn that computer on and you start dealing with it, it's gonna be depressing." Nevertheless, she hasn't bothered to get counseling for herself. "This is my counseling, right here," she says, motioning to the action center conference room around her. "These guys are a big, big source of [the] glue that holds me together."

A decade ago, it was Audrey's job at the plant that held the splintering parts of her personal life together. She had been a stay-at-home mom with three children. But when her husband, a recovering alcoholic, started hitting her, she took off—"I broke his nose before I left," she notes with some satisfaction. In her thirties by then, she got a job at a fruit market, making just $7 an hour but refusing to go on public assistance. "I was making enough to be able to survive," she says. "I didn't have to take it from somebody else."

Then she landed a position at the plant. Barely able to withstand the physical exertion of the plating line, Audrey cried herself to sleep for a week. But she stuck it out. *The money's better than what I've been paid my whole life,* she kept telling herself—$14 an hour, money that she and her kids needed. "Chromeshield saved my butt," Audrey points out. (Chromeshield also wore down her body: she has gone through multiple surgeries for her wrist, thumb, and knee, and still suffers from asthma "because of all the chemicals.") At the end of her ten years working there, she was making $21 an hour, plus good benefits, plus a company contribution to her retirement account. "I'm never gonna find a job like this again," she says.

Now Audrey is starting over again, seemingly at the very bottom rung—taking classes to obtain the high school diploma she never bothered to get as a teenager. She had planned to go on to college, before Ontario tightened their retraining program's criteria and slammed that door shut. "So now I'm looking at maybe massage therapy."

After a year out of work, Audrey is still unsettled about her future, another trait she shares with her peers. "I don't know how many guys we put through school that sit there and say, 'How do I pick what I want to do for the rest of my life? I don't know.'" There is a certain irrationality to the idea of sending a fifty-year-old out to struggle in the classroom again, she points out. "And for what? For a job he may not get because he's gonna be too old for it anyway?" As for her, Audrey is in her forties now, an overripe age for an entry-level worker, and she has few illusions that she'll be able to get anything, pitted "against a twenty-three-year-old" just out of school. Education has become the decisive factor, she says. "It's what you've done, where you've gone to school, what you take, and what your credentials are. It's business."

When Audrey was growing up, the rules were different. "People quit school to get into the factory with their moms and with their dads," she says. "Generations upon generations are in these factories." A good standard of living did not require a good education, so many people didn't bother to get one.

"Factory life was easy," Audrey says, wistfully. "Man, you went in and you threw bumpers around and you went home. Now it's not—in today's world it's not—a job. You're going for a career."

CHAPTER 3

Decline and Fall

Hardship, Race, and the Social Safety Net

An aged man is but a paltry thing,
A tattered coat upon a stick, unless
Soul clap its hands and sing, and louder sing
For every tatter in its mortal dress

—William Butler Yeats, "Sailing to Byzantium"

It was a frigid December afternoon, two days after Christmas. It had snowed the night before, and the roadways were freshly plowed, the sky a blank canvas of clouds. D.J. Packer told his wife he needed to get out of the house and take a walk. Ali knew he was upset. They had not argued, but they had been together for twenty-five years, and they sensed each other's moods.

D.J. hobbled down the road, favoring his good right knee. It took him twenty-five minutes—stepping gingerly over snow and ice—to get to the bridge. He sat down on a stack of wooden planks behind the guardrail and watched the eighteen-wheelers creep by, weighed down with huge coils of steel.

D.J. knew the trucks well. They came from the piers alongside the Detroit River, where the freighters docked, and where he used to work, more than a decade earlier, hauling the same steel coils off the ships and onto the trucks—two to a flatbed. A longshoreman's job was seasonal: man the piers for $11 an hour until the winter waters freeze, and then live off a government unemployment check until spring when the freighters pull into port again.

D.J. left that way of life for the more reliable paychecks to be had in the auto industry. In 1997, he started working as a temp at the Chromeshield plating company in Windsor, throwing greasy, fifty-pound bumpers onto racks. His foreman liked his uncomplaining attitude, and six months later, he was hired full-time. With those good factory wages, he and his wife raised their daughter and paid off the mortgage on their ranch house.

As the years went by it seemed that this would be his last job, and his decades-long career of hustling and hauling would end in a comfortable retirement. On that score he hoped for better luck than the rest of his family. D.J.'s father had just retired after three decades at the Canadian National Railway when he had a heart attack. He died on the way to the hospital. After working for Ford for twenty-five years, his brother Gene took a buyout and then shortly afterward died of bowel cancer. D.J. and his youngest brother discovered Gene's body in his apartment after he had gone missing for days.

One day at work, D.J.'s foreman handed letters to everyone on the factory floor. The letter stated that the plant was shutting down in two months. D.J. just stood there, clutching the paper in his hands.

"Frums, how can they do this?" he finally asked his foreman. "We've got a number-one ranking in plating in North America and they're closing our doors?"

"It's nothing personal," the foreman said. Flex-N-Gate wanted to cut costs. The truck bumpers that D.J. and his coworkers had been toiling over would now be handled by the company's Chrome Craft plant, across the river.

The day the plant closed, D.J. felt as if someone had taken a sledgehammer to his chest. In his mind, he had let down his family. He could no longer support them. Losing his job, he said, "took my dignity and just slapped me in the face with it." That was when the insomnia began. Every night, D.J. would sleep for two hours at a time, then wake up. His mind constantly churned through his anxieties about the future—the mounting bills, the bleak job market. "You can't keep going without sleep," Ali told him. "You're going to kill yourself."

He worried about how he would care for Ali and his teenage daughter, Emily. Ali was a homemaker and caretaker of her elderly mother, who lived nearby. Everyone depended on his income. He asked Ali if he should head out west, to the tar sands of Alberta, to get a job in the oil industry. She told him no. "I'd prefer to have you here and us struggle to get by," she said, "rather than have you halfway across the country."

But there were no more jobs in Windsor for someone with his skills. The global recession had wound its way to southwestern Ontario, leaving mass layoffs and broken companies in its wake, and the metal finishing plants that had not yet closed were in no position to hire. D.J. wasn't the best candidate, either, for manual labor of other kinds. He had ruined his body at the plant. One day he was turning a corner, a heavy bumper in his arms, when he slammed his knee into a pole. The momentum flipped him over and shattered his knee cap. Surgeons plucked thirteen shards of chipped bone from the joint. D.J. came back to work after six months.

Desperation led D.J. here, to the bridge near his home. It was one o'clock in the afternoon, and he sat on his roadside perch in a bleary haze, watching the semis roll by. He was tired. Used up. A husk of nerves.

He had worked out the blueprint in his mind that morning. The length of the bridge was curved, highest in the middle. Until a truck cleared the top, the driver would not be able to see down the other side. *All I've got to do is take one step into the road and he can't stop.* Wrapped up warmly in his jacket and hat, D.J. found himself trembling. He studied the ice-slick asphalt, his unruly thoughts running in the same unending circuit. *You're useless. Your family would be better without you. Why are you wasting their time? Look at you.*

He eyed the coils of steel loaded onto the truck beds and appreciated the irony. He had blinked, a decade had passed, and he had gone nowhere. He was almost sixty, with nothing to show for it. He was back to the prospect of $11-an-hour jobs, back to living off the fickle generosity of government bureaucrats, back to getting up in the early morning with nothing to do. Except this time, there was no one waiting to hire him back when spring came. There was nothing at the end of all those years of work. Shivering on the side of that road, all he could think about was how he had let down the people he loved.

The minutes slipped by. By now, it was four o'clock. D.J. had been sitting there for three hours. *You know what? If I'm going to do this, I'm going to do it.* He stood on the curb of the highway.

A semi roared up the incline. A strange, distant sensation overtook him. He imagined himself jumping in front of that truck, a mass of flesh and bone brushed away by a larger mass of steel and rubber, and he realized that at that moment he felt no fear. Nothing at all.

This was the moment. His heart beat furiously. He braced himself to jump.

But he didn't. His knees would not release; his feet failed him. He watched the truck sail by, the driver catching his gaze at the last second.

He turned around. "I can't do this," he said to himself. "This ain't right."

He followed the highway back home. He told Ali what he had done. "We had a big cry," he says, recalling the moment a year afterward. "And she told me, 'Don't ever think like that again.'"

. . .

After his vigil on the highway, D.J. went to see a therapist. "You got to a point where you had put yourself down so bad that you felt you were nothing," said the therapist, Frank Trevelyn. "What you need to do is start giving yourself credit for your life." After that first session, D.J. sat down with Ali and told her he wanted to continue the therapy. "I need this. *We* need this," he said. But D.J. had lost his health insurance when he lost his job, and Canada's vaunted single-payer health system doesn't cover therapy. D.J. would have to pay $200 out of pocket per session.

D.J. worked out a deal with Frank. He would pay half that, and make up the difference later. But even that hundred-dollar rate was still a huge drain on the family's income from unemployment benefits. Ali told her husband it was all right. "If the bills don't like it, tough on them," she said.

Frank taught D.J. to stop obsessing over the negative aspects of everything. Slowly, D.J. shifted his thoughts away from his layoff and lack of education, silencing that echo in his head, as Frank described it, that impugned every accomplishment in his life. As he began to focus on his family and home and the other small-bore triumphs of a workingman's life, his depression lifted. But the therapy bills continued to pile up. That first month, D.J. spent $2,000 on his multiple sessions every week. On top of that, the loss of his health insurance meant that D.J. had also started paying almost $500 a month for his diabetes medication. (The universal Canadian system has another blind spot when it comes to prescription coverage.)

Fortunately, D.J. had more help at his disposal: the action center. As I discussed in the last chapter, action centers are government-funded support centers for unemployed workers that are set up following large layoffs. D.J. discussed his situation with the coordinator of his center, Tammy Anger. A short, vivacious woman with sunny blonde curls who comes to work in hospital scrubs (she is training for a new career as a nurse), Anger had been a line operator at the Chromeshield plant. She talked to the company and convinced them to pay D.J.'s insurance premiums for two years. D.J. could afford to keep seeing his therapist. As he regained his footing, he also turned to Anger and other staff at the center—peer helpers trained to assist their former coworkers at the plant—for more casual offerings of empathy and acceptance. The connection he already had with them made it easier to open up, he says. "They understand what I'm going through because they're somewhat in the same position."

Of course, advice and counseling can only go so far. Like any psychological blow, the hurt of unemployment has its absolute and relative dimensions: the reality of losing one's job and living on a lower income, and the mind's perception of that reality. As he freely admits, D.J. needed to change his way of looking at his troubles. At the same time, it helped that his reality was not deteriorating further as he was trying to get help. In addition to the innovative interventions pursued by his action center, D.J. benefited directly from generous education benefits and income supports. Currently, he is completing his high school diploma through an online course, and in two months he will begin a college program in addictions and community services. The government is paying his tuition. Meanwhile, a temporary federal program targeted at workers with long work histories is providing up to two years of unemployment benefits—more than twice the typical limit—while D.J. goes to school. The checks will keep coming even after he graduates, so he can search comfortably for a new job.

When I started my research project, I imagined that the Canadian policy advantage here would be decisive. The picture was more mixed, however, due to the extraordinary measures that the Obama administration and Congress took when the financial crisis hit, along with the gradual weakening of the Canadian safety net over the past two decades. Racial differences were also important. My African American workers could rely less on their social networks of family and friends to stay afloat as their forays into unemployment deepened. Nevertheless, as I describe in concrete detail in this chapter, in general, well-designed policies can give those without jobs a real and reliable foundation on which to rebuild their lives.

In understanding the social safety net's impact, it is important to look not just at the tangible ways it reduces financial hardship but also at the psychological rewards it confers by keeping incomes stable and dreams intact. While the absence of coverage for his prescriptions and therapy was a major problem for D.J., the social safety net as a whole gave him the time and space to deal with his depression before it dragged him down a much darker path.

Five months after he came close to suicide, D.J. paid off his tab with Frank. Today his mental health is good, he says. He is grateful for his family, especially his wife Ali, whom he credits as his source of strength. He is grateful, too, for the help he's been given to get his life back on track. Going back to school on a government scholarship has provided a much-needed roadmap for his unstructured life, downsizing his daily worries to a manageable burden revolving largely around homework and tests. Meanwhile, receiving his extended unemployment benefits every two weeks allows him to feel that he is still contributing to the household, even though he doesn't have a job. "I don't feel ashamed that I'm on unemployment because I'm providing for my family and we're living," he says. In fact, now that he is training for the career he's long wanted, his life has a hopeful forward momentum. "I feel like I'm on the verge of a new adventure."

YOU CAN'T GET SICK NOW

Vincent Formosa's father was a Tennessee sharecropper, a man of a flinty farm stock. Although he'd lost a leg, he somehow tended the cotton fields and supported his large family. "He could drive anything on the farm," says Vincent, fifty-three. "Very strong." The family was poor. Neither of Vincent's parents made it past the third or fourth grade. But the kids—five girls, ten boys—"never went hungry," Vincent says. In elementary school, Vincent started picking cotton and caring for pigs, cows, chicken, and geese. He never did finish high school.

Shortly after Vincent married his wife, Renee, the couple left Tennessee to go to Pontiac, a city just north of Detroit. His brother-in-law had found work in a GM plant there. Vincent, then in his early twenties, put in an application and was called in. But he failed the physical. His blood pressure was too high, he was told. Come back when you get it down. ("Never did happen," Vincent says.) He struggled to find a job. Those first few years were hard for Vincent and Renee, and for a time they were on public assistance. Vincent eventually landed a job as a delivery-man at a furniture company, where he stayed sixteen years. The owner of that company knew the owner of the plating plant, then a family-owned business, and recommended Vincent. He was hired.

Vincent worked the 3 to 11 P.M. shift, pouring chemicals and hoisting bumpers out of their baths in the plating tanks. Sometimes the stench got so bad that he would start choking and have to hurry outside for air. In the morning he would wake up to find his pillow stained yellow from the chemicals that had soaked into his hair the previous day.

Working at the plant was bad, but not working there has been worse. "I'm going through hell, man," Vincent says. He owes a $600 balance on his water bill, $400 on his gas bill. His family is living unemployment check to unemployment check, with just six dollars in their bank account—"just enough to keep it open so my direct deposit can go in there." Desperate, Vincent and Renee recently applied for food stamps. They have also started visiting food pantries at churches.

The family's financial woes are not unlike those of their city, Pontiac, which has seen its industries shrivel up over the years and in 2009 went into receivership. Their green colonial house sits not far from the railroad tracks, on a desolate strip littered with boarded-up, bombed-out, burnt-up homes. After their neighbor died a few years ago, Vincent notes, the house was stripped of everything—including the garage door.

On a snowy evening Vincent sits at his dining-room table, dressed in a dark gray sweatshirt stained with drips of white paint. He is a heavyset man with prodigious, bearded jowls, deep worry lines etched under each eye, and a huge belly, the top portion of which puffs out when he stands—a hospital intern told him he has a hernia, which he dismisses contemptuously. "I've had that all my life," he grunts. "Them doctors, they don't know everything."

As Vincent tells his story, he cracks jokes and laughs heartily at his own misfortune, eyes mischievous behind the squared frames of his glasses. But other times the anger washes over him like a wave. His eyes narrow to slits and his forehead crinkles, giving him a fierce look. His voice quivers with rage, and he bangs his hand on the table with a threatening emphasis. Little things have a habit of bothering him these days, he admits. He's always had a temper, but never like this. "Get the hell out of my way," he'll snarl at his wife or children, for no reason, his head reeling with raw emotion.

Impotent but consuming, such rage bears within it a core of judgment, a belief that someone, somewhere, has violated the meritocratic order. For his part, Vincent is mad at management for shuttering the plant and abruptly leaving him and his coworkers without livelihoods—even without severance pay—after years of loyalty to the firm. He feels humiliated, and yet helpless to do anything about it. He lashes out at the government, too, for the indignities it has put him through whenever he and his family have sought help.

But in recent days, what has gotten Vincent most riled up is his inability to get the health care he needs. He suffers from severe arthritis and has painful gallstones that need to be surgically removed. Unfortunately, even with a federal subsidy, he can't afford the hundreds of dollars a month it would take to extend his family's health insurance policy through the COBRA law, which allows laid-off workers to keep their previous coverage for a limited time. Because of his unemployment benefits he doesn't qualify for Medicaid, though the social services office said he should start collecting his unpaid medical bills to show them at the end of the year, and maybe he'd get a Medicaid card then. In the meantime, when he sees his family doctor for a typical visit, he pays $144 out of pocket—a quasi-copay—and the social services office takes care of the rest.

Vincent can hardly afford even that much, he says, but the alternative is worse. Four months ago, the pain from his gallstones suddenly became excruciating. He was urinating blood. His doctor told him he could no longer treat him if he didn't have insurance. He would have to go to the local hospital and see if they would provide charitable care. The hospital gave him a list of three surgeons to call. He called all three, and each one told him that if he didn't have insurance, they wouldn't operate. "What am I going to do now?" he asks, his voice shaking. Without surgery, the only thing he can do is continue to pop painkillers, and he's run out of the Vicodin that the hospital gave him for free—three pills at a time. Meanwhile, he can no longer afford the medications for his other chronic conditions: high cholesterol, high blood pressure, asthma, gout. "What if he just gets half?" Renee asked the pharmacist on a recent visit. He paid $40 for half the supply, and he made do. "I'm in limbo," he says. "It's hard to do this, hard to do that."

A month ago, Vincent headed to a free clinic to get treated. What transpired was something out of a black comedy. Vincent sat on the table in the exam room for three hours ("people coming in and out—nobody's telling me shit"). His temper began to smolder as he listened to the staff at the front desk conversing and joking. ("Everybody out there laughing. I'm the only one in the damn room!") Finally, someone came in to take his blood pressure and found that it had skyrocketed—Vincent was irate. Where was the doctor? "He'll be in—in a few minutes," he was told.

After twenty minutes, the doctor stepped in. He was of South Asian descent, and spoke with a barely understandable accent. Vincent tried his best to explain the problem, but the doctor was more interested in having him take off his socks so he could examine his legs. "I didn't come in here for that," Vincent snapped. He was ready to explode, but held his ex-factory worker's tongue—the clinic's policy was not to treat people after the third incident of profanity.

After some waiting, Vincent received a pill to lower his (now heightened) blood pressure. After more waiting, he got his prescriptions refilled. When his appointment was finally over, Vincent complained about the wait. The staff apologized. "The second time won't be as long," the receptionist told him.

"I hope to hell not." He stormed out.

This is America's health care system for the uninsured—overburdened, callous, infuriating—and now that he has lost his job, Vincent finds himself mired in its bureaucratic games and petty indignities.[1] The stress of his futile search for decent health care is compounding the stress of his other preexisting condition, unemployment. He has applied to feeder plants in the area, but hasn't gotten any interviews. "A lot of jobs I'm not going to be qualified for. I don't have the education." And yet Vincent, now in his fifties, doesn't have the savings to retire early. He knows he is not alone on this score, either. As the pension risks once borne by corporations get offloaded onto workers, there is no shortage of senior citizens standing behind store counters and greeting people at Walmart. "Now you've got twenty-one-year-olds working, sixty- and eighty-year-olds working," Vincent says. "Something's got to give, man."

When the anger returns to knot up his thoughts, when his head prickles with that dull pain, Vincent will go outside for a smoke to calm himself. He confesses that he has few friends to turn to. "I don't go nowhere," he says. "Nowadays you got people you really can't trust, man. You can't call everybody your friend . . . especially now . . . because everything's so fast-moving now. People just take everything—take *you*—for granted."

Every night he picks up his Bible and reads a dozen verses, hoping for serenity. He long ago gave up on church ("I want to go to hear the Word—I don't want to go to see what you're wearing"). His brother, a Baptist preacher, told him to keep reading. "Keep your faith," his brother says. "Don't give up. Something's got to give, sooner or later."

. . .

More than half of Americans receive their health insurance through their jobs. As a result, unemployment is often a one-two punch of job loss followed by insurance loss. Not having coverage makes it difficult for people to get regular, preventive care, aggravating whatever illnesses they have. And with or without insurance, being without a job is itself linked to health problems such as alcohol use, heart disease, mental illness, and suicide. The financial strains that spike after a layoff poison the home environment and raise anxiety levels. The unemployed tend to become isolated from family and friends, losing their social supports even as they endure shame and idle temptations to engage in harmful behaviors.[2]

For unemployed workers like mine, adequate care is even more critical. The health and life expectancy of manual laborers and workers without a college education are worse than those of all other workers.[3] Years of work in a factory breaks down the body. Many of my workers had carpal tunnel syndrome, damaged joints, or herniated discs. A few had more catastrophic ailments such as severed fingers and severe arthritis. They had worked routinely with toxic materials; some had developed asthma, while others were worried about what would happen years from now. (They had some reason to be concerned. One of my workers was receiving treatment for a metastasizing cancer, which he blamed on his exposure to chemicals over a decade.)

During the recession, health insurance for most unemployed workers rested on two foundations: COBRA and Medicaid. My fieldwork took place before the Affordable Care Act ("Obamacare") dramatically expanded Medicaid—especially for childless adults—and set up state exchanges where people could buy private plans with the help of government subsidies. Provided that the legislation survives its unending siege, these policy changes are likely to equalize the situations on the two sides of the border quite considerably. But back in 2009–10, Medicaid coverage of adults was meager in Michigan. What's more, as the economic downturn dragged on and enrollments surged, Michigan and a host of other financially strapped states responded by slashing the program's benefits and doctor payments. During this time, adults needed to have household incomes way below the poverty line to qualify for Medicaid, which meant that most unemployed workers were not eligible until long after their unemployment checks had stopped coming. (The income tests were much less strict for children, who were covered by Medicaid and another government program.)[4]

Under the federal COBRA law, laid-off workers can keep their coverage for a year and a half. However, their employers no longer have to pay their premiums. One study found that the average monthly COBRA premium for families is more than fourth-fifths of the typical worker's unemployment check. (For individuals, it is about one-third.)[5] During the recession, the federal government chipped in to cover these costs, paying two-thirds of the premiums for more than a year after workers became unemployed. An even larger subsidy went to workers covered by the federal retraining program (described in the last chapter) that helps workers who lost their jobs due to foreign trade.[6]

Even with the subsidies, most of my American workers said they could not afford health insurance.[7] Ken Brennan, a forty-seven-year-old former parts worker, spent seven days in a hospital last year after a blood clot traveled from his leg, through his heart, and into one lung. "You could be dead right now," a doctor told him. He recovered, but he wound up with a $1,400 bill even though he was insured. Ken still hasn't paid that back—and now he has lost that insurance, meaning that the next emergency could bankrupt him. The government recently sent Ken a COBRA notice: $316 a month to continue his insurance. "I can't get it. Hell, I can't even pay a bill sometimes," he says. The drugs for his high blood pressure, heart disease, and chronic anxiety alone cost him a hundred dollars a month. With no way to pay for them anymore, Ken has turned to the Salvation Army. They recently called his doctor and ordered him $300 worth of pills. When he runs out, he will have to call them again and hope the generosity continues. Ken tried applying for the state insurance program, but he was told the funds had dried up. They said they would call him when they started accepting enrollees again. Until then, he won't able to visit his doctor, he says. Just an office visit costs $110.

As months and then years passed without steady work, Mal Stephen eventually got coverage through the same program that Ken sought out. But shortly afterward, the fifty-one-year-old former Chrysler worker was told that the state, now broke, could no longer afford to cover adults like him. Mal is bitter about that. "I paid lots of money in taxes in the last ten years. Come on."

Some of the Americans were lucky enough to have health care coverage through their spouses' jobs. However, they soon realized just how good their fringe benefits had been. In almost all cases, their new coverage was worse—not surprising, given that the kinds of good jobs they once had have largely vanished from the corners of the labor market that they and their spouses reside in. One ex-Chrysler worker said he used to pay $20 to see a doctor. Under his wife's plan, he has to pay a $2,000 deductible before their insurance even kicks in. "So, believe me, I don't plan on seeing a doctor," he says.

Charlie Calhoun, a forty-nine-year-old former parts worker, hasn't even bothered to get insurance through his wife. Nelyn is a price adjuster at a box store, and her insurance policy isn't worth using, he says—with the high deductibles, "you end up paying everything anyway." Charlie says he could technically afford to extend his old plan through COBRA. But rather than be underinsured and poor, he has chosen to be uninsured and a tad less poor.[8] He points to a counter decked with bottles of vitamins, which he takes every day to stave off any illness. He can't afford to be even stressed, he says. "That'll get you health problems, and you get health problems, you ain't got no damn insurance. . . . You can't get sick now, shit."

Workers like Charlie gambled on not getting sick. They had other pressing bills to worry about, and since paying for insurance was optional, they could leave it out of their already stretched budget—however irrational a decision that sometimes turned out to be. Obamacare is addressing this problem through its individual mandate, which requires individuals to have insurance or pay a fine. Since the government-run insurance exchanges opened up in 2013, the percentage of Americans saying they are uninsured has dropped—considerably, according to some measures. Perhaps the law's carrots and sticks will convince unemployed workers like Charlie to purchase coverage and thereby shield themselves from the economic costs of serious illness, which for the uninsured must frequently be paid by hospitals and doctors—and, ultimately, by the public, in the form of higher premiums.[9]

There is one area where America's patchwork system of public insurance goes beyond even single-payer Canada, offering a fully socialized health care network of facilities owned, operated, and paid for by the government: the Department of Veterans Affairs and the broader military health care network.[10] While the VA suffered a major scandal in 2014 that highlighted, among other things, its long wait times, the system has reduced those waits over the years and has also received plaudits for the quality of its care. The handful of American veterans I talked to who had access to it said they were grateful for what was available. Forty-year-old Van Tranchina, who served as a petty officer on an aircraft carrier, is separated from his wife and unable to afford COBRA. "Only thing that . . . I could really depend on right now is the Vet," says the former parts worker.[11] But that coverage has its limits. Recently, Van wound up in the emergency room with a sudden bout of severe inflammation in his back and side. He ended up with a $1,000 bill he has yet to pay. "I'm gonna have to," he says, "because I know I'm gonna need them again."

Whether they are poor or middle-class, elderly or young, a parent or childless, military or civilian, an emergency trip to the hospital does not end up costing Canadians $1,000. Shortly after his layoff, Mitch

Beerman, a thirty-three-year-old former parts worker, developed an ulcer. He blames it on the stress from the loss of his job and the constant fights with his wife. One day last summer the pain hit him so intensely that he veered off the side of the road into an oncoming lane of traffic and smashed the front of his car. He was rushed to the hospital in an ambulance. Fortunately, Mitch was not injured in the crash. And as a Canadian, he paid nothing for the medical care.

My Canadians generally had a much easier time getting and affording care—which they ended up needing quite often, given the toll that long-term unemployment took on their health. Mitch and Van—two unemployed parts workers who separated from their wives shortly after they lost their jobs—were both going through a hard time because of their layoffs and marital situations, but at least Mitch did not have to worry about paying for his health care. In fact, very few of my Canadian workers ran into problems with medical bills, and all of these cases had to do with areas that the Canadian system does not fully cover: mental health therapy, vision and dental care, and prescription drugs.

Audrey Calvin, a forty-four-year-old laid-off parts worker, has developed dental problems that she can no longer afford to treat. She has a habit of grinding her teeth, which has worsened amid the stress of looking for a job. "I can tell before I get up in the morning how bad my night was because my mouth will ache," she says. The constant grinding wound up dislodging one of her fillings. Three months later, she has not been able to get it fixed. "Now it's cracked," she says. "If I had to go get this pulled at a dentist right now without coverage, it would probably be a couple hundred bucks." When she was working, her insurance paid for $1,800 in dental expenses a year.

My workers could get some coverage for prescription drugs through a province-wide program. It pays for medications for people who don't have private insurance—provided they pay a sliding-scale deductible and $2 copays. Even with this assistance, however, some of my workers still couldn't afford the medications they needed. A doctor told Tom Moon, a fifty-four-year-old ex-Ford worker, that his enzyme levels were off-kilter. The problem was, Ontario's program only covers certain medications, and Tom was told that the drug his doctor prescribed wasn't one of them. He didn't have $60 to pay out of pocket. So he ended up not getting it. He has no idea whether this will cause any problems later. Struggling as he is to pay his mortgage, Tom has other things to worry about.

Beyond paying for care, of course, the length of time patients wait to get treated is also a key metric in how effectively the health-related patch of the safety net catches downwardly mobile workers. According to one study, about a third of Canadians wait six or more days to see a doctor or nurse when they need care. In America, that figure is 19 percent.[12] For my Canadian workers, however, onerous wait times were generally not a problem. Tom was one of a few exceptions. He started going to clinics because he couldn't stand the three-week wait to see his family doctor. Upset, his doctor threatened to drop Tom as a patient. If it's an emergency he'd see Tom right away, he said. "That's a lie, 'cause I had an emergency a while ago and I called him and couldn't get in to see him," Tom says.

On the whole, though, cheap care that may take longer to receive seemed more valuable to my workers than expensive care supplied relatively quickly. They were already dealing with steep drops in their income. Without a safety net of public insurance beneath them, more of my Americans were forced to ration their care. They got fewer pills than they were prescribed. They chose less costly options, or went without. They waited until the last minute to see a doctor—in a sense, forfeiting any advantage the faster U.S. system might offer them. And when the problems became too risky to ignore, they sacrificed their financial health for their physical health, letting exorbitant medical bills go unpaid.

DOWN TO REALITY

Henry Rico lost his job at the feeder plant eight months ago. With just an unemployment check to rely on and little in the way of savings, the forty-one-year-old American has pared down his expenses dramatically. In the middle of a Midwestern winter, he barely heats his West Side bungalow, wearing a fleece at the dinner table. He survives on two simple meals a day: cereal during the day, and a bacon, egg, and sausage biscuit at night. "I used to be able to get spaghetti and meatballs and all that kind of living," he says, "but that's been cut down to the basics."

Nevertheless, his situation is manageable, he adds. "I just got to keep it a real tight ship. . . . As far as the major stuff, everything's okay." It doesn't bother him too much that his car's transmission is slipping or his tires are worn or the sewer line out back is leaking into his basement. He can make do for the time being, and in any case he doesn't have any children. "I don't know if it's a gift or a curse," he explains, but "I consider it a blessing right now that I don't have that."

What does bother him is losing the identity he has had ever since he was nineteen, when he started working full-time at a hotel, washing dishes for $5 an hour. "I know it's not my fault," Henry says about his layoff. "But . . . I always prided myself as a working man, if you will. They say there's no better feeling, other than to get off from work. When you punch out, ain't no better feeling but to have somewhere to punch out from. And without that? The sense of just . . . drifting in the wind."

. . .

A job is a marker of status—both social and moral. "You are what your job is," as one of my workers put it. When people are out of work, their sense of self-worth suffers, even as their fears for the future grow. Being unemployed turns you into "a different man," says Van Tranchina, the former parts worker going through a separation, who is struggling to pay his bills and also to cover expenses for his two daughters. "When I was working, I may have walked around with my head way up in the air, and now it's kind of like looking down," he says. "It brings you down to a sense of reality."

As their time without a job grows longer, the situation that my workers find themselves in does not just claw away at their dignity. It also leads some unemployed workers to feel self-blame (a topic I will return to in chapter 6). And it makes their lives less structured and more isolated, potentially worsening whatever depression or anxiety they may have.[13] Over eleven years at his Windsor plant, D.J. Packer's mind and body became accustomed to the routine. He still wakes up at seven o'clock every morning, ready for a job he no longer has. He also misses the sense of belonging he had at the plant. "There's nothing I can say bad about the guys I worked with," he says. Losing his job has meant losing touch with many of those friends. It has also tarnished his friendships outside the plant. A friend who worked at Chrysler once chided him for wearing secondhand clothes. "If you really feel that way," D.J. replied, "then you don't need to come over and see me." The bowling buddies drifted apart soon afterward.

Many workers grimly noted the number of funerals they've gone to since the layoffs in the industry began. "We've had guys that have taken their lives because . . . they feel that there's no way out," says Liz Jung, a recovering alcoholic who has struggled with depression herself. For her, the "way out" was going back to school: at the age of forty-six, the former Ford worker is now getting her university degree. When Liz goes to social events and gets asked, inevitably, what she does, at least she can say she's a student. When you say you're unemployed, she points out, "It's almost like you're a nobody."

For those workers like Liz who could get into school, that status helped them retrieve a sense of self-worth that unemployment had beaten down. That said, Liz is quick to point out that working at the plant was no paradise, either. "When you come in and you do the same thing for eight hours a day, eighty hours a week . . . you're no different than the robot that they replace you with at the end of the day. And they teach you not to think, right? Don't ask any questions, just do what you're told." She clocked in such long hours at the plant that it started to mess with her head. The "brain-numbing" work in the plant deepened her depression over a divorce and aggravated her drinking problem, which ultimately led to a suicide attempt. Liz counts herself lucky to be out of that environment—but, then again, she has yet to begin her job search.

In her study of American autoworkers at a GM plant, Ruth Milkman found that those who took buyouts were more satisfied with their lives after they left the factory gates. In retrospect, most were happy with their decision; like Liz, they did not miss the alienating discipline and punishment of working the assembly line. Some started businesses and exulted in being their own bosses.[14] When Milkman conducted her study, however, the economy was in relatively better shape. My workers were out of work at a time when the very existence of the auto industry seemed in question, and the economy was shedding massive numbers of jobs. With the greater severity of their financial troubles, as well as their despair about the dismal job market, the outlook of my workers was much worse—particularly among the lower-paid, less protected, and involuntarily terminated parts workers, a more vulnerable population that Milkman did not happen to study. More broadly, it may be that in the two decades since her research, the prospects of these less educated workers have worsened, through the more intensive sorting in the labor market I have described. Indeed, several of my workers ended up getting new jobs, but their wages were nothing like the ones they had left behind in the factory. Those who started their own businesses likewise struggled to make money and overcome their anxiety about making it on their own—a sign of the times in an economy where the self-reliant ideals of the independent contractor and self-employed entrepreneur free the fortunate, but impoverish those unable to deal with its inherent uncertainties.

In both countries, about a third of my workers admitted to being depressed or anxious, and several of them were on antidepressants. The

Americans had much more difficulty paying for their medications, and very few of them were able to find someone to talk to about their problems, either a therapist *or* a family member. Strikingly, none of these Americans were under the care of any psychiatrist or therapist for one-on-one counseling; they were simply getting pills from general practitioners—a hint of the makeshift nature of their care. On the Canadian side, help was more readily available, and a few workers were seeing specialists.

For fifty-four-year-old Hannah Frey, a long and luckless job search has left her anxious and demoralized. "It kind of makes you feel useless," she says. Last year, when things at the plant and in her home were particularly bad, she was taking a moderate daily dose of Cymbalta. After leaving her verbally abusive husband, she weaned herself off the antidepressant—which is a good thing, she adds, because she can barely afford her other medications, which include a cholesterol drug that without insurance costs $300 a month. Extending her company insurance would set her back ten times that amount, for just six months of coverage—which is simply out of the question, she says.

As her unemployment lengthens, Hannah finds herself slipping back into a funk. "I'm scared. I'll be ending up in the hospital somewhere in the garbage heap because I'll be indigent," she says. She used to live in a pleasant suburban neighborhood north of Detroit, where she felt safe enough to leave her back door open to let the dogs run in and out. But without the support of her husband, a Ford worker, she couldn't afford to pay the mortgage. She decided she had no choice but to turn to a "man friend" who offered to let her stay at his home in a low-income neighborhood outside Detroit. Her old neighborhood was like the Garden of Eden compared to this one, she says. "I lived in a $200,000 home. I had everything that I needed and wanted. I was secure." Now, there are drug dealers plying their trade next door. Police cars with lights streaming through the streets at all hours of night. Men throwing fists on the sidewalk right outside her window. "I just am not used to that anymore," she says. "I want out of here so bad." With all the stress and anxiety, Hannah can't sleep. She wakes up in the middle of the night and anguishes over what to do. Full of regret for the decisions she's made, she berates herself. "I'm a loser," she says.

Navigating the health care bureaucracy is a special burden for the depressed, who by definition are sapped of motivation and vigor, and yet who desperately need to find the right therapist and medication for their particular problem and personality. Ontario's government-sponsored action centers make sure that out-of-work people going through a rough patch get the help they need. Peer helpers who used to work in the very same factory or office call them at home to see how they are doing. While the peer helpers are not licensed counselors, they can put workers in touch with free or low-cost therapy and also provide an informal source of advice and understanding. The medium here—a trusted coworker—is part of the message. "There's a familiar face," says Mark Van, a Canadian with years of experience advising workers and companies on how to take advantage of Ontario's adjustment services. "If we hired professional counselors, then the only way the professional counselor would ever see them is when they walked in the door. A peer helper can call them. 'Haven't seen you at the action center. Come on down. We've got so much for you here.' Or they know the ones who are at risk. They've heard through the grapevine that somebody's drinking themselves into oblivion, so they show up at their house."

The centers are welcoming places: an unemployed worker can stop by the office, grab a coffee, and chat. When I talked with my workers, I was struck by how much they appreciated the personalized support. They had faith in their peer helpers. A former coworker, they said, could understand what they were going through better than the typical caseworker at an impersonal agency could. This kind of "moral support," D.J. Packer says, helped him get through the hardest period of his life. (In his case, the help was more than moral. If the center hadn't lobbied the company to extend his health benefits, he might not have been able to continue with his therapy.) Even now that he has overcome his bout of severe depression, he appreciates being able to just pick up a phone and hear a familiar, helpful voice. "These guys down here," D.J. says of the center, "are just a lifeline."

In the United States, laid-off workers often have to head across town to a state job center in order to get help. Lynn Minick, a workforce development specialist for the National Employment Law Project, points out that these so-called One-Stop Career Centers tend to serve a wide variety of people—from welfare recipients to recently terminated workers with long work histories—and that creates a barrier for some people. "They say, 'I don't want welfare, that's not me,'" he says. "They think that's what it is. They walk away from it." But if they hear about the available government services from someone they know, Minick adds, they will at least consider getting help. In these ways, peer programs bring people through the door and then keep them inside the system—helping laid-off workers become comfortable asking for help, giving some of them a personal reason to keep coming back, and reaching out to others who fall by the wayside. This last group, Minick says, gets all but ignored by the social safety net. "The system tends to serve those who are standing in front of them, not those who are not in the building." Laid-off workers who aren't assertive about getting the available benefits and supports "fall through the cracks," he adds. "There's no follow-up—the system can't serve them all anyhow."

My parts workers dealt with more depression and anxiety than my Chrysler and Ford workers, much of it revolving around their desperate finances. Losing their lower-paid jobs hit their already stretched family budgets harder (as I will discuss later). But money issues were not always decisive. A few of my workers managed to keep their spirits up even as their incomes plunged, through sheer will and resourcefulness or the unconditional support of family and friends. And others who could pay off their bills still felt upset and isolated because of their declining status. This is unsettling because it points to the fact that the mere condition of not having a job is cause for concern. Individuals internalize society's belief that being unemployed is degrading, and their mental health and social ties suffer as a result. Regardless of how much they receive in benefits, the unemployed are less satisfied than those with jobs. Even in countries with generous unemployment insurance, the unemployed tend to die at a younger age.[15] Policies to provide health care and income to the unemployed are important, but they cannot fully address the problem. Instead, we need a more vigorous approach to creating, and connecting workers with, jobs—a subject I will return to in the last chapter.

ROBBING PETER TO PAY PAUL

Health care is one area where the policy differences between the two countries were especially stark. In terms of benefit checks, however, the picture is more complicated. As I've mentioned, emergency measures the United States put in place after the recession struck narrowed any gap. But that gap had already been shrinking in the decades prior. Once boasting one of the world's most generous programs of unemployment insurance, Canada wound down that generosity beginning in the seventies. Under the leadership of governments of the Left and Right alike, the replacement rate—what percentage of a worker's previous earnings she would get back in unemployment benefits—dropped substantially.[16]

In both countries, the duration of these benefits lengthens when rates of joblessness shoot up, though the threshold for extending this assistance is normally much higher on the U.S. side.[17] Once the Great Recession began, Canada raised the limit to 50 weeks in the hardest-hit areas. For experienced workers, the maximum became 70 weeks—and a little over two years if those workers were taking classes. On the U.S. side, the federal government began funding extensions in all states. In areas of the country walloped by unemployment, like Michigan, that meant an unemployed worker who qualified in full could stay on unemployment for 99 weeks.[18] When the checks stopped coming, workers who qualified for trade-adjustment retraining, discussed in the previous chapter, could receive another year and a half of unemployment benefits. In other words, if covered by all the extensions and in school, a Michigan autoworker could receive almost three and a half years of unemployment benefits. (For workers fifty and older, a different federal program pays wage subsidies once they get new jobs, though none of my workers used this program, largely because most of them hadn't yet found jobs.)[19] The federal government's role here meant that the unemployed on the U.S. side ended up doing relatively well, benefit-wise, during the recession.

Yet the time limit was steadily shortened as the economy began to crawl back to health. Now that the various extensions have expired, it is back to 26 weeks in most parts of the United States, and actually less in some financially strapped states, including Michigan, that decided to pare back their programs.[20] In Canada, the current maximum in the most economically depressed areas is 45 weeks. Even in parts of the country with few job losses, the limit is 36 weeks, 10 weeks more than what states typically provide south of the border. The advantage is now clearly on the Canadian side—though after winning power in 2012 the Conservatives toughened the requirements for benefits.[21]

Canada officially has a two-week waiting period before unemployment benefits begin. But the delay ended up being longer for my workers. Yul Kane, a forty-two-year-old former Ford worker, waited eight weeks for his first check to arrive. He insists that he filled out the application correctly—before his time at Ford, he used to work in the government office that handled unemployment claims. Chrysler and Ford were both going through layoffs, Yul explains, and the system was severely backed up. By the time the money came in, Yul was $3,600 deep into overdraft and being socked with fees.

The wait on the U.S. side tended to be shorter. Michigan does not impose any waiting period, one of a minority of states to do away with it. Almost none of my Americans had complaints about the system. One ex-Chrysler worker points out that the bureaucracy is more tolerable than it was a generation ago, when he was last on unemployment. "I remember them long, long lines," he says. "I used to go to the unemployment office and be there a whole day.'" Now he just has to phone in.

In Michigan and many other states, eligibility depends mainly on the income that workers used to make, a standard that puts those with low wages at a disadvantage. Canada has a more lenient threshold, based on hours worked. This may help explain why many more of Canada's jobless file for unemployment benefits (though the proportion has fallen in recent decades).[22] Furthermore, Canada also tops up the benefits paid to low-wage workers. And even when they do not qualify for unemployment compensation, they can turn to Ontario's retraining program, described in the previous chapter, which offers living allowances for those currently studying. (A union-sponsored study of laid-off Canadian autoworkers found that those going through retraining found income supports to be the most important consideration in enabling them to go back to school.[23])

Once the unemployment checks start rolling out, the policies on the two sides of the border do a fairly comparable job of buffering the income shocks of losing a job. For certain households, however, Canada offers much more in the way of help. I will discuss the most important difference—the ways that Canadian policies target single-parent families—in the next chapter, along with other, smaller tax credits that matter in both countries. In the rest of this section, I will focus on how the largest income supports in dollar amounts—unemployment insurance and mandatory severance pay—affected my workers.

Because of their middle-class wages, my workers all qualified for unemployment benefits, and almost all received the largest amount possible, which was about the same on both sides of the border.[24] Mandated severance pay, however, tips the policy advantage slightly toward the Canadian side. Ontario requires that companies with large payrolls or substantial layoffs furnish workers with a severance package. (Normally, Canadians cannot receive severance and unemployment benefits at the same time, but a temporary federal initiative allowed some experienced workers undergoing training to do so—amplifying the Canadian policy advantage even further for this group.) My Canadian parts workers had all made good wages at the plants, so their weekly severance pay was more than what their unemployment benefits paid out. On the American side, the Chrysler workers received special, union-negotiated cash payments and car vouchers as part of their buyout packages. The American parts workers, however, did not receive any severance. Michigan law does not require it, and the company chose not to pay any (though the UAW was seeking to remedy this when my field-work ended).[25] In both countries, laws required that employers give advance notice (or equivalent pay) before they terminate workers, which helped to ease my workers into their new, lower-income reality. The forewarning that my Americans and Canadians received was about the same.[26]

In both countries, unemployment benefits amounted to only half or less of the paychecks my workers had been bringing home. With little in the way of savings, most of my parts workers experienced financial hardship after they lost their jobs for good. A large minority skipped bill payments; a handful lost their homes. An expression they often used was "robbing Peter to pay Paul"—shifting money from one overdue bill to the next. On the other hand, the circumstances of the former Big Three workers were generally better. Over the years, their unions had negotiated contracts that had created a private safety net of sorts, pro-viding not just buyouts to those severing their ties to the company, but also supplemental unemployment benefits for those who were instead on indefinite layoff with the (uncertain) chance of being recalled.[27] In the rocky years leading up to the auto industry's collapse, these extra payments cushioned the financial blow of the temporary layoffs these workers experienced, allowing them to avoid depleting their savings earlier on. The parts workers did not have these protections, even though they were represented by the same national unions.

That said, all of my Chrysler workers and some of my Ford workers took the buyouts, which meant that, at least on the U.S. side, they did not receive any unemployment benefits—from the company or the gov-ernment. While the buyout packages more than made up for the loss of these benefits, these lump-sum payments could be a mixed blessing because workers often did not understand how difficult finding a new job would be. They did not leave enough cash to pay for day-to-day living expenses as the weeks turned into months. Instead, many of them spent down their buyout packages rapidly—for frivolous purposes, sometimes, but also to pay off large debts such as car loans, mortgages, and credit card balances.

Timing was everything. Mal Stephen was laid off from his Chrysler job in 2007, and five months later he decided to take the buyout. The package was $100,000—$60,000 after taxes—which he used to buy a house and car. Over the course of a year the remaining money dwindled away, and Mal wasn't able to find a job. Then the "economy tanked," he says, and things went from bad to worse. His bank account and his retirement savings shriveled up quickly. Eventually, he had to turn to food stamps.

Mal doesn't regret using the buyout to clear off his mortgage—if he hadn't, he says, "for sure I would have been living with my mom"—but after the housing market crashed it became impossible to downsize his housing. He hasn't been able to keep up even with the utility payments, and his gas has been shut off for a while now. He heats his house with kerosene. "I cook on a hot plate and I got every electronic cooking device probably known to man," he says. To wash himself, he heats water in a two-and-a-half-gallon pot and then takes a "pot shower." "You take your big pot full of water, pour the water all over you like a shower, soap up, do it again." With the survivalist zeal of a former military man, Mal has adapted well to his current situation. And yet his day-to-day existence is a "whole 'nother life," he notes, from the one he once lived, when he was gainfully employed at Chrysler.

While most of my families on both sides of the border said they had difficulty paying their bills, my American parts workers tended to be in the worst financial straits. They had larger debts, and were more worried about losing their homes or declaring bankruptcy—in spite of the more lenient bankruptcy policies and the targeted mortgage assistance on the American side.[28] Randy Simpson, forty, has had to scrounge for extra cash. He lost his job at the feeder plant eight months ago. He cleaned out his bank account and now has just a few hundred dollars left in his retirement fund. Randy lives with his mother, who suffered severe, disfiguring burns from a cooking fire and receives disability payments.[29] Unfortunately, his unemployment check and her disability payments don't go that far, even with the food stamps they now receive. Randy is grateful that their mortgage terms were recently modified, which drove their monthly payments down to a more manageable amount—though it tacked on another $20,000 to their $100,000 housing debt.[30]

Randy remembers the time he spent in the eighties struggling to find steady work as a janitor. People kept promising him that if he kept at it he'd get hired full-time, but that never happened. He finally got a job at the plating plant, but again, working as a temp. Eventually, he gave up—and gave in to the temptation of selling drugs for quick cash. He spent three years in jail. When he got out, he went back to the plant. Now that he's laid off, Randy dismisses the idea of going back to his old ways—at forty, "that ain't no life no more." Still, he has no idea how his family will climb out of their financial hole. When he was dealing, Randy points out, "I was never broke."

A smaller number of Canadians parts workers found themselves buried under growing liabilities as the length of their jobless spells grew. One key reason was the severance packages they received. Under their union-negotiated contract, the Chromeshield workers received two weeks of pay for every year of seniority—twice what the law requires. The Canadians could use that pot of money to pay off the debts that overwhelmed many of their counterparts across the river.

Another reason is the different racial mixes of the two groups. My American sample was predominantly African American, while my Canadian sample was predominantly white (though four out of ten of the Canadian parts workers were first-generation immigrants). Since black Americans in general tend to have fewer savings to rely on and worse employment prospects, it may be that the greater hardship I observed on the U.S. side is a story of race interpreted as a story of policy. This is a limitation of my study's design. But, as I've mentioned, the income assistance for unemployed workers tended to be only slightly more generous in Windsor than in Detroit. Health care and retraining were the main areas where there was a Canadian advantage, and in those areas the effects of policies on individuals could be traced more clearly. Before they lost their jobs, black and white households largely shared the same health care plans paid for by their employers. After their layoffs, interactions with the action centers and retraining programs on the Canadian side led to tangible courses of study and concrete instances of counseling. The absence of free health care on the U.S. side led to specific, onerous medical bills. Furthermore, comparing just my white workers on the two sides of the border, the Canadians fared much better in terms of accessing health care and retraining. (The same was true for just the nonwhite workers.) In the next section, I will discuss several specific ways that race worsened the experience of unemployment for African American families in particular.

THE MIGHTY HAVE FALLEN

Royce Terrell's grandfather moved the family from Alabama to Detroit in search of jobs in the booming postwar plants. He found a job at the historic Ford River Rouge Complex, a sprawling campus built in 1928, at one time the largest integrated factory in the world. Grandpa Ed ended up working there for four decades. He managed to get his son, Uncle Jason, a job at the River Rouge as a security guard, and it looked like Royce's father, Mike, would follow next. But one day Jason got caught using drugs while sitting in his security booth. After that happened, Grandpa Ed decided he'd had his fill of the family. "He didn't want to put his name out there for anybody else," Royce recalls. "He had an opportunity, too—it was plenty of times that Ford was hiring." Ed had worked hard to establish himself, an African American, in the predominantly white Ford workforce. Once burned, he wasn't going to risk his reputation again. Son Mike Terrell wound up getting his own job at GM's Hamtramck plant. Grandson Royce Terrell ended up at a lower-paying parts supplier. Royce remembers repeatedly asking his grandfather for help in getting him work at Ford, only to be denied. When Grandpa Ed died, he was still the only Ford man in the family.

The elites of Michigan industry, UAW autoworkers are used to being selective about whom they help, deluged as they are with entreaties from relatives and friends. But now many of these autoworkers, having lost their jobs, find themselves on the other side of the equation: asking a high school friend for job leads, or an uncle for extra cash.

Help from family and friends—whether in the form of cash assistance, childcare, or career advice—can make a crucial difference for unemployed workers. So it is troubling that the black unemployed workers I interviewed were, on the whole, less able than their white (or other nonwhite) counterparts to tap family and friends for job leads or gifts and loans of cash during their unemployment. This finding accords with other recent research that looks at personal networks and concludes that white job seekers can take advantage of more—and better— referrals from friends, family, and teachers. (It is worth noting, too, that recent research continues to find that employers discriminate against African American job candidates who are equally—or even more— qualified than white candidates.) Among low-income blacks in particular, few receive useful leads from their networks. The fortunate, employed individuals in their social circles, sociologist Sandra Susan Smith argues, distrust the competence and reliability of their relatives and friends. They fear that their own reputations will suffer if these slouches put their names on a job application.[31]

The situation of my unemployed black autoworkers bears further scrutiny, however, because these are the former job holders who were themselves once wary of the job seekers around them. Helping them should not pose a reputational risk. They worked hard, paid their dues, and proved themselves worthy employees. But now they find themselves in a position of no small irony in having to ask others for help—and getting rejected.

As it turns out, many of their friends are also unemployed. There is little they can do for each other. About half of Henry Rico's friends don't have jobs, and so far the unemployed African American parts worker hasn't gotten any promising leads through the grapevine. His stepfather, who is a custodian at a private school, said he'd let Henry know if anything opened up at the school—nothing has come of that so far, though. It's not that Henry is setting his standards too high, either. He'd be willing to push a mop if he has to, he declares.

Henry is working his network as much as he can. A good friend of his also lost his job recently. They used to chat on the phone regularly, doing postmortems of football games and joking around. But nowadays Henry knows to keep it short and to the point: "You got a hookup for me?" It's a waste of time to converse about anything else, he says. "I can hear it on the phone how he's hurting"—and Henry is struggling, too—so why pretend? "He's a man looking for work just like I am, and you can't laugh like you used to without work. . . . And stuff you used to talk about seems so irrelevant now. . . . There's no thrill about it because I need work. I ain't got time to worry about football games. . . . If you ain't calling about a job, or you're hurt or worried about something, why call? . . . Don't call me about no, 'Did you see the score?'"

In terms of financial help, black workers couldn't tap as deep a reserve of family funds as other workers could. James Channing, a white Canadian, was able to stay out of a homeless shelter because his mother let him move in with her. The former parts worker has borrowed about $10,000 from his family members. They are sympathetic about what he's going through and haven't pushed him to repay. But he still feels ashamed. "I'm forty-three years old and living off my mother," he says bitterly. "How long is my mom gonna put up with this, you know?" Meanwhile, he feels terrible about not being able to provide for his twelve-year-old daughter, Gloria. His unemployment benefits ran out in December, and he gave virtually the entire amount of his last check to Gloria so that she could have the Christmas she was used to. "She's my daughter. I don't need nothing for Christmas," he says. "When am I gonna get the chance again?"

In spite of all the problems James is dealing with, he points out that he is lucky to have family willing and able to support him through his personal crisis. Even when comparing families at the same income level, the median white family has seven times the wealth of its nonwhite counterpart.[32] For the unemployed the consequences of this gap are particularly great: cash transfers between relatives and even friends can be lifelines for their families. James Channing's family has savings to give him—no strings attached—to keep him from falling into further misfortune. Gary Jansen's family—an African American household—does not.

Eight months after the twenty-nine-year-old parts worker lost his job at the plant, Gary has had to take out a few thousand dollars in loans to keep up with bills. What has most traumatized his family, however, happened around Thanksgiving, when thieves broke into their home. They stole a water cooler full of change. They seized the fireproof safe where Gary was keeping cash from his unemployment checks. And they even ran off with his children's things: their Xbox and Wii, their clothes and shoes. All together, Gary figures the family lost almost $4,000 worth of possessions and cash. The kids, ages ten and seven, were distraught and frightened. "Why would they do that to us? Why would they take my stuff?" asked his son, a fifth-grader, whose room was ransacked. Last Christmas, Gary wound up spending more money he didn't have, to buy them back a piece of normalcy.

Nowadays Gary is trying to work out an arrangement with the electric company to pay off a hefty unpaid balance. But their terms keep changing, and they somehow expect him to fork over large sums right away, he complains. "I really feel for any other Americans going through anything like this. We're working so hard trying to come up with the money to pay these people. They don't care at all." When Gary was making money, he didn't have to worry about being at the mercy of customer service agents and government bureaucrats, groveling for a bit of leniency from strangers. But now he has to, and he doesn't have well-off family or friends to help pull him out of his predicament.

It's not that Gary hasn't tried to reach out for help. When he asked, his family wouldn't step up. His friends did, modestly. He borrowed $1,500 from three of them. "I'm sure I probably wore that welcome out by now," he says. He points out that only three of his friends actually have jobs. Everybody else in his circle is unemployed. "I try to be as independent as possible. I try to keep my strains and stresses from screwing up the other people's lives as much as possible. So it was hard to ask people for help." With no one left to turn to, Gary puts his faith in the *deus ex machina* of modern times: the Mega Millions lottery. He buys a bunch of tickets once a week, sometimes twice a week, every month forking over $40 for a chance at salvation from his mounting bills. So far, he's only won $10 on a scratch-off ticket.

African American workers like Gary Jansen and Henry Rico are hit harder by unemployment than their white counterparts because of their less helpful social networks, which include fewer stable, gainfully employed, middle-class family members or friends. As Royce Terrell points out, he is unique in his family for having—well, he had at one time—a high-paying job. "My family isn't very educated and rounded. No one's ever been outside of Detroit, and [the] motivation isn't really there. . . . My family can't come out here. My uncle has a car, doesn't have a driver's license. So he just drives from work and back. My grandmother, aunties, sister—no one has a car. The money is not really there. So as far as when it came to visiting, it was always me going to them."

Now that he no longer has an income or a working car, those visits have stopped. There are few people in their extended family that he or his wife Elena can turn to. Royce's uncle lent him $200, though Royce points out that over the past decade he has been giving money regularly to his uncle—a middle-aged man who has worked as a cook at a chain restaurant for two decades—so that gesture was really just payback. What aid the Terrells do get tends to be in kind. Elena's mom helps pick up the kids from school and stuffs their refrigerator with packs of chicken every week. It helps, but it's not nearly enough. "A lot of times, some of the kids don't eat well," Elena says. "We don't tell her."

In any case, Royce knows he can't really latch onto his family when they're just barely afloat themselves. The other day he met up with another uncle, who is unemployed and lives in the basement of Royce's grandmother's house. Royce had $2 in his pocket; his uncle asked him for a buck, and he handed it over. "It's hard for me to say no to somebody when I got it," he says. "Even though I know I don't have it—I don't even know where it's going to come from next. All I know is I have it now, and somebody needs it, and I'll worry about me later."

Royce is a fairly typical representative of the black middle class, which on the whole—controlling for income—is more generous than its white counterpart in loans and gifts of money bestowed on family and friends. Generally speaking, the networks of mutual expectations that connect family and friends should circulate benefits to everyone, including transfers of cash when needed. And yet, to a degree, the obligations placed on workers like mine by their less well-off kin have held them back financially—thus serving, in this narrow sense, as a form of negative social capital.[33] As Royce knows well, he was one of the privileged few—those rare scions of the ghetto who could obtain well-paying union jobs (unions that historically had been closed to blacks) and ride that wage scale into the middle class. It was their very privilege that obligated them to be generous to their many kith and kin—jobless and McJobbed alike—who came out of the same downtrodden neighborhoods. Yet, when these once-envied Chrysler sons and Chrome Craft cousins ended up losing their own jobs, their social networks were starved of the kind of affluence that could marshal aid back in their direction. They could not expect much in the way of resources—whether in terms of extra cash, job leads, or just the sympathetic ear of another middle-income person who could truly understand what they were going through. The pathway of assistance, in other words, was painfully one-way.

On the Canadian side, I interviewed only two black workers, one formerly at Ford and the other a former parts worker. Neither was receiving help from friends or family, though both households were experiencing serious difficulties paying their bills. I can't make any claims about how my black Canadians compare to the other groups of workers I interviewed, but I should note that both of these households relied on substantial government help. Social policies covered the tuition and living expenses of the Packer family that I profiled at the beginning of this chapter. The other black Canadian household, the Sewells, received government assistance of a quite different sort. Hubert, a thirty-eight-year-old former Ford worker, says he and his wife Julie have struggled financially in the four years since he lost his job, but he recently landed a part-time job driving a Zamboni around a town skating rink. He is still looking intently for full-time work, but he considers himself lucky to have found a sixteen-dollar-an-hour public-sector job—one of the few left amid the government cutbacks of recent years.[34]

When social networks underperform, the state can step in with compensating social policies or public-sector jobs that employ the less educated. In this way, government assistance may provide a useful corrective to the way race and class unequally distribute society's informal resources of cash assistance and job leads from family and friends. And that help can reach beyond those directly targeted. Strengthening each node—each relative and each friend's household—creates a stronger network able to mobilize more in the way of resources for those, like my workers, who found themselves groping for a hand up.[35]

For their part, unemployed black autoworkers tend not to grouse about the fact that family and friends aren't lining up to repay them for those earlier years of charity. When they do think of the people around them, it is more often with a feeling of embarrassed remorse rather than righteous self-pity. With their hard-won union wages, they had once hoisted families and friends onto their shoulders. But now they have lost their grip in the labor market, and the many people who relied on them are being dragged down as well. Indeed, the cynic's take on minority workers—last hired, first fired—understates the damage that happens when the unemployment of these once-proud workingmen and women reverberates throughout their social networks.

In turn, their fall from grace is a blow to these workers' very identities as steadfast friends, loving family members, and decent human beings. They had reveled in their role as neighborhood paladins. Henry Rico, the former parts worker, never used to wait for his relatives to ask for help. Sure, sometimes they would say something—"reluctantly," he says—but he took pride in volunteering to pitch in. He used to help his aunts regularly. And then there was his cousin Danny. The two grew up together and are close. Danny, a married father, got laid off from his job and struggled to pay his mortgage. Henry stepped up with $200 here, $200 there. He continued to help out even months after his layoff. But recently his finances have sunk to the point that he's had to cut off all his family philanthropy.

Another of Henry's cousins ran over a possum in the street a few months ago and wrecked her car's radiator. "Normally, I would jump right in there—'Hey, let's get this repaired,'" Henry says. "That used to be one of my joys—just try to help people out. Can't really do that no more, like I used to."

EQUALITY AND THE SOCIAL SAFETY NET

For my workers, social policies played a vital role in smoothing away the market economy's rough edges. The Canadians' single-payer, universal health care system and the personal touch of their action centers ensured that their health problems—physical or psychological—were competently treated and did not lead to as many grim financial consequences. While the Canadian system had blind spots in its coverage of mental health therapy, dental care, and prescriptions, overall my workers there found it easier to get the care they needed and to pay for it.

However, my comparison of the social safety nets on the two sides of the border cannot be boiled down to a simplistic finding of Canada stronger, America weaker. In terms of direct monetary benefits, there was less of an advantage up north. On the one hand, companies had to pay severance on the Canadian side, providing valuable help to my workers and their families. However, the total income transfers were only slightly lower on the U.S. side, thanks to the extraordinary measures that the government took when the financial crisis hit. Federal extensions meant that unemployment benefits actually lasted longer here. (As I mentioned, the expiration of these extensions since the time of my fieldwork has changed the picture dramatically.) Some workers received extra help thanks to trade-adjustment policies. The overall financial situation of my American parts workers tended to be worse than their Canadian counterparts, though this had something to do with the large number of African American workers I interviewed, who experienced unemployment in a more desperate fashion than the other groups I talked to. They had few savings to start with and could not tap networks of family and friends for assistance as much as the white workers could. This meant that they were less able to sustain themselves within the seething waters of the economy, leaving them at the whim of a stunted meritocracy and a culture of judgment, both hostile to workers like them—with deleterious consequences for their sense of well-being and worth.

In most cases, Canadian unemployed workers had a window of less than a year—the length of their unemployment benefits—to secure employment. Without further income or savings, they would quickly descend into poverty in the second year, and eventually find themselves resorting to welfare payments and other stigmatized forms of government assistance. This make-or-break approach in the first year may be the most efficient use of resources: provide a strong infusion of support early on, so that the unemployed worker is not worrying about rising debts and can concentrate fully on her job search. As I discussed earlier, the chances that a laid-off person will ever find employment diminishes considerably as his spell of joblessness grows longer. Furthermore, in both countries, most people avoid hitting the wall: they are typically able to find new work before unemployment benefits end. It makes sense, then, to frontload benefits.[36]

For a handful of my workers—all of whom had been unemployed for more than a year—social policies for the poor became relevant. Research shows that when the unemployment checks stop coming, household incomes drop by a third and the poverty rate doubles, with food stamps and other safety-net programs softening the financial blow only a little.[37] But that is only half the story. As my interviews suggest, there is also a psychological price to be paid in moving off the unemployment rolls and onto the welfare rolls. One advantage of receiving unemployment is that workers can at least make the argument that they paid into the system. Welfare, on the other hand, is utterly reviled. The public associates it with laziness and dependency.[38] For the unlucky few among my workers who followed this path, turning to public assistance dealt a major blow to their dignity and compounded the emotional damage caused by going so long without work.

. . .

Tom Moon was laid off from Ford in 2005 and since then has struggled to hold on to jobs. No longer covered by unemployment benefits, he now lives off social assistance payments of $650 a month—and what peanut butter and days-old bread he can get at food pantries. It is a world apart from his past life as a Big Three autoworker, making $90,000 in a good year, golfing and vacationing in Jamaica, never worrying much about money. Now he worries about losing his home, an ancient Windsor bungalow where he's lived for thirty years. The place is so old the bricks are starting to fall apart, and the back porch is rotting away, but it's home. Tom still has his golf clubs, and to relieve stress he'll go to the backyard and smack a couple balls into a net.

He needs the reprieve. Every month, Tom is in a desperate race to pull together his $1,000 house payment, which includes a second mortgage he took out after his layoff. Lately, he has been driving a beat-up 1991 Ford Windstar around town running under-the-table errands for people, even though the minivan's Check Engine light is on, the air conditioning is broken, and the brakes are ground down. "I go around the parking lot in reverse, hit the brakes, and it ratchets them up, makes them a little tighter," he says. "Does it work? Not really, but it makes me feel better." Creditors hound him for the $6,000 he owes on a now cut-up credit card. They siphon away his funds whenever he sets up a bank account to pay his home loan. "You try to go to different banks and open new accounts. Hopefully they don't catch it."

All the contortions that Tom goes through to keep his home will probably be for naught: he expects an eviction notice any day now. "I'm gonna try to keep it going until winter. I don't think they'll evict you in the wintertime." His son Bo recently paid two months of Tom's mortgage. Though Tom was desperate, he waited seven months to ask his son for help. "It made me feel like shit. Having to take money from him so that I can survive? He's having a hard enough time on his own." Tom says he won't ask his son again. There's not much anyone can do at this point, he says, to save his home.

"I never thought I'd be getting welfare," he adds. "Fifty-four years old and on welfare. I used to think everybody on welfare was a head case. A lot of them are, but . . . there's a lot of them that aren't." When he was employed, he never gave a second thought to the poor people on public service announcements struggling to pay their electricity bills. "I just thought, 'Oh, if this guy really wanted to work he could work.' Well, now I'm at a point where I really want to work, and I don't got a job."

The frustration eats at him. Throughout the summer of 2009, Windsor's municipal workers were on strike, protesting cuts to retirement benefits. Trash piled up on the streets, and parkland grass grew into thickets. Comments on newspaper websites assailed the "greedy" union, a sign of the anti-union anger—justified or not—present even in a factory town like Windsor. At the time, Tom happened to be searching for ways to supplement his welfare check, so he agreed to haul away a load of concrete in return for a few bucks. He had just packed the concrete into a trailer attached to his van and was getting on his way when a driver stopped, leaned out, and yelled, "Strikebreaker!" Tom slammed on his brakes. "Get the fuck out of the car!" he screamed at the man—who, wisely, stayed put.

"I was gonna beat his fucking head in," says Tom. In his trailer he had concrete, which the garbage trucks would not have taken anyway. He wasn't scabbing. But "this guy," he says, "thought I was hauling garbage." Tom is not an imposing man, but his shaved head, bushy eyebrows, and missing top front teeth give him the look of someone you'd be foolish to cross. "I think it would've been a real big mistake if he would've gotten out of his car," he says quietly.

As Tom's unemployment has dragged on, episodes like this one have become more common. He'll "fly off the handle" if someone cuts him off on the street. "When you put your clothes on and you go looking for somebody to fight, that's not good," he points out. It's not that Tom is a cheerless man. He speaks gruffly and sparingly during our conversation, propping his chin up pensively on one hand, but at times he laughs and shakes his head wryly—as if he cannot believe the ludicrousness of his own predicament.

Nonetheless, his relentless spasms of anger have made it less likely that Tom, an older worker already deeply scarred by long-term unemployment, can hold on to any job. After Ford laid him off, he briefly worked at a canning factory. One day a coworker complained he wasn't doing his job right. "You can't come in after fucking forty minutes or whatever sitting in the lunchroom . . . and tell me I'm not doing it right," Tom snapped. He lasted a month in that job.

During the day, when he is driving around town, scrambling to make a dollar, he is too busy to listen to all the antipathies teeming in his head. But at night, as he sits in front of the television, numbly watching whatever is on, "all of a sudden it fucking just starts," he says. The rage at where he is in his life, what he has become—who he has become.

Recently, the fury reached a point that Tom knew he needed help. "I thought my fuse had burned out," he says. "I was mad at everything, everybody." He called his doctor. Tom has had problems with depression for about forty years, but he had never mentioned it during his past visits. "Why didn't you tell me?" his doctor asked him.

"You never asked me," Tom said.

"It's not something I ask."

"It's not something I talk about."

Tom agreed to follow his doctor's advice and see a psychiatrist—for the first time in his life. "I'm wondering what he's gonna be thinking about it after he sees me," he says, and then laughs dryly. The good thing is that his consultation is at a hospital crisis center that his doctor referred him to, so it won't cost Tom anything.

Growing up, Tom never told anyone about his depression. It was understood that you didn't talk about such things. Nobody knows about his visit to the psychiatrist. "That's not something that we're supposed to do in my family," he says. Anyway, his friends would probably snigger if he told them. Factory workers aren't the most sensitive lot. "'You're going to see a psychiatrist? Oh my God.' That would've been me talking about somebody else."

CHAPTER 4

Half a Man

Fragile Families and the Unmarriageable
Unemployed

The strongest poison ever known
Came from Caesar's laurel crown.
—William Blake, "Auguries of Innocence"

Half of Royce Terrell's face is frozen.

It's not a stroke, Royce explains in his cautious and deliberate cadence, supremely conscious of the slurred edge to every other word he utters. It sounds as if he has been drinking, or busted his lip, but actually it is Bell's palsy: paralysis of a nerve running below his left ear and across his cheek. He has had the condition for more than three months. There is no cure, and doctors tell him there is no telling when it will go away. The cause, too, is unknown. But Royce thinks it no coincidence that he woke up with this stricken visage two days after he lost his job at Chrome Craft. He had worked there for seven years, and it was the best job he ever had.

He is thirty-one years old, a tall man with soft brown eyes and long lashes that make him look younger than his age. He sits at his kitchen table in a long-sleeved gray T-shirt and denim shorts, his jowls and throat unshaven, his goatee uncombed. At times he rubs his slight paunch with either hand, leaning back in his chair with a look of dejected weariness lingering on the still-expressive half of his face.

His left eye won't close. The wet pupil glints, motionless, even as he blinks the other. It will tear up constantly, he says, so people think he is crying. "You know why your face is like that now?" a friend told him recently. "You can no longer hide how unhappy you are. So you might as well start letting your feelings out."

"And that's what I'm doing now," Royce notes. "I'm broke down."

These days, he broods over long-past mistakes and beats himself up constantly, mercilessly, for everything that's happened. For not being more prepared for the possibility of losing his job. For not recognizing the dangers in the auto industry before the market sank. For not being able to provide—as he always had—for his wife Elena and their four children. "Not being able to work, that is mental anguish for him," Elena says.

He had always worked. When Royce had started hanging out with a rough crowd on Detroit's West Side, his family shipped the teenager to his father's house outside Atlanta. There he nominally attended high school, but spent his afternoons and evenings and early mornings at a warehouse, driving a forklift and loading trucks. "I fell in love with the money that could be made by working," he says. "School and going to college probably left my head around sixteen." Once he had dreams of becoming an architect, but after he brought home his first $1,400 pay-check, he became an overtime junkie, plowing through fifty to sixty hours of work every week. He slept through his first-period math class. But in that affluent suburb, where teens drove to school in BMWs and Porsches with gleaming rims, and his peers derided Royce's neighbor-hood of fine townhouses as "the projects" and "the ghetto," the new kid from Detroit felt a need for respect—the kind that money could buy. "I remember going to school with big knots of money in my pocket," he says. With that cash he paid his phone bill, he bought his clothes. One thing he had learned from his father was that he needed to fend for himself. "My Dad wasn't really fond of taking care of his boys."

Returning to Detroit, Royce worked a low-wage peonage for nearly a decade—Pizza Hut, a department store, factories, the post office—before landing a job at the plating plant. It was a temporary gig that paid $8 an hour, but he stuck with it. There was plenty of overtime ("I like overtime"), and they promised to hire him after ninety days.

Nine months later and still a temp, Royce was dragged by coworkers to a club on the East Side. It wasn't the kind of place he cared for, and he thought he had better ways to spend his hard-earned cash. But that night, he met Elena. She was tall and beautiful, smart and ambitious, and—in a word—"opinionated." She thought he could do better than temping. "You go in there busting your butt every day," she told him. "You need to just leave that company." So he quit, telling his boss that he was upset the company hadn't hired him as they promised, even though he was working, as he puts it, "like a slave."

Three weeks later, the company offered him a permanent position.

He moved in with Elena and her three children. They got married. Their own baby boy, Keith, followed. By then he was making more than he ever had, with health insurance and a company contribution to his retirement account. The couple was in love, the kids were happy, and Royce was doing well compared to the rest of his family in Detroit—who, not surprisingly, beseeched him for a piece of that good fortune. Royce handed out dollar bills where he could, and was glad he could do it.

But then the layoffs began, starting in 2007. Production at the plant had stalled, and Royce, with his low seniority, was out the door. Fortunately for the Terrells, a year earlier Elena had started a job in a property management office. Now they could depend on both Elena's income and Royce's unemployment checks to tide the family over. Still, he took the loss of his status as breadwinner hard. Subconsciously, it ate at him, his wife says. "When I worked, that added to his mental state." But Elena, nearly forty and with no experience in real estate, was flourishing in her new career. A quick study, she eventually worked her way up into management.

In 2008, the layoff ended and Royce was called back to the plant. A month later, his manager offered a sanguine assessment. The company's Windsor plants were shutting down. Royce's plant was going to pick up their work—five years of guaranteed employment. "I literally ran through the whole plant, jumping up and down," Royce recalls. "I got on my knees and was praying and thanking God. I was happier than I had been in a long time."

But shutting down the Canadian plants was not the end of Flex-N-Gate's downsizing. Headquarters decided that it could trim even more fat from its global chain of production, so it shut down Royce's plant next and shipped the work elsewhere.

Laid off once again, this time for good, Royce started looking for a new job. Over the months he has applied to dozens—auto and janitorial, thrift stores and restaurants—without any bites from employers. It doesn't help that, with his car's throttle out of commission, and without $1,200 to fix it, he has to take the bus to the state job center to use their computers and search for jobs. Once a week he walks there, which takes an hour but saves him the $2.25 fare. Meanwhile, his family's finances are collapsing. With Royce no longer receiving unemployment benefits, their income has been cut in half. They have fallen months behind in payments on their mortgage, car loans, utilities, and credit cards. They have plumbed the bottom of their overdraft privileges at the bank. Recently, Royce pawned the diamond-encrusted gold ring that Elena had given him on their wedding day. He got $200 for it.

Their marriage, too, is in hock. Royce's perennial unemployment—and Elena's burgeoning real-estate career—have driven the two former best friends apart. He is no longer the person she fell in love with, she says. When she calls him from work, he gripes about being home and "cooking and cleaning." He is cold and distant in the evenings when they're together. She says it's because she's coming home from work, and he's not. The provider for some seven years, Royce is now the dependent one, and it has devastated his pride.

Royce acknowledges he has a problem. Month by month, he has seen himself withdraw from life, his once-gregarious personality weighed down by a leaden harness of stress. These days he feels foreign to himself, he says: instantly irritable, sensitive to every slight. Nevertheless, Royce maintains that he doesn't mind Elena's job. What bothers him, he says, is that she will make comments about his inability to provide. When their arguments boil over, she will declare to him, "This is my house! I pay all the bills! I put all the food in the house!" The words will wrap around his thoughts for weeks, and fester. He never said those words when *he* was the provider, he insists. They argued every now and then—twice a month, maybe. Now it's every day, usually over the bills. Royce wonders aloud whether they argue more frequently just because they see each other more.

Their conversations will sometimes drift into joking and playful banter, but always there is an undercurrent of venom—a reckless, deep-seated need, Elena suggests, to make the other person feel pain. With each caustic exchange, "sorry" has become an endangered word in the Terrell household. "Back in the day," she says, "he was the one that always came with 'I'm sorry' first. That was an attribute of him that I loved."

"But now I'm like, 'Damn, I ain't sorry no more! I didn't do nothing!'" Royce says, practically shouting. "I was saying sorry every day for a long time. I say sorry for stuff that you do. I say sorry when I really ain't sorry, just for it to be—"

"My apologetic approach never helped, never was acknowledged, never was accepted," Elena interrupts.

He, in turn, believes that his wife is capable of plenty of sympathy toward other people, but is somehow unwilling to extend that compassion to him—for being unemployed, for being sick, for being depressed. Once, when he was feeling self-conscious about his face, she told him, bluntly, "Ain't nothing wrong with you. Stop having pity on yourself."

She says she was only trying to convince him that most people couldn't even notice the slight palsy, so there was no reason to be embarrassed. Whether it's his sensitivity or her callousness, the constant friction between them has made him bitter, so much so that in recent months a visceral hostility seethes inside of him whenever she's around. "I know that in this relationship, I am a different person, and I don't like the person I am."

There is little communication between them now. Royce deals with his depression alone. He saw a therapist years ago, but he hasn't talked to anyone recently—and now that he's lost his insurance, he can't afford it anyway. "I don't have any outlets," he says. "Not a hobby."

"There is an outlet. Me," says Elena. "[You] dump it on me through nonverbal gestures, looks, rejection. You don't realize it. This is what *I* deal with."

As with many married couples at odds, the most trivial matter becomes an opportunity for settling scores—what Elena calls their "constant competition." The other day it was over her purse. She asked him to get it off the kitchen chair. He got up and shuffled out the room, with exaggerated, plodding steps. "You notice I'm taking my time, because I want to aggravate you," he joked. Five minutes later, she noticed he still hadn't brought over the purse. Angry, she stormed into their bedroom and locked the door. He knocked and asked to be let in. She ignored him. "I did not want it to go to the next stage," she explains to him the next day.

"I've been the vulnerable one," he counters, testily. "And that's why I might slip a little thing like not bringing your purse." Since he was laid off last year, the fights have escalated to the point that she starts slapping him—four or five incidents so far, he says. "So me saying, 'I'm gonna walk slow to get your purse'—after being hit, being physically hit and not hitting you back, that's the least!"

"That's in a typical day, week, or month that you're hit?

"See what I'm saying? It shouldn't be ever."

"It shouldn't be ever that I feel I have to get physical and slap the mess out of it." She admits that at times the anger wells up in her, like a wave, and she needs to push him away from her. "I will try to knock him out, and knock him out the door," she says. Several months, Royce says, the fighting got so bad he called the police. He didn't tell them she hit him—"I didn't want her to get locked up"—but she had locked him out, it was cold, and he needed to be let back in. She has kicked him out of the house and changed the locks several times, he notes. He still does not have a key. "She has a box of locks—a *box* of locks," he says. "I'm not a person that sleeps around."

She has never slept around, either, she points out. And the reason she changed the locks the last time was because he decided, after a heated argument in their car, to walk all the way home, pack up, and—without a phone call to her or their children—move out. "I do everything. I work like a slave," she says, her voice cracking. "I can work ten hours, and come home and work another four hours, and it's never recognized."

The older children have now grown used to the constant bickering in their home. The youngest, five-year-old Keith, not so much. During one of his parents' recent yelling matches he fled to a corner of the living room. He cowered behind the leather ottoman, covered his head with his hands, and started wailing.

"What we're doing is too damaging—for our kids and for ourselves," Royce says. "We love each other. That's not always a reason to stay together."

. . .

The story of marital woe is age-old, but the weak economy has deepened its reach, as millions of men and women find themselves waylaid by financial uncertainties and wracked by the stresses and fears that come with not having enough money. If a couple has no constructive way to cope, there is always the "outlet" of the other person, or their children—but in Royce Terrell's family, the negative energy unleashed by those arguments lingers on, like a perverse law of thermodynamics, poisoning relationships to the point of alienation and separation.

Even when the anxiety of tight finances and the gloom of unemployment do not fracture domestic life, they force unemployed workers and their families to question the future. Whether or not a new job materializes, will they be able to maintain the standard of living they have enjoyed up until now? Since the recession, depressed housing values have made it harder for ordinary families in many parts of the country to borrow against their one major asset, their homes, to finance the skyrocketing costs of college tuition and health care. When a worker loses his job, these financial commitments become an even heavier lift. "You're always trying to do one better for your children than what was done for you," says Yul Kane, forty-two, an ex-Ford worker with a ten-year-old son. But "the cost of hockey has gone up. The cost of everything has gone up, except for the value of your home." Just a few years ago, Yul had cleared off the remaining debt on his line of credit. But after being unemployed for so long, now he is $30,000 in the hole again. He and his wife Sara would like to sell their home and downsize, but that means taking a huge loss. With his financial situation so grim, Yul no longer believes that he'll be able to save up enough to send his son Nick to the top schools. "That's going to make me feel bad. . . . [But] how is it we're going to retire in twenty or thirty years?"

In this way, the tightening vise of financial insecurity that families like mine find themselves in hurts the chances of the next generation. Without a good education, the children of workers like Yul will begin their working lives mired in the mud of the low-wage economy, and probably stay there.[1] If a parent's layoff propels families toward lower income brackets, it also propels their children toward a higher risk of unemployment themselves once they venture into the working world. Although the recession highlighted this problem, it is not simply a matter of a temporary dip in the business cycle and a temporary crimp in savings. Rising inequality is the broader backdrop to what happens to households when someone loses a job. Trends that disproportionately harm their less advantaged families have made the situation of my unemployed workers worse than it otherwise would have been.

In the middle decades of the last century, the family helped preserve the egalitarian outcomes that a booming (if exclusionary) economy produced. At a time when the sole breadwinner was the norm and two-parent households were more common, families in need of extra income could send the spouse working at home to work in the labor market, providing a backstop of sorts for the unemployed.[2] The abundance of good jobs for the less educated meant that ordinary factory workers could pass their bounty down to the next generation, through the income that paid for decent housing and schooling or the family connections that landed a young worker a plant job. Even today, the few unionized jobs that remain continue to serve as an engine of upward mobility. Though most of my workers' older children have gone on to manufacturing and service jobs, many have gone to college and found good white-collar jobs—which, though they typically pay no more than what their Big Three parents made, keeps the younger generations from worrying about getting grease on their hands.

In the postwar economy, women depended on male breadwinners in sometimes hurtful and cruel ways.[3] Fortunately, today's households have moved in the direction of gender equality, with women and men playing a wider range of roles in the home and office. At the same time, the family as an institution has become more inimical to *economic* equality.[4] Changes in family structure—whether a household has one or more earners, whether there are children to care for, and so on—have affected different social classes to different degrees. Separation and single-parent-hood have become much more common among workers like mine, in part because a good partner (that is, one with a decent-paying job that can support a family) is harder to find. Many unmarried working-class parents live together, but even as cohabitation becomes more prevalent and accepted across society, the outcomes of the children raised by these couples and lone parents alike still lag far behind those of kids in married households. Meanwhile, the growth in two-earner households, while a major advance in women's rights, has further widened the gap between highly educated households (more likely to have two incomes) and less educated households (more likely to have just one). These disparate trends, over five-odd decades, have concocted a strange brew of gender equality and family inequality. "Since the 1970s, families have become more egalitarian in their internal relationships," historian Stephanie Coontz writes. "But inequality among families has soared. Women have become more secure as their real wages and legal rights have increased. But families have become more insecure as their income and job instability have worsened."[5] In other words, the challenges facing my workers amount to an inverted version of James Fishkin's triangle, discussed in chapter 1. Low levels of education, rising inequality, and a family environment of breakups and single parenting build upon each other to deepen and entrench the disadvantages that they and their families face.

In this chapter I discuss the ways that changes in family structure shape the experiences of the unemployed, and the ways that long-term joblessness, in turn, affects families. First, the movement away from marriage and toward cohabitation and single-parenthood in recent decades has worsened the economic and emotional fallout of losing a job. Here, I do not wish to romanticize two-parent married households, which are themselves plagued by problems of domestic abuse—as the experiences of many of my autoworkers, female and male, attest to—or a generally oppressive climate in which the male breadwinner imposes his will. However, it is important to recognize that these trends have placed greater economic strains on households, especially those going through a prolonged period without work. Lone parents find it harder to cope with the loss of income. Unmarried couples find it easier to split up after one person loses a job. Furthermore, single-parenthood and cohabitation are especially common among less educated households. Already weighed down by a lack of marketable skills in today's economy, these families experience unemployment in a more desperate fashion. In contrast, more educated households, which tend to have fewer single parents among them, fare better when they go through the loss of a job. These differences further deepen the divide that separates society's advantaged and disadvantaged families.

In turn, unemployment can easily break the bonds in less educated and therefore more economically vulnerable families. Within these households, the rising economic fortunes of women workers have helped (albeit in a limited way) make up for years of declining wages for their men.[6] But when a partner loses his or her job, any pretense of stability disappears. Now that getting well-paid work is a more uncertain proposition, unemployment is especially likely to make the emotional climate noxious—more corrupted by the fears and shame that drive the bickering between couples like Royce and Elena Terrell, the husband and wife who were at war over who was providing. Likewise, when every dollar counts and there are few savings to rely upon, the stakes rise for workers scrambling to get good jobs so that they can remain "marriage material" in their partner's eyes.

Third, social policies can lighten the disadvantages borne by unemployed single parents, especially those with little education. This is the area in which the Canadian social safety net excels. Government benefits are more generous there for single parents and other households reliant on a single earner, giving them a sturdy shoulder to lean on as they adapt to their job loss. It can help single parents maintain their standard of living and compensate for the flimsiness of their support networks, thereby protecting their children's well-being—and their own sanity.

Even in areas as personal as depression and health and as idiosyncratic as divorce and housing, the economic distress that families face inevitably trickles down into sufferings of other kinds, which are less measurable, but no less real, in the manifold ways that they deplete and pollute a family's natural reservoir of love, understanding, and pride. While my fieldwork can only hint at possible patterns, it does raise the question of whether the dollar amounts that social policies extend to households have real-life consequences that go beyond pushing down national statistics of unemployment and poverty—whether they can, to some degree, soften the emotional distress of families going through a harrowing episode of long-term unemployment.

UNEQUAL FAMILIES, UNEQUAL UNEMPLOYMENT

Kirsten Dinnall once thought she was going to have it all. A forty-year-old divorcée with two young children, she had found a good job at the

Chrysler engine plant in Detroit. She had also found a new man, Chaz, whom she adored. They had gotten engaged. Kirsten was already providing well for her two young children, and with her fiancé's help, she reasoned, things would be even better.

But as the relationship became serious, her fiancé became abusive. Matters boiled over early one morning, after Kirsten came home right after her shift. Her fiancé demanded sex from her. Kirsten refused. Chaz started slapping and strangling her in front of their two young kids. He tried to throw her out of the second-story window. Their son called the police, and Chaz fled. Kirsten went to work at the engine plant the very next day, with black-and-blue bruises all over her face and throat.

A single mom again, Kirsten was tempted by the Chrysler buyout. "I wanted to get away from that," she says of her abusive relationship. Taking the buyout, she reasoned, would give her more options in the long term—assuming that she quickly found another job. The buyout also meant that she no longer had to put up with family-unfriendly factory hours that made life difficult for her young kids. And the atmosphere at the plant, with the constant layoffs and downsizing, was becoming toxic, she adds. "I didn't want to take that stress out on my kids."

But now, sixteen months later, Kirsten finds herself with no income and no job prospects, a decade of retirement savings all but cashed out. Besides Medicaid, Kirsten says she doesn't receive any help from the government. She can't apply for food stamps until "my bank account is empty," she says. So Kirsten resorted to hawking her possessions. The $7,000 she raised went toward bills, but to little avail. Many months behind on her mortgage and credit card payments, she is now considering bankruptcy. She has also sunk into a depression. Last month, she started taking Cymbalta, an antidepressant, to quiet the black thoughts that run through her head. Her doctor urged her to see a psychiatrist, but she has yet to do that. Instead, she obsesses over her decision to leave Chrysler. "If I could pay to get my job back, I'd take it back in a minute. I didn't know times were so hard."

Kirsten also has two adult sons. Now that she has lost her job, she tells them they have to fend for themselves. "Okay, baby, you got your own job," she tells the younger son, who is in college, when he asks her to buy something. "You're going to have to save up and get it. If Mama had it, I would do that." The truth is, parent and children have swapped places in the family's economic order. She will make indirect appeals to her older son, who works on cruise lines, that he should pitch in with the shopping for her and the little ones. "I'd probably throw a hint, like, 'Mama like that!' Or 'Mama could use that.'" It is hard for her to ask him outright.

"When I was working at Chrysler I had nothing like that to worry about," she points out. It shames her to know she can no longer provide for her family in the ways they are used to. Meanwhile, her stepfather, a retiree living solely off Social Security, constantly chides her for taking the buyout. Every time she sees him, it is the same refrain: "Oh, you wish you had stuck it out at Chrysler, don't you?"

"Yeah, Daddy," she will sigh, her self-esteem shriveling just a bit more.

. . .

Raising children outside of marriage has become much more common in America, across racial groups. In Canada, the growth in single-parent households has not been as dramatic as it has been down south, and rates of single-parenthood are lower—though in comparison to most of Europe, they are much higher. Importantly, having a critical mass of single parents has taken away the opprobrium once directed at them and their "illegitimate" children, opening up possibilities for countless individuals who have sought to leave behind abusive marriages and stultifying relationships. Yet, the rising numbers of single-parent households have also been linked to growing levels of child poverty and a growing divide between well-off and struggling households. To some extent, the entry of many more women into the workforce and the widespread push to acquire more years of schooling have counterbalanced this trend, tamping down any rise in inequality. But the severity of the last recession has cast doubts on whether those countervailing forces can carry much more momentum, now that families face a foreseeable future of slow economic growth and rising tuition.[7]

The well-educated—no more than a third of the working-age population in either country—have so far resisted the broader march toward single parenthood. While the sexual revolution altered their behavior for some time, they are now more likely to marry in the first place, and less likely to divorce, than those with less education.[8] Nine out of ten mothers with college diplomas are married, compared to roughly half of women who have just a high school degree. These trend lines have been largely flat for college graduates since the seventies, even as the coupling and childbirth decisions of the less educated have undergone a dramatic transformation.[9] Their children are more likely to be born outside marriage. Their live-in partners are less likely to be married to them. And what partnerships they do form are more likely to fall apart.

If the conventional wisdom blames cultural factors for this divergence, a key and underappreciated factor is the paucity of good-paying jobs for the less educated, who have taken the brunt of the "creative destruction" that has devastated manufacturing and immiserated the lower tiers of the service sector. Couples with dim economic outlooks more easily collapse from strain or fail to pledge vows in the first place. Because the men available to them have little in the way of wages, and little prospects of better, even struggling single mothers hesitate to take a chance on marriage, given the risks of getting trapped in an unhappy or abusive relationship, or weighed down by yet another jobless dependent. Meanwhile, children who are born outside marriage and see changing faces among the adults they live with tend to do worse in school as well as elsewhere in their lives, research shows—which means that the next generation may enter the work world even less prepared, human capital–wise, than their parents were. In short, single-parenthood adds another layer of inequality to the already stratified labor market I described in previous chapters, one in which median incomes are growing weakly and the soaring wealth of elite professionals and managers is pulling them away from everyone else. What's more, now that the college-educated marry only the college-educated in increasingly self-selective unions, coupling across the class divide is yet another egalitarian irregularity that has been sanded away by economic and cultural forces, along with well-paid jobs for the less educated.[10]

The changing makeup of today's families has increased inequality. Add unemployment into that mix, and the consequences are particularly severe. When unemployment strikes single parents, it is often hitting the most vulnerable kinds of households. The income statistics alone are telling. Married couples with children boast high median incomes—often thanks to both parents' working outside the home—that might as well place them in a separate reality: $81,000 for married couples in 2012, versus $25,000 for single mothers and $36,000 for single fathers.[11] The disadvantage is stark—and it becomes more so for those who lose their jobs.

In both America and Canada, families with two wage earners on the whole weather the financial shocks of unemployment better than other types of households. These are families like the Hardings, a married couple with two young children who live on the outskirts of Detroit, in a brick bungalow nestled in the shadows of an ancient tree that squirrels have been ransacking for food—sending gem-sized walnuts showering onto the roof of their pickup truck. "I hate that tree," mutters Darius, a thirty-seven-year-old ex-Chrysler worker. But the rodent antics forty feet above seem to be the extent of his family's problems. "The buyout was a blessing," he says. "I was able to pay everything off at once." The lump sum—$47,000 after taxes, along with a car voucher—finally gave him the means to square away his car loan and other outstanding bills. The federal government is paying for him to get trained and certified as an aircraft mechanic, a long-time interest of his. Meanwhile, his wife Ellen, a schoolteacher, continues to bring home $4,500 a month, allowing Darius to focus on his studies instead of scrambling to find more work. They have had to cut back considerably on their expenses, but so far Darius has successfully curbed his addiction to souped-up cellphones and computers. And now that he's not working full-time, Darius can be fully involved in his children's lives. Working until midnight at the plant, he hardly saw his son and daughter and could never make it to his son's football games. "Now I'm here for everything," he says.

As the story that began this chapter made clear, losing a job when you have a partner can severely test that relationship. But generally speaking, married two-earner households that plunge into a spell of joblessness can rely on the other partner's income to soften the economic impact. (Among the few workers I interviewed who had live-in partners but were not married, their financial hardship tended to be less serious than that of the lone parents, too, though on the whole they fared worse than their married counterparts.) Those couples without children tend to be the best-off of all. They need not fret about feeding and caring for dependents; they avoid not just the extra monetary burdens but also the shame and self-blame that come with failing to provide for one's kids. They do not have to worry about plotting out child care during a potential job's working hours and dealing with those employers—common in the lower tiers of the labor market—who resent time off to tend to young kids.

In these particular settings, older workers actually fare better than younger ones. As I noted in chapter 2, unemployment was generally harder for my older workers, who had greater difficulties adjusting to an economy that had changed radically since they first ducked into the factories. At the same time, they had one advantage over their younger coworkers: the ability to call themselves "retired" rather than "unemployed." With his five-plus decades and graying hair, ex-Chrysler worker Paul Young finds it easy to pass as a retiree. "To look at me, no one would know it," he says. His attitude is much different from that of my younger workers, who have decades to go in the labor market and face pervasive social expectations to be productive citizens. It is important to note, however, that the guise of "early retirement" was only helpful to a very particular group of my older workers: those who had spouses with stable incomes—and who also did not have dependent children. Paul's wife Gwen, a salaried worker at Ford, is currently supporting the two of them. There may not be much of a government safety net for Paul, but Gwen is his safety net. Without that kind of material support, unemployment becomes poverty, with all its stress and shame.

Generally speaking, my single workers who didn't have dependent children were worse off than their counterparts in two-earner households. For some of them, not having the safety net of a spouse's earnings meant that their finances quickly and catastrophically fell apart, as I discussed earlier in this book. But others found that they could make ends meet relatively easily in spite of the loss of their jobs.

David Vihan, a former Ford worker who lives near Windsor, finds he has more peace of mind now that he no longer has to worry about supporting his wife, Tracy. They separated a year earlier. "It is easier for me because now I'm on my own," he says. "I don't have kids to deal with." When David and Tracy were together, they landed in serious debt in part because of Tracy's desire to house, feed, and outfit her thirty-year-old son, as well as his partner and kids. "This kid was a loser," David says. "He cost us so much money. . . . We're talking about a guy with three kids of his own." (As I will describe later, the extended dependence of the younger generations—living in their parents' homes for longer spells because of either a lack of ambition or a dearth of job opportunities—is another family burden that weighs heavily on less affluent households.) David and Tracy had gone to marriage counseling, and even the counselor had told Tracy she needed to let her son fail. "She kept saving him," David says. Family ties, in his case, caused much grief. Nowadays, David compares himself with other laid-off workers he meets at the action center. He feels blessed to be free. "They're all stressed out about how their wives want them finding jobs. I don't have that now."

In both countries, my two-earner households did relatively well, and my single, childless workers did relatively worse. But the national differences were more pronounced for my single parents. While those Americans like Kirsten Dinnall, the divorced mother described above, often fell quickly down the economic ladder, the single parents up north generally did better, thanks to a set of Canadian policies—the focus of a later section—that are targeted at households like theirs.

Even single workers who don't have custody of their children face special challenges as they seek new jobs. If they intend on remaining part of their children's lives, the limbo of divorce or separation limits their employment options. Van Tranchina, a forty-year-old American, says he would be better off moving to Atlanta or Las Vegas, where the jobs are more plentiful. But the former parts worker is separated from his wife and has two daughters, ages seventeen and nine. His older daughter, Natasha, is a senior in a Detroit high school, and, he says, "I gotta make sure I can see that through" to her graduation. Of course, married couples face roadblocks in moving to opportunity, too: when one worker loses her job, she may be unable to relocate because her spouse already has a job. But if marriage presents challenges, divorce and separation present impossibilities, since the idea of moving the kids where the jobs are becomes a nonstarter with an ex-husband or ex-wife.

Another challenge for laid-off workers cut off from their families is their legal or moral obligation to divide their available funds across two households: his bachelor household and the household of his estranged partner and children. That adds not insubstantially to an already full plate of economic and psychological woes. "In a sense, I'm taking care of two households," says Van. "It can get rough at times." Still receiving unemployment, he is struggling to survive on half the income he had before he lost his job, and yet also continue to pay more than half the mortgage on the house where his wife and kids reside. Finances have become so tight that he has had to move in with his older sister, into a grim concrete housing project with the claustrophobic feel of a prison.

Like Van, Mitch Beerman also pays the mortgage on a house he's not living in. He, too, would like to move somewhere where there are jobs—Alberta, in his case, which boasts a labor-intensive oil industry—if he could only get custody of his kids. "That's pretty much the only thing that's kept me here," he says. Being separated from his wife hinders his job prospects in other ways. His one interview so far was for a $15-an-hour job at a Windsor factory that polishes aluminum balcony rails. The human resources manager asked Mitch whether he was going through a divorce. He answered truthfully. "Sorry," said the manager. "We're not going to be able to use you, because we need someone that's going to be here every day." The legal process would suck up all his time, the manager claimed: "I know because I've already been through it." Whether or not this kind of discrimination is legal, it is another example of how divorce and separation can drag down unemployed workers unlucky enough to find themselves in foundering family vessels.

Just as the family is a prism that refracts the prospects of most employed workers into separate streams of high-income, stable households and lower-income, fragile families, the unemployed experience their job loss in starkly different ways depending on their family arrangements.[12] For those of my workers who were single with children, unemployment tended to unleash a much harsher blow. In turn, the disproportionate harm it caused them widened the substantial income gap that already existed between them and two-parent households. While dual-earner couples without children tended to do the best, those couples who had children could at least rely on a second income or free child care—the married couples, more dependably so—giving them a built-in economic advantage that insulated them from the worst shocks of unemployment and kept them from resorting to outside help.

In this way, marriage (and, to a lesser extent, cohabitation) spread out a private safety net that may lessen the need for a public one—although it also means that some women have to deal, as did several of my workers, with outbreaks of domestic abuse that were hard to escape without the financial independence of their own well-paid job. In any case, if the market economy continues to generate greater inequalities, there is reason to doubt that even marriage can prevent the decline and impoverishment of two-earner families enduring one family member's long-term unemployment. The jobs available to less educated workers like mine are becoming less remunerative, or fewer in number, or both. More and less educated workers are coupling with others like them, so that the loss of one worker's poor job means relying on a spouse with a similarly lousy one. Meanwhile, their adult children are wavering in a more brutal labor market especially hostile to the less educated, eventually returning home to lick their wounds—and burdening their parents with ever-extended financial responsibilities. As a result, even a few of my two-earner families, American and Canadian, found themselves little able to shoulder the loss of just one income.

. . .

After a year out of work, Audrey Calvin is living "check to check," she says. Three months after her layoff at the Canadian parts plant, she and her husband downsized their housing, moving into a smaller ranch home and lowering their mortgage payments by $200 a month. "Now the fun is keeping it," says Audrey, forty-four. Her unemployment benefits run out in two months. Her husband installs home alarm systems and other electronics, but he is struggling to get hours at his company and nowadays pulls in just $400 a month. At the moment, one of their adult daughters also lives with them, chipping in a little bit every two weeks in rent. Twenty-year-old Stephanie works at Tim Hortons, a coffee-and-doughnuts shop known throughout Canada for its low-wage workforce. Meanwhile, Audrey continues to keep space in her cramped house in case her other twenty-something daughter, Angie, should "boomerang" home, too.

Parents like Audrey feel an obligation to stay involved with their grown children, given how tenuous a hold these unseasoned workers have on their jobs. (For her part, Angie is living off public assistance.) Thanks to growing risk and inequality in today's labor market, each younger generation has to run faster to keep up with the fiercer fight for jobs and the higher costs of education and housing. Even the college-educated are learning to depend on mom and dad nowadays, as the less educated have long had to do. As a result, the obligations of many parents persist long into their children's adulthood—and into their own old age.[13] But the parents are not necessarily secure in this economy, either. Audrey worries that, with her declining fortunes as an unemployed factory worker, she can no longer help her kids. "I can't be there for them like I used to be," she says. Before, she could fork over $20 to a daughter who needed money for groceries without a moment's thought. But two days ago, Angie asked her to get some Motrin for the baby. "I don't have any money to buy any," Audrey told her. "My [unemployment] hasn't come in. My phone's shut off."

In the early twentieth century, society came to prize the economically "useless" but emotionally "priceless" child, sociologist Vivian Zelizer argues.[14] Children became increasingly dear for their sentimental and moral value and for the social status they imparted. But as the employment prospects and living standards of today's working- and middle-class families stagnate, this culture of "pricelessness" is colliding with a contemporary economics of scarcity. As much as they wish to, many workers living in this age of diminished expectations are no longer able to "do one better" for their kids than the previous generation did for them. Her own father had slipped her money when Audrey was struggling as a single, divorced mom, and it pains her that she can't do the same for her children. But Audrey's financial situation in her forties is much rockier than it was for her father at that age, not just because she doesn't currently have a job but also because today's market has relegated her and her husband to a spot near the bottom of the economic food chain.

"That is hard, to say no to my grandkids," Audrey says. "That's the hardest thing in the world. Because they're just as defenseless as mine were when my dad was there doing it for me." But the money isn't there. Audrey downsized her holidays, too, this past year. She bought a three-foot-tall tree and forced herself to be grateful for an equally Charlie Brown–sized Christmas, too: her daughters got slippers and socks. The other day she saved her electricity from being shut off with a last-minute payment. Meanwhile, the unpaid balance on her credit cards alone has swollen to $10,000. "I even stopped paying those," she says. "They're gonna be coming after me."

In any case, Audrey has other things to worry about. Her relationship with her husband Ethan has suffered because of the added stress of her joblessness. "I don't know if it's because we're separating—or we're growing away—or if our future is just so unreadable," she says. "It's hard to look toward something when there's nothing to look towards to."

MARRIAGEABLE NO MORE

A year after he lost his job at Chrysler, Mal Stephen separated from his wife Leah. The couple has a nine-year-old daughter. Isabella is not biologically his, but he adores her—"I named her, I cut the cord." Isabella and her older brother Markus now live with their mother. His empty nest has made the fifty-one-year-old despondent. The holidays were the nadir. He didn't see the children. Leah said she was too busy to bring them over.

Mal broods over the fact that he is not the man he used to be. He can't help thinking that his older sons, from a previous relationship, look down on him. "They don't come and see me anymore. They don't call me," he says. "They need to use some of my stuff, they'll ask, but other than that? I can go two to three weeks without talking to either of them." Perhaps it's just the usual teenage and twenty-something issues, but Mal notices a change.

As for the little ones, Mal wonders what they think of the fact that their father doesn't have a job. "Daddy, why are you home all the time?" they will ask, followed shortly by "Daddy, can I have a dollar?" I don't have a dollar, he'll tell them. The kids say they understand, but he thinks their confidence in him has suffered. "They know I can't do those things for them that I used to be able to do. They still ask."

His inadequacy is not just in his head. Leah has made that plain. "I've got no money and now she's got a job," he says. "All credibility is out the tubes when you can't pay the bills." Leah started cheating on him. He still loves her, but now Leah lives with an older man who pays her bills and showers her with gifts. "You should see the bracelet he bought her for Christmas," he says. "Man, it made me so mad. It's about five carats of diamonds." He doesn't know what this man does, whether he is an autoworker or a professional or something else—"I don't ask," he says. All he knows is that he buys Leah things he no longer can.

In Mal's view, the situation is straightforward: "A man came up with money. That's pretty much it. . . . Put up or shut up. I shut up. He put up."

. . .

While unemployment tends to be hardest on single parents, family structures are not always static. A couple under strain can quickly separate, leaving husband or wife to deal with the consequences of joblessness alone. In other words, a "before" snapshot of Royce and Elena Terrell, the couple bickering over roles and responsibilities at the beginning of this chapter; an "after" shot of Mal Stephen, the one-time worker and husband now dropping headlong into poverty. Of course, even in the absence of financial difficulties, some couples will find constructive outlets for a marriage's unavoidable pageant of frustrations and insecurities, and others will let the procession of stresses overwhelm them in spectacular fashion. But whenever paying the bills becomes an issue, these conflicts tend to become more intense, as research on stress and its effect on marital quality attests.[15] In some cases, isolated instances of rage boil over into the kind of "constant competition" that Royce and Elena are engaged in: a perverse desire to win each argument and make the other person suffer.

As I mentioned in the previous section, marriage by its very definition pools economic resources, and not surprisingly, married and cohabiting couples tend to do better financially during a long spell of unemployment. But the causal arrow points in the opposite direction, too: prolonged unemployment drains a couple's bank account, which causes tensions that may bring about the relationship's end—which, ultimately, creates even more financial hardship for the unemployed worker now left on his or her own. Among my workers, it was striking that those whose relationships fell apart after they lost their jobs invariably blamed financial struggles for corroding those bonds. Perhaps the couples who stayed together were more committed to each other, or perhaps they were more affluent to begin with—meaning the loss of one partner's job hit them less hard. This distinction matters because it is unclear whether it is marriage itself, or the economic resources of marriage, that matter more in determining how well a particular family copes with unemployment. (In other words, if our goal is to alleviate the material and psychological blow of losing a job, do we promote marriage, or do we promote economic assistance for couples?) My research obviously cannot settle this question. But it suggests that long-term unemployment may generate a vicious circle in which households splinter because of financial strain, forcing now-single workers to fend for themselves—with their inability to find a job, in turn, making it less likely that they can find or maintain another long-term relationship.

With the widespread entry of women into the labor market, the role of the male breadwinner would seem to be less important. Among other things, marriage as an institution has changed. Its sacred promises of permanence and security have become less vital than the satisfaction and meaning it brings, leading to a modern view of marriage as "self-expansion," a means to broaden one's knowledge and experiences.[16] In the upper tiers of the American workforce, we can speak of the rise of meritocratic marriage: a rigorous selection of the best candidates for long-term partnership (not necessarily "best" in terms of income potential), given a person's position in the sexual marketplace. In this competition, as in the labor market, the selection is increasingly segregated by education, with college graduates pairing with other college graduates: self-expansion is less likely when your significant other lacks a comparable education or profession.[17]

Anthropologist Carrie Lane notes that men today no longer deal with as much reproach—from themselves or from others—for not being a family's provider, a cultural change that is striking among the unemployed tech workers she interviewed. The women among her interviewees, however, spoke at length about their shame about no longer having a career. Among these elite workers, meritocratic marriage can cut both ways; the male "breadwinner" is viewed as less essential, but both partners are expected to be "successful" people who fulfill each other's need for self-growth.[18]

A good partnership, in other words, is about romance and compatibility—the "soul mate" paragon that Hollywood thrives on. But generally speaking, the less income a couple have at their disposal, the more hard-nosed exigencies intrude on that romantic ideal. My blue-collar workers had clearly different experiences from those of the highly educated tech workers Lane studied, and here their class status—and their families' relatively meager financial cushion—may have been decisive.

For workers discarded from dying industries into a beggared new world of Walmart wages, the dangers that unemployment poses to their relationships—before and after marriage—are especially great. Their prospects of finding a new job that can offer pay and benefits remotely close to what they once had are so slim that losing that good factory job permanently lowers their value as a provider. Meanwhile, if a relationship bears a substantial risk of falling apart anyway, as today's more casual ties of love do, it's only rational to be focused on the bottom line. There are, of course, other important factors at work in any relationship, but a partner's gainful employment does matter, and families with fewer means do not have the luxury of ignoring this hard fact.[19] Indeed, my workers and their partners were at times quite explicit about it. In this day and age of quick, relatively painless exit from relationships, they said, why waste time with a "deadbeat" who can't pay the bills?

At its most extreme, this prevailing attitude places my workers in a no-win situation. They have not just become unemployable. They have also become unmarriageable. Here I am using a term from sociologist William Julius Wilson's influential research on poor urban neighborhoods, where young men are not able to marry because they cannot find decent jobs. I argue that this term can be applied in the opposite direction, too. Men who are already married and once had good jobs become less marriageable, as their unemployment becomes a long-term condition of helplessness and shame.[20]

It is worth noting that the changes in the institution of marriage in recent decades—above all, the ease with which marital bonds can be sundered—may be affecting the less educated in different ways than they do better-off couples. The contrasts here are similar to what we see in the job search. More educated workers are expected to possess sufficient stores of cultural capital—traits that establish their "chemistry" and "compatibility"—to be successful in the labor market and marriage market alike. For less educated workers, cultural capital does matter, as I discussed in chapter 2, but more straightforward capacities tend to matter more: in the workplace, the ability to contribute to the company's bottom line, and at home, the ability to feed the shared bank account. Because of the different expectations that households have for the cultural and economic contributions that each partner makes, the loss of a job is more of a *social* problem for the tech workers that Lane studied—that is, not being the "interesting" working person who will be attractive to a spouse and on an equal footing with friends. It is less of a *financial* one. For this very reason, when these workers are unemployed, they can continue to bring other, less tangible, benefits to their relationship that compensate for their lack of income.

The less educated, on the other hand, are expected to "come up with money," as my worker Mal Stephen put it. Research suggests that the shift away from the long-term bond of marriage has prodded poor women to become more economically instrumental in their relationships, and a similar thing can be said for the partners in families like mine, which were relatively better-off—but still not positioned well for success within today's labor market.[21] Given the growing number of families in both countries who live together and don't marry, it is also worth noting that my workers who were cohabiting felt pressures much like those faced by their married counterparts. Randy Simpson, an American former parts worker, lived with his partner and hoped to have children with her. But after he lost his job, she broke things off. Randy insists "she wouldn't have went nowhere" if he had still been able to help her out financially. Instead, she started going out with other men, he says. There's no loyalty anymore.

For the most part, men were the targets of blame for not fulfilling the role of a breadwinner. While there were still arguments over money, my women workers with partners often found that they could take up a respected support role as a stay-at-home mom, a co-owner of the home business, or another kind of household helper. But there were some exceptions, which speak to the fact that households depend more and more on two incomes, male or female. Hannah Frey, a fifty-four-year-old American, separated from her husband, Zaza, after escalating arguments about her lack of income. "Jesus Christ," she told him once, "I didn't think that our relationship was based on the amount of money that I brought in." But anytime she was on temporary layoff—which was often, in recent years—"he got pissed," Hannah says. Once loving, she says, Zaza began to abuse her with comments about her weight. Eventually, she mustered the courage to leave him. But without his income, her financial situation quickly deteriorated. Interestingly, she decided to move in with a man with whom she's romantically involved but whom she does not call her boyfriend or partner. To a greater extent than their male counterparts, my unemployed women can still attract partners, even if the expectations today are more pointed regarding how much they, too, can contribute.

Losing their jobs appeared to make my Americans in particular "unmarriageable." Only two of my Canadians separated or divorced following the loss of a job. Among my Americans, however, this was a fairly common occurrence. (As I will discuss later, the racial difference may have again played a role here, given higher rates of single-parenthood and divorce among African Americans.)[22] Even if there were other, idiosyncratic reasons for each of their breakups, it became clear in my interviews that many of them had problems relying on the financial and emotional support of their partners, largely because their partners resented their failure to pull their weight.

These different reactions on the two sides of the border may reflect distinct views of individualism and the family. The United States is unique, sociologist Andrew Cherlin argues, in the importance it places on two seemingly contradictory impulses: "its strong support for marriage, on one hand, and its postmodern penchant for self-expression and personal growth, on the other hand." While Americans idealize marriage, they also insist on the freedom to seek out a "successful personal life"—a freedom that implies being able to end relationships that are seen as unfulfilling or unsupportive. This eclectic concoction of attitudes is the reason that close to 90 percent of Americans will end up marrying, but nearly half of marriages end in divorce—a higher rate than elsewhere in the Western world, including Canada.[23] In few other advanced industrialized nations, too, is the successful working spouse so essential and esteemed—or the jobless "scrub" so reviled.

Perhaps because of these cultural differences, whenever household finances imploded, the pressure placed on relationships in Canadian homes was less severe. In fact, D.J. Packer, a sixty-year-old former parts worker, saw his family come together after he lost his job and considered suicide. Ali, his wife, admonished him not to spare any expense for therapy—even though the insurance was no longer there to pay for it. When he talked to Emily, his fifteen-year-old, about what had happened, she told him she would give up "everything that we had bought her" to help out, D.J. says. Afterward, she started taking more of an interest in the family, asking questions and opening up to her parents. "Before, we didn't have that openness, that communication. We're really close now. She'll come in and sit down next to me and she'll say, 'You got anything you want to talk about?'"

More so in Canada, families used unemployment as an opportunity to come together and rethink their priorities and purpose. Such a non-materialistic attitude helped tremendously in the Packer family's adjustment to unemployment. D.J. says he is pursuing a career as a social worker, even though the starting pay is just thirteen dollars an hour, because his family is willing to make do with less. "We can live on that," Ali assured him. "That's not a problem." D.J. says his wife has been a powerful source of strength ever since he lost his job. "I get up every morning and she's there, and I'm thankful that she is."

More of my American workers expressed materialistic values.[24] For example, when asked what they missed about their jobs, they tended to say "money." (My Canadians were more likely to mention the camaraderie and lifestyle of a working person.) Among those who were parents, their older children were sensitive, too, about how the lack of money would affect them. Van Tranchina, the laid-off parts worker, has two daughters. "It's hard for them to take in the reality of what's really happening, because they've never known me to not work," Van says. He misses going bowling with them, and he dreads telling them, when they want him to go with them somewhere, "Daddy don't have it." Older daughter Natasha, a typical teenager, had become "used to certain things" of a material nature, he says, including being able to attend class trips and other social events. The loss of his job really hurt her, Van says. "I think it hurt her more than it did me." As for his estranged wife Helen, his inability now to chip in with the girls' expenses has not gone unnoticed. "She . . . can't understand that I don't have it like I used to have it," Van says. "A lot of times, I just won't have it. . . . And so, it's like, kinda putting a little strain on the relationship. It does." His contributions are sporadic, once causing Natasha to hand in her class dues late and suffer embarrassment. Her grades have also slipped. "I know it's gotta be bothering her, more than she maybe lets on."

. . .

The youngest child in the Terrell household, Keith is a wiry five-year-old with expressive, light-colored, almost Asiatic eyes—long-lashed like his father's. Wearing a blue Sponge Bob T-shirt and checkered shorts, Keith floats around the kitchen table, grabbing his father's head affectionately and holding onto his arm at times. While Royce talks he is rarely motionless. He climbs onto his father's lap and plays with his cell phone. He draws a green tank and blue submarine in wavy marker strokes and hands it to his dad for an appraisal.

A report card from his kindergarten class notes that Keith "has great potential but needs to work more quickly."

The conversation goes into the evening and it's time for bed. Elena leads Keith away, but cries from the bathroom indicate that he isn't following his mom's instructions all that well. "He favors me," Royce explains; it has been that way since the boy was born. "I don't want to go into the shower!" his son wails, making an appearance in the kitchen doorway. Keith rubs the tears from his eyes gingerly with his fingertips. His father comforts him. "I want you to go to sleep happy so you have a happy dream," Royce says. "What you want to dream about now?" Keith is placated. Dutifully, he heads to the shower.

Clean at last, he returns to the kitchen. Royce tries to shoo him affectionately into his room. "When I click my fingers, go!" His son shrieks and farts at the same time, then runs off with heels flying. "Goodness gracious!" Royce says, chuckling. "Whenever he has a good laugh, he passes gas."

Royce may not have a job, but there are other things in his life to compensate for that loss. He stresses that he is grateful for his family, especially his son. "Every day he develops and grows and shows me something new," he says. He has become a doting, hands-on father, even as Elena has become more occupied with her career. As for the other children, he notices that Rasheea has become more standoffish when he's around, which may have something to do with the constant arguments between him and Elena. She naturally favors her mother, he says, since he is the stepdad.

As bedtime arrives, Royce leads Keith over to his bedroom. On Keith's door hangs some artwork: a bright-red fire truck with black tires and a somewhat abstract-looking ochre fire hydrant. Keith squats in his racecar bed, a huge poster of Lightning McQueen from *Cars* hanging over him.

Keith whispers advice into his father's ear as we talk. "Dad, tell him you're rich," he says.

"But I'm not rich," Royce answers. "You may make me rich, but I'm not rich."

"So just tell him you're rich," Keith insists.

• • •

Cultural differences probably play an important role in determining how much long-term unemployment frays relationships at home. But it may also be the case that the weaker social safety net for single-earner households south of the border makes breadwinners of either gender more essential—and thus makes the focus on the material more consuming. It is important not to overstate this possibility, and the cases of my workers are merely suggestive. But as they themselves pointed out, social policies that offered income and education gave hope and needed stability to their families.

As I mentioned in the last chapter, the American and Canadian policies for the unemployed were not as different as I had first expected, thanks to emergency assistance on the U.S. side and government retrenchment on the Canadian side. But the Canadian social safety net did do a much better job of keeping unemployed single parents—and single-earner families more generally—from hurtling into poverty. (Generally speaking, single parents tend to fare better in Canada, where 43 percent of children of single mothers are in households with incomes of less than half the national median income, compared to 51 percent in America.)[25]

In the next several paragraphs I compare the two sets of policies and their effects on particular types of households. The appendix includes tables with the exact dollar amounts of each benefit.

I should point out at the outset that my analysis compares the policy situations of two areas that are not necessarily representative of the rest of their countries. That said, compared to other states and provinces, Michigan and Ontario offer unemployment and public assistance benefits in the middle range of generosity. In any case, I prioritized giving a detailed, on-the-ground view of the situation in specific localities rather than a broader national picture that would vary considerably in the ways that real families experience real policies.

For households in which two adults were working, the income supports are quite similar across the border. Consider two unemployed workers, one American and one Canadian, each married with two children and a working spouse who makes $40,000 a year in U.S. dollars. Both worked for ten years before the loss of their jobs, making the same amount in annual earnings as their spouses. In the first year without a job, the American family would reclaim 57 percent of the jobless worker's lost income through government transfers, while the Canadian replacement rate would be 60 percent—a difference amounting to just $1,000. (However, this gap would have been larger if not for a temporary $400 credit for American workers). The Americans would receive almost the entire amount from unemployment benefits. The Canadians would receive *most* of their transfers from unemployment benefits, but a significant portion would come from mandated severance payments.

Now consider the same family, but with a spouse who makes low wages—in this example, $20,000 a year. The replacement rate would be about the same for the Americans and the Canadians: 62 percent. This is because of the various benefits that kick in for the American families at this income level—most importantly, earned-income tax credits. (Canada has a similar credit that it is more generous to single, childless workers, but much less so for families.)

For another family of four—similar in all ways except that the spouse doesn't work outside the home—the social safety net in America is much weaker. The replacement rate here is 63 percent, compared to 76 percent in Canada, and the gap has grown to over $5,000. Child tax credits on the Canadian side provide substantial relief: from the "baby bonus" given monthly to poor and middle-class households alike, to credits specifically targeted at families with low incomes or young kids. Less affluent Canadians also receive sales-tax refunds that put hundreds more dollars in their pockets every year. In comparison, the corresponding social safety net across the border is rather flimsy. Importantly, America's federal child tax credit is not refundable for families whose income comes from unemployment benefits. Congress expanded the food-stamp program (now called SNAP) after the recession began, but even if we ignore the fact that it is an in-kind (not cash) benefit, its income boost remains relatively small compared to what happens up north.

But the Canadian policy advantage is most apparent if we look at an unemployed single-parent family on either side of the border. The American households have 56 percent of their income replaced by government transfers, while the Canadian ones have 75 percent replaced, for a gap of $7,700. Again, what is decisive here is the significantly greater income provided by the various Canadian child benefits.

Because of the importance of child tax credits for the Canadian social safety net, the policy advantage for a single unemployed person *without* children is not so stark on the Canadian side. The replacement rate for Americans is 52 percent, compared to 58 percent for Canadians, a difference of about $2,100. On the U.S. side, this childless worker is ineligible for food stamps; on the Canadian side, she gets little in the way of sales-tax refunds. Neither receives an earned-income tax credit, because unemployment benefits are not considered earned income.

As can be seen across the examples above, Canadian households across the board tend to have a slightly stronger social safety net. And among those households with children and just one (now unemployed) wage earner, the amounts of cash furnished over there are much greater.

Compare the situation of Kirsten Dinnall, the unemployed and struggling single mother I profiled earlier in the chapter, with Alice Parrott, a single mother like her who happens to live on the Canadian side. Alice had an alcoholic husband who abused her verbally and later moved on to hitting, breaking her nose and blackening her eyes. Fortunately, Alice landed a job at Ford around the time the violence escalated, and those high wages were her ticket out. "I wanted to leave," she says. "That's why I started at Ford—to get the money [to get] out." The job was her lifeline: the day after her husband beat her black and blue, she still showed up at the plant. "Couldn't afford to miss work," Alice says.

Alice is in some ways a mirror image of Kirsten Dinnall: a forty-something single mother of two, an unemployed ex–Big Three autoworker, a divorcée who thankfully bailed out of an abusive marriage with the help of her union-negotiated wages, an engine plant worker who took a buyout and cut her ties with the company. Unlike Kirsten, she has sizeable debts, including $30,000 on a line of credit at the bank and $9,000 on her credit cards. Despite these financial burdens, though, the Canadian is doing relatively better, owing in part to her good fortune in being matched—with the help of her action center—to a college program that is training her to become a nurse. Her regular unemployment benefits have long since run out, but Ontario's retraining program is covering her tuition and also paying her almost $700 a month for living expenses while she's in school. She lives on that, her savings, and two other government transfers: a child benefit of $125 a month (which arrives via direct deposit), and a sales-tax refund for low-income families of $150 every three months (here I've used U.S. dollars throughout).[26] She is still "broke," Alice says, and the creditors call up now and then. But she is upbeat about her new career, and in spite of all she has suffered through—from the humiliating abuse to all the low-wage, dirty jobs she has endured over the years to make a buck—at age forty-three she can finally report a degree of happiness. "It's going the right way," she says of her future.

In the first year of unemployment, the wide range of income supports provided on the Canadian side—unemployment benefits, mandated severance pay, tax credits—made a noticeable difference in the ways that single-earner families there experienced unemployment. This was part of the reason that these households suffered less hardship and were less likely to resort to debt, foreclosures, and other painful means of coping with a steep drop in income. Another factor, discussed in the last chapter, was race. Kirsten is black, and Alice is white, and to some extent racial differences in financial well-being may account for the different trajectories they and other workers experienced after they lost their jobs. It may also account for the higher number of American families I observed whose marriages fell apart during long spells of unemployment. However, as I mentioned earlier in the book, in recent decades working-class white households have been looking much more like black households in terms of their family structures.[27] Furthermore, I deliberately compared households with the same family structure and comparable levels of savings and debt—some of the pathways where the racial difference might be expected to play out—and the divergent outcomes remained clear: less hardship on the Canadian side.

Just how much social policies matter to families can be seen in the case of D.J. Packer, who is black. As I described in the last chapter, his family's upbeat attitude amid his prolonged unemployment has, by his own admission, something to do with the fact that D.J. receives substantial benefits that cover both his tuition and his household living expenses. Besides the government help I've discussed above for single-earner families like his, D.J. is receiving additional assistance from a federal pilot program that extends his unemployment benefits while he's in school. Meanwhile, the intense anxiety on the U.S. side about saving up for a child's college education is milder across the border, thanks to the stronger support for public education (discussed in chapter 2), which means that D.J. and his wife have to save up less money to send their teenage daughter to college—and that D.J., as the breadwinner, faces less pressure to bring home a hefty paycheck.

. . .

For D.J. Packer, an unemployed autoworker who is recovering from a bout of severe depression, sizable government supports helped out in a domain we wouldn't normally expect to be affected by the push and pull of policy: the intimate relations and family dramas that inhabit the home. And for Alice Parrott, a jobless and indebted autoworker with teenage children, they helped arrest the downward fall of her family. If a stronger social safety net can make a difference in these ways, it may be worth stepping beyond the perennial debate over "handouts" versus "hand ups" for deserving or undeserving workers. Instead, we should focus more intently on the impact of policies on entire families. It is vital to consider what will happen to the children caught in the middle as their parents' marriages unravel, and whether social policy can help lower the high stakes of the ever-tougher search for marriageable men (and women) among less educated workers. After all, government intervention here serves not only a moral and social purpose in keeping families together, but also an economic purpose in safeguarding the younger generation's long-term prospects by keeping them in stable, two-parent households that provide the best foundation for future health and success.

THE FAMILY AND THE CYCLE OF INEQUALITY

In the past, the institution of the family helped shore up the economic gains of workers like mine. As resources trickled down from parent to child—from the homes in decent school districts that provided a good education, to the blatant nepotism of factory hiring that provided good jobs—multiple generations rode up an economic escalator. Good jobs, in turn, built a foundation for stable, two-parent households. But in more recent decades, the cycle has reversed. Dwindling opportunities in the labor market discourage less educated workers from marrying, and encourage them to cut off ties with partners who are just one more mouth to feed.

Likewise, while unemployment hits all families hard, it is a particularly brutal blow for the kinds of families I've described here. It's not just that less educated workers are more likely to become, and remain, unemployed. As they lose the well-paid employment they were once lucky enough to possess, they also lose—perhaps for good—the middle-class livelihoods they once bequeathed to their children. Even if they get a new job, the income gap between them and their more educated counterparts is likely to grow, thanks to both the disappearance of that now atypical breed of well-paid factory job and the dwindling ability of their households to compete with households who feature two well-educated and well-paid earners. In fact, families like mine are more likely to be single-parent households that are the most vulnerable to the economic and psychological shocks of losing a job. With fewer family resources to draw upon, the hardships of unemployment are all the harder to bear. While the more educated segments of the middle class, too, have been confronted with stagnant wages and rampant downsizing, their relatively good incomes and their steady rates of marriage and childbirth in marriage work in concert to shield them from the worst of unemployment's consequences, improving the odds that their initial spell of joblessness will not become a long-term trap of poverty.

Meanwhile, the loss of a good job makes couples all the more hesitant to marry or stay together. In the families I got to know, fights over money multiplied and relationships withered after the loss of a job. These scenarios came up more frequently among male workers who lost their jobs, though there were also instances of women whose unemployment contributed to tensions in their marriage and, eventually, its dissolution. Just as national trends in marriage and single-parenthood may reflect different cross-border attitudes, the distinct ways that my families responded to unemployment can be chalked up to the culture divide between more individualistic and status-conscious America and more collectivist and egalitarian Canada.

That said, the ways that social policies blunt the financial impact of losing a job may also improve the rapport between struggling partners and between struggling parents and children. A parent's unemployment does not harm the future of the next generation as much when government intervenes in a robust fashion to prop up faltering incomes. When the intervention is strong enough, the economic role of the family, for better or worse, can become less crucial. More materialist values make sense in a society where material hardship is a more present danger.

In this way, the size and the strength of the social safety net may have a subtle say over cultural understandings, such as our notions of masculinity, and societal values, such as our pointed rejection of partners without good employment prospects. (Of course, the process can work in reverse, too.)[28] If governments cover the costs of tuition, for example, mothers do not have to search so single-mindedly for men who can underwrite their kids' college educations. But where there is little in the way of support for struggling families, it matters all the more if a member of the household is unemployed, because that lost paycheck must be replaced if the state does not replace it.

This places huge pressures on a family experiencing unemployment, pressures that further ramp up the high-stakes competition within the modern economy's stunted meritocracy, as former breadwinners desperately try to regain their identities as worthy and productive partners. It also aggravates the self-loathing that the long-term unemployed perhaps already feel within a dominant culture of meritocratic morality, as they see their personal failures and flaws reflected in the eyes of their spouses and children.

So far, the trends I have identified have not had as much of an impact on college-educated households. However, as the economies in both countries continue to become more demanding of those in the middle tiers of the labor market, white-collar families may start behaving more like blue-collar ones, with intense financial strains encouraging them to focus not on a partner's chemistry or compatibility but on his or her ability to provide.

. . .

Three years of off-and-on unemployment have eroded the foundations of Royce and Elena Terrell's relationship. It is not just the fact that they are in debt, or that Royce no longer feels like much of a man. Their roles are now reversed, bringing about confusion and resentment. Once the workaholic teenager who thrilled at the feel of wads of hard-earned cash in his pockets, in recent years Royce has shifted his attention to his kids, as layoff has followed layoff and his drive has dwindled away. Once the stay-at-home mom, Elena is now hungry for recognition in the world outside. They fight over these priorities. "Who's tending to the kids?" he will question her. "He's big on that," Elena says. "So am I. I'm also big on my position in the company . . . and really wanting to look good. Because that's just how I am. Wanting to look good, wanting to feel good."

Elena is well aware that the culture—the country—values winning above everything, and she enthusiastically reflects that ethos. "I'm a very high performer in my field," she says with certainty. She is America's rugged individualist: a problem solver; a pragmatist; a warrior. "Whatever happens in my situation, I attack it. I find the source." For a time, attacking the problem meant pestering Royce to agree to marriage counseling. But Royce refused. At that point he didn't think Elena was serious. "You only asked about that after you done put your hands on me," he snaps. He was reluctant to let a stranger get involved and tell them how to behave in their relationship. In any case, they no longer have insurance.

Elena's passionate focus on performance and merit means other, less tangible ends get neglected, Royce insists. His wife is "aggressive," he says—when she rages, an elemental "force"—and sometimes he would like her not to act but to understand. When he struggles with the Bell's palsy, he doesn't want her to say, "You got to suck that shit up." When he is fruitlessly calling around for job openings, he doesn't want to hear, "I'm the one putting all the food on the table." He wants her to listen and empathize, but, he says, Elena always finds a way to make the conversation turn back to her. Royce offers an example: when he was in the hospital with spinal meningitis several years back, she hardly visited him—and was upset that his other family members did, as if she envied the attention.

Remember the context, she blurts out: she had just given birth to Keith. She was bloated and irritable and exhausted. "None of that matters—none of that is even considered when I apologize. The apology isn't even taken seriously."

"You never apologize!"

"To this day I will just let him feel the way he feels," she says, ignoring him.

"That's what we come to. You feel what you feel, and I—"

"It is what it is."

But now the unexpected happens again. Elena is laid off. Her firm has decided to downsize. "I don't want to say they've let me go, but basically, yes, they did," she says, quietly. "I guess I'm in denial." When she first got the bad news, Royce was supportive. ("That was a time that *I* felt closer," Elena says.) Yet the antagonism soon returned, as bitter as ever.

"There's things that's been said that can't leave your mind," Royce says. "There's situations—there's great situations that we're in—and some might trigger what we've said to each other."

"Anything that will hurt. The most hurtful thing that you can say," Elena adds.

"There's no blame, I don't think."

"We are just reacting—reacting to a situation."

Royce has been hitting temp agencies. He wakes up and calls five or six of them every morning, to see if any jobs have turned up. Every day they tell him no. So he steps up his game. Instead of just asking if they have work, he starts to market himself more. He makes small talk over the phone. He drops by their offices. Little things, he says, to make them remember who he is. It's what he needs to do, Royce has learned, in today's labor market. And the extra effort pays off: he gets a call about a job at another plating factory. But it's a temp position, and it pays just $7.75 an hour. "They might not need me next week," he points out. Nevertheless, working again, even temporarily and for low pay, has improved his mood. It is, he says, an outlet for him.

But it is one step forward, two steps back: with Elena's job gone, their financial security has taken another blow. They are now five months behind on paying their credit cards. Two months behind on their mortgage. Two months behind on a car loan. The water and electricity are both due to be shut off next month. And they owe another $1,800 for what was originally a $600 payday loan. The other day the bill collector was knocking on the door.

All nonessentials are out of the question now. Keith wants to take a karate class and trumpet lessons, but his father tells him no. Last month Royce promised to take the boy to a dinosaur exhibit, but it didn't happen, either. "No one can depend on me," Royce says. "I'm not able to make promises to my kids. And that was a big part of who I was when I was working." He was the reliable and involved father; he was the successful nephew who could help out here and there; he was the fortunate son of black Detroit who did not forget the family and friends around him. But now he sees his hard-fought gains trickling through his fingers, as the industry he placed his hopes in—stupidly, he now declares—pushes out uneducated grunts like him, and as the once-plentiful jobs that could sustain families like his disappear, perhaps for good.

His little son can't really comprehend what's going on, Royce says. All he knows is that the family needs money. Keith's school recently began a fundraiser for the American Heart Association. Keith had his eye on one of the toys—a pair of stilts—that he could get in exchange for raising money from family members. "Dad!" he said, waving the brochure in his hand. "Do you have a—" He stopped in mid-sentence. "Never mind. You don't have any money."

At first, Royce was upset that his son felt that way. But at five years old, Keith won't let such thoughts bother him for long, and his joyful buoyancy is infectious. When Royce is despondent, he sits with Keith and chats, and in a moment Royce will swear he is talking to an old soul. The boy will wrap his arm around his father's neck—real tight—and start consoling him, as if Royce were the son and he the father.

"Dad, it's okay," Keith tells his father. "It's going to be all right. Dad—you're going to get a job."

CHAPTER 5

Vicious Circles

*The Structure of Power and the Culture
of Judgment*

The awful thing about life is this: everyone has their reasons.
—Jean Renoir as Octave in *The Rules of the Game* (1939)

When he first got laid off, Alex Wynn waited two months before his first unemployment check came. The recession had struck, and Windsor firms were laying off workers in droves. The government agency in charge of the benefits was swamped with applications. Without any income, Alex had to tell his landlord—twice—that he couldn't pay his monthly rent. "He was visibly upset," Alex recalls. "He was just ranting and raving." Alex pleaded with him, pointing out that he'd never missed a payment before. "If I could have avoided this, you know I would have," he said.

The landlord let Alex stay. When the money finally came in, Alex paid up.

More than a year later, though, Alex is a month behind on his rent again—and this time, there's no check in the mail. His unemployment benefits have expired; a while back he burned through his retirement savings. Still unable to find a job, Alex has been doing construction projects here and there for a contractor friend of his, praying every month that the under-the-table cash will cover his expenses. Meanwhile, he and his wife Charlotte have separated. For the time being, she's living with her sister in another town. "It was hard on us, financially and everything else," says Alex, thirty-two. "She didn't make a lot of money." Charlotte had also lost her factory job, so Alex parceled out some of those retirement savings to help keep her afloat.

Their separation has also meant that Alex sees his stepson, eight-year-old Jasper, less often. "It kills me," Alex says. The two share a close bond. When the family was together, he'd spent every night after work hanging out with the boy. He describes Jasper as a sensitive boy—like his mother—and Alex worries about how he's processing the troubles of the adults around him. Jasper's grades have slipped, and he keeps asking his mother when Alex will be around next. "It's hard on him," Alex says. "He really starts to get broken down over that."

It's the first time in his life that Alex hasn't had a job. The son of a Ford worker, he got a job at the plating plant after a brief stint in college. He had developed a drinking problem while in school—at his worst, he could down two bottles of whiskey a day—but after struggling with it for a few years he went to rehab and cleaned himself up. The job at the plant kept him rooted. He made $21 an hour, enough to help out his cousin's family with cash here and there, and enough to pay for an apartment big enough to house his father and stepmom while they sorted their own issues out.

It's a two-bedroom apartment in a yellow-brick house, not far from a rowdy bar whose fistfights sometimes spill out onto the street. The rooms are decked out with mismatched and rickety furniture, including an ancient bookshelf filled with his grandfather's thirty-year-old encyclopedias. On the wall hangs a picture of Jasper, sporting sunglasses, in a frame printed with the words "Little Prince." Alex is tall and thin, his scruffy brown hair tucked under a cap, a light growth of facial hair circling his mouth. As he talks about his stepson, his hazel eyes begin to tear up. He takes off his glasses and wipes the reddened lids with his fingers. "It's very stressful," he says. "It can get to the point to where I just break down and cry some nights, you know. I got no choice—I got to let it out somehow."

If he could just get another job, perhaps he could—as Alex puts it—"regain the family environment we had." But in spite of the six dozen or so applications he's sent out, nothing has turned up yet. There are too many people searching, he says—"It's like a thousand vultures at one carcass, you know what I mean?" Nonetheless, he keeps plugging away. Unable to afford a car, he rides the city's unreliable public transit buses everywhere. "It's no picnic trying to go look for a job in the freezing cold."

These days, Alex takes whatever help he can find. His mom has bought him a few hundred dollars worth of groceries. His dad forks over packs of cigarettes and some cash to get him through the week. A friend let Alex borrow his propane stove when the electric company cut off his power for a week; another friend loaned him money to pay his bill and get the lights turned back on. Not everyone has been supportive, though. Recently, an aunt mocked him during a family get-together, telling him that he might have to go on welfare. Alex was incensed. "You're putting me down to that level already," he says, "and I haven't even reached that yet."

In fact, if Alex had his way, he'd have nothing to do with any of the government's inept bureaucracies. When his unemployment benefits got delayed, he tried calling around for answers, only to get fed up with the agency's feeble attempts at customer service. "The government hires a lot of people that barely even speak English," he says. "You get some of these guys on the phone—you can't even understand a word they are saying to you." He doesn't understand why the government won't devote more resources to the agencies that are supposed to help the many jobless workers out there. "They're cutting back so that they can try to save money or something," he says. But the delays spiral into further problems that end up costing taxpayers even more. "If you waited eighteen weeks to get your first unemployment check, well, how damaged are your bills? How damaged is your credit?"

If Alex can't count on the government, he doesn't have much faith in the labor movement, either. He thinks auto unions will continue to lose ground in the years ahead. "But I think that's a good thing, because they're gaining too much ground, to the point where they're almost becoming the auto industry itself," he says. "That's not what unions were intended for." The unions go "gung ho" too often, making unreasonable demands for higher wages and more generous benefits with every contract, he says. "You have to make allowances for the company, too." At the same time, Alex avidly supports his own union local. He is grateful for the sense of camaraderie it fostered at the plant. "There was a lot of brotherhood and sisterhood going on there." He starts to tear up again, and apologizes. "I do get very emotional, because that was my life in that place, you know. These were my friends." But now they're losing their homes, he says. Prolonged unemployment has sucked the life out of them. "A lot of these guys, they're not the same people."

Neither is Alex, for that matter. "Mentally it's draining, and physically it's boring," he says of his forced idleness. His body isn't used to it, and so on most nights, he can't sleep. He cleans his house and yard incessantly, trying to keep himself busy. He smokes more—a pack a day, twice what he used to. And he pays attention to the news less. Alex used to be a political junkie. He and Charlotte would flip through the cable news networks every night. Nowadays, he doesn't bother. "Unless they're gonna tell me that people are gonna start getting their jobs back . . . what is the point?"

. . .

Following the Great Depression, North America and Europe saw the rise of broad political movements determined to transform an unfair economic system. They successfully fought for potent policies and bounteous contracts that swallowed many of the risks of the market for the average citizen. Strong unions promoted a "moral economy" by assailing inequality in public pronouncements, lobbying for progressive social policies, and negotiating rules favorable to workers. Activist governments lifted the floor on wages, opened up possibilities for workers to organize, and reined in capital and corporate behavior. The trauma of depression and war and the surging power of leftist organizations and ideologies helped bring about relatively egalitarian attitudes and more enthusiasm about collective approaches to society's problems.

After the Great Recession, the worst economic crisis in eight decades, the response was much different. Many governments responded with austerity measures. Countries on both sides of the Atlantic saw glimmers of populist protest like that of the Depression era—grass-roots coalitions of students, workers, church members, and others upset with corporate greed and government inaction—but they also raged with nativist and antigovernment sentiment.

Clearly, the political tide has turned on workers—most obviously in America, but in Canada and other countries as well. Unions have seen steep declines in membership, and left-wing ideologies everywhere have flamed out. Fortified by trends of globalization and automation, a pro-corporate movement has successfully pushed its message that unions and government are evil. As a result, the institutions that once helped bend public attitudes toward egalitarian ends have been severely weakened. While at times governments have been able to halt its momentum, the *long-term* thrust of the economy since the postwar period has been toward unfettered markets and away from any spirited efforts to reduce inequality and increase employment through union or government meddling.

In short, when seen across decades, the arc of economic policy has bent toward pro-corporate conservatism. Even in their moments of electoral triumph, American and Canadian administrations on the political left have largely hewed to this consensus, pressing for market means to achieve liberal ends.[1] In Canada, it was the Liberal Party that pushed forward reforms in the nineties that shrank the size of the state; in more recent years the Conservative Party has continued that work, attacking public-sector unions for good measure. In America, Democratic lawmakers since at least the nineties have focused more on policies that place a floor on the downward mobility of the working and middle classes—that is, helping the "deserving" and preventing the very worst outcomes in the labor market, rather than aggressively supporting unions and pursuing egalitarian outcomes through more explicit shows of government power. While important, the implacable opposition of their political adversaries can only explain part of this reluctance to do more.

Indeed, while the political Left has done relatively well in U.S. presidential elections over the past two decades, the economic liberalism of the Clinton and Obama eras is altogether different from that of labor's heyday. In his 1996 State of the Union address, Bill Clinton pronounced that "the era of big government is over," and his administration's policy approach toward the labor market made good on that promise. It entailed individual training accounts, lifelong-learning credits, and the earned-income tax credit—market-friendly efforts to help people help themselves, rather than vigorous interventions in the market. Barack Obama has pushed somewhat more successfully—within a narrow political space—for a stronger safety net and tougher "rules of the road" for business, but the situation remains a world apart from the postwar period. His administration's most obvious success in addressing income inequality—ending the Bush tax cuts for top earners—was merely a return to Clinton-era tax rates. In spite of all the White House's rhetoric about addressing soaring inequality at the very top, politicians in both parties have put forward few serious ideas, having given up on past proposals for assertive government action, such as policies to achieve full employment and a guaranteed national income—proposals that were once supported by Republican leaders like Richard Nixon.[2] At least among Americans, concern about inequality has grown somewhat. Yet inequality has grown much more, especially in the United States, but in Canada as well.

Perhaps public opinion has played just a small role in what has transpired in recent years. The Wall Street banks whose market manipulation contributed to the meltdown have not received much in the way of punishment, but that outcome may have less to do with any deficit of public outrage and more to do with the ways that the pro-corporate movement has captured the loyalties of elected officials and government regulators alike. Likewise, the largest economic disaster since the Depression did not lead to an egalitarian reordering of the economic system on the scale of the New Deal, but here, too, the attitudes of ordinary Americans and Canadians may have mattered less than the professional preference for less interventionist approaches that prevails among the elite circle of policy technocrats, who worry incessantly—and perhaps excessively—about the tradeoff between efficiency and equality. Further back in time, politicized rulemaking also appears to be a better explanation for the fact that union membership dropped in the latter half of the twentieth century in America but not (at least for a time) in Canada.[3] Changes in institutions, rather than public opinion, have often been decisive in these cases.

That said, institutions do not emerge out of thin air. It is hard to imagine that the overall ideological climate has not influenced the economic experts and political operatives who have enacted recent policy changes—even as these elites have molded the broader context, too. More importantly, it is difficult to see how a labor movement that gains its power primarily by organizing people rather than money can grow in the long run when a pervasive ideology turns a significant segment of the population against that movement's aims. The political partisans who dictate economic policy clearly express more extreme views than ordinary citizens, and yet I was surprised by the extent to which my unemployed workers—left-of-center in their politics and recently members of powerful unions—agree with the views that today's elites take as the norm. Much of the reason they feel this way is that they are just realistic: this is the way today's market works. But there was also a sense among some of them that this is the way it *should* work—a point of view with consequences for how they coped with their inability to find jobs anything like the ones they once had.

In this chapter I tackle three questions. First, are workers like mine skeptical of the collective institutions that are supposed to help them— thereby moving in the direction of the self-reliant white-collar professionals and managers described in notable studies of past generations? Second, to what extent are their views driven by an ideology of individualism and critical judgment, as opposed to a simple realism about how today's market works? Along these lines, one argument is that blue-collar workers fail to champion their economic interests because they have abandoned "class consciousness" for "false consciousness"— no longer identifying or siding with the working class and instead internalizing an antilabor and antigovernment ideology that serves elites.[4]

Finally, given the widespread trends of globalization and government retrenchment, how do the views of Americans on opportunity and institutions compare to those of Canadians?

Both powerful ideas in the culture and weak institutions operating on the ground shaped the attitudes that my workers held about the labor market. Their experiences with other people and their exposure to mass media instilled in them a set of beliefs from the available, changing selection that society offers. These ideologies seemed to be connected to certain attitudes toward government and unions and certain responses to unemployment. In this way, perhaps, culture matters. And yet individuals do not simply parrot beliefs handed down to them. My workers were also responding to real-world circumstances, adapting their beliefs as the situation changed.[5]

NOTHING TO FALL BACK ON

Travel down East Grand Boulevard in northeastern Detroit and you will find—sprawling across two full city blocks—the empty, rotting shell of the once-famed Packard plant. Built at the beginning of the twentieth century, it was one of the most state-of-the-art industrial complexes in the world: seventy-four buildings spread out over 3.5 million square feet, the first structurally reinforced concrete factory ever built, designed by the city's preeminent architect, Albert Kahn. Packard was the country's top-selling luxury brand through most of the 1920s and '30s. But after a hiatus to build aircraft engines during the war, Packard frittered away its image with lackluster models, and the mass market deserted the brand. The plant assembled its last Packard on June 2, 1956. Never demolished, it continues to stand in its solitude of concrete and brick, its drab skin of graffiti almost as weathered as the old Packard lettering on the walls, its long banks of smashed windows fixed in a toothless leer—looking in its perfect decrepitude like some totem to a postindustrial god.

Ken Brennan's father toiled in the Packard plant for two decades. After the factory shut its doors, he never really worked. He developed tuberculosis, and had a lung removed, then developed cancer in the other lung. He died in 1978, when Ken was a teenager. Ken's mom struggled to support the family by herself. "I had six brothers and two sisters, so we had it rough growing up," says Ken, forty-seven. "No Christmases, no none of that." He was a troubled kid. When Ken was seventeen, a driver almost ran him over, and in a fit of wrath Ken smashed the car's windshield with a baseball bat. His record barred him from joining the Army when he tried to apply several years later.

In high school Ken met a girl named Sue. They fell in love and married young. Ken dropped out of school to work as a house painter. That job didn't last, so Ken bounced around other low-wage positions. Around this time, Ken's older sister was murdered. Her husband, a felon, had run afoul of prison friends of his. They came to the house and stabbed Ken's sister and two nieces, ages fifteen and nine, to death. The killers were caught, but Ken was devastated. "When her birthday comes around it's hard for me," Ken says. He motions to a photo of the nieces with his sister, twenty-seven, beautiful and ageless. "She would be in her fifties now," he says.

"You can't trust too many people out here," he adds. "Sometimes I'm scared to go out in the world. It's kind of cruel."

Ken and Sue settled down in their hometown. Sue worked at a cleaning company, for eight dollars an hour and no benefits, always just a few hours shy of full-time. ("If you were full-time you had insurance," Ken notes.) For a number of years, Ken worked at a parts supplier, where tensions between labor and management ultimately reached a tipping point over wages, benefits, and the outsourcing of work. A few hundred workers, Ken included, went on strike. "The company was being stubborn, and the union was being stubborn," Ken says. "And you're a union member. What are you going to do? If they go on strike, you can't go there and work." The strike became a lockout, and Ken and his coworkers lost their jobs. Afterward, as everyone struggled to get new jobs, a friend of his committed suicide.

More recently, Ken was working at a supplier that made solar panels for cars. He drove a forklift for $11 an hour. This time, there was no union.

One day, Ken had an accident at the plant. He was driving a forklift when someone pushed a ladder into his vicinity, out of his field of vision. He reversed and bumped into it, sending it hurtling down. Nothing was damaged, no one was hurt, but immediately afterward he could not shake the thought that he would be laid off. *I'm going to lose my house. My wife's going to be totally pissed off.*

"That's exactly what happened." Four days later he was fired.

Ken claims that his accident was just an excuse for the company, which had seen orders taper off and wanted to cut its workforce. He consulted a lawyer about a wrongful termination suit but was told he was an "at will" employee—which meant they could fire him for wearing the wrong clothes if they wanted. Ken says he is still baffled by what happened. He was never late, he did what he was told, he worked hard. But nowadays, you can't make any mistakes. "One accident and I'm gone."

When Sue heard the news, she was furious. "You shouldn't have had an accident," she told him.

"Well, that's why they call it an accident," Ken said.

Sue wanted him to get a job right away, and when nothing turned up, they bickered some more. It's not that easy, Ken tried to tell her. Eventually, she told Ken she wanted a divorce. He decided not to contest it. They had been arguing regularly over money. "She's tired of struggling, and she can do better by herself," he says.

Now Ken is waiting for the foreclosure to come. Without the two of them pooling their wages, there's no chance of keeping their home.

It is a small house with weather-stained siding, flanked by two leafy trees. The plants out front are yellowed, but the lawn is well trimmed (Ken mows lawns for extra cash). On the door hangs a decorative wooden heart with the words, "Welcome Friends." Next door is a sullen white bungalow with a faded realtor sign in the window; Ken says it's a short sell.

Ken's "new" car sits in the driveway, a slate-blue 1991 Oldsmobile with a rusted-out left taillight and 113,000 miles. After his wife left him and took their car, he bought this one so that he could get to interviews. But the brakes went out, and to fix them he needs another $200 he doesn't have.

Inside, Ken leads his guest to the kitchen table. Impeccably polite, he offers homemade pastries and coffee before stepping into the doorway of the laundry room to puff away at a cigarette ("I don't want to bother you," he insists). Nearby, a cabinet displays a crystal-studded pendant bearing his mother's silhouette and an urn with her ashes. Ken says he couldn't afford a burial. His mother died of congestive heart failure, two months after one of Ken's brothers, a truck driver, died of a heart attack. "They're probably in a better place," Ken says, almost enviously.

He has been thinking of his mother lately, and how she raised her kids on welfare and food stamps. He swore he would never turn to that, but the loss of his job and the end of his marriage have left him, he says, with no options. "I'm dependent on the government right now," he says. "That's degrading, but I gotta eat." Ken is quick to add that he worked for three decades. "I paid into it. I should be able. I've always worked." In any case, since he doesn't have kids, he can't get much in the way of benefits, he notes. Ken actually wanted to have children, but he and Sue weren't able to.

Besides prescriptions, the Salvation Army has furnished him with gas cards to fill up his car. Now that it's no longer running, he rides his mountain bike everywhere. Ken has applied for a hundred jobs so far, but he hasn't landed a single interview. "If you had a high school diploma a while ago, you could get a job," he says. "Now they want college." He maintains that he isn't being picky. "If I have to shovel dog crap, I would"—so long as he can get insurance, he adds. In the meantime, he waits—for employers to call back, for bureaucrats to get around to his case file, for his divorce to wind its way through the courts. At least he has something to do once a week: for his church's Sunday school he volunteers on the bus, singing songs and otherwise entertaining the children. "It helps to be around young people."

Ken says he can't blame the company for his accident. "I'm a man. I man up. I did it. What am I going to say, I didn't do it?"

Ken used to think of himself as, in his words, a "happy-go-lucky" guy. But his downward momentum has driven him to despair. For a time, thoughts of suicide drifted regularly into the prickly core of his consciousness. His ears would ring; his head would swim with sudden bursts of hatred. Ken has not able to see a therapist or psychiatrist because he can't afford health insurance. But he has seen his family doctor, who prescribed Paxil, an antidepressant. "I'm not going to try to fool nobody," he says. "I have depression." He can't eat. His weight has shrunk several pants sizes. But if he takes the pills, at least his frenzied mind slows down. Without the medication, the anger creeps up, the senses narrow, the reason blurs; the urge not to suffer anymore seizes him again.

Ken can't turn to his siblings for help, he says. They have their own financial woes. "It's your problem, little brother," they tell him. "Deal with it." In truth, he's glad that his family doesn't pry; he is ashamed to tell them what's going on. As for Sue, Ken knows their marriage is just ashes now. "We're tired of each other. People fall out of love, is all I can say."

They have known each other for so long. Ken threw her a party for her sweet sixteen. They adored each other, then. But the years have gone by, fruitlessly, and now the two of them are worse than strangers: fuming over the slightest infraction, at war over the few dollars in their bank account. Sometimes, Ken brims with resentment. "I'm done. I'm a free man. No woman is going to tell me what to do again." Then his mood becomes somber, almost plaintive. "She don't love me no more, so I can't make her."

Once in a while, Sue drops by the house to pick up clothes and other things. She heads to her room without speaking a word, slamming the door shut. The rage returns, itching in a corner of Ken's skull, and he has to struggle to master it.

Ken went to the state job center and asked about counseling services. There was a two-month waiting list for anyone to see him, he was told. "You can commit suicide tomorrow," Ken points out. But "it's the sign of the times of Michigan—they take who they can take."

His own story is also a "sign of the times," Ken says. From protected union employee, to at-will worker fired for no good reason. From a married man with a spouse and extended family to lean on, to a lonely bachelor living off government aid and what medicine and gas he can beg from the Salvation Army. From a hard worker whose decent blue-collar wage made him an essential breadwinner, to a laid-off has-been of no use to his employed wife. He's not alone, Ken knows. When the plants began shutting down decades ago, when fathers like his started losing jobs that gave "too much" pay for "too little" skill, when mothers like his went on welfare and sons like him quit school to get a paycheck—perhaps it started back then, for Ken, for his generation, for the generations that followed.

Politicians get on TV and make lofty promises of "no worker left behind," but Ken knows better. He can't rely on the government. "[I'm] trying to get aid, but like I said, they ran out of Medicaid," he says. Desperate, Ken finally decides to start going to a local church for group therapy. The only sessions available are for Narcotics Anonymous. Ken doesn't have a drug problem, but he starts attending anyway. "They'll talk to anybody," he says of the program. "They'll let anybody in." At each meeting, he will tell the recovering addicts there about his struggles with depression. They seem to understand what he's going through, he says. "But nobody has an answer."

. . .

Unemployed workers like Ken have learned that government policies that are generous on paper differ in practice when you're dealing with their sluggish, strained bureaucracies. States and provinces frequently do not have the funding or staff to fulfill their promises. Churches and other private organizations at times step in to fill in these gaps, but the help is often inferior and ad hoc—in the case of Ken, a non-addict resorting to the off-label assistance of Narcotics Anonymous, it's a hammer when he needs pliers.[6] And so he relies on himself, hustling every way he can to make a buck. "I'm strong," he says. "I'll make it. I'll be all right. I'm not going to let nothing get to me. . . . I'm not ready to check out. I'm not ready."

In previous chapters, I've described the numerous frustrations that my workers experienced dealing with poor government institutions. Clearly, the Great Recession placed huge strains on these agencies. Americans searched for public health care options in vain. The few programs that actually existed were overwhelmed and underfunded. Without any coverage, my workers were forced to endure the degrading treatment and labyrinthine procedures of the health care system for the uninsured. In Canada, unemployment benefits were delayed by weeks, leading to nail-biting waits as bills piled up and that first unemployment check still hadn't come. And in both countries, surging demand led to huge waiting lists and service cutbacks for government-funded retraining.

Nevertheless, the weak infrastructure and implementation my unemployed workers encountered cannot be blamed just on the economic downturn. Government bureaucracies have long been criticized for ineffectiveness, delays, and poor service. In America, the much-touted initiative during the nineties (headed by vice president Al Gore) to "reinvent" government was a tacit acknowledgement of the extent of the problem. In more recent years, government services have been outsourced to private firms. In-person assistance has been replaced by call centers and websites. And for-profit schools have swallowed up a larger chunk of the retraining dollars.[7] Whether these changes have succeeded in making government sleeker and smarter is debatable. For their part, my workers were not big fans. They were especially upset about how profit-hungry training centers snapped up their government tuition checks but provided a poor education in return.

Half of my workers on the American side had troubling experiences with another critical institution: labor unions. Many of my workers were simply upset by the union's failure to stop their layoffs. But some of them also pointed to specific instances of favoritism. Even in organizations like unions—groups that in theory are rooted in the egalitarian creed—some people are inevitably "more equal" than others, because of friendships, political connections, or cultural affinities. (This rift between the leadership and the rank and file has long bedeviled the labor movement.)[8] One ex-Chrysler worker points out that her union had its own pecking order. Although she was a good worker, she was never invited to the UAW's Black Lake retreat and golf resort in upstate Michigan. Only friends of the local's officers went, she says. "If you really weren't friendly with them, you didn't get the chance to go." The old boys' network didn't care that she was dedicated and reliable on the line. Another former Chrysler worker remembers working alongside a union representative who was flat-out lazy. "I had to do his work," she says. "He'd just leave when he want to, and here I am doing his job and two other jobs." The union let his behavior go on unpunished, she says.

Because most of my workers were not working, they had to deal with government bureaucracies for their benefits. Amid the collapse of the auto industry, they saw their unions in their weakest and least helpful state. It is worth noting that I also interviewed several workers who had found new jobs by the time I talked to them, and among this group the skepticism about government was less intense—though they shared many of the ideological concerns about unions that their unemployed counterparts had, as I will discuss later in this chapter.

Among the unemployed workers, however—especially those with particularly frustrating encounters with government and unions—it was striking how little interest they had in politics, union organizing, or other means to change either the labor market that had left them without jobs or the social safety net that floundered in helping them. As other researchers have found, unemployment does not necessarily lead to political engagement, much less radicalization.[9]

My workers' views of government tended to be less ideological, and more pragmatic, than their views of unions. But there was little sense, especially among the Americans, that government was there to take care of them, or that they could depend on those institutions in any substantial or sustained sense. In addition to the government-sponsored action centers, a handful of my Canadians got involved in politics—mainly through the workers' party, the New Democratic Party—and that provided another collective outlet for their energies. But on the American side, the country's political parties had no such following among my workers. Again, this speaks to their social isolation. It also may reflect the demise of local party politics—the party machines that had once integrated struggling immigrants and given them the power to defend their interests—as political reforms and the rising power of wealthy donors and self-financed candidates have shunted them aside.[10]

With no alternatives, my Americans explicitly focused on self-reliance: overcoming their bouts of unemployment through their own efforts. Vincent Formosa is fifty-three and unemployed. He says he lost interest in politics after he lost his job at the parts plant. He voted for Obama and the Democrats in 2008, but "they didn't do shit for us." The government bailouts enraged him—not just the bailouts of Wall Street banks, which let corporate executives stick around and receive "million-dollar bonuses," but also the bailouts of the Big Three. "There ain't no sense in getting all these big corporations all this money," he says. He is equally fed up with unions, which he feels just look after the interests of union officials. "You know what? If I didn't get another union job I wouldn't even care."

In any case, Vincent has more immediate concerns than what is going on in Obama's White House or the UAW's Solidarity House. As I described in chapter 3, Vincent is struggling to pay for his prescriptions and get seen by a doctor for several chronic health conditions. His family has been on food stamps since he lost his job, though the benefit was recently pared down because the government said he made too much money—which Vincent finds ridiculous. Whenever he receives a letter from the social services office, anger instantly grips his thoughts. "I know it's something they're nitpicking about—'We're going to cut you off for this, or we're going to cut you off for that.'"

The kind of help that the government provides comes ensnarled in bureaucratic strings, Vincent says. His hot-water tank broke right after he was laid off, and he didn't have $400 to replace it. He turned to the social services office for help, and they said they would chip in—provided he got three different estimates of the cost, and then waited a month. If he were fifty-five years old, they added, he would qualify sooner. "What's fifty-five got to do with me getting a hot water tank?" Vincent asked, incredulous. The caseworker tried to explain, but by now Vincent was seething. "I don't even want to hear it." He hung up, called his brother, and asked him to wire the money. "I'm not waiting no month."

Vincent is outraged by the long delays and hostility he encounters whenever he tries to get help. So instead, he relies on himself. He is vehement that he will find a way out of his family's predicament, with God's help and his own sweat. Hard work makes a difference, he insists. He points out that he was raised in poverty. But decades of grinding through shifts at Walmart, a furniture company, and then the auto plant pulled Vincent out of that trap. "It made me the person I am," he says. "I could have been dead, in jail." He holds on to that same faith today. What else can he do? "I ain't got nothing to fall back on," he says.

And yet Vincent, who worked hard for thirty-six years, can't find anyone willing to hire him. "The only thing I've got going [for me] is my work ethic. If you give me a chance to prove myself, then I'm going to do the best I can." He pauses. "I ain't run across nobody like that. . . . You can't really blame them. But then again, you say, 'What the hell?' Just give me a chance, that's all I ask."

When the institutions that are supposed to help them let them down, workers like Vincent come to the rational conclusion that they are really on their own. Their lived experiences show them they have no other option.

Family, nonprofit organizations, and religious institutions are potential alternatives to the self-reliance my workers turned to. The failure of government and unions, then, may simply lead to a greater dependence on other parts of the private safety net. As they were in earlier times, families and charities could become the proper—and, perhaps, preponderant—sources of support for the long-term unemployed, with the privatization of economic *assistance* advancing alongside a privatization of economic *suffering*—as the plight of workers becomes seen as a private concern, not a public one.[11] (This is the once-and-future scenario advocated by some on the right, including America's Tea Party.) Regardless, my conversations with my workers suggest that these options are no real replacements for strong government policies and strong unions. Inequality plays a role here, too: blue-collar, lower-income, and less educated workers in general are more socially isolated than white-collar, middle-class, and more educated workers, meaning that they get involved less in voluntary associations and other organizational alternatives to unions or political parties.[12]

Their extended families offered to help the families I got to know, as I described in chapter 3, but in most cases (especially for the black households) there was not much in the way of resources to give. In any case, asking for their assistance was degrading, my workers routinely said. One benefit of government benefits is that households can receive them on the down low. As for charities, Ken Brennan was fortunate enough to receive prescriptions and gas money from the Salvation Army, but the rest of my workers received little in the way of tangible help: mainly groceries from food pantries and the occasional holiday gift card from the union. The meritocratic ideology generated a sense of guilt here as well, undermining the value of any outside help they did receive. Several of my workers, for example, said they refused to go to a food pantry because of the stigma attached to it. Food stamps, on the other hand, could be used with a relatively inconspicuous swipe of a card at a checkout counter.

As for religion, many of my workers—my Americans in particular—spoke of their faith as a means of getting through their personal crisis. But few went to church regularly. Religion for them was mainly a matter of individual faith and self-reliance, rather than a collective struggle for social justice. "With God's help," they believed, "*I* will get through this." Even those who attended black churches—traditionally strong reservoirs of social-justice sentiment—did not draw from that aspect of their faith.

Fewer of my Canadian workers had unfavorable encounters with their unions or government agencies. As I discussed earlier in the book, the action centers funded by the province and their former employers made a favorable impression on my workers. Peer helpers who were their fellow union members provided personalized counseling, burnishing the union's image. The centers guided my workers through the maze of government bureaucracy and lobbied officials on their behalf, alleviating some of their frustrations and making what government assistance they did tap more effective.

If the action centers improved the experiences that my Canadian workers had, the differences between the two nations in this area should not be overstated. Social spending in both countries, I noted earlier, has converged, with the Canadians becoming stingier. The labor movement remains stronger in Canada, but unions in both countries have been losing power. Meanwhile, the pro-corporate movement has had success even up north in its campaigns to deregulate markets, defund government, and rationalize labor. These trends have degraded the institutions that workers encounter in their day-to-day lives, perhaps leading to more similar experiences and responses in the two countries. For instance, as dedicated as the peer helpers were, they could do nothing to alter the sluggish pace at which the government paid out its unemployment benefits. They could not alter bureaucratic decisions to tighten an overwhelmed training program's requirements and to exclude many workers. In these and other ways, there were limits to what determined individuals could do to address the frequent structural strains endured by fraying social safety nets.

Those of my Canadian workers who did not have much contact with the action centers felt much the same way as the Americans did. Tom Moon, a fifty-four-year-old Canadian and former Ford worker, got on public assistance after his unemployment ran out. His encounters with bureaucracies have been universally bad. The government offers no real solutions for people like him, he says. "Are they gonna step in and give me $3 or $4 million to make my life better? No." (And yet they give corporations billions not to go bankrupt, he adds with disgust.) Meanwhile, the help he does get is half-hearted. "Welfare doesn't give you enough to live."

Their exposure to faltering institutions gave my workers good reasons to be skeptical of government and unions. But more broadly, they also acknowledged that the economy has changed. It was only practical to change with it. In 2009 and 2010, the auto companies and unions were on the brink of collapse. Government agencies were broke and cutting payrolls and benefits. My workers were responding to this extreme climate. At the same time, in both countries they were also well aware that long-run economic and political trends have not been moving in their direction. Unions have grown weaker, and corporations have grown stronger.

Unions were once important, Tom says. They won good wages and benefits for their members when they had bargaining power years ago. But nowadays, he says, autoworkers are getting paid too much relative to what the market will allow. "You're at a point where you have to give something back. And now everybody's saying, 'The union is doing this, the union is doing that.' No, they're not. The company is deciding what they're gonna do." Unlike the workers I mentioned earlier, Tom wasn't mad at his union for specific instances of favoritism. He was just being realistic.

As for corporations, many of my workers angrily attacked their former employers for making poor or dishonorable decisions that led to job losses. (This was especially true among my parts workers, whose plants had already been shut down.) That was not surprising. What *was* surprising was that a substantial minority of workers in both countries—again, former members of powerful unions—stressed how important it was to see things from the company's point of view.

Tellingly, they prided themselves on their knowledge of what is necessary to run a profitable business. At the end of the day, the decision to close the plant made sense, says Allen Lee, an American ex-parts worker. He was upset with how the company treated its employees right after the layoffs, but he sees the wisdom of transferring production to more modern, integrated, profitable facilities. "I can't get mad with what they did, 'cause it was a good business move," he says. Other workers "hate" the company's owner for what happened, but he knows a "good businessman" when he sees one. "I know sometimes you gotta make decisions that everybody ain't gonna coincide with," he points out.

Workers like Allen have a folk understanding of economics.[13] To some extent, they have adopted the viewpoint of those higher up in the labor market's hierarchy, who point out that companies are in business "to provide a service or a product," not "to hire people."[14] They realize that companies cannot survive if their expenses exceed revenues. They appreciate the competitive constraints that companies operate under. They become skeptical of unions and other collective action to deal with the consequences of those "good business moves."

This kind of market realism could be seen on both sides of the border. Americans and Canadians alike talked about how companies had moved their factories overseas, how automation had excised certain positions and upped the skills required for others, and how their government and union leaders had been either unwilling or unable to stop the loss of jobs. Free trade, automation, and politics had led to this dire situation, and they were helpless to do anything about it. And yet because hard work and further education are always things that (supposedly) will lead to a good job, they could pursue this individual strategy—and perhaps suffer the self-blame that came when their failures piled up.

Their personal experiences and personal understanding of the changed economy pushed my workers toward one course of action: relying on themselves. For the most part, then, my workers do not exactly fit the concept of false consciousness. They are acting rationally.[15] Policymakers, with their ineffective and incompetent bureaucracies, have failed them. Unions, with their cronyism and powerlessness, have failed them. They can't count on these institutions. They can only count on themselves. Rather than do nothing, they should be hitting the pavement, looking for jobs. Rather than wasting their time retraining for careers in growing industries that probably won't hire the likes of them anyways, they should be sending out résumés, making phone calls, and praying that there are factories that still want them.

MORALITY PLAYS

With his faith in God and the support of his wife, Eddie Frank has so far been able to take his unemployment in stride. Thankfully, Maria has a good job as a restaurant manager. They go to church every Sunday, and Eddie firmly believes that God will handle whatever may come. "He been doing it all my life," says the American ex-autoworker. "Everything is even probably closer to Him now than ever." Still, at times the stress ramps up. Things can seem "gloomy," he says. "You got to pay everything on time, but at the same time, you got to spend."

It bothers him that he can't help support Maria and the kids. "A man's got an ego," he says. "So . . . I'm a little bit more humble." If he could get even an $11-an-hour job, he says, he'd take it. But so far nothing like that has presented itself. Meanwhile, their tight finances mean that he and Maria have no margin of error in their spending decisions. "It's like a chess game," Eddie says. "You got to be cautious on what kind of move you make now."

Eddie is a muscular man in his thirties, with a neatly trimmed beard and close-cropped hair. He worked for almost twenty years in the industry, and has a ruined shoulder to show for it. Nevertheless, he counts his blessings. He compares his situation to those of many of his former coworkers, who didn't put money away, and whose partners, if they have any, are unsupportive or lazy. "It's like you just defeated the purpose of you working hard," he says. "If you don't have nothing to show for all that time, shame on you."

It's not that he doesn't see the desperation around him. When Eddie moved into his Detroit home, he lived in a good neighborhood. But hard times have brought it down. Now, many of the houses on his block and elsewhere are shuttered, abandoned by their owners. He and Maria have an alarm, a fence, and a guard dog protecting their home. "I never had an incident, thank God." But if you park your car on the street at night, he adds, "forget about it. You wake up in the morning, they broke the glass." People will rip off parts and sell them easily in this car town.

Eddie doesn't know how to even begin solving these kinds of problems. Workers need education to get jobs, but a lot of his former coworkers are already middle-aged, he points out. What are they going to do? Companies no longer have any patience for anyone but the most productive workers. "They don't care if you're struggling in your house," he says, "or you ain't got no money to feed your kids. The only thing they worry about is . . . they don't want to lose no money." As for unions, they will be "gone in a minute," he insists. Corporations are steadily rooting them out. The recession just provided another opening for management. "They want somebody that's gonna go in there and work with their rules, you know, not with the union rules."

To some extent, he understands the companies' point of view. "As soon as you hire somebody that's in a union in a company, then you pretty much gave up your right as a businessperson, because they're gonna find that loophole for them to get less work and get paid more money." Unions helped a lot of people "back in the day," he points out, but nowadays they go "overboard." "As every year goes by, they renew their contract, they want more, more. How much more? . . . And then, on top of it, what do they do? Sit and eat donuts in the local?" It's not fair that some unionized workers get paid better than people who spent their time and money getting an education, he says.

Since he lost his job, Eddie has been busy taking care of his kids and cleaning up the house while Maria works. Meanwhile, he waits. He'd like to get a commercial driving license, which would allow him to get a job as a truck driver. He applied for the state retraining program, which would foot the thousands of dollars in tuition. But the program ran out of funds. "So what am I gonna do, you know?"

He understands that times are tough. The government only has so much money to spend, he notes. He can't blame them for needing to economize their resources. Still, if it's not going to help out, it would be better if the government could at least step out of the way. Years ago he worked as a barber, and these days he cuts his friends' hair for extra cash. But state regulations mean that he can't make that into any sort of living. "You got to be licensed," he points out.

Maria describes her husband as a "workaholic." For two decades he was up before anyone else in the house and out the door, headed to work. "If there was overtime, I was getting it," Eddie says. "It was not a day that I was home saying, 'Oh, I don't want to work.' Even [if] I'm sick, I'm going to work because it's just—that's the kind of person I am."

If things are going to work out, he's going to be the one to make it happen, he says. As for the union, they're useless. "They call and say bad news." He laughs. "That's what they help me on."

. . .

National surveys have consistently shown that Americans endorse the virtues of self-reliance, willpower, and individualism. Past scholarship has dubbed this set of interconnected beliefs the "American belief system" and the "achievement ideology." But even as it spurs ordinary Americans to extraordinary accomplishments, the ideology has consequences for those who falter along the way. As other scholars have argued, it focuses attention on how individuals, rather than the system, have failed, leading people to criticize others—and themselves—when they stay stuck in poverty and unemployment. Success, in this view, is a sign of moral virtue, and failure a mark of sin.[16]

For a span of decades in the middle of the last century, there were powerful and persistent alternatives to this meritocratic viewpoint. Strong labor unions emerged, rallying working men and women under the banner of solidarity and collective struggle. More radically, leftist political movements captured much of the world's imagination. Communism ended up being brutal and oppressive of the people it was supposed to lift up, but for a time it did offer a worldview that glorified ordinary workers. Under the Marxist ideology, they could see themselves as key players in a broader historical struggle, rather than just cogs in the market economy's perpetual-motion machine. And under its threat, capitalist societies were forced to respond to their demands—ironically, more so than was the case in totalitarian communist societies, which were hostile to independent labor movements.

It is important to note that, in America at least, what blue-collar workers once had going for them was never a socialist wonderland. As Kay Lehman Schlozman and Sidney Verba point out, blue-collar workers in the 1930s were somewhat more class conscious than was the case four decades later, in that more of them—though never a majority—identified with the working class and supported aggressive government action to further their economic interests. When Schlozman and Verba conducted a survey in mid-seventies, amid stagflation and worries about American decline, they found that even the unemployed held persistently onto the American Dream ideology, and blue-collar and white-collar attitudes had converged, largely moving in a more conservative direction. Even during these years of relative union strength, blue-collar Americans had conflicting attitudes about success, and about who was to blame for the lack of it.[17]

Nevertheless, the power of their unions to win good wages—beyond what their educational credentials would have paid—was a source of pride. "You got people working in offices, they might consider themselves . . . a little better than the workingman," says a shop steward in Robert Lane's 1962 study of the political beliefs of ordinary Americans. "But nine times out of ten, the workingman is making more money than he is." In his later study of plant workers, David Halle tells the story of a high school dropout whose daughter told her teachers how much he earned. "They didn't believe it, so I Xeroxed a pay stub for her to show them!" he gloated. An egalitarian combination of institutions and ideologies insulated these workers to a significant degree from the self-doubts and self-blame that accompany low status. It encouraged these workers, in turn, to take a collective response to unemployment. In the eighties, Katherine Newman found laid-off plant workers to be a "brotherhood of the downwardly mobile," who stood together against corporate downsizing. A culture of meritocracy did thrive then, Newman says, but it was relevant to elite white-collar managers, who justified the startling inequality that placed them on top by pointing to their own "sheer ability and hard work." A decade later, Kathryn Marie Dudley described white-collar professionals who welcomed the closing of a Chrysler plant in their community. They believed that economic advancement should depend on individual credentials, not collective bargaining. Nevertheless, Dudley's unionized autoworkers still defended the value of organized labor.[18]

Looking across the border, Canadians have traditionally been more collectivist than Americans. In many ways, the two nations share quite similar cultures that harken back to the frontier lifestyle of the New World. Nevertheless, as sociologist Seymour Martin Lipset famously described, Canada and the United States emerged from distinct sets of political values. Canada grew into a communitarian nation that envisioned society as a mosaic of groups, while America evolved into an individualistic country that emphasized laissez-faire competition and meritocracy.[19] America's racial diversity, its ideology of the American Dream, and its unfettered markets have long meant that its citizens espoused a more self-reliant view of opportunity and government.

In recent decades, however, as the flow of ideas across national borders becomes increasingly costless and effortless, the American Dream is becoming a somewhat universal dream, even as cross-Atlantic concerns about inequality also percolate into the American consciousness. (Interestingly, Martin Whyte uses survey data to show that meritocratic views are the very strongest today in China, where the Chinese leadership boasts about the so-called Chinese Dream.)[20] For this reason, the terms *American belief system* and *American Dream* may be outdated. Scholars have proposed other, less insular terms. As I mentioned in chapter 1, I build on the work of Katherine Newman and use the term *meritocratic morality*, defined in opposition to three other kinds of moral ideologies: egalitarian morality, fraternal morality, and grace morality.[21] I will have more to say about these various perspectives in the final two chapters of this book. But first, I want to discuss what, if anything, public opinion surveys can tell us about possible changes in attitudes concerning individual opportunity and collective institutions.

If we think of the meritocratic perspective *just* in terms of hard work leading to success, support for this view has fluctuated slightly but remains strong. For example, posed the question of whether individuals get ahead by dint of hard work or the intervention of luck or other people, two-thirds of Americans over the past four decades have told Gallup they believe "hard work" is responsible—a proportion that has drifted upward. The less educated believe more strongly than their well-educated counterparts in this idea, although the differences are not large. A Pew Research Center poll on the same topic finds similar results: a strong, and slightly growing, belief that success is within our control. (Contradicting these other surveys, however, the World Values Survey finds a decline in this way of thinking over two decades, though the survey is not conducted as frequently as the others.)[22]

However, whether someone believes that "people get ahead by their own hard work" is not the best measure for the meritocratic thinking I have in mind, which as I've explained involves a more complicated understanding of what we understand merit to be. In addition, those who believe that people get ahead through hard work may simply be responding to a labor market that is no longer shackled by high degrees of nepotism and discrimination. They may or may not believe that people *should* rise and fall based on their effort and ability, but here the question is asking them what actually happens in the labor market. Finally, the idea of "luck" as an alternative to hard work is a nebulous one, as sociologist Leslie McCall points out. When luck is put in more concrete terms, she writes, a "significant minority of Americans (just under half) say that things such as social connections and coming from a privileged background are essential or very important factors in getting ahead." McCall argues that the fact that Americans acknowledge these barriers means that they are—contrary to scholarly stereotypes—concerned about the lack of opportunity for all to succeed.[23]

A different measure of meritocratic morality is how much people believe that education leads to success. According to one international survey, Americans overwhelmingly believe that education is important in "getting ahead," regardless of the amount of schooling they personally have, and this proportion has increased slightly over the years. But when we look at the public's view of how important education and training "ought" to be in deciding pay, the trend is in the opposite direction. It is not clear what to make of this divergence. On the one hand, it may be the case that any *pay* advantage of education is less salient for workers like mine—"getting ahead," which implies being gainfully employed, is the more pressing concern. It is worth noting, too, that the less educated are equally or slightly more supportive of the view that education *ought* to matter in deciding pay—denying, it seems, their own deservingness.[24] On the other hand, these trends may suggest (at least for the U.S. population) that realism, rather than ideology, is at work here: people increasingly acknowledge that education *does* matter, though they increasingly think it *shouldn't* matter.

The picture is further complicated by Americans' complex attitudes toward inequality. In 2009, for instance, two-thirds of Americans believed that income differences in their country were too large, slightly higher than the proportion a decade earlier. That said, the public's concern about inequality peaked in 1992, at 77 percent, and has remained below that level since—in spite of the rapid income gains of the top 1 percent over this period of time.[25] McCall points out that during the nineties the economy boomed and shared its bounty widely, which may have dampened concerns about inequality. Given the recent explosion in inequality, however, the lack of a larger and clearer shift in public opinion is puzzling.

Furthermore, on some questions, the public's views are a bit incoherent. For example, a third of Americans in 2009 agreed that government should reduce differences in income between people with high incomes and those with low incomes. However, when the same survey used a question with different wording—instead asking about income differences between the *rich* and the *poor*—half of Americans agreed. (Clearly, question wording matters, and popular views are not always ideologically consistent.) On the first question, support for government intervention has declined, but on the second question, it has increased. Meanwhile, a little more than a third of Americans have consistently said that it should be the responsibility of government "to provide a job for everyone who wants one."[26]

How do the American public's views compare with those across the border? In their views on the importance of hard work, one international survey finds that the attitudes in each country have moved a bit closer to those held across the border. In the middle of the last decade, for example, 76 percent of Canadians approved of the statement "Hard work usually brings a better life," compared to 77 percent of Americans— a one-point gap, compared to a seven-point one in 1990. Very similar numbers of Americans and Canadians said that education was essential or very important in getting ahead, in the one year that a survey was conducted in both countries. In terms of how much it *should* affect pay, however, Canadians believed substantially less in the importance of education, though the gap has shrunk over time.

In both countries, a majority of the population is concerned about inequality. More Canadians than Americans agree that government should reduce income differences between rich and poor, but this belief in intervention has risen in both countries since the mid-nineties. In terms of unemployment policy, about the same proportion of Canadians— four out of ten—believe that government should provide a job for everyone who wants one.[27]

Overall, then, Americans and Canadians tend to have fairly similar views about the importance of hard work and education in getting ahead, but they differ on how much they think education *ought* to matter and how much government *should* get involved in addressing inequality. The fact that Americans believe more strongly that education should be important suggests that there is a bit more ideological support over there for the kind of meritocratic labor market I have described. At the same time, this view appears to have declined over time in America and Canada alike, while support for the belief that education *does* matter has risen—suggesting that today's workers may be responding more to changing realities than to a changing culture per se. In terms of policy preferences, Americans tend to be more skeptical about direct government interventions in the market, with the exception of providing jobs (which still gets the support of only a minority of people in both countries). McCall, however, points out that, in line with their strong belief in the principle of equal opportunity, Americans do support spending on education, and that support has grown. I will return to this point in the last chapter.[28]

. . .

The workers I interviewed tended to come from less privileged backgrounds. Their stated politics were overwhelmingly liberal or moderate. And they were unionized blue-collar workers—a group that has long represented the upper bound of class consciousness in both America and Canada. For these reasons, I did not expect to hear the narrow individualism and self-blame that many of them expressed. In fact, I had begun my research with a focus on social policy, and without any particular interest in meritocracy. But the rhetoric my workers used prompted me to expand my study to try to capture what was going through their heads.

Of course, other groups express more extreme meritocratic views than my workers do. The Tea Party movement that rose to prominence in the 2010 U.S. elections has been driven in part by an especially uncompromising form of the ideology, most apparent in the movement's disdain for those reliant on government assistance. Likewise, anthropologist Karen Ho has studied the radical individualism of Wall Street investment bankers, smug in their knowledge that they are the superior exemplars of the meritocratic creed: intelligent, hard-working, and extraordinarily talented.[29]

Tea Party members may have an enthusiasm for dismantling the welfare state, and Wall Street bankers may extol the ruthless actions of corporations, but my more liberal workers didn't put forward such hard-line views about government or corporations. In fact, the American and Canadian autoworkers largely expressed support for *stronger* policy interventions to improve the economy.[30] As I've described, if they personally turned away from government agencies, they had little choice in the matter: their personal experiences had taught them that they could not rely on its underfunded and faltering bureaucracies. In other words, realism, and not the meritocratic ideology, appeared to drive my workers' views of government. Likewise, my workers expressed disgust with corporate executives. They were universally mad that some CEOs were receiving million-dollar bonuses even when their companies were falling apart. They fiercely criticized the careless and half-witted business decisions of the Big Three and other corporations, which many said contributed to the auto industry's ruin. And they were outraged by the corrupt and selfish actions of Wall Street during the economic crisis.

At the same time, ideology did matter in other, more subtle ways. The prevailing culture of judgment forces less advantaged workers to adopt a defensive posture, regardless of whether they espouse its meritocratic tenets. In the case of my workers, the broader narrative about the evils of big government was very much on their minds. They were sensitive to the extreme meritocratic viewpoint, adopted by some conservatives, that there are two classes: the makers, and the takers. They expressed great shame about receiving government benefits. They constantly sought to refute any notion that they were freeloaders. The bank bailouts were overwhelmingly unpopular among them, and yet their support for the auto bailouts was surprisingly tepid. This defensiveness about government was common among my Americans and Canadians, parts workers and Big Three workers.

Likewise, my workers in both countries felt the need to attack their own relatively high compensation even as they attacked overpaid corporate executives. Both management and labor were to blame because they didn't "deserve" what they were getting: the virtuous link between skill and compensation had been sundered. "The fact that they're paying a lot of these auto executives millions and millions of dollars and offering CEOs millions and millions of dollars in buyouts—I think it's asinine," said a Canadian worker. But he felt that the workers at his unionized plant were paid too much, too. "They gave it to us because the executives were getting it. That money should have gone back into the company for product development and research."

There did seem to be a more ideological tinge to my Americans' views of corporations. On the Canadian side, plenty of anger was directed at the inequality that corporations promoted. James Channing, a forty-three-year-old former parts worker, thinks it ludicrous that companies can pay their bosses million-dollar bonuses and still get upset that their workers are making $23 an hour. "I'm not talking a line worker should be gettin' CEO money, but there's no reason for anyone to get a $10 million bonus ever, for anything," he says. On the American side, however, workers more often couched these criticisms in the narrower terms of meritocratic morality (if with a more politically liberal cast), arguing not that too much wealth or power was necessarily a bad thing, but that elites had done bad things that proved them to be undeserving. "When you screw up and you're making a million dollars a year or better, they don't fire you," says Johnson Cheney, a former union steward at Chrysler. "They just say, 'Well, okay, we'll give you ten million dollars and you go on home.'"[31]

The broader culture of judgment did not always convert my workers to a meritocratic view, but it did force them to plead their case against its criticisms. In his postwar study of autoworkers, Eli Chinoy noted that the "defensive measures" that workers adopted back then were only "partially effective" in stopping the ideological onslaught of "guilt and self-depreciation."[32] Since then, however, the situation has grown worse for ordinary workers, through the trends of growing labor weakness and heightened market competition I have described. They have to fight against the now commonsense notions that the free market should be allowed to work its creative destruction unhindered, and that workers with little skill should not be paid much. In the next section, I will explore how the prevailing ideology colored their views of a third set of institutions, ones that traditionally have been bastions of collective action: labor unions.

A UNION OF THE DESERVING IS NOT A UNION

Because he's a hard worker, Mitch Beerman sees no point to unions. "I can't see which way they've actually helped me in the past up until now," says the thirty-three-year-old Canadian. "If I could stay away from unions, I probably would." In his thirteen years at a feeder plant, Mitch had to turn to the union exactly twice—once because the company stiffed him on some hours, and another time because it wouldn't give him a modified work assignment after he developed tendonitis. Other workers were always getting suspended and having the union bail them out, Mitch points out. "I never miss time, nothing. I stay out of trouble. I go and do my job. I go home."

Mitch does not see unions surviving in the long term—and in fact, he is "kind of hoping" they will go down. "All they do is they fight for the people that actually need the union—the ones that always get into trouble," he says. "They're the ones that save their butts."

These days, though, Mitch could use someone to save him. When he lost his job at the plant a year ago, his wife Kendra picked up a second, part-time job to help support them and their two young girls. After a short while it became clear that she resented the situation—bitterly. She would come home from work and start yelling at him, unprovoked. He was lazy, Kendra declared. He needed to start paying more bills. The two eventually decided to split up.

"You deserve somebody better than me that ain't gonna yell at you every day for no reason," Kendra told him.

Four months ago, Mitch moved back in with his parents. They are both retired, and they say they don't mind, but Mitch hasn't lived at home for a decade. Staying there grates at his pride. Even though he pays $150 a month in rent, "I still feel like I'm intruding," he says. But he has nowhere else to go. He has already spent the $10,000 he had in retirement savings. His bank account has run dry.

Mitch is deeply depressed. His weight has dropped twenty-seven pounds. "I just eat enough to get me by," he says. He feels guilty using up his parents' groceries. Unable to sleep more than a handful of hours at night, Mitch will crawl into bed during the day. When his mood sinks to its lowest, he will find himself sitting in front of the TV, aimlessly flipping through channels, a monologue running through his head: *What am I going to do? My parents are only going to let me live here for so long. Am I going to lose my Jeep? Is the bank going to take my house? Why can't I find a job? Is there something wrong with me? Is it my résumé? Am I just not smart enough to do this?*

Mitch doesn't blame himself for losing his job, but he can't help being hard on himself as the employer rejections pile up. "It's never taken me this long to find a job," he says a year after his layoff. When he was younger and bouncing between menial positions, he never thought to go on unemployment. "I'm usually someone who is right back in it."

Even though he, a diligent worker, suddenly finds himself jobless, buried under debt, and struggling to pull himself up again, Mitch wholeheartedly agrees with the idea that hard work brings a better life. "I've always felt like that," he says. He doesn't point to any structural flaws in the economy that hinder his chances or those of other hard-working men and women; the economy is bad right now—and that's temporary.[33] Things will get better "sooner or later," he adds. "I truly believe it. Things will start to turn."

For the moment, though, things are headed sharply downward. Recently, the utility company shut off the gas in his former home because the bills had gone unpaid. He asked his parents for the money to get it turned back on so that Kendra and his daughters wouldn't freeze. Later, Mitch had to go to the hospital for a severe respiratory infection. His father paid for the Percocet painkillers that the doctor prescribed.

"I've never asked for help all the way up until this year," Mitch points out. "And it takes a lot for me to actually ask somebody for help, because I feel embarrassed."

He should be the one providing—to his kids, above all. He still upbraids himself for what happened this past Christmas. The only things he could afford to buy his daughters came from the Dollar Store: coloring books, crayons, colored pencils, puzzles, workbooks. "I didn't get my brother or sister anything. Nothing for Mom and Dad." His daughters didn't mind so much. "They were just glad they had things under the tree." But he felt like "crap," he says. "Still do."

. . .

In recent years, anti-union activists and their corporate backers have won a telling string of victories. Around the time of the federal bailouts of the auto industry, commentators blasted unionized autoworkers as the undeserving recipients of taxpayer assistance, their intransigent opposition nearly dooming the industry to liquidation. Public-sector unions—a rare bright spot in the modern labor movement—came under fire for their generous pensions and other benefits, which their detractors said had put unsustainable pressures on government budgets.[34] In both countries, a significant segment of the population expressed support for these criticisms. In 2011, 48 percent of Canadians said that strikes by public-sector unions should be banned and settlements imposed by arbitrators, in step with recent efforts by the federal government to exert greater control over when those unions can and can't strike. That same year, 39 percent of Americans told Gallup that they supported the governors in Wisconsin and elsewhere who sought not just to force concessions from public-sector unions but to hobble their very ability to negotiate. And a year later, the unthinkable happened: Michigan—the home turf of the UAW—successfully passed a right-to-work law, the twenty-fourth state to do so. One poll before the vote found that the state's residents were evenly divided (47 percent in favor, 46 percent opposed) on the new law, which dilutes organized labor's power by allowing workers in unionized workplaces to refuse membership.[35]

In 2014 organized labor took another beating—this one involving the UAW itself. Employees at a Volkswagen car plant in Tennessee agreed to a vote on whether to unionize. Volkswagen, which was used to working with Germany's strong unions, pledged neutrality. With the employer standing aside, the Volkswagen drive represented perhaps the UAW's best opportunity ever to break into the labor-unfriendly South, where in recent decades foreign-owned plants employing nonunion workers have multiplied. But in the end, the UAW could not beat back an aggressive and well-funded opposition led by conservative lawmakers and lobbying groups. The plant's workers rejected the union.

We should not read too much into these recent defeats. To some extent, the public's disdain for "overpaid" government workers has to do with naturally tightfisted (but temporary) attitudes during a period of economic turmoil.[36] Likewise, the legislative victories of anti-union activists may say more about how much money today's pro-corporate movement is willing to pour into their cause, rather than any long-lasting groundswell of public opinion in their favor.

That said, current trends in public opinion cannot be very comforting for the labor movement. During the Great Depression and war years, unions were widely seen as champions of the underdog.[37] When the Gallup polling organization first asked about them, in 1936, only 20 percent of Americans disapproved of unions, while 72 percent approved. Aggressive strikes amid labor shortages gave even management a grudging respect for them—so much so that in the 1940s the president of the U.S. Chamber of Commerce could venture to say, "Labor unions are woven into our economic pattern of American life, and collective bargaining is a part of the democratic process."[38] A decade later, public approval of unions stood at record highs in both countries: 75 percent in America, and 69 percent in Canada.

Today, majorities continue to approve of unions, and surveys indicate that Americans and Canadians alike desire more representation at work than current union membership rates might imply.[39] Yet, in America at least, public approval has dropped significantly since the middle of the last century. The rate began to fall in the 1960s, recovered some of its lost ground around the turn of the century, and then collapsed dramatically in the years after the recession—when, for the first time, less than half of the country approved of unions.

Furthermore, the public's *disapproval* of unions has risen even more sharply than approval has fallen. This is because fewer people today, when polled, express "no opinion" of unions.[40] Since its peak in 2009, anti-union anger has simmered down, yet not enough to bring it back to its level just a decade ago. In Canada, comparable data doesn't exist for more recent years, but what is available paints a similar picture—indeed, approval rates in the two countries have largely moved in lockstep.[41]

As for my workers, a little less than half of them expressed ambivalent or hostile attitudes toward unions. The discontent was slightly higher in the United States, and much higher among the parts workers. To some extent, the fact that my workers were *former* autoworkers explains these harsh assessments. For my parts workers, the closure of their plants soured their views of the union. And losing their jobs during the worst economic crisis since the Great Depression added to a sense of bewilderment and fear that made them question institutions in general. Nevertheless, I did not expect to hear such intense discontent in my interviews. I found most of my workers with the help of the unions. If anything, I had expected them to be pro-union. Even more surprising, these men and women had recently been members of two of the most powerful labor organizations in North America, unions with proud histories of organizing and agitating on behalf of worker rights. Yet, a substantial number of them were skeptical about the very organizations that had won them years of good wages and benefits.

Earlier in the chapter I talked about how much of my workers' skepticism of unions was practical rather than ideological. A few of them pointed out that organized labor has a problem with corruption. They might not oppose unions in principle, but when they came across instances of blatant favoritism, it was hard to feel any loyalty to the cause. In this way, fraternal and self-serving pressures ruptured the union's egalitarian ideal. At the same time, other workers said the labor movement has too *little* power. They questioned whether, in today's economy, unions could continue to defend their interests given the steep declines in membership in both countries. If the views of my workers were likely colored by the fact that they were union members—or, contrarily, the fact that they lost their jobs during a severe downturn—in these areas they expressed attitudes not much different from those of the rest of the public. Majorities of Americans and Canadians have said that there is too much corruption in unions, and that unions are becoming weaker.[42]

Such assessments might imply that the problem is one of implementation. With honest leaders, unions could be governed better. With the right strategy, organized labor could claw back more power from corporations. However, my workers' criticisms sometimes went beyond a sober recognition of the weaknesses of today's labor movement. It was not just that unions are powerless, but that they are inefficient. It was not just that they happen to be corrupt, but that they—almost by definition—help the undeserving. Unlike the realism I discussed earlier, this perspective seemed to have less to do with the ups and downs of the market, and more to do with ideological conviction, or defensiveness, in the face of a dominant, anti-union narrative.

The public's focus on corruption is not surprising, given the long history of organized crime's dealings with organized labor—vividly dramatized in the late fifties by the McClellan Committee congressional hearings, with their endless procession of taciturn labor leaders invoking the Fifth Amendment. But the mafia organization most entangled in unions, Cosa Nostra, has seen its power wane from its peak in the sixties and seventies. Since the McClellan hearings, the U.S. government has monitored the activities of unions more closely and prosecuted corrupt leaders. And organized crime never had as strong a labor racketeering operation in Canada as it did in America.[43] So if there are modern-day concerns about union corruption, perhaps they have more to do with the kinds of minor-league corruption my workers experienced—episodes of union leaders looking out for themselves and their buddies.

Or, there may be deeper concerns at work. "Corruption" tends to be a catch-all term that people use to express any kind of disenchantment with public institutions. Meritocracy is the moral right; corruption is the moral wrong. This is the standard narrative of muckraking journalists: officials of a particular institution defy the law or bend the rules for the benefit of themselves and their friends.[44] As media scholar Jay Rosen observes, among news professionals the romantic image of the journalist is the "hard-boiled detective, ferreting out lies and corruption and moving on to the next town"—that is, not the pointy-headed commentator examining the workings of institutions and the sweep of social trends. In other words, the problem with focusing on corruption is that it distracts us from structural problems—problems with the system itself, rather than the people or groups who currently run it.[45] We root out the bad apples rather than tending to a sickly tree. In their criticisms of corporations, as I noted earlier, my American workers tended to adopt this narrower viewpoint, leveling their displeasure at corrupt business leaders rather than the larger structure of corporate power. In a similar vein (though a completely different domain), they would some-times complain about union "corruption," but what they were really talking about was the way their own values clashed with the union's egalitarian spirit.

When meritocratic morality is taken to its logical conclusion, it leads to a particular viewpoint: I'm a hard worker and responsible for my own success, so why do I need a union? Burak Oya, a Canadian and a former Ford employee, has a more colorful way of expressing this view. He believes that the union's egalitarian rules penalize hard workers. "If you and I are doing the same job, but I'm busting my ass and you're not, why are you and I going to make the same pay?" he says. "Union thinks everyone should be paid in accordance with their job description, but there's a lot of dog fuckers out there, and I don't want to carry their ass." By clinging to unfair seniority practices and inefficient work rules, unions contradict the meritocratic society's essential principle: that peo-ple should be judged on their effort and ability.

Some of my workers said that they didn't "need" the union because they were just good workers, the kind that management respected and retained. They saw their union membership purely in instrumental terms—help when you're in trouble—and since they were never in trou-ble, there was no point to it. Others maintained that the union was important but that they wanted a union of workers who "deserved" protection—not the reprobates and malingerers and lackeys who were currently free-riding on the backs of dedicated workers. "I'm not so sure if it is good to have a union all the time," says a Canadian former parts worker. "Because there's a lot of people that take advantage of it . . . and the union allows that." Unions these days are antiquated, he adds, because education is more widespread and important. "If you're hired by a company that has a well-educated management, I think you don't need a union." A few of the people I interviewed who had found new jobs shared these critical views of organized labor. Though she sup-ported the UAW, one (now white-collar) worker said, it drove her crazy that the union would defend those of her coworkers who missed work. "That was the only thing I didn't like about the union," she says. "It did protect the bad workers as well as the good workers."

Johnson Cheney, the former union steward, told me about how he had had to defend lousy, incorrigible workers—the "fuck-ups," as he calls them. It bothered him that he spent his time helping them instead of workers who did their jobs well. ("I've got to treat everybody the same, you know?") So did the fact that some workers managed to get plum assignments that paid more, even though they didn't put much effort into their jobs. "The harder you work, the less you make, right? And the less you do, the more you make," he says. Even for those who ascend into the lower ranks of the leadership, unions can be double-edged swords, cleaving an arbitrary line between favoritism and fairness.

Part of what bothers these workers, both Americans and Canadians, is the fundamental nature of the union—the fact that the union protects *everyone,* and not just those who "deserve" it. But in criticizing organized labor, they neglect a simple strategic reality: a union of the deserving isn't really a union.[46] There is a reason that unions operate mainly according to rules of seniority, and not job performance. Any cracks in solidarity mean that the union's only power—its power of numbers—will come crashing to the ground. Yet, under the meritocratic perspective, critics of the union often ignored or dismissed what their unions had accomplished, and instead focused their ire—narrowly—on fellow workers who had violated the moral code of the workplace. To this extent, they exhibited false consciousness.

This disdain for protecting the unworthy may explain part of the public's perception of unions as "corrupt." Helping the undeserving is favoritism in the eyes of meritocrats, but solidarity in the eyes of a union, whose very legitimacy and influence are derived from the sum of all its members. In other words, undeservingness is to egalitarianism as inequality is to meritocracy (or as favoritism is to fraternity, or as permissiveness is to grace)—an unavoidable price of doing business.

Another of my American workers, Laura Leistikow, says it was infuriating to witness the lackadaisical attitude of her coworkers at the Chrysler plant. "A lot of people would take that pay and benefits for granted by not wanting to do their job, or screwing around, not coming in on time, because they had that 'buddy-buddy' system going on in the union," she says. What's more, her coworkers "trashed" the plant, and the janitors (also unionized) cared nothing for the quality of their cleaning. The bathrooms in particular were filthy: "You walk in there and you almost want to have a hazmat suit." Once, she found a janitor asleep on the job. "I'm telling you, you can't know how many times I've almost called. But if you call the Health Department, then you're ratting on a union brother or sister." With brothers and sisters like these, it was hard to feel a sense of solidarity.

What made Laura's view particularly interesting was that she also had problems with her black coworkers. Asked whether there was favoritism in the union, Laura, who is white, volunteered an explanation. "Definitely! Black favoritism. I'm being totally honest." African Americans were a third of her plant's workforce and were represented high in the union's leadership. Several times she heard her coworkers make racial comments that convinced her she was not really a union sister in their eyes. What's more, the union members who were black were able to leave their posts on the engine line for stints of training, she claims. "I always had to stay on the line while everybody else, it seemed like, was moving."

It is difficult to build group solidarity in a multiracial setting—a hurdle that American unions in times past sought to sidestep by excluding (and even demonizing) nonwhites. Some research suggests that a diverse populace is less likely to support policies to assist the poor: the "undeserving" become all the more so when they have different-colored skin.[47] Race can twist notions of deservingness in the workplace as well, making it harder for workers to see the union as their champion—or, for that matter, to acknowledge their coworkers as true "brothers and sisters" worthy of help or cooperation.

. . .

The meritocratic ideology fed a particular narrative that explained the travails of today's labor movement. If unions are weak, some of my workers said, it is because they were once too strong. They overreached. They asked for too much, more than the market would allow. If this view is somewhat self-contradictory, it speaks again to the ability of human beings in general to be of two minds (or multiple minds) on the same topic.

Market logic leads to the view that unions are anachronisms in today's dynamic economy. The only reason that union members turn to labor power is that they can't get ahead on their individual merits. According to a detailed 1996 survey of public attitudes toward unions, majorities in both countries agree that the "wage demands of unions don't reflect economic reality" and that "unions enable workers to get away with being inefficient."[48] In other words, the criticism of unions is in part pragmatic—what they ask for does not "reflect economic reality"—and in part judgmental—they "get away" with doing less than they "should."

If the public truly believes that union members are overpaid, that view may be in part a reaction to the excesses of the old (and disappearing) "labor aristocracy" and their "gold-plated" contracts. Private-sector unions are virtually nonexistent in the United States, which means that UAW-level wages and benefits seem all the more ludicrous in comparison to those elsewhere. Based on this logic, Perry Lew, an American and ex-Chrysler employee, vehemently disapproves of the benefits that his former union won over the years. "It's messed up because our parents messed it up," he says. "It got too plush. You know, the Jobs Bank—what is that? There's no work, go home. . . . I'm paying you the same price, and you sitting in a break room watching movies, reading books, and playing cards?" As Perry sees it, the union's reckless persistence led to its downfall. And rightly so, because Big Labor failed to live within its means.

Even a few of my workers who call themselves staunch union supporters express misgivings that their unions did *too* good a job: winning wages and benefits that were ultimately unsustainable. Katherine Sergio, a Canadian, says she is fed up with the way certain corporate executives made out like bandits during the financial crisis. All the bank bailouts did, she says, "was line the executives' pockets." As for the auto industry, free trade "killed" it. And yet this self-described "union girl" also believes that organized labor bears some blame, too. "Unions put us in this predicament because of higher wages that are unreasonable," she says. "That [cost-of-living] percentage got put onto your wage before you even negotiated a new wage. Some companies were going up six bucks an hour." Katherine recognizes that the company needs to live within its means, labor costs included, if it's not to go bankrupt—like two out of the Big Three actually did. "You're not going to get retiree benefits anymore. We're all gonna have to pay for them, because companies that do have that turn out to be like GM." This is the way the market works, she points out. You have to be realistic.

As she continues talking, however, it's clear that Katherine is doing more than stating the new facts of life. Thanks to the economic crisis, the auto industry will never be the same, she says—and that may actually be a good thing. "There's not gonna be the twenty-one-dollar-an-hour job. We're gonna get back to reality and basics. We don't need the money for our boats and Ski-Doos. We need the money for our food and our homes and our utilities." Meanwhile, she empathizes with the company to some extent. "If anything, we probably owe the company because we robbed a lot of overtime hours out of them."

By calling for moderation, my workers are commenting on the modern-day limits of the union's ability to advocate for much higher wages. And yet their perspective is not just about realism. To some extent, it is also about ideology. They are falling in line with a specific, common-sense notion of what workers like them really deserve. It doesn't matter that a labor union's very reason for existing is to fight relentlessly for the best deal. By asking for too much, their unions violated the accepted moral standard of what workers like them merited in pay—the "natural" wage derived from the workings of the free market. In this way, a culture of meritocracy changes the moral calculus, shifting its focus from what decent wage employers should pay you and your coworkers, to whether you were "smart" enough to get enough education or experience to be valued in the labor market. Human capital replaces worker solidarity as the main, *moral* means of leverage in the workplace.

Ironically, though, the fact that they didn't just let the free market have its way is the very reason that these unions brought about egalitarian outcomes. For decades, they had successfully distorted the market in favor of higher wages for unskilled work, corroding the link the market forges between an educational credential and a job. The power of collective bargaining—and the threat of the strike weapon—in this way gave many ordinary workers access to the good life. And yet, to some extent, unions also allowed workers to be more inefficient, as the public widely believes.

It is important to understand that the choice of this one segment of experience to harp on—worker productivity and its effect on company profits and losses—is fundamentally ideological, too. I do not see the influence of ideology as necessarily a bad thing; it inevitably plays a role in any endeavor, for one thing, and in any case the structure of our economy should reflect the values we believe in. However, in this particular case the prevailing ideology promotes a narrow concept of efficiency that excludes other senses of the concept—for example, "efficient," or healthy, households and communities, ones that avoid falling into costly dysfunctions thanks to the stabilizing presence of employed people with good jobs.

If union disapproval was strong on both sides of the border, the other half of my workers followed large numbers of their fellow Americans and Canadians in supporting their unions. They pointed out the ways that unions could be a check on management's own penchant for abusing power. However, their defensiveness was, again, telling.

Even in a blue-collar city like Windsor, anti-union sentiments have trickled down so deeply that the public thinks today's autoworkers are "only getting what was coming to them." "We had so many people in the opinions column in the *Star* going, 'Haha! . . . It's about time you guys lose your thirty-two-dollar-an-hour jobs. Now you're really gonna know what the real world's like,'" says Liz Jung, a forty-six-year-old ex-Ford worker. The union never wished this kind of fate on the people now sniping at it, she points out; it wanted to pull all workers up, not push others down. For her part, Liz believes she and her coworkers earned every dollar that the union negotiated for them. "People always say, 'Well, you guys have it so easy, you make so much money,'" she says. "And [I'm] like, 'Yeah, come and play for a while and see how wonderful it is.'" Despite the union's ardent objections, people in the community continue to bash autoworkers, blaming them for the region's economic woes, and it is hard to ignore the critical chorus, Liz says. "When you have a city beating up their own, I think that's where the guilt comes from. Because you're always defending yourself."

"Even though it's a union town, it's not a union town anymore," says Ziggy Dordick, another former Ford worker. These days, Ziggy tries to steer clear of conversations about politics with acquaintances or even family, because inevitably they will start fulminating against unions. They work nice office jobs; they think union members are lazy and uneducated. "They've been lucky or whatever it is," says Ziggy, forty. "But at some point, they're going to feel the same thing." It bothers him that white-collar professionals want job security, too, but just don't want to give it to the "little guy." "If we didn't have unions, what would we have? We'd all have to have lawyers?"

James Channing, the unemployed parts worker, is separated from his wife and struggling financially after a year without work. He says being unemployed makes him ashamed. Yet he doesn't believe that good wages should go only to the well-educated. A former CAW member, he insists he is not "a big-time union supporter," but he thinks that the wages unions have won are fair. If the workers had not been organized, he says, it would have been "hell" at his feeder plant, because an unchecked management would have gone wild. "People talk about autoworkers like we were a bunch of greedy pricks. Like union people killed everything. Meanwhile, if it wasn't for unions, it would just be turnover—you know, 'You're fired. You're fired. You're fuckin' fired. Get out of here.'"

Though his factory job is long behind him, James Channing still bristles at the public's judgment of union members. "When we were in negotiations for contracts, if they couldn't afford to give us that money, they wouldn't have gave it to us. So now people are saying, 'Well, you know, you made too much money.' Well, what do you mean? What is too much money? You want everybody in Canada to make $8.50 an hour? Everybody's gotta make minimum wage? That's not right."

Even those workers who were critical of unions did not want minimum-wage jobs, of course. Like everyone else, they wanted decent jobs with decent pay. But their pragmatism and the broader meritocratic ideology made many of them question their unions. Among the half who were critical, some felt that less educated workers did not deserve the flush contracts their leaders had negotiated. Some felt that the union rewarded the undeserving. Almost all of them pointed out that times had changed—and unions, wrongly, had chosen not to change with them.

. . .

The attitude that unions let workers "get away with" bad behavior has consequences, in turn, for organizing. The battle over popular opinion that unfolds with every strike action becomes harder to fight if the public views union members as privileged "haves," their wage demands as unfair, and their very status as members of the middle class—attained through bargaining, not education—as undeserved.[49] Indeed, as they described how today's unions are too well-fed and contented for their own good, a few of my workers explicitly compared their union's rousing past with its more picayune present—which suggests they don't have a problem with unions per se, just with the lavishly appointed ones they happened to join. A century ago, when the UAW was waging bloody strikes to win recognition and living wages, there was an idealism and purpose to the struggle, they say. It is not just that earlier generations had it tougher in the plants; it is also that they were out there striking in droves, crowding the picket lines, scuffling with the police and Pinkerton detectives. "People died for our benefits," says Laura Leistikow, the American ex-Chrysler worker. "They actually laid their lives on the line to give us the privileges that we had." When autoworkers like her look back at those storied days, today's labor struggle seems bureaucratic and pedestrian in comparison, the benefits of union membership less clear, the dues subtracted from each paycheck more loathsome.

The generation that fights the good fight develops a devotion to its cause through the baptism of political struggle. Later generations find it harder to keep that faith.[50] "There's no real, 'One for all, and all for one,' anymore," Laura says. "It's part of that buddy-buddy system now that doesn't work for everybody, it just works for certain people." The UAW's long string of successful contracts over the decades may have come at the price of complacency and internal divisions, along with the loss of the underdog status that once won it widespread public sympathy. Without shared experiences of struggle and community, it is harder for workers to maintain an ethic of egalitarianism, and it is easier to dismiss the labor movement as irrelevant to their lives.

If unions continue to vanish, perhaps the public will eventually come to miss them. Any past of perceived excess will recede from the public consciousness. How much workers value unions may grow in response. Right now, though, public opinion polls give us little reason to believe this will happen any time soon.[51] Even as union membership in both countries continues to fall, large numbers of Americans and Canadians express the view that Big Labor remains too big. In 2011, six out of ten Canadians agreed that unions had too much power. That same year, four in ten Americans believed the same—a startling number, considering that today only one in ten American workers is unionized.[52] While the labor movement remains stronger in Canada, since the nineties even unions there have seen large membership declines. Meanwhile, Canada's networks of progressive advocacy organizations and think tanks have suffered from cuts in government funding. As a result, even up north there are fewer prominent voices making the case for collective solutions to society's problems.[53]

In fact, an alternative view is that organized labor's declining power does not make unions more enticing, but simply digs a deeper hole. After all, if UAW members in earlier times were truly principled, steadfast adherents of the egalitarian faith, a strong union organization helped make them so. The labor movement heralded norms of equity throughout the industrial and political realms, altering policies and also culture. It gave ordinary workers dignity and decent livelihoods, as well as opportunities to be leaders and agents of historical change. It is striking that in the late 1930s, a time of growing labor militancy, there was a stronger relation between the objective circumstances that the unemployed experienced and their expressed political attitudes. Engaged unions may have provided the institutional means to channel disparate frustrations into concrete political views and on-the-ground mobilization. But today's labor movement is bleeding membership. As its clout continues to weaken, so too does its ability to engage the imagination of broad segments of the workforce. In this climate, unions find it harder to foster solidarity among their members and also among the broader public. That cannot bode well for their popularity or membership rolls into the future.[54]

For their part, many of my workers—critics and supporters of the union alike—responded to the hostility of the surrounding culture by hunkering down. In this they were not unlike the black job seekers that sociologist Sandra Smith studied in poor Chicago neighborhoods, who avoided reaching out to family and friends for help.[55] What Smith calls "defensive individualism" is a survival strategy, a way to maintain pride and manage expectations in the face of daunting odds. But for Smith's workers as well as mine, this method of coping is tragically flawed. It means that some workers lose their faith in government or union solutions. It means that others ignore the structural barriers to their success and direct the blame for their long-term unemployment at themselves. The irony is that these are some of the workers who should be the most upset by the structure of today's economy. As the great transformation of our economy and culture has progressed, they have fallen farther than most.

THE CULTURAL CONTRADICTIONS OF SELF-RELIANCE

My research draws mainly from interviews and observations during the recession, and therefore it cannot make any strong claims about any historical change. The patterns I observe can only be suggestive and must be tested further. As I have described in this chapter, a mixed picture arises from the limited survey data now available. The international surveys find a strong (and realistic) sense that education matters in the labor market, in America especially. They describe some concern in both countries about inequality, though it is still below its peak levels—a somewhat curious finding given the spectacular rise in the top 1 percent's income and wealth in recent years. And they reveal the public's ambivalence about labor unions, in spite of the drastic deterioration of the U.S. labor movement in particular. That said, these various surveys do not fully capture the shifting cultural understandings of merit that are key to my argument about change over time. More exhaustive analysis of the available survey data and historical records is needed.

Being unemployed during the Great Recession clearly made my workers more cynical about government and unions in special ways.

But they also understood that these institutions faced considerable challenges in a market economy that relentlessly cuts costs. Their personal experiences, too, reinforced a perspective of hardheaded realism. They were desperate for help, but many of them—especially the Americans—found little support from tottering unions or starved bureaucracies. Even though their social safety net and unions have also grown weaker in recent years, my Canadians' peer-staffed action centers improved to some extent their encounters with government and unions.

A rational appraisal of their situation led my workers toward self-reliance and away from the collective strategies of government and unions—pushing them a few steps in the direction of Newman's white-collar managers of old, and Lane's tech workers of today. Rather than relying on government or unions, they emphasized how their own courage and determination would get them out of the hole that the loss of their jobs had pitched them into. In today's labor market, a stunted meritocracy purged of labor unions and activist government policies, this course of action makes much sense. Clearly, over the past several decades the dominant institutions have changed in pivotal ways. Ordinary workers have lost the protections that once established sheltered (if sometimes sluggish) markets, and the social norms that once encouraged sheltering (if sometimes oppressive) families. The pro-corporate movement has gained in strength. Countervailing institutions—not just unions and governments, but also political party machines and church-led social movements—have seen their influence wane. With them has gone the ability to offer alternative visions of the economy and society.

With resignation, workers like mine recognize that corporations have the upper hand, and there is not much to be done about it. As management has gained power at the expense of labor, and as offshoring and automation have ramped up, they no longer have much faith in organized labor's ability to prevail at the negotiating table in any sustainable way. They come to the conclusion that they, and unions, can no longer ask for much. Instead, they have to sink or swim on their individual merit, a merit captured in the résumés that measure their accumulated experiences and skills—or lack thereof. Faced with systemic problems, they look, either falsely or just fatalistically, to individual solutions.

While past research has looked at how, for example, social networks and race shape views about opportunity, in this chapter I have focused on another, less studied domain: the effects of personal interactions with formal institutions of government, unions, and corporations.[56] Policymakers tend to look at these institutions from a bird's-eye view. I showed how they are experienced on the ground, from the point of view of the unemployed. This kind of approach focuses our attention on an important but neglected policy dimension: implementation. In addition to benefit levels, we need to consider how well-meaning government policies are actually implemented. In addition to membership numbers, we need to look at how well-intentioned unions are actually organized. More broadly, the strategy that leaders adopt in response to economic and political trends also matters. In the face of globalization and automation and a powerful pro-corporate movement, the U.S. government long ago decided to turn away from robust interventions meant to bring about full employment, redistribution, and income security. In more recent decades, the Canadian welfare state has retreated as well. These high-level decisions have, among other things, impoverished and diminished the institutions encountered by ordinary workers.

At the same time, the broader culture of judgment acts to worsen the situation of ordinary workers. From the perspective of meritocratic morality, success in the labor market depends on acquiring skills and education, not on winning "undeserved" high wages through "unnatural" collective bargaining. When taken to an extreme, meritocratic morality conceals the collective nature of the problem of inequality and weakens the very institutions that could do something about it. To the extent that they adopt it, workers do not stop to consider whether organized labor's willingness to ask only what it "deserves" entrenches inequality. What they lack, in other words, is a sociological understanding to go along with the economic mindset: an awareness of how our culture's prevailing attitudes shape our expectations about what is the "right" wage—and what is the "right" way to get it. Nowadays, as waves of outsourcing start to threaten jobs at Silicon Valley tech firms, hospital radiology departments, and corporate law firms, this go-it-alone strategy is becoming questionable even for those elite workers at the very top of our stunted meritocracy. But that is the implicit consequence of an absolutist ideology of individualism: the right to rise, yes, but also the right to fall.

I must emphasize that a significant gap remains between the views of workers like mine and those of elite workers and conservative activists. My left-of-center union members did not attack government dependency and did attack corporate malfeasance. They did not necessarily internalize the meritocratic viewpoint. But ideological criticisms trumpeted by the media and the people around them put my workers on the defensive and (as I will discuss further in the next chapter) overwhelmed their sense of worth. While my Americans and Canadians alike generally supported government intervention in the economy, they were ashamed about receiving benefits and sensitive to the critiques of government largesse. The Canadians expressed more concern about growing inequality and corporate power, while the Americans, if also quite critical of corporate executives, tended to focus in a meritocratic fashion on management's poor decisions. Both, however, recognized that the economic vitality of corporations was important to their own well-being. Meanwhile, though a good number of my Americans and Canadians believed that the labor movement faces daunting, even overwhelming, odds, some of their skepticism was more pointedly ideological, revolving around their sense that their union brothers and sisters were undeserving, and that their own unions had overreached.

To the extent that my workers attacked the guiding philosophy of unions, rather than just acknowledging their weaknesses and foibles, and spurned the possibility of collective action, rather than recognizing their common interests, false consciousness exerted its influence on them. That said, it is difficult to disentangle true adherence to the meritocratic perspective from simply a sensible assessment of the weakness of particular institutions. Their realism was particularly striking among my workers, especially the Canadians, but to some extent what factor is dominant—experience or ideology, realism or morality—is also in the eye of the beholder. And that is the point: both realism and ideology are at work here, interacting with each other in a feedback loop. Their real-world experience and knowledge convince workers that institutions are powerless or inadequate to their needs, and that they are better off on their own. In this way, the failures of government and unions push unemployed workers toward a disenchantment and self-reliance that fits well with the meritocratic ideology. That ideology, in turn, instills a market logic that channels their frustrations toward one set of the possible responses to institutional failure—that is, an individualistic approach of self-blame, skepticism of unions, and rationalization of the actions of corporations. These two mechanisms build upon each other, in an interactive and iterative process.

In this sense, the recent decline of unions and retrenchment of government present us with a vicious circle. A weak infrastructure of institutions leads to alienating personal encounters at union locals, state job centers, and other key bureaucratic contact points. These negative experiences lead to disenchantment and hostility toward government and unions, helping to support a reactionary politics that defunds and weakens those institutions further.

The meritocratic perspective, in turn, makes any opposing political force harder to sustain by sowing divisions within the broader society. Amid the attacks on the "undeserving" recipients of redistribution, the public looks not with sympathy, but with schadenfreude, on the plight of unionized workers, those once-favored sons and daughters now being laid off in droves. They are suffering, but their suffering is deserved because they received pay that was too high given their education. Meritocratic morality places the burden of responsibility squarely on the individual. With its perspective narrowed so, the public fixates on how government and unions stand in the way of liberty. With its ire directed at a dissolute and parasitic underclass, it has less enthusiasm for having public funds go toward building a stronger social safety net, much less intervening directly to create jobs for the jobless. It dwells on the moral decay of the "dispossessed" masses—the cable TV subscriptions and out-of-wedlock children of this or that poor family, the credit card debts and high school educations of this or that laid-off factory worker— but not, as Daniel Bell noted, on the "calculated chicanery" of groups of political and economic elites.[57] In this way, meritocratic morality deflects anger downwards, toward those least able to bear it—and away from the man behind the curtain.

. . .

When he started working at the plating plant in the late nineties, the first thing that Sarmad Dakka noticed was the stench. The carbon that filtered the liquid nickel filled the factory air, a dark cloud of dust. When he sneezed, black soot would come out of his nose. He had a mask, but it barely helped. After he had been there a while, his sense of smell and taste disappeared.

At the time, he lived with his parents, immigrants from the Middle East who had come to Canada to escape war. One day he found his mother crying in the laundry room. "Mom, what the heck is wrong with you?" he asked.

"I see what you go through," she replied, gazing at his dust-stained shirt, pants, and socks. "I feel so bad for you."

"Mom, it's not that bad of a job."

But it was, Sarmad admits. The plant was filthy. His friends asked him why he did it. It was the best option he had had after dropping out of college. Burdened with student loans, he signed up with a temp agency and got a job at the plant. It was just a ninety-day assignment, with the expectation of being rotated out, but one day he buttonholed his manager and begged for a real job. "I had my back to the wall," Sarmad notes. "I'll never forget how badly I wanted to have that job there. That's something I won't forget, that they let me work there."

He pauses. "Maybe they weren't doing me a favor, though."

Thirty-one, Sarmad has a boyish charm about him, expressed effortlessly in his easy smile, bright eyes, and smooth way of speaking. At the plant his people skills landed him a position as a union steward. He enjoyed the job, but the troublemakers he had to deal with every week—his feckless coworkers—wore down his nerves. "Nine out of ten times I was dealing with the same six or seven employees," he says. It made him wonder whether unions were doing right by their members. "A lot of times they're just defending the losers, the bums, the vagrants—the people that didn't deserve a job, the people that didn't need to be defended, the people that didn't appreciate it," he says. "A good employee that did what he was told was the minority, and in the meantime they could bypass him, or use him." It felt at times that the union was "helping the wrong people," he says.

When the company announced that the plant was closing, most of the workers were upset but went on with their work. A few of them, however, took their anger a big step further. "Some of the crazies vandalized things and smeared feces on the bathroom wall," Sarmad says. Workers sabotaged the line, trashed the union office, and stole curtains, files, even a modem. Sarmad was angry, too, but the vandalism was beyond stupid, he says. "They thought that this was a decision that a manager made. . . . It's completely out of his hands. It was the economy."

After he lost his job, Sarmad went to the local job center to talk to a career counselor. "They're overwhelmed," he says. "I think I talked with her for seventeen minutes, and she had forty-three messages waiting for her in those seventeen minutes." Sarmad wanted to pursue a one-year training program for border security officers, but the counselor kept insisting he consider woodworking or welding. She was perfectly nice, Sarmad adds, but "she just saw a blue-collar guy sittin' in front of her."

He ended up enrolling anyway. What's allowed him to go back to school, he says, is a federal pilot program that has extended his unemployment benefits until the end of his course of study. It's made a huge difference for him and his wife Carolyn, who can't support them by herself with her income as a hair stylist. While he's grateful for the help,

Sarmad wonders how many other people who could have used this benefit didn't know or didn't bother. There was only a short window in which to apply, and the program wasn't well-advertised, he points out. Self-reliance, self-initiative, and luck made all the difference here. Maybe the government didn't want the program to get overwhelmed, he says, but still, it makes no sense that a rich country like Canada can't do more to help its own. "In writing it looks great, but how many people did you really help?"

Although being back in school helps his mood, Sarmad deals with depression from time to time. "I'm still a young guy," he says. "There's still a lot of things I wanna see in the world and none of these things are available to me now because I'm not employed." Sarmad has what he needs—their financial situation is stable right now, he points out—and yet he doesn't have what he wants: the trappings of middle-class propriety, the level of affluence and opportunity whose bar rises with every generation. He thinks about the days when he and Carolyn could travel: Mexico, the Dominican Republic, Las Vegas. "It's nice to be together, to experience things together as husband and wife," he says.

He looks back on his decision to drop out of college with regret. When he was eighteen, he wasn't mature enough to realize how important his education was, he says. And it's not enough these days just to have a good work ethic. Yes, working hard in school pays off, he says. "But simply being a hard-working line operator? No, that will just leave you as a line operator."

CHAPTER 6

Loser

The Failures of the American Dream

It belongs to human nature to hate those you have injured.

—Tacitus, *Agricola*

This world is what you make of it. That is what Art Moreno learned, working in the sweltering pit of a Ford foundry decades ago, slogging through overtime shifts and heading into the plant even on his off days. Never missing a day of work. Born in Tennessee, Art had come to Detroit and built a life for his family of seven. The recession of the eighties dulled the sheen of Art's American dream, but just temporarily: when the plants were shuttered, Art found a job driving a truck. He didn't look back.

His oldest daughter followed him into the factories. At first, Art did not want Tamar, a petite, seemingly dainty girl with long manicured fingernails, to step into a car plant. But he hadn't wanted her to play basketball either, which she did in high school, having jostled and juked her way onto the West Side courts alongside her brothers. When she started a job at Chrysler in the nineties, Art relented, but with a word of caution. "Tamar, don't miss no time," he told her. "Do what you're supposed to do."

Over sixteen years in the plants, Tamar had perfect attendance. "That's what this man instilled in me," she says. Routinely, she put in sixty, seventy hours a week. The daughter of an autoworker, she wasn't rattled by the taunts and cockiness to be endured in a factory fueled by testosterone. "Once you shoot somebody down, they'll leave you alone." Some women, she adds, came into the plant with a clinging attitude, expecting their male colleagues to do their work. "I didn't

196

expect nobody to do mine," Tamar says. "That guy ain't going to take my paycheck."

One day at the plant, Tamar was shutting down a machine when a coworker asked her if she was working that weekend. Tamar turned to answer when she slipped in a pool of coolant. Her knee slammed down; she heard the insides pop like a rubber band. At the hospital, they diagnosed her with a torn meniscus.

She was still on crutches and taking Vicodin for the pain when her supervisor insisted that she return to work—not even to do her job, but to sit in the locker room. Tamar decided that was ludicrous; she would rather go back to the factory floor and work through the pain. She was upset by how she was treated, by the company but also the union. "If you wasn't in their little clique," she says, they didn't help you. When she objected to being forced to work, the union told her Chrysler was within its rights. "What do I need you for?" Tamar asked, bitterly. "You're not even going to fight?"

Other than this issue with her medical leave, though, Tamar never had reason to complain about management. The way she saw it, workers like her didn't need the union. She had won the trust of her supervisors through her ironclad work ethic. If she had a doctor's appointment, or her teenage son Tony had a basketball game, her supervisor would let her leave early. Sure, line workers and supervisors sometimes clashed, but Tamar had sympathy for middle management. "You've got to realize that it's not them—it's coming from somewhere else," she says. "They just do what they're told to do."

Her stellar work record bore other blessings when Tamar found herself preoccupied with family matters. Her father, Art, then in his seventies, was in the early stages of Alzheimer's disease. Tamar moved into his home to take care of him. One morning, Tamar was at the stove making pancakes while her father and son were watching TV. Suddenly, Art stood up, buckled, and keeled over. Tamar called 911. An ambulance rushed him to the hospital. "He's having a stroke," the EMT told her.

Art never fully recovered. Several months later, he developed a blood infection. And shortly after that, Tamar remembers walking into a manicurist shop after her shift and getting the phone call. "I knew," she says.

Tamar still gets worked up over how the union acted after her father died. Typically, they take up a collection and send flowers. In the case of Tamar—an outsider to the union's "clique"—that didn't happen. Tamar had harsh words with the local president. "I didn't even care about the collection," she says. "I cared about the flowers." The next day, a house plant appeared at her front door.

Amid all the anxiety and grief of that year, at least Tamar didn't have to worry about any problems with management. "When you have good attendance and something like that comes along, you don't have a problem," Tamar notes. This younger generation of plant workers, she adds, doesn't realize the consequences of skipping work and not playing by the rules.

She is quick to contrast her own diligence with the lack of it she sees in her ex-husband, Victor. He had always been somewhat of a shady character, from the time of their first meeting. Smitten after spotting her driving by, he followed her so closely that Tamar pulled over. After she rebuffed him, he followed her to a club. "See, it was meant for us to talk," he said coyly when he "bumped" into her there. Her friends were leery, but Tamar started dating him.

If only she had listened to them. By the time Tamar got the job at Chrysler, she knew well that her husband was, in her words, "lazy." It wasn't that Victor was a complete loser: he was a manager at a box store. But he seemed to think that a father's job description didn't include changing diapers. He refused to pick up Tony from the babysitter. "You just write down stuff," Tamar groused. "You ain't tired." Eventually, Tamar decided she could do better on her own.

Yet all her hard work did not insulate Tamar from the turmoil in the auto industry. After Tamar was laid off indefinitely—with no return date penciled in—she decided to take a buyout.

She had assiduously put away money over the years, so that nest egg plus her buyout money turned out to be more than enough. In fact, Tamar ended up buying a new home shortly after her layoff. "That tells you something right there," she says.

"If you plan it right, you can do things right," Tamar stresses. She compares herself to other Chrysler workers who squandered their buyout money. "They didn't pay their house off, they didn't pay their cars off, and that is awful." Her coworkers were using the cash to go shopping, she says, or trading it in for casino chips.

It is not that Tamar is indifferent to the suffering of people down on their luck. Her father spent his weekends fixing cars, mowing lawns, and cooking up barrels full of barbeque for people in the neighborhood. Her grandmother says that Tamar has a "big heart," too. It is just that Tamar expects people to earn that generosity. She will give a meal and hot chocolate—never cash—to a homeless person. "I've had one man say, 'I don't want no food,'" she says. "So, that meant he was going to take my money and go buy something wrong."

As Tamar sees it, she worked hard and saved up and did things the right way, and that is why she is dealing with this extended period of joblessness just fine. Others were tempted and failed the test. They are rightfully suffering the consequences. "The casinos ain't no help," Tamar says—but ultimately, the blame rests with the individual. "You put yourself in that spot sometimes." Her advice to her former coworkers who are "addicted" to gambling and shopping and other spendthrift ways is simple: "Quit. You've got to think about what you're doing."

As for the unemployed, they could get a job if they really wanted one. Whenever she and her son have headed out to buy him the newest pair of Air Jordans, the mall has always been packed. "If there's no money, then why is everybody shopping?" Tamar asks. "I keep hearing, 'There's no jobs out there,' but everywhere you look it says, 'Now hiring.'"

People can always find something to do, she adds. "You just might not be able to do what you want to do, but you can still get a job."

. . .

In her own life, Tamar Moreno holds fast to a personal code of virtue that would be familiar and admirable to many people. She, and her father before her, put this faith in its plainest terms. *You can do what you want to do. Plan and do things right. Make your own way.* This is the essence of the American Dream: the notion that through hard work all Americans have a decent shot at achieving success. Those who persevere can achieve any ambition: from the simple pleasure of a home of one's own, to the adulation of peers, to the wealth of enterprise—all markers of the individual's superior character.

The American Dream and its belief in rugged individualism have been with us for a long time, of course. But today we may be seeing a different, less egalitarian understanding of its tenets take root. As the economy and culture have evolved, the definition of "merit" has broadened, an expansion that Richard Sennett and Jonathan Cobb described decades ago—and yet has further grown and intensified, I argued earlier in this book, in the years since then. Today hard work still matters, but the experiences of my workers in the labor market suggest that other criteria increasingly matter, too—from cognitive ability to social skills, from having self-initiative to being a team player. As the determinants of what Sennett and Cobb called "badges of ability" have multiplied, the alternative "badges of dignity" that working men and women once

boasted—their strength and stamina amid grueling work on the line—
have become tarnished.[1]

As I discussed in the last chapter, the meritocratic ideology affected
my workers to an extent that I found surprising. These were the kinds of
workers who should have been the *most* resistant to its intense individualism: unionized autoworkers who throughout much of the modern
labor movement's history have been part of the cavalry leading the collective charge. But as their job searches dragged on, my workers nonetheless struggled against the sense, cultivated by politicians and coworkers alike, that they were to blame for their prolonged unemployment. A
broader ideology of meritocracy reinforced the individualistic perspective that failed institutions had already pushed my workers to adopt. It
led to a virulent self-blame for some, even as it forced others to defend
themselves, with varying degrees of success, against its cutting criticisms.

NOT A GOOD WAY TO BE

At Ford, Tom Moon used to scare away partners on the line with his
uncompromising work ethic, he says. "I figured I was there, I was getting paid $30 an hour—I'll do my job." His coworkers, he adds, did not
want to work hard. "Then they'd fight because they don't wanna be my
partner." He laughs. A lot of good that hard work has done him: no
steady work, on welfare, a house on the verge of repossession. "What's
it got me? It's got me to a point where I don't know where my next thing
is coming from. I have no faith in the harder you work, the better it's
gonna be for you. That's horse manure."

Without anyone or anything to rely on, Tom trains his energies on his
pet schemes to get extra, under-the-table cash and stay one step ahead
of the bill collectors. Anything else is a daydream. "When a thousand
people band together it makes a difference, but just by myself, no. . . .
They're gonna tell me what to do anyhow, so let's go along with it.
Don't make waves." But Tom's skepticism of institutions brings him
again and again back to his personal initiative—and his personal failure
to seize that initiative. He complains about the unfairness of it all. He
tries to tell himself that he's a hard worker, that the reason he can't get
a job is just because he's too old, not because he's no good. But at the
end of the day, when he's alone with his thoughts in the home he's about
to lose, he is the one he rips into. "I should be able to find employment," he says. The self-doubt is crushing. "I couldn't even get a fucking job at a worm farm."

After applying for hundreds of jobs and never finding anything that lasted, Tom Moon is becoming resigned to his circumstances. "I'm willing to work as hard as I need to, but now . . . I don't really give a shit," he says. "You can only beat your head over it so many times." When he was laid off, at first Tom kept telling himself that he was going to get another job. Soon. Eventually. Someday. But now, he no longer bothers trying to convince himself. "I know I'm not gonna get a job," he says flatly. The brief stints of work he's managed to get so far have meant dealing with the bureaucratic hassle of getting off welfare and back on it after the job ended. Better just to stay in the system and coast—to anywhere, or perhaps nowhere. "I'm just getting to the point where I'm just willing to accept what they're gonna give me and that's it," Tom says. "I'm gonna sit down for the rest of my life and I'm not working."

He pauses. "It's not a good way to be."

. . .

Tom Moon exemplifies some of the seemingly contradictory aspects of the self-blame that afflicts the long-term unemployed. First, Tom does not believe he is lazy. He has always had a strong work ethic, he says. His inability to advance has made him question the idea that hard work leads to success. At the same time, he doesn't bother much with any critique of the system. In fact, now that his unemployment has extended into years, he directs the blame squarely at himself. It's not about his lack of effort per se. It's about being a failure in the face of all the requirements that the labor market now demands of anyone who wants a good job.

Of course, jobless workers have long been the target of blame, from others and from themselves. For centuries societies have divided the poor into camps of "deserving" and "undeserving," a practice that the historian Michael Katz argues has served to legitimize the market economy and deflect popular discontent. In earlier times, being a virtuous and valued member of society had more to do with social and spiritual propriety—your adherence to the accepted rules regarding diligence, sexual behavior, honesty, violence, religious ritual, and other conduct relevant to your class or clan. But in the labor market, what mattered for ordinary workers was hard work.[2]

We can still come across this emphasis on effort alone in some circles today. Rich Boyer, the former president of the UAW local that represented Chrysler's Detroit Axle Plant (now closed), likens autoworkers to professional athletes. "They get paid because their bodies are beat down for the service they provide," says Boyer, a burly Mexican American man with a mustache and gray-streaked, greased black hair, who worked his way up from the plant floor to a post in the union's leadership. "Well, these folks provide a similar service, and their bodies are beat down at the end of the day. And if you say because I've got an education, I deserve more money, how bad is your body going to be sitting behind a desk for thirty years as opposed to you jumping in and out of a vehicle for thirty years?" In this view, college-educated white-collar workers are no more hard-working, and therefore no more worthy, than those toiling on the assembly lines.

The key difference between professional athletes and factory workers, of course, is that these athletes have reached the top of their sport. Their high skill level is clear. Factory workers have difficulty making the same argument. If before they could point to the backbreaking work they did on the assembly line to justify their high wages, nowadays they lack the skills that really matter to employers. On the other hand, the public and the markets alike venerate the celebrity pantheon of musicians, actors, and artists, who are not begrudged their phenomenal wealth because they presumably have the talent to match it.[3] Even corporate executives can lay a claim—one with a patina of moral justification—to generous compensation packages. It's not just because they work hard, they insist. It's also because of the rare leadership abilities they bring to their positions.

This suggests that the American Dream has been updated. As I described in chapter 2, the stunted meritocracy increasingly demands more in exchange for its good jobs. In the white-collar world in particular, this means both quantifiable competencies and nuanced people skills that convey the individual's wealth of human and cultural capital. While the situation is not as extreme for them, even workers in the lower tiers of today's labor market face greater expectations. Educational credentials are key markers of skills that prove them to be persons of worth. In turn, they are responsible for how much education they get, which is a function of not just how hard they work but also whether they have the initiative and savvy to pursue and complete further education.

The path up the mountain remains open to all because merit can—in theory—be attained by persevering in school or other forms of self-improvement. To the extent that it exists in the modern marketplace, then, moral virtue is less about social propriety and more about the excellence described by the Greek term *aretē*—being the best in some measurable quality of material, social, or professional achievement, from the excellence of intelligence, to beauty, to coolness. Mediocrity, the market's cardinal sin, leads to guilt. Here we see the modern-day culmination of philosopher Jean-Jacques Rousseau's concept of *amour-propre,* our prideful self-love: a society of ever-greater size and anonymity pushes individuals, in their search for personal dignity, to endlessly compare themselves with others—and thus endlessly fixate on their failings—to an extent that, Rousseau suggested, men and women in their natural state of grace did not know.[4]

The evolving definition of merit can put workers like mine at a disadvantage and debase their self-worth. If we compare factory workers who toil long hours at the plant and law students who toil long hours in the library, it is clear that both groups "work hard." But one group is limited to doing "grunt work" on an assembly line, while the other has both the capacity and drive to do intellectually demanding labor—work that, in B-school speak, "adds value." One group was paid more than they were "worth," while the other took out loans and "sacrificed" for their education—even though that brief sacrifice is more than made up for by lifetime earnings that far outpace those of factory workers.

From the meritocratic perspective, a few of my workers went so far as to see the economic crisis that devastated the industry and unions alike as a necessary corrective, a flood to wash away a world of economic sin. "You get a lot of low-life people working in there," says Laura Leistikow, an American, about her old Chrysler plant. "They don't care. They're there for one thing, for the money. They could give a shit if they do a good job." It infuriated her to see coworkers shirk their responsibilities. "Here I am, a conscientious worker . . . and these people are sleeping. Or they're bitching because they have to do a job." In her view, the auto industry's collapse may have been a good thing: cosmic retribution landing on the heads of coddled workers. "They're finding out now what it's like to be in the real world," she gloats.

When taken up with such fervor, the meritocratic ideology saps the ability to empathize with those who are suffering: these people "deserved" what happened to them.[5] With this moralizing view, coworkers, spouses, children, and friends faulted some of my workers for their long-term spells of unemployment. They really weren't trying hard enough, the criticism went. They had been foolish to drop out of school. They should have shored up their finances and employment records before the storm struck. The tendency is for the fortunate to think that what works for them will necessarily work for everyone else. *I was able to get an education, so you can, too. I saved up, so you should have, too.*

As I've discussed, today's labor market is generally more accepting of diversity—across race, gender, sexual orientation, and so on—than was the case in past generations. Such tolerance speaks to our progress as a society. But our condemnation of other people continues—perhaps in an even more concentrated form. The evaluation of intelligence and skill remains an appropriate basis for criticism, and that criticism is widespread and unrelenting, visible everywhere from high-stakes testing for high school students to the anonymous incivility of the Internet town square, where the terms *loser* and *fail* have become choice epithets in a culture intolerant of failure. For the long-term unemployed, this censure takes on a particular form: If you can't retrain, you deserve the punishment to come. The path was there, but you refused it. Unemployment and poverty are your just deserts.

And yet, as their time without a job lengthened, it became harder for my workers to pull themselves out of this state of transgression, in part because they faced the negative judgment of another important group: employers. Whenever they throw their résumés into the ring, the long-term unemployed routinely suffer discrimination. As research shows, firms are likely to favor a job candidate with *no* relevant experience over one with experience if the green candidate has been out of work for only a short time. In a culture that reviles personal inadequacy, it is no surprise that these workers—discarded, disdained, and damaged by their unemployment—can find no one willing to give them a chance.[6]

THE MISTAKES I MADE

In his teenage years, Gary Jansen, the son of a Chrome Craft worker, ran through a pointless gauntlet of low-wage jobs before his dad took him aside and asked him if he wanted a job at the plant. It was a dingy, rickety building, with the stench of chemicals in the air, rust falling from the ceiling, holes everywhere—when it rained outside, it rained inside. But Gary was just eighteen, and the alternative was just another $6-an-hour fast-food job. There was no arguing with that UAW wage.

Gary's dad retired early. His father had nearly three decades at the plant before it beat him down. Gary had been working there just two months when his glove got caught in one of the machines and an industrial-sized chain ripped the ends off three of his fingers. The tips were reattached, but a decade later they remain misshapen and painfully sensitive. Gary can't stay outside on a wintry day for more than five minutes before the burning is too intense to bear.

Even after the accident, Gary stuck with the job. It was just too hard to give up those wages.

Now the plant is closed. Eight months have gone by, but Gary is still figuring out how to cope. He started his job search confident that he would land something. A hundred failed applications later, Gary now applies for "everything—anything."

He disparages himself for never finishing high school. As a kid, he thought fun and independence were more important than a diploma. He worked long hours delivering pizzas, until he had to drop out. "I had to sacrifice my good grades for better paychecks," he says, ruefully. Gary wanted to make up his last few credits at night, but his manager demanded that he work every evening. He eventually quit the job, but by then, his education had been derailed.

Gary tried again when he was working at the plant. He started attending night classes at a community college. The building-trades program he was enrolled in would have also given him his high school diploma. But eight weeks into the twelve-week course, his supervisor handed him a slip telling him to start reporting for the 3–11 P.M. shift. Once again, Gary fell off the academic track. The irony was, the company sent him back to the day shift a short time later.

Now that he is unemployed, Gary is giving school one more chance. At the age of twenty-nine, he is working toward an associate's degree through another fast-track program at a community college. But after a decade in the factory, he feels directionless. A career counselor convinced him to take a test to determine what career would be the best fit. These kinds of evaluations are the epitome of the new technology of meritocracy—measure people's skills and temperament, and match them, with scientific precision, to the occupation ideally suited for them. Unfortunately, the career test told Gary he was ideally suited for low-wage jobs. "The ones that you are a good fit for, are not well-paying enough to support your lifestyle and your family," he says.

Gary insists he is trying his hardest to find another job. Yet that supreme confidence he used to feel has left him. "There was a point in time where I really felt like a good provider," he says. "And I don't feel like that as much anymore." The judgment of the people around him—or what he perceives to be their judgment—wounds him at times. "That's the worst part about it," he says.

Gary and his fiancée Ruby, a full-time student, have gone through a rocky period since he lost his job. They argue much more than they used to—always about finances. "Sometimes it's just a little comment or remark," Gary says. "Sometimes it can blow up." When they fight, Gary feels his self-respect slipping away in the glare of Ruby's contempt. If he's by himself, his unemployment does not bother him as much. He is not a sociable person by nature, and when he is alone he can view his predicament with some clarity and objectivity. It is when he is among other people that the current state of his life becomes unbearable. It makes him feel low, he says, when his son and daughter ask him whether he's found a job yet, or when they bug him for toys or outings he can no longer afford—or when they just give him that *look* after they get home from school. "Sometimes it's like, 'Dang! They're tired of seeing me around here all regular, too!'" he says. "Sometimes I'd like them to hear me say, 'I'm going to work.'"

Gary broods at night, managing just a handful of hours of sleep, constantly thinking through his problems and trying to figure out ways to "make it all work." He worries incessantly about money. When he drives he fixates on how much gas he's using, keeping doggedly to local roads and driving in a straight line to his destination. "Each gallon count now. Every mile count."

At times, Gary feels an urge to disappear and leave his troubles behind—"just be a bird and fly," as he puts it. "I don't think I'm a harm to myself or my family," he adds quickly—but he knows he probably should be seeing a therapist. The trouble is, Gary can't afford health insurance. For him and his wife and two young children, the government safety net is rather frayed.

Gary insists that he had no control over the loss of his job, and yet when he talks to his family and feels their disappointment, he can't help blaming himself. He should have worked harder. He should not have been so young and stupid. Always, in the background, is the moral of his sad story: This downfall was deserved. "To an extent it's not my fault," Gary says. "Then, I think about my past, and mistakes I made—like the time that I felt getting money was more important when I was in high school instead of my education. Man, if I had focused my attention somewhere else I could *be* somewhere else now . . ."

. . .

In a sense, anger is to our modern age what sentimentality was to the Victorian age: the logic of the underlying ideology taken to its emotional extreme. When the full fury of the meritocratic worldview is directed outward, it is expressed as a righteous anger at other people's personal failings. Turned inward, it manifests itself among unemployed workers as disgust with bad decisions, shame about being uneducated and unproductive, and a self-image of themselves as "losers."

The well-documented stigma of unemployment affected many of my workers. Four out of ten said they were ashamed about being unemployed. Not surprisingly, this feeling was most common among those who had been unemployed the longest. Their sense of self-worth plummeted in tandem with their social status. Mal Stephen, a fifty-one-year-old Chrysler worker, has gone three years without steady work. He has come to see it as a kind of hubris that someone like him, who never got a college degree, once made $72,000 a year. "I've had to come down from my high horse," he says. "I'm not going to make $30 an hour any more. . . . I used to think in such big numbers. I have to stop that. I have to think in regular numbers, like regular people."

For my Americans, their shame was more likely to be manifested as self-blame. Let us distinguish the two concepts. *Shame* is a state of pain, discomfort, and stigma arising from one's perceived unworthiness and low status. It brings about a sense of oneself as a social outcast. But though shame can related to one's actions, it is not always. One can be ashamed, for example, of a disfigurement that one had no control over. *Self-blame* or *guilt*, on the other hand, implies that the individual could have avoided a wrong action.[7] At its most basic level, self-blame is not necessarily a bad thing. Taking responsibility for a wrong action is an important part of learning from a mistake. However, when shame and self-blame are combined, they create a particularly toxic concoction. In what the sociologist Pierre Bourdieu has called "symbolic violence," they draw from the dominant narrative of success, convincing workers that "they owe their scholastic and social destiny to their lack of gifts or merits."[8] Ultimately, as workers become trapped in their unemployment, they come to view themselves as, in their words, "losers," "failures," or "fuck-ups."

My workers overwhelmingly did not blame themselves for becoming unemployed. The layoffs, they pointed out, were not due to any fault of their own. On both sides of the border, they pointed the finger at free trade (and government policies in favor of it), the poor economy, and bad decisions by management and unions alike. But as the length of their unemployment stretched out, their perceptions started to change. Workers who didn't blame themselves for *losing* a job started to blame themselves for *not finding* a job. A third of my Americans, and almost half of my parts workers, expressed self-blame.

As Carrie Lane points out, unemployment has become somewhat "normalized" over the decades, as workers come to see it as a temporary interlude—or even a "fresh start"—in the upward ascents of their careers.[9] But when unemployment becomes long-term unemployment, these rationalizations begin to fray. Royce Terrell, a thirty-one-year-old American, went through a period of depression as the weeks went by and no new job materialized. He was upset that he was not able to provide for his wife, their young son, and his three stepchildren. "Being responsible for as many people as I was, I wasn't feeling that I was doing my part," Royce says. He continues to dwell on certain regrets. After the first round of layoffs at the parts plant ended, in his euphoria he went out and treated himself to a Jaguar XJ8 sedan—albeit a used 2004 model. That was one of several decisions about his finances and career that he would later spend nights ruing. "I would do a lot of like backtracking, thinking of what I could have did, and should have did," he says. "I think I could have been more prepared. . . . It's a lot of decisions that I made that constantly beat up on me, like buying that car when I did."

My Canadians dwelled less on past decisions and more on their low status. Yul Kane, a forty-two-year-old ex-Ford worker, prides himself on his dedication to the job. "If you're lazy, get away from me," he says. "Don't even bother with me because it means that I have to work twice as hard to cover your ass." But it's been almost two years since he left Ford, and Yul has nothing to show for his job search. As he sees it, he doesn't have the kind of merit that today's employers really respect—a merit that today has less to do with hard work and more to do with education. "My stepsister has a hell of a lot more options than me, being a microbiologist," he says. "One week she's in Frankfurt; next week she's over here or over there doing symposiums. I want to have that—I want to be wanted." But in this economy it's "getting tougher and tougher to be wanted," he adds. After he lost his job, Yul felt shame for no longer being able to support his family. "I felt like I was less of a man because I wasn't providing the way that I had in the past."

Being unemployed made Yul feel inferior, though his low status was not tied to regret for a specific course of action he failed to take. This distinction is important because the workers I talked to with the most intense problems coping with unemployment had a high degree of regret and, therefore, self-blame. Those who started taking antidepressants during their period of joblessness, for example, pointed to specific decisions they had made—the "stupid" decision they made to take the buyout, a car purchase they now "beat" themselves up over, a "mistake" in their youth to choose cash in their pocket over a diploma on their résumé. While stressful and pernicious as well, shame did not lead to the same degree of despair.

In his study of the long-term unemployed—white-collar workers and blue-collar workers, Americans and Israelis—Ofer Sharone finds that the way the hiring process is structured can determine whether the unemployed blame themselves or the broader system for their failure to get jobs. Staffing agencies, widely used in Israel, provide a central location where white-collar job candidates are screened based on relatively impersonal and transparent criteria. If they do not get hired, it is clear why. In a similar way, blue-collar workers in the U.S. tend to be hired through a rigid filtering process, one focused on straightforward criteria such as reliability, compliance, and work ethic. As it does for the Israelis, the formal and predictable nature of hiring in their corner of the job market encourages blue-collar workers to keep applying for jobs even if they fail at first, Sharone argues—and that persistence sometimes pays off. The way the system is set up for white-collar Americans, however, multiple rejections are more likely to leave them feeling discouraged and dejected. How sociable or how much of a team player they are—a less tangible sense of their cultural goodness-of-fit—factors heavily into the hiring equation. With more personal investment and more uncertainty in their job hunt, they tend to blame themselves when they do not land a job, paralyzed by the sense that something is fundamentally wrong with who they are.[10]

Sharone makes a persuasive case that the presence or absence of particular institutions, rather than national culture or social class, is most important in determining how workers react to long-term unemployment. But even if white-collar workers are quicker to blame themselves, this does not mean that blue-collar workers do not engage in these behaviors as well, as the many instances of self-blame I found among my workers suggest. Furthermore, the *nature* of their self-blame seems to be different. For white-collar workers, it is about failing to get jobs they're qualified for—ones they should get but, for some inexplicable reason, don't. For my blue-collar workers, the problem is more fundamental. They have a sense of shame that they are not valued, productive members of society. They are not so much discouraged as denigrated. They keep applying for more jobs, but they can get only lousy jobs— ones much worse than what they had at their old plants. And they are woefully aware of what that fact says about their own worth. For some, the Americans and parts workers in particular, there is an added sense that they somehow deserve their lot. They regret specific decisions they made in the past—sometimes decades back—particularly around their choices to pursue, or not to pursue, education.

Here it is useful to bring in, again, the work of Eli Chinoy, who conducted an influential study of employed autoworkers in the middle of the last century. Even back then, Chinoy saw evidence of a meritocratic perspective among his workers, who took responsibility for their low status in life and tended to ignore the fact that they lived in a world of only limited opportunity. Under the dominant ideology, their failure to rise was due to their own deficiencies of character.[11]

Nevertheless, Chinoy's autoworkers could take refuge in other areas. They could pour the personal ambitions that had been blocked in their own lives into their children's lives. They could define their own progress not in terms of their advancement within their workplace but their "quantitative" acquisition of material possessions—the American Dream as the house with the two-car garage and the souped-up entertainment system. These alternative metrics of success—private meritocracies of home and hearth—were not as easily tapped by my workers, who by the very fact of their unemployment did not have the income to consume or provide adequately for their children's futures. (That said, the Canadians were somewhat better able to focus on the second area, their family life, as I explained in chapter 4.)

The differences between my workers and Chinoy's go beyond their employment status, however. Since the time of his study there have been at least four developments in the market and culture that make the situation of my workers distinct, and may have made the influence of shame and self-blame stronger. The first is changes in the institutions underpinning the dominant culture, especially the decline of unions and the pro-corporate movement's other political adversaries. The second is the technological progress that has given individuals the increasing ability to rise based on their talent alone. These two factors affect the *intensity* of self-blame among my workers. The third change involves the labor market's greater emphasis on education for ordinary workers and, more broadly, its expanding understanding of what merit is. The fourth has to do with the increasing technical ability of employers to measure that merit. These last two factors—again, one cultural and one technological, and both rooted in institutions—affect the *capacity* for self-blame. Each of these factors influences the other. For example, the dearth of egalitarian institutions means that ever-higher demands for what elites "ought" to be paid are not rebuffed, individuals are pragmatically forced to rely on themselves, and competition (and therefore evaluation) deepens. In turn, the growing cultural, economic, and technological power of the talented worker puts her in conflict with collective approaches that could rein in that power.

The intensity of self-blame depends on what other narratives exist to explain a person's prolonged condition of unemployment. Technologically speaking, new tools have emerged that allow everyone to compete on a more or less level playing field, leading to a much-heralded "flat" world where entrepreneurs in Bangalore can dream the same dreams as their counterparts in Silicon Valley. Culturally speaking, the diminishment of (albeit still formidable) social barriers such as racism and sexism has also opened up possibilities for a lone worker's advancement. Here, too, culture and technology directly build upon each other. Market power enhanced by technological innovations encourages a reconsideration of social norms, and the loosening of cultural impediments allows the individual to make full use of the available opportunities. On the other hand, as Michael Young pointed out decades ago, the very existence of those opportunities makes it harder for individuals to justly blame the system, as they more easily could in past, benighted eras of gilded privilege and glass ceilings.[12] With so much more computing power and networked resources at an individual's disposal, and with fewer obvious barriers to success, the excuses for failure have disappeared.

Meanwhile, the demise of universal left-wing ideologies and the decline of labor unions have left an ideological void, taking away alternative worldviews that individuals could use to understand their situation in a less reproachful way. As perilously flawed as it was, communism provided a compelling language of class consciousness. Unions provided the institutional muscle not just to advocate for (less radical) policies of egalitarianism, but also to encourage laid-off workers to see their plight as collective, rather than individual, and direct their anger outwardly to an external enemy—the corporation.[13]

Because the labor markets in the two countries are fairly similar, as I explained in chapter 2, the ideological gap between the two countries perhaps accounts for more of the self-blame we see among my Americans and parts workers than the other three factors do. That gap, in turn, is rooted in institutional differences. Savaged by fierce worker competition and dogged corporate resistance, union membership dropped particularly early and precipitously down south. In Canada, a third of workers today are members of unions, almost three times the proportion in the United States. As American unions have disappeared, leaving their ideological terrain undefended, the pro-corporate movement has gained ground. Its mass-media framing of inequality continues to shape the public's understanding of who is deserving and who is not. In Canada there is a smaller ecosystem of conservative organizations. No right-leaning media organization has nearly as much scale and clout as Fox News has across the border.

How do race and ethnicity, in turn, shape these attitudes of individualism and blame? Michèle Lamont argues that working-class African Americans embrace the morality of the "caring self," a fraternal creed that emphasizes solidarity and compassion and stands in contrast to the domineering, responsibility-oriented "disciplined self" of white workers.[14] As Lamont points out, these contrasts between white and black workers are ones of degree only. Black workers, too, value the disciplined self, even if they place less emphasis on its dictums of hard work and responsibility. As useful as this cultural perspective is, however, it did not seem to make much of a difference in how my workers reacted to being out of a job for so long. My black workers did not blame themselves any less than my white workers for their failure to find new work.

A more noteworthy difference was that those who identified strongly with their unions tended to feel less self-blame. By trumpeting the righteousness of higher wages, unions encouraged them to see themselves as deserving of good jobs even if they didn't have an education. (Unions were also heavily involved in staffing and running the action centers that improved my workers' personal experiences in Canada.) When workers felt no kinship with the labor movement, however, they lost this ideological armor. With a more inhospitable environment for organized labor on the U.S. side of the border, as well as the less favorable experiences they had with unions after losing their jobs, my Americans in particular felt estranged from organized labor. My parts workers, who generally had weaker union representation (manifested in poorer contracts and less attention paid to their concerns than for the Big Three workers), also felt greater distance.

John Hope, a fifty-five-year-old American who used to polish bumpers at the plating plant, points out that he made more money back when the company paid per piece polished. He blames the union for protecting the interests of mediocre workers. "All the lazy people want to get back on the clock," he says, rather than getting paid for what they actually do. He was also fed up with the union's leaders for helping out their "buddies" and not caring about who was really qualified. "They were all for themselves," he says. In the end, John had harsher words for the union than for the company that had laid him off. Yet, after he had sunk into a long bout of unemployment, his inability to side with the union against a corporate enemy meant that the anger eventually fell on him. "It's all my fault," he says of his joblessness.

In the period that Chinoy was writing, when the labor movement was in its prime, autoworkers could think in more collective terms. "They have come to see that their future well-being lies in a collective effort to achieve common goals, for example, general wages increases, rather than in the private pursuit of success," Chinoy notes. This "common objective" would "give meaning and significance to both great achievements and the faithful performance of humble tasks." Collectivism, in other words, would shield workers from the shame and self-blame of their lowly status and personal failures.[15] But today, the bulwark of power and hope that their unions once provided workers like mine has cracked, and the culture of judgment has swept in.

The capacity for self-blame has also grown in the long run. As employers move from a weak form of meritocratic idealism (merit as hard work) to a strong form (merit as hard work and talent), more ordinary workers fall short of what is expected. This may help explain why workers like mine experience a self-blame that was not as readily apparent in past periods of comparably massive unemployment.[16] A lack of education in particular generated this wounding self-criticism among my workers. The worst of it could be found among my parts workers, who started at a lower point in the socioeconomic ladder and possessed fewer credentials and other markers of merit.

In shaping these self-perceptions, both institutions and culture—both realism and ideology—appeared to matter, though my workers more clearly expressed a realistic viewpoint. Pragmatically, they admitted that it would be "hard" or "impossible" to find the kinds of wages and benefits they had once enjoyed. In today's economy, people with little in the way of education get paid less. And if they had failed to grasp that reality early on, when they could have obtained those credentials, it was their fault. At times, however, my workers' self-rebukes also tapped into a moral viewpoint—that workers like them *should* get paid less, because they were less *deserving* of high pay.

Here, of course, the line between realism and ideology becomes blurry. A "sinner" has done something wrong, and yet a shared culture shapes the very idea of what that sin is—and is not. As for the meritocratic ideology, its claim that the less educated are less deserving is grounded in the simple reality that these individuals *do* lack the skills that companies are looking for. But it is also important to note that the ideology itself sets the rules of that game: what the labor market should value ("smartness" over a "strong back"), how merit should be judged (economic rewards over social ones), and what should be the proper way to succeed (education over organizing). In this way, how much pay is "too much" for an unskilled worker is socially constructed and contested.[17]

It was striking that even African Americans—a group that, as I noted, tends to be more collectivist—acknowledged that manual labor was not deserving of high pay. Johnson Cheney is an African American ex-Chrysler worker who previously served as a union steward. He has a meritocratic, commonsense view of what autoworkers deserve to make. "You got factory workers that didn't have a fifth-grade education, right, living next door to doctors and lawyers, in Bloomfield and Novi, in $600,000 houses. Here's a guy that says, 'I'm a doctor and I spent . . . $100,000 . . . for an education, for me to get this doctor degree,' and you got a guy that moved out here that can't speak plain English—he still barbequing on the front porch. You know, it's like this has got to cease."

Even black former union members like Johnson have internalized the belief that they don't deserve a good standard of living. And it's because they don't possess the kind of merit that's now appreciated in this labor market and in this culture.

My Americans were more inclined than the Canadians were to see high pay for low skill as unjustified, in line with the stronger public consensus down south that education "ought" to be decisive in setting pay—a more ideological view that the culture of weak unions and strong conservative media perhaps, in turn, promotes. Of course, the problem with this blinding focus on education is that access to such opportunities is unequal: the more affluent and educated the household a person grows up in, the more likely she is to pursue higher education. Meanwhile, the speedup (described in chapter 2) of required human capital and cultural capital—a rising bar of education and personal traits—continues to make the likelihood of this success more theoretical than real for many workers. Ordinary workers are supposed to keep up, and so they struggle (importantly, like everyone else) to get more education and to be more proactive job seekers, but they do not, as a group, get anywhere. Today's workers tend to ignore these realities, however. Meritocratic morality provides ideological cover for the fact that the system fails to deliver on its promises of upward mobility.

Indeed, the main way that the dominant ideology contributes to shame and self-blame is not about making ordinary workers parrot the meritocratic moralizing of the Fox News crowd. Rather, it is about narrowing the individual's field of vision so that she does not see the structural circumstances that hem in her ability to succeed: that is, the stunted nature of the stunted meritocracy. While at times they were more brazen in their meritocratic judgment (usually of other people, as the next section will explain), in most cases the stance of my workers was a defensive one: attempting, rather unsuccessfully, to ward off the blows to their self-esteem that the meritocratic ideology rained down on them. They can no longer take much refuge in the moral virtues of hard work and the alternative ideologies that once glorified their position in the world.

The other factor that has boosted the capacity for self-blame is the growing technical capacity to quantify ability and performance. (Again, these two factors—expanding merit and the enhanced measurement of merit—are intertwined, each supplying the other with further possibilities to grow its domain.) New and improved metrics allow tighter sorting. More avenues for individual improvement emerge—and with them, more opportunities for criticism. Failure to meet the expanding criteria now used for evaluation creates self-blame to an extent that did not exist among past generations of blue-collar workers. Just as the low score that parts worker Gary Jansen received on his career test suggested that he was worthy of only a low-wage job, the expansion of metrics more broadly means the expansion of evidence that proves my workers to be inferior.

Against the backdrop of these cultural and technological changes, the self-blame that afflicts workers is similar to the self-blame that afflicts consumers. As the market system evolves, more products can compete for the attention of companies and consumers alike, and choice abounds, enhancing freedom and thus overall welfare. Yet, as psychologist Barry Schwartz argues, one consequence of having more choices is that the psychological price of failing to make the *right* choice is steeper. In earlier times, a bad choice in the market was not an occasion for self-blame, since there were few or no other options. The system was to blame, for not supplying the optimal good or service—and it couldn't be helped. Today, there are more opportunity costs for going one way and not the other, even as the proliferation of choices raises expectations that one or more of them should fit the buyer's preferences perfectly. With all the options available, the individual could have chosen better. In other words, there is more reason for regret, and less patience for error. Thanks to this so-called paradox of choice, more freedom through more choices does not lead to more happiness.[18]

We can observe a similar "paradox of skill" in the job market, where today's workers focus on the growing pile of things they, too, did wrong. As the pathways to success and the criteria for excellence multiply, the opportunity costs of the paths not taken—the schooling not pursued, the various skills not acquired—become more legion and vexing. The regrets for coming short become sharper. With all the career possibilities now available, the luckless job seeker knows he could have chosen better in life. With all the competencies now required, she can see more plainly where she is deficient—that is, the extent to which she is a "loser." In today's labor market, there are more ways to fail, and more reasons to feel like a failure.

CONTEMPTIBLE CONSUMPTION

Even back in Eli Chinoy's time, the auto industry was pushing aside the career ladders that line workers could use to ascend to management. As a result, their chief outlets for their stymied ambitions were, as I noted, family and consumption. "As long as possessions continue to pile up," Chinoy writes, "the worker can feel that he is moving forward; as long as his wants do not give out, he can feel that he is ambitious." The shift in emphasis away from production and toward consumption thereby opened up another avenue for the accumulation of merit—and self-blame.[19]

While they had their union-won wages at the plants, my less educated workers could aspire to catch up with the white-collar Joneses, living in tony suburbs and buying pricey flatscreens and furniture—even if some still preferred their pickup trucks and "barbequing on the front porch." But the loss of their jobs has given the lie to the notion that they were ever in the same league. The hedonic treadmill has stopped. There is no more overtime to tap, and no new jobs on the horizon that can, for unskilled applicants like them, reclaim their old union wages. All their spending through the boom years—the constant competition they engaged in to latch onto a higher quality of life—now takes on the dim moral cast of profligacy.

Consumer choice and worker merit are flip sides of the coin of capitalism, and not surprisingly, meritocratic morality is used as a cudgel against not just the talentless worker but also the spendthrift consumer. Many of my workers understandably criticized coworkers who frittered away their paychecks and left themselves woefully unprepared for an extended period of joblessness. "A lot of people overspent, built big homes that they didn't need to be building," says a Canadian former parts worker. "Surprise! You're gonna lose that house eventually . . . unless you get another job." For people like him, who played by the rules, it is galling to see such little regard for personal responsibility.

As has long been the case, society condemns those individuals who fail to live within their means. And yet achieving "perfection" in one's household finances has also become more difficult amid the pressures and temptations of modern life. As sociologist Daniel Bell has argued, an ever-more sophisticated consumer culture pushes people into debt to buy the latest fad or status symbol, eroding the austere and frugal character— the Protestant work ethic—that once rooted capitalism and allowed it to flourish. Yet meritocratic morality continues to expect human beings to be saints as they walk through capitalism's pleasure dome. Even worse, they must be saints one moment, and sinners the next. "Against the fear of going into debt, there was now the fear of not being credit worthy," Bell writes.[20]

Again, this kind of moral judgment leaves out certain aspects of reality. In a more flexible economy, more advantaged workers will generally fare better, having not just the talent and skills that make employers bid for their attention, but also the knowledge, initiative, and discipline that allow them to be superior stewards of their personal finances.[21] More educated and informed, they naturally do better in the game of saving and investment, racking up higher credit scores that mark them as meritorious consumers (the credit score itself being yet another new metric of meritocracy). Meanwhile, the growing personal-finance industry and the broader push toward an "ownership society"—one in which everyone owns property, and thus everyone benefits from rising returns on wealth—have widened inequality in this area, inundating the market with capital, meting out more in the way of rewards to those better able to go after them, and giving households more choices in how to invest their savings—and thus more reasons to fault themselves should they make the wrong ones.[22]

When they were making union wages, heavy spending was quite common among my workers. "You think differently when you're tired," says Ziggy Dordick, forty, a former Ford worker who used to rack up dozens of hours of overtime whenever production ramped up. "You always just say, 'You deserve it.' You know, 'What am I working for?'"

There is plenty of blame to go around, but it is worth pointing out that attitudes toward spending depend on context. Individuals look to the actions and expectations of the herd around them. When everyone starts running up debts to get in on a good thing, it is those who stand aside who are seen as "chumps." Then, when the bubble bursts, moral perceptions shift to label the risk-takers as rash and dissolute. In other words, the sinfulness of profligacy (or austerity) depends on which and how many people are doing it. Attitudes about how much spending is enough, too, depend on your peer group—the friends and neighbors who make judgments about the size of your house and the cut of your lawn.[23]

At the level of national policy, meritocratic morality helps make the case for painful austerity measures that further serve the interests of antigovernment activists. It transforms economics into a morality play, as ordinary citizens conclude that the present-day malaise arises from the excesses of debt and dissipation in the past.[24] Yet, too many people saving up too much money can ruin an economy, too. If no one—including the government, the spender of last resort—is spending, no one is making money. Indeed, the extravagant ways in which some autoworkers used up their paychecks helped prop up their communities. "They make the money, they get drunk and eat," says the owner of a Windsor bar that draws about three-quarters of its business from autoworkers. "They're not educated. And they spent the whole paycheck." What was wasteful to some was income for others.

When the recession hit, the bar started closing earlier, and a few servers were let go. The economy has improved since then, but those customers who remain are unwilling to spend like they used to. "They're worried about their pensions," the owner says. "There's a fear in them. They're scared to spend money." Taken too far, zeal for thrift and anger at extravagance are disastrous for local businesspeople, who can't keep their doors open and their staff employed without a degree of "wasteful" spending.

THE HIDDEN INJURIES OF SELF-BLAME

Many of my workers were ashamed about being without a job for so long. My Americans and parts workers, however, felt more of a particular kind of shame: self-blame. It was not just that they did not have a job. They regretted their failures as uneducated workers and spendthrift consumers. These assessments were rooted to a large degree in reality—the reality of today's stunted meritocracy. Amid the changing requirements of the labor market and the grim prospects for collective solutions, it was clear to these workers that they would have been more successful if they had gotten an education. Nevertheless, the broader culture of judgment appeared to worsen their self-blame, by emphasizing their personal failures over the system's failures.

In a postwar era of strong unions, the autoworkers profiled in Eli Chinoy's work could realistically devote themselves to collective struggles that justified their worth as workers and shielded them from self-blame. Many decades later, identifying with the labor movement can still alleviate some of the wounds of economic competition, as I saw among my workers. Those with closer ties to their unions tended to deal with their unemployment in less psychologically injurious ways. But, for the rest, the pent-up anger grew and grew—at times, to the point of implosion. The expanding criteria used to judge them as inferior and the demise of any alternative ideologies or rationalizations for their circumstances seemed to make their self-blame more possible and potent. After all, in a meritocratic society, where today's hard-working and talented have supposedly limitless opportunities to advance, the labor market's losers have only themselves to blame.

It is important to reiterate that my focus is on the experiences and attitudes of the long-term unemployed, rather than workers more broadly. Those going through prolonged periods of joblessness have different points of view from their employed counterparts. Among other things, their very status of being unemployed makes it tougher for workers like mine to use alternative measuring sticks of their self-worth, such as their (now diminished) ability to buy the accoutrements of middle-class life or letting their (now dimmed) ambitions for their children substitute for their own. While Chinoy's workers could turn to family and consumption to bolster their dignity, my jobless workers largely could not. This may explain why the views of my workers differed from those that other (mostly employed) workers expressed in the classic studies of blue-collar families. Nevertheless, if unemployment and underemployment continue to become more common and chronic conditions for ordinary workers, whom they hold responsible—or blameless—will become even more vital to understand.

. . .

The irony of the meritocratic ethic is that, as with most moral codes, its saints are hard to come by. Tamar Moreno, the ex-Chrysler worker we met at the beginning of this chapter, stresses the fact that she helps only those who can help themselves. She "can't imagine" neglecting, as some of her former coworkers did, to set aside a wintertime reserve for her family. Yet the truth is that Tamar is not too proud to take government assistance. Next month, she will begin a two-year course in electrical work, plumbing, heating, cooling, and carpentry. The federal Trade Adjustment Assistance program will pay for the entire thing. What is more, Tamar has started receiving child support. After her father died, Victor—her deadbeat ex-husband—finally got in touch, which allowed the authorities to track him down and start garnishing his wages. Tamar is now receiving $512 a month in child support, which she uses to take her two sons out to dinner every week and buy the expensive athletic shoes Tony craves.

Tamar says she wouldn't even take a job right now if one were offered to her. Her grandmother is now ninety-one, and Tamar worries about her. The siblings rotate the responsibility of watching over her, but she often wants Tamar—or, better yet, her "baby," Tony. ("He just makes her light up, I tell you," Tamar says of her son.) So, after three uninterrupted decades in the labor market, Tamar is willing to "lay back and take it easy" for a spell. With her contacts and track record, it will be easy for her to find a job, she says, when the time comes for that. And the truth is, she doesn't miss heading to a factory every day. She still wakes up in the wee hours of the morning, as is her habit, and finds plenty of work for her—and her sons—to do. "God, I wish they'd call you back," her sons grumble whenever she orders them into the cellar to rummage through boxes from their recent move.

Tamar the rugged individualist is studying thanks to a government scholarship, living off her union-won buyout, and relying on child support enforced by the state. Since leaving the factory, she has prospered—but not just because of her past conduct of prudent saving. A present-day government safety net has also intervened in her favor. Her reliance on public help suggests that Tamar is not exactly the picture of uncompromising self-sufficiency her words might imply.

Of course, such a disconnect between ideology and reality is quite typical. Even beneficiaries of such storied government policies as the GI Bill, which helped build a postwar middle class by providing college scholarships and financial assistance to veterans, were able to couch their success in stark terms of individual merit.[25] This is the moral myopia that often afflicts individuals in a meritocratic society: a circumscribed view of the world that puts into sharp focus their own achievements and abilities, while obscuring the policies and organizing that shore up their prospects. In Tamar's mind, people are responsible for their own position in life, and she pays less attention to the assortment of advantages that muddy this simple truth. After all, she struggled for what success she has. She put in long hours at the factory and raised two boys with little help from her husband.

Tamar may be glad for the child support she's now receiving, but she is also glad that her reluctant benefactor, Victor, has left her alone. When Tamar thinks back on her past with him, it is, she says, "a forgetful season" for her. It would be better if segments of that life could be clipped out altogether, the mistakes avoided, the hurt averted. But a child, the idiosyncratic outcome of those long chains of personal history—however shameful and unpleasant they were—gives an unconditional reason not to regret that past. That is the way Tamar sees Tony, the baby of that unfortunate union. She finds comforting traces of herself—and her father—in that boy. He shares the same unrelenting work ethic. Up early, Tamar will hear the lawnmower snarl alive. She will look up and see Tony pushing it through the backyard, without having been asked. An honor-roll student, the tenth-grader sometimes can't breathe when he gets a B, she boasts. A high school point guard, he was recently ranked in the state. "I work hard and he's coming right behind me," Tamar says. Tony is the one who will secure the family's place in the world, a third generation of strong merit and morals to carry on what his grandfather started and what his mother built into a solidly middle-class existence.

Victor disappeared when Tony was just two, Tamar says. Recently, her ex-husband was diagnosed with muscular dystrophy. "Pretty much now he needs them in his life, but you closed that door by yourself," she says. When Tony graduated from eighth grade, Victor called and asked to speak to his son. "What am I going to say to him?" Tony said. "He never did nothing for me."

Perhaps for the better. Grandpa Art filled the void that an absent father left. Tony called him "Daddy." Art, in turn, doted on the boy. "That was his whole world," Tamar says. When there was a heavy storm, Art would call and ask if Tony was okay. "Tony? What about me?" Tamar blurted out once.

Tony was devastated by Art's death. He mourned by inking a tattoo into his arm: "Rest in peace, Daddy." In his will, Art left everything to the boy. His death also left Tony with nightmares. He had seen his grandfather fall stricken before his eyes, and the bad dreams still come, two years later. Some nights Tamar will "look up and there's some kid laying next to me," she says. "I dreamed about Granddaddy," Tony will say, simply. Tamar will let him lie there with her.

He is a strikingly sensitive boy, yet the unflagging dedication with which he does everything awes Tamar, and motivates her to respond in kind. Nowadays, with no more overtime to pay for guiltless purchases, Tamar has grown used to saying no. "We don't have any money," she will tell her sons, fixing her most implacable face. (Tony will give her a scathing look—he doesn't buy the idea that his mother, the consummately frugal householder, doesn't have the extra cash squirreled away.) That said, Tamar will make exceptions to reward her hard-working son. She routinely sets aside money for each new addition to the Air Jordan line. The shoes have become Tony's rewards for good grades. In the Moreno family, as in many families, the report card is childhood's metric of success, a proto–job evaluation that bears gifts and punishments in its two hands.

The older son, Manny, is the opposite of Tony in many ways—which Tamar is quick to count. At the age of twenty-six, Manny is still living off his mother's largesse. After high school, he never bothered to continue his education. He found a job cleaning fish tanks through Tamar's brother, but then the economy flatlined. Nowadays Manny fritters his days away with a TV remote snug in hand. "He got his father, and the other one"—Tony—"got me," Tamar says. Sometimes she will ask Manny to cut the grass. "It's not long enough," he will mutter in reply. Tamar will have to ask her boy—this grown *man*—three times before he starts to move. Manny, she concludes grimly, is a "bump on a log."

There is no fattened calf waiting for the prodigal son—no Air Jordans, and if Tamar had her way, no free rent and food, either. "What would you do if I told you you had to leave?" she asked Manny one day.

"I don't know," he mumbled.

In the end, though, Tamar listened again to her father. "Don't put him out, girl," Art told her. "Where he going to go?" So, at the age of forty-seven, Tamar still has two dependent children under her wing—and little faith that the older one will ever be able, or ever want, to leave the nest. Fortunately, Tony appears on track for college. She offers him the advice her father once gave to her: "You can do what you want to do. Make your own way."

That's not to say that a bit of luck doesn't help. As much as she believes in her hard work and ability, Tamar plays the lottery, too. On a visit to her grandmother in the suburbs, she stumbled across a gorgeous twelve-bedroom estate, a house so big "you need a bike to ride through." If she hit the jackpot, that is what she would buy. "My grandmother says it's too big, but, man, it's beautiful." She and her sons could each have their own side of the house. With luck like that, there would be more than enough to share.

CHAPTER 7

There Go I

Does it matter? Grace is everywhere. . . .
—George Bernanos, *The Diary of a Country Priest*

David Vihan looks the part of a factory worker: tall and burly and imposing, blonde bristles running down his chin and throat, slightly unkempt
hair sprouting from under a University of Michigan cap. Today he wears
a navy-blue T-shirt with a picture of a Model T car, a huge truck engine
strapped onto its roof. "The heart of the Ford is the engine," it reads,
along with the epitaph, "1981–2007, Essex Engine." That was the plant
where David spent a decade of his career, before the economy faltered and
Ford shut the place down. David used to work on the motor line there
"pounding pistons," as the workers called it—by consensus the most
demanding job in the plant. He and his coworkers would thrust fifteen-
pound pistons into the bores of engine blocks. They had to time the motion
precisely to keep up with the pace of six to eight seconds per engine, applying just the right touch so that the impact didn't crush their shoulders.

David grew up in Windsor, the son of a postal worker. He went to
college but dropped out after his drinking got in the way of his grades.
He eventually found a job at a ski pole manufacturing firm applying
artwork screens to the poles. He was good at it. "It was the best job I
ever had," he says. "It wasn't physical or nothing. It was all using your
head." But by then, David could no longer deny how serious his alcoholism had become. "I was going to die probably from drinking. I could
really go at it hard."

That's when he met Tracy. The two fell in love. David vowed to curb
his drinking, and he did. Tracy and David got married. A metal fan,

David insisted on playing the Black Sabbath song "Warning" at the wedding.

A few years later, David "hit the lottery": on the advice of a friend who worked at Ford, he applied for a job there and got it, seemingly winning himself economic security for life. But for all its white-collar wages, the job never let him forget that he did blue-collar work. One day, he was twisting his torso back and forth to keep up with the fast-moving line when he heard a snap. He doubled over in pain. He had blown out the cartilage on one side of his chest.

When he came back to work, David was moved to a desk job. The pain in his side was chronic; it felt like someone was constantly sticking a thumb under his ribs and jerking it upwards.

His injury at work was just the beginning of David's health troubles. Two years later, he was showering when he discovered a lump in his groin. On Tracy's birthday, David headed to a cancer center in Windsor to get the results of the biopsy. His doctor told him it was Hodgkin's lymphoma. It had already spread. "We're starting chemo in the morning," she said. David was stunned. He was only in his thirties, just getting used to life again after his debilitating chest injury. Suddenly there was no more time.

David's grandmother had died of throat cancer, and he had watched her waste away in agony, the chemotherapy burning away her insides. "I ain't doing that," he told his physician, Dr. Joelle Horwich.

"Without it you're going to be dead in two weeks," she replied. She slapped his chest X-rays on a board and lit them up. "You couldn't see nothing," David recalls. "It was all spiderwebs." The cancer was everywhere.

His doctors began a massive course of chemotherapy. David's skin became as white and smooth as a baby's; just slapping his wrist could cause a bruise. The chemotherapy ate away at his bones, which ached constantly. His body was numb from the waist down. He had intense headaches and couldn't sleep. "Even my worst enemy I wouldn't want to go through what that was," David says. "It was brutal." David's weight shrank to 150 pounds. "Some of my friends couldn't even look at me."

At one point, the doctors moved him into hospice care. His parents thought they were going to lose him. In the middle of his treatment, they took him out for his birthday at a Chinese restaurant he liked. Their present was an Xbox. "You've always said you wanted one," his mother said.

He finished a six-month course of chemotherapy, and his doctor asked him to try another month. Then another. David agreed. "I knew the worst thing a parent can have is a kid die before them." The cancer finally seemed to be responding to the treatment. But ten months in, David said he was done. Dr. Horwich told him it was okay to halt the chemo. David moved on to radiation treatment.

Three months later, David's cancer was in remission. Several months passed, and Dr. Horwich said his tests remained clean.

By now, David had been away from the plant for two years. Eventually, Dr. Horwich leveled with him. He needed to start living his life again, she said. At first, David was reluctant. "I didn't see myself going back," he says. "It was surreal." He returned to the plant later that year.

But even as his health improved, things had started to fall apart elsewhere in David's life. The economy was sinking into a recession. Ford plants were dropping shifts. David was laid off. A short time later, he came home to find his home cleared out—the furniture, the car, gone. Tracy had decided to leave him.

They had been struggling for quite some time. While David was delirious from his chemo, Tracy allowed her son, his girlfriend, and his three children to move in with them, and poured the couple's savings into keeping them all afloat, David says. After his stepson started stealing his hardcore painkillers, David decided he had had enough, and kicked him out. "That made my wife sour, basically, and that was the beginning of the end," he says.

By the time they separated, the couple had racked up a six-figure debt. David had been paying out of pocket for expensive naturopathic medicines to supplement his cancer treatment. Meanwhile, Tracy had been spending extravagantly on credit—unbeknownst to him, David says. "I knew it was tight, but again the whole year I was out of it." When his home's furnace broke down that winter, he couldn't afford to fix it.

That was it for David. He handed back the keys to his home and walked away. He filed for bankruptcy shortly afterward.

The Big Three autoworker, who had once made $70,000 a year, ended up having to ask his parents for money to buy a used car. "I kind of just lost it then," David says. "I broke down crying a few times. That's the first time I did that since I found out I was going to die supposedly." David moved in with a close friend. He started attending group therapy sessions for the divorced at a local church. He had come to the realization, David says, that his anger and bitterness were eating away at him.

Over the next several years, David rebuilt his life. Government assistance made a difference. Bankruptcy wiped away his debt. After several years of waiting for the bureaucracy to turn its wheels, he finally qualified for worker's compensation for his old chest injury at the plant, which started paying 85 percent of his Ford earnings, tax-free. With a government-funded scholarship, he went back to school to study medical accounting. The help, David notes, was a lifesaver. "I could concentrate on myself instead of having to worry about, 'What am I gonna do for my next meal?'"

I spoke to David shortly after his fifteen-month extended bankruptcy period ended. He was upbeat. He was unemployed, divorced, just out of bankruptcy, and a cancer survivor, but he was back in school and learning a new, respectable trade. He was paying his bills now, and he had cleared away his debts. "My life is probably as cruddy as it could possibly be right now, and yet I'm at the most peace," David said.

When I talked to him again in 2014, though, the future remained uncertain. Two years out of school, he had still not found a job.

• • •

If history repeats itself, it always finds a way to vary the tune. The second-greatest economic crisis in a century's time, the Great Recession forced many countries to reckon with the vulnerability of their working and middle classes, the result of years of stagnant wages and accumulating risk. The crisis has receded, but the essential facts have changed little. Economic growth remains sluggish, the income gap is widening, and many families remain apprehensive about the future—while others have already sunk into the desperation of long-term unemployment or low-wage labor. Karl Polanyi argued that these outbreaks of widespread suffering under the rule of intransigent market laws would inevitably lead to a political countermovement. And so they did in the wake of the Great Depression, with a vicious ideological extremism sprouting up in some corners of the globe, but also a turn to a more egalitarian economics emerging in America, Canada, and elsewhere. As I described in chapter 5, however, the aftermath of this more recent crisis has been entirely different. Countries have reverted to the old free-market ways. Regulation remains weak; and, as in earlier days, austerity continues to be hawked as the remedy for all ills. Antigovernment and nativist outrage drowns out alternative voices.[1]

The events of the past few years remind us of capitalism's existential problem: deepening inequality. The stunted meritocracy of the modern economy has raised the fortunes of a well-organized elite while leaving ordinary workers on their own. Those who falter in the high-stakes competition over good jobs find themselves stranded in deep and ruinous unemployment, cut loose from the mainstream economy—and, with time, from mainstream society.

It does not have to be this way. Nations do not have to be passive victims of market forces. Smart political decisions can strengthen the social safety net and ease the suffering of many. As this book has described, even modest variations in benefits at the national and regional levels—the difference between the policy landscapes on the two banks of the Detroit River—matter mightily in the ways that individuals and families experience the loss of a job. But if markets and meritocracy lead inevitably to a growing social divide, as I have followed other scholars in arguing, then much more forceful interventions—from substantial taxes on wealth, to the direct government creation of jobs, to the automatic provision of basic incomes—will eventually be necessary.

After all, the experience that my autoworkers went through after losing their jobs was not just a product of a long recession or one industry's upheaval. In the next few decades we can expect concerns about good jobs to proliferate throughout the labor force, perhaps outstripping the ability of the social safety net to help. As I noted in chapter 2, technological progress is leading to ever more sophisticated machines that can accomplish not just routine tasks but also the kinds of mental labor that today's skilled professionals handle. Technology has always created jobs to replace those it destroyed. But present-day advances may be qualitatively different, in that ongoing advances in artificial intelligence and robotics—already visible in computers that win game shows and cars that drive themselves—may lead to net losses of *good* jobs.[2] The highly skilled workers who design, build, and repair these technologies will do well, but the future of ordinary workers across the economy, white-collar and blue-collar alike, is in question. And even if technology continues to create good jobs *ad infinitum*, the trends I describe in this book mean that the skills employers expect from them will keep expanding, leaving less advantaged workers, as a whole, behind. Retraining is helpful, but no cure-all.

The advocates of the unfettered free market used to say that there is no alternative. In this sense perhaps they are right. If the market economy generates ever starker inequalities, either democracy disappears or one day the majority takes hold of the levers of popular power to transform the economic system and put an end to their further impoverishment.[3]

When most everyone is unemployed, the public may clamor for a greater government role.

But with labor unions weak and even politicians on the left merely talking about a return to an earlier generation's tax rates and regulations, the short-term prospects for significantly expanding the social safety net are poor. Meritocratic morality worsens those odds. With its commonsense persuasiveness, it excuses social divides and paints collective strategies to address them as unrealistic and counterproductive. It upholds individualistic goals of personal and family success—meritocracy and parental autonomy, self-actualization and responsibility, personal growth and ideal (and idealized) marriages. Above all, it prizes liberty—our freedom as individuals to cultivate talents and achieve the success we are capable of, as well as our freedom as parents to provide fittingly for our children and bestow on them a portion of our life's hard-won riches—so as to "do one better for your children than what was done for you," as one of my workers put it to me. This viewpoint is intuitive and in many ways admirable. But it has a price: a growing inequality that celebrates society's winners and immiserates its losers. Under its influence the public, like some of my workers, may react to widespread, entrenched unemployment not by protesting or organizing but by sinking into apathy, despair, and self-blame.[4]

Policy books by social scientists usually conclude with a list of thoughtful policy recommendations that would dramatically improve human well-being if enacted. Unfortunately, no one—sometimes not even the author—believes that they are politically feasible. I have such a list below. But most of my thoughts in this chapter will be on a topic other than policy, narrowly defined. Below, I argue for a *morality of grace*—both as a means to egalitarian ends and, more importantly, as a vital end in itself.

Before you close this book in search of pie not in the sky, let me state three reasons for my point of view, two of them wholly pragmatic. First, the kinds of hard-hitting policies needed to deal in any long-term way with inequality cannot be sustained in this political climate.[5] If enacted, they will eventually be squeezed away in the vise of the market economy and the narrowly meritocratic ideology it promotes. Treating the malignant consequences of the market economy therefore requires not only changes in policy but also a gradual transformation of morality—built piece by piece through organizing efforts and mass media. The path to this cultural change is admittedly long and arduous. Given limited resources, it may seem simpler and more practical to focus just on policy. Nevertheless, when we look at past periods of reform it appears that a coherent ideology—made real and vivid in the culture through the work of intellectuals and orators, artists and activists—is essential in bringing about enduring policy change.

Second, I make the case that the culture of judgment must be tackled—head-on. As I have discussed in this book, to some extent the meritocratic ideology sways even the kinds of workers we might expect to be the most hostile to its claims—for example, unionized blue-collar workers who lost their job during an economic crash. But if their public pronouncements are any indication, it energizes elites to an all the more fevered pitch. They attack policies to reduce inequality, calling them not just hindrances to a dynamic economy that grows the pie for all, but also immoral attempts by society's deadbeats and whiners to grab the hard-earned wealth of those who actually pay the government's taxes and create the economy's jobs. In a world that has decisively stepped away from the communist nightmare, the egalitarian ideology has difficulty fending off these accusations of class warfare.

One alternative strategy would be to sidestep that criticism and adopt a framing that could appeal to rich and poor alike—that is, both the winners and losers in the economic game. This would involve downplaying the economic and material concerns that animate the meritocratic and egalitarian ideologies alike, instead taking up what I describe as the morality of grace. Although personally I am not religious, I find this perspective compelling. Grace is fundamentally about an attitude of nonjudgment and nonmaterialism, one that happens to connect with many religious and ethical traditions even in libertarian America. Strands of this perspective can be found intertwined with egalitarian efforts everywhere: from the agenda-less compassion that drives Americans and Canadians to give generously to the homeless and hungry, to big-tent campaigns that seek to raise the minimum wage—not necessarily in order to promote class consciousness or equity or even to "save the middle class," but simply because it is the right thing to do.

In the ideological conflict over rising inequality, grace morality presents a few tactical advantages. Unlike egalitarianism, its goal is personal redemption, rather than social justice, and its perspective is fundamentally spiritual, rather than economic. As a result, it moves us away from the zero-sum conflict of egalitarianism, even as it encourages a society where economic competition becomes less important and shared prosperity becomes more possible. For these very reasons, grace morality can help build coalitions across party lines. It can persuade even some of society's well-off to consider the kinds of redistributive policies that might otherwise clash with their natural bias in favor of a narrower, self-justifying morality. In short, I see grace morality as a good complement to the egalitarian approach that unfortunately, in recent years, has failed to gain much traction.

Grace is an attitude that a few of my workers expressed, each in their own way. For them, it was about not letting affluence or status define them, and not caring about the competition that put some on top and others, including them, at bottom. It was about finding a sense of acceptance and peace within a frenzied society that is always sorting good from bad. Of course, as the story of David Vihan makes clear, policies are necessary, too: by alleviating painful scarcities of income, they can lay the soil for a sensibility of grace to bloom. Again, my research emphasizes the substantial role that policy can play in fostering values, by reintegrating jobless workers, sustaining their households, and keeping temporary labor-market problems from spiraling into the more pernicious failures of bankruptcy, divorce, illness, and hopelessness. Grace and egalitarianism thereby build upon each other in a virtuous circle.

And yet I also see grace as much more than a strategy. This brings me to the third—and for me, the most compelling—reason for grace. Meritocracy is a jealous god, bearing manna in one hand and a sword in the other. Those who fail are struck down, assailed by a censure all the more painful because it is deserved. They suffer, as do those who love and depend on them. For a time society may continue in its contest, ignoring the discarded, but as their numbers grow, and as the divide widens—to paraphrase the philosophers, and quote the prophets—the kingdom is brought to desolation.[6]

I wholeheartedly believe that grace adds a sense of proportion and balance to the soulless conversation we are currently having on issues of equality and justice, which is so focused on winners and losers and whose group prospers at the expense of others. There is a hunger in our society, I think, for more—for a sense of purpose beyond achievement or justice, and for a sense of connection beyond class and clique.

A TALE OF TWO SAFETY NETS

When I was doing my research for this book, I expected to find a good deal of financial hardship among the unemployed workers I interviewed, but in many ways the less tangible consequences of losing a job turned out to be more important. Long-term joblessness and failed institutions had driven some of my workers to desperate measures: taking showers with pots of water heated on the stove, making do with half or none of their prescribed medications, attending Narcotics Anonymous meetings for affordable therapy. Even for those who could make ends meet, though, the loss of good jobs that had supported families and liveli-hoods, and the poor prospects of finding new jobs just as sustaining, were brutal blows to their sense of identity and worth. What I could not get out of my head was how these men and women felt about their situ-ation: bewildered, frustrated, despondent, cast aside.

While one school of thought stresses the powerlessness of government in the face of globalization and related economic shifts, and another tends to see an expanded welfare state as a panacea for social ills, this book stakes out a view somewhere in the middle. As millions of the long-term unemployed go through the stress and despair of losing their incomes and identities, generous and well-implemented policies slow, and sometimes even reverse, their descent. And yet the vulnerabilities of the modern-day social safety net continue to grow, due to mounting costs that national governments struggle to pay, escalating global competition, and a pervasive culture of judgment that justifies society's growing inequalities even among the labor market's apparent failures.

I have argued that the long-term unemployed face two key problems in today's labor market. First, getting a good job requires that ordinary workers—white-collar and, increasingly, blue-collar—bring more to the workplace than just a good work ethic. From certificates to college degrees, from cheerful personalities to networking skills, they need to show clearly that they possess the kinds of human and cultural capital necessary for the remaining jobs that pay well. Second, workers with less education suffer from a relative disadvantage in seeking out these jobs because the standards for credentialing and job-search sophistica-tion keep rising. What I call the capital speedup—the higher bar of required human and cultural capital—means that their efforts to catch up with their more advantaged rivals often come to naught.

In Canada, government-funded action centers and other generous government policies of retraining and support helped address the skills mismatch that hindered my workers in the job market. They encour-aged more people to go back to school and acquire the knowledge they needed to compete in burgeoning industries. Yet, their futile job searches, sometimes even after their second-chance stints in school, sug-gest that training policies alone will not solve the problems faced by these workers. There simply are not enough good jobs to go around, and these workers will, on the whole, fall behind in the race for employment. Also needed, then, are policies that will generate more good jobs for workers from all backgrounds.

During the recession, the Obama administration's emergency measures meant that the unemployment benefits that Americans received were about as generous as those on the Canadian side, and the Americans actually received their checks for much longer. Because unemployment benefits ended in Canada after just a year, the long-term unemployed there had to rely sooner on public assistance and other stigmatized forms of aid. However, the policy situation has reversed dramatically in the years since my fieldwork, so that now the advantage is back on the Canadian side. In terms of health care, my American workers had a much harder time affording visits to the doctor or emergency room after they lost their jobs, which meant that their health emergencies at times spiraled out of control. Canadians also dealt with problems getting medications and care that the single-payer system did not cover, but overall they had many fewer problems with medical bills, and peer helpers at their action centers helped them cope emotionally as their unemployment lingered.

Debt and other forms of financial hardship were most severe among my American parts workers. However, the racial mix of my interviewees, which on the U.S. side came disproportionately from a more disadvantaged black population, may account for the worse outcomes to some extent. I argued that African American unionized autoworkers—an older and more privileged group than has been studied in recent research—experienced the shocks of unemployment all the more severely because their extended families could mobilize relatively few resources for them. Although they had well-established employment records, they found their social networks of little assistance in finding new jobs and making up for their lost income.

The policy differences I observed are complicated—perhaps skewed in favor of Canadian outcomes, due to the racial mix of my sample, or perhaps skewed in favor of American outcomes, due to federal emergency measures and my focus on a politically powerful group of manufacturing workers who were the beneficiaries of generous trade-adjustment policies. Yet there is one area where Canada clearly excels: its vigorous support of single-parent households, as well as single-earner households more generally.

The lower rates of marriage and higher rates of single-parenthood among working-class households mean that losing a job hits them much harder. Indeed, my workers who were single parents tended to fare the worst as their unemployment deepened. Workers without children did fairly well, and interestingly, older workers whose partners earned decent wages did best of all, thanks to both the financial security of the other person's paychecks and the psychological defense of "early retirement." Married or cohabiting couples with children, on the other hand, had mixed outcomes. Quarrels over finances and other kinds of stress tore apart some of their relationships, especially on the U.S. side of the border. More materialistic values may have made partners there more impatient with meager contributions to the shared bank account. On the other hand, my research suggests that income assistance and state-subsidized educations for families also help lower the stakes of joblessness for those unemployed workers—especially, but not exclusively, men—who wish to remain "marriage material" within households at real risk of poverty and bankruptcy. Regardless of their effects on marriage, Canada's targeted measures to help struggling households did keep many of my families from falling precipitously down the income ladder.

This book has also proposed a new concept—*stunted meritocracy*—that helps us understand the highly competitive and yet fundamentally inequitable situation that ordinary workers find themselves in today. The labor market, I have argued, is under the sway of two separate organizing principles: fraternalism and meritocracy.[7] In the fraternal capitalism practiced at the top, elite professionals and managers pursue both market and family advantage—banding together to wall off their markets or professions from competition, intervening to give their children an enduring head start, and otherwise tilting opportunities toward themselves and their families. In the lower and middle tiers of the labor market, however, the economic and political means that ordinary workers once used to exert strategic power, such as organized labor and activist government, have largely been swept away. What matters now for them is the size of the personal store of human and cultural capital they have accumulated. Hard work matters, but it is no longer sufficient.

Finally, this book has examined the ways that workers like mine understand what it means to be unemployed and what they need to do to escape their condition. A substantial minority of my workers expressed shame or self-blame, which grew as the length of their unemployment grew. My workers recognized that they no longer were considered meritworthy in today's economy, which prizes education and other markers of ability. In both countries, this led to a sense of shame regarding their low status. The Americans and parts workers, however, were quicker to feel self-blame—a sense that this status was deserved.

Their self-blame drew from a realistic acknowledgment of their deficiency but also arose, in part, from an ideological perspective that I call *meritocratic morality*.

This widespread system of belief, I argued, fosters a culture of judgment that encourages self-blame and diverts any outbound anger toward the very institutions that might combat society's inequalities. I think the term has four advantages over previously used concepts. First, I distinguish it from other kinds of ideologies within a coherent moral typology. Second, I believe that *meritocratic morality* best captures the essence of the dominant ideology, which is about individualism but also about a certain type of critical judgment regarding success and failure. Third, the term encourages us to think of the American Dream as a universal moral vision held by people throughout the world. Indeed, by opposing any sort of biases except those relevant to personal ability and effort, the meritocratic ideology presents a cosmopolitan and inclusive character that well suits today's rational and interconnected global economy.

Meritocratic morality shapes the ways that workers distinguish right and wrong in the distribution of spoils in the labor market, while downplaying the trade-offs of the deregulated market: greater inequality and less security. While this perspective has historically been strongest among white-collar professionals and managers, I find that it affects the thinking of even unionized blue-collar workers like mine. I suggest that its nature may have changed in ways that lead to greater self-blame among the unemployed, due to technological and cultural changes that include the decline of unions and leftist ideologies, which provided an alternative language of class consciousness, and evolving understandings of merit and its measurement, which degrade the value of less advantaged workers. The existence of strong (if declining) unions in Canada helped bolster the self-worth of workers there, while the importance given to educational credentials and other markers of merit undermined the status of my parts workers in particular.

There are other, subtle ways that meritocratic morality influences how individuals view institutions. My workers—particularly the Americans—responded to their unemployment by withdrawing into themselves and putting faith in their own ability to find new work and pull themselves out of their predicament. They were upset and demoralized by the mediocre service of government bureaucracies implementing social policies. They were also angry at the ways their unions played favorites. In view of these frustrating encounters, some of my workers were skeptical that these institutions could provide any kind of solution to their problems. On the Canadian side, peer helpers who used to work at the same plants provided my workers with personal advising that made their experiences with government programs better, placing less of the focus there on self-reliance. However, there was only so much these grass-roots organizations could do, given the high-level policy decisions that constrained them. For their part, my workers understood that the economy had changed, and they had to adapt. Beyond a simple displeasure with certain institutions for failing them, however, they expressed a defensive acknowledgment, and sometimes even an internalization, of the dominant ideology. At its most extreme, their criticism of unions and corporations was cast in ideological terms. There was not a similar critique of government.

The way that workers see organized labor is a particularly critical consideration for those seeking to build a more egalitarian society. Unions, some of my workers said, violate moral principles by helping people who are not worthy of that help. In this way, meritocratic morality assaults the very legitimacy of organized labor, weakening a union's ability to recruit or retain members even as it energizes anti-union activists. In turn, the political push to eliminate unions devastates the very institutions that, with their organizational and ideological potency, are best able to spread the egalitarian gospel.

Indeed, the real-world circumstances that government and unions deal with in both countries have worsened considerably in recent years, thanks in part to shared trends of globalization and automation. In the United States there has been a decidedly stronger pro-corporate movement, which has worked to promote the meritocratic ideology and attack the political leadership and unions that champion principles of shared prosperity. In Canada and Europe, on the other hand, the economic and political environment remains more amenable to egalitarian solutions. Today, we can look to Sweden for a model of a strong welfare state that intervenes forcefully in people's lives, and to Germany for powerful labor unions that win high wages for the great mass of workers. But even in those countries, the welfare state is slowly being chipped away. As I have noted, labor unions and pro-equality advocacy organizations have been steadily declining in Canada. In Switzerland, a country with less income inequality than Canada, jet-setting industry magnates have recently taken up a familiar banner—"the politics of envy"—in attacking (with some success) limits on their pay.[8] In other words, they are following a path long trodden in America, where socially isolated and politically savvy elites have attempted to push public opinion and policy away from government intervention and labor rights. In turn, for ordinary workers everywhere, the diminishment of egalitarian institutions dims the prospects for a decent livelihood and sharpens the self-blame of long-term unemployment.

As the market economy gains in strength, meritocratic morality crowds out its ideological rivals. Yet the meritocratic ideology is ultimately contradictory: its promise of equal opportunity is eventually dismantled as the winners of the race stamp out any budding competition and safeguard their gains. This is the fundamental paradox of meritocracy. Without tough measures to stop elite workers from gaming the system and elite parents from passing down their advantages—measures that imply strong egalitarian institutions and some rollback of parental and market freedoms—the reality of inequality eventually overtakes the rhetoric of meritocracy.

A LIST OF POLICIES—AND A PROBLEM

What can we do to help the last-place finishers in the meritocratic race—the long-term unemployed? On the Canadian side, my workers were too quickly shunted off into the welfare system, acutely undermining their sense of well-being and their drive to reenter the labor market. Because the hardship of unemployment often revolves around the toxic effects it has on mental health—even in the absence of severe financial problems—the question of framing policies as "deserved" (unemployment insurance) or "undeserved" (welfare) is perhaps more important than policymakers realize, not just to win the support of voters but also to avoid further harm to the individuals being helped. Americans, in turn, could emulate the ways that Canada makes it easier for low-income workers to qualify for benefits and tops up the benefit levels for those with children. More concretely, letting severance and buyout recipients tap their unemployment benefits earlier, as a Canadian pilot program did, would provide these households with a more dependable revenue stream and improve their ability to plan for an extended bout of unemployment.

Americans can learn something as well from the faithful commitment that their northern neighbors have to peer programs and workforce development more generally. In America's patchy and underfunded system, states can get away with providing little in the way of information or assistance to workers who lose their jobs, and "best practices" like peer programs get knocked about by political winds, if they are considered at all. In contrast, a robust and rapid response to layoffs—as is the routine approach in Ontario—not only ensures that unemployed workers get the help they need quickly. If done early enough (thanks to government-mandated advance notice), it can also give the employer and employees the chance to work together to avert at least some of the layoffs, through wage concessions, employee ownership, job sharing, or other strategies.

As they hunt for jobs, the unemployed can also benefit from having a familiar and welcoming place to turn to, one where dedicated peer advocates, rather than unknown bureaucrats, work on their cases and help them deal with any confusion or shame they have about getting government services. By tapping and strengthening personal connections already in place—in other words, leveraging and growing social capital—government-funded action centers provide more personal and personalized forms of assistance, making sure that workers don't get ignored by a strained system that inevitably favors the loudest and most persistent voices.

Social policies targeted at single parents are controversial because of fears that they will encourage couples not to marry. But we also have to consider the reality described by the cases of my struggling families. If there is not much in the way of a public safety net, then a partner's paycheck multiplies in importance—leading to the sorts of instrumental behaviors that wrenched some of my families apart. Finding ways to keep families together is essential, and it is perhaps best achieved through income supports for families with children, period—single-parent as well as two-parent. By doing so, we will avoid pushing spouses to stay in unhealthy and abusive relationships, a matter of great importance to workers like mine. On the Canadian side, a number of universal benefits are targeted at the parents of young children—poor and middle-class alike—not only winning broad public support for these measures but also helping couples of all types manage the work-life balance early on—and therefore helping them stay together. Likewise, America could follow Canada in vigorously assisting two-parent households with one wage earner, making more realistic the *option* for someone—either male or female—to stay at home and take care of young children. (The cultural work I describe later is obviously critical in this area, in encouraging men to choose this option, too.) This old-fashioned model could be revamped for a gender-equal age, and it does have certain advantages in terms of unemployment, in that the stay-at-home parent can choose to go back into the labor force to make up for the family's lost income—an option not available to already tapped-out two-earner couples. Of course, its family structure is not very sustainable if too many households choose the two-earner model instead, driving up the cost of living for all and making it harder to get by on just one income. That is another reason that social policies and the incentives they create are crucial.

Some of the most noteworthy policies now in place to help lower-income families, such as the earned-income tax credit and the refundable child tax credit, only help families with wages. Considering jobless benefits to be earned income for some purposes would allow these carefully targeted programs to better help the unemployed. As they are in Canada, tax credits for struggling American households should be paid out across the year, not just offered through an annual tax refund, so that unemployed workers and their families can better rely on the income and use it wisely. Finally, American workers would clearly benefit from having more affordable options for health insurance after they lose their jobs. This is a shortcoming that Obamacare's expanded Medicaid coverage and state insurance exchanges are already helping to address, assuming they survive the ongoing political assault.

The social safety net, however, should not be judged just on the size of its benefit checks. It also matters how well the benefits and regulations are implemented. Labor unions and government bureaucracies—on both sides of the border, but particularly south of it—fail to make good on their promises and principles. Reformers need to find ways to make them more accountable and responsive.[9] After all, how people experience policies is just as important as what those policies are. Some would suggest that government mimic the private sector and their best practices in customer service—or even outsource those activities to private firms.[10] Governments on both sides of the border are already taking up these approaches, and clearly there is much the private sector can teach. But the easiest and quickest way to help the unemployed would be to follow the coworker-staffed model of Canada's action centers. A departure from the stereotype of ossified and unresponsive government bureaucracies, this strategy to help laid-off workers is flexible and pragmatic.

While the social policies I have just described can make a huge difference for struggling households, in another sense they are limited. As I've noted, jobless workers suffer not just from a deficit of income and health care but also from their very status of being unemployed. They pay a steep social and psychological toll for not achieving what a society obsessed with success expects of them. In this sense, the problems of isolation and stigma that frequently afflict the unemployed cannot be solved by checks—or even counseling. People are proud of having good jobs, not of receiving good government benefits.

Critics of a strong social safety net for the unemployed have gone further in arguing that it is counterproductive. Such efforts to combat inequality, they say, will shrink the economic pie for everyone and bankrupt the state. Historically speaking, unemployment has tended to be lower in America than in European countries with even costlier welfare states and stronger unions than Canada's. Continental firms are loath to hire because of restrictions on job terminations and minimum wages, and lavish unemployment benefits discourage workers from finding work. As a result, the critics say, government intervention may diminish some people's immediate hardships while worsening the broader problem of having too many unemployed people.

Too much is made of this trade-off between social protection and job creation, as the recent recession—which brought widespread unemployment to America's laissez-faire labor market—reminds us. Market economies of whatever variety of capitalism can engineer their fiscal, trade, and monetary policies in ways that spur growth and create jobs. Meanwhile, a moderately strong social safety net is not necessarily a drag on economic activity. One study of the extension of unemployment benefits during the Great Recession, for example, found that it reduced rates of reemployment by only a small amount. And even if we assume that a "dynamic," deregulated economy does create more jobs, it is not clear that society is any better off if it winds up creating shoddy forms of employment that cannot support families and must be propped up with government subsidies. In fact, research finds that a bad job can be even more soul-crushing than no job at all.[11]

One way to help the unemployed get *good* jobs is, of course, education. In addition to education's moral value as an end in itself, government support of retraining makes good financial sense. A large population of poor people with few marketable skills hems in economic growth.[12] A faulty educational infrastructure is just as much an impediment to a high-powered economy as decrepit roads and bridges. Germany's recent prosperity speaks to the advantages of this strategy. While the rest of Europe floundered, Germany weathered the global economic crisis relatively well, in part because of its innovative and efficient manufacturing plants run by highly skilled workers. High-quality training and education for all has helped this dominant sector maintain a capable workforce, one organized by powerful unions and worker councils.

The Trade Adjustment Assistance provided on the U.S. side is the most generous retraining program I came across. However, it only applies to workers in the manufacturing sector who can prove they lost their jobs due to foreign competition. Retraining a much broader segment of the unemployed population would probably entail a program like Second Career in Ontario, which has less generous benefits than the U.S. federal program but assists all sorts of workers—including those in the vital and growing service sector—and doesn't have as many logistical hurdles, such as the need to certify a worksite. Even Michigan's innovative No Worker Left Behind program pales in comparison. America could learn from this model.

Another way to connect unemployed workers to jobs is to reduce the discrimination they face in the job market. Governments should provide more in the way of incentives to hire the long-term unemployed. Besides tax breaks and the like, governments could pursue various forms of class-based affirmative action, weighing unemployment status or low socioeconomic status in their decisions about hiring job candidates and selecting students, and encouraging the private sector to do the same. In general, what we consider merit when we decide between job or college applicants can be broadened and loosened to some extent, so that more people from disadvantaged backgrounds—the long-term unemployed or minorities—will get a second look.[13] Finding ways to prod businesses to make their HR practices less prone to bias would help minority job seekers in particular.[14] Israel uses third-party staffing agencies extensively, which tend to make hiring decisions more transparent and impartial, and which can also reduce self-blame among the unemployed by clarifying the reasons they were passed over.[15]

But as important as retraining and antidiscrimination measures are, rising inequality dilutes their benefits. With job growth mainly at the top and bottom of the labor market, the new jobs accessible to disadvantaged workers tend to be of the worst kinds. For the limited number of good positions, the competition has intensified, and while some of these workers will manage to do well, most will not. These are more intractable kinds of challenges, which a more broadly meritocratic labor market or a couple years of government-funded training—however rational and useful for the *individual* worker—do not really address.

Shrinking this class divide would mean targeting tuition and income supports at the very neediest workers. Investing in better education for lower-income children would perhaps have an even larger payoff, particularly education in the earliest years, when the benefits are tremendous.[16] Some studies have found that even children from poor house-holds, when targeted with forceful educational interventions early in their lives, can perform just as well as children from more advantaged backgrounds.[17] But efforts to scale up many promising approaches to bring quality education to all have not yet been successful. It may be that more affluent households naturally respond to any well-intended efforts to equalize opportunities for the poor in ways that preserve their relative advantage.[18] Upper-middle-class children, for instance, have learned to dominate SAT assessments of college readiness through private tutoring, gaming the system and neutralizing the threat.

By the same token, government-subsidized retraining for less advantaged workers may very well be matched by increases (unsubsidized or subsidized) among the more advantaged. This privileged group can also distinguish themselves to employers in the arena of cultural capital, retaining their edge in the labor market through more prestigious schooling and more sophisticated networks. In any case, rising tuition and the growing burden of student loans hint at the future limits of this strategy of "college for all."

Another targeted strategy to reduce inequality more directly is encouraging savings by less advantaged households. Automatically setting up savings accounts for each child and topping up the amounts given to lower-income families would lessen not only wealth inequality but also racial inequality, given the huge disadvantage in assets between black and white households—a particularly stark problem for my African American families, who could not rely on as much assistance from family and friends. Again, however, the fact that households with greater education tend to have greater financial literacy (and elites game the financial markets in more pointed ways) means that the wealth divide—tremendously wide already—maybe be quite resistant to these attempts to reduce it.

Capital speedup works across these various divides—educational quantity and quality, human and cultural capital, worker merit and investor acumen—to maintain existing inequalities. In these ways it sabotages egalitarian interventions that are meant to intercede in the free market with a light touch. Without policies to create enough good jobs for all, or other robust attempts to address the relative inequality that continues to consign workers from poorer backgrounds to poorer education and poorer skill sets, less skilled job seekers who retrain may still find themselves outclassed, shut out of the labor market in favor of their savvier competitors. And yet this problem is not confined to the labor market's grimmest corners. White-collar workers increasingly find their livelihoods jeopardized by automation, outsourcing, and offshoring as well. While many of the unemployed will go on to get decent jobs, millions of others will not, as today's recalcitrant rates of long-term unemployment make painfully clear. That is a tragic outcome that needs to be addressed—and not just in terms of quick fixes.

These unequal outcomes remain important regardless of the level of economic growth because, as I noted in chapter 1, we now live in a society that has attained a considerable degree of affluence, so that what increasingly matters in determining people's happiness is *relative* success.[19] Even if a booming economy brings more prosperity to all, those at the bottom remain at society's bottom, assailed by the doubts and criticisms that I have described throughout this book. Only by finding ways to employ them—and, more broadly, to compress social inequality—can we take away this sting.

There are two ways to deal more directly with the fact that ordinary workers cannot get good jobs. However, they are not so good at leaving the waters of the market unstirred. One strategy involves reducing overall inequality—thereby transforming the economy's bad jobs into relatively better ones. In the long term, this would entail aggressive policies of economic regulation and progressive taxation to level a playing field distorted by elite power, such as estate taxes to reduce the transmission of advantage from one generation to another, higher taxes on capital gains, and stronger regulation of other streams of income that elite workers—particularly those in the financial sector—rely upon. To bridge the gap in pay between ordinary and elite workers, the labor movement needs to be revived through reforms in the law—to give it a fighting chance in today's globalized economy—and also through reforms in the ways unions are governed—to make sure these organizations help workers more generally rather than the interests of certain narrow groups. In the short term, shrewd policies can nudge employers to improve the quality of their jobs. Paul Osterman and Beth Shulman have put forward a sensible platform for how this could be achieved. Many of their recommendations require that government collaborate with firms—or at least recognize their need to operate efficiently and profitably—in order to appeal to the private sector's long-term interest in employing productive workers with high morale. Their ideas range from establishing standards, regulations, and industry norms that not only improve pay and work conditions but also make the business environment less uncertain, to finding ways to provide low-wage workers with training and career ladders up to better-paid jobs. They also see moderate increases in the minimum wage—a policy change popular even with the American public—as a powerful means of improving the quality of jobs. The research, they point out, shows few or no negative effects on employment (perhaps because it reduces turnover and other kinds of costs) and yet substantial gains even for workers with wages higher than the minimum (given that employers typically react to wage increases at the bottom by raising pay higher up as well). The overall goal of these various approaches to dealing with inequality is, as Christopher Jencks argues, not to obliterate competition but "to change the rules of the game so as to reduce the rewards of competitive success and the costs of failure."[20]

The second strategy is to reduce unemployment more directly, but in a way that promotes equality at the same time. The focus here is on growing the demand for labor—that is, *creating* good jobs that less advantaged workers can actually get.[21] Investing in infrastructure projects that provide well-paid jobs to workers with little education is one way of doing this. Even in the United States, there are prominent and potent examples of this interventionist approach: FDR's Works Progress Administration and the Civilian Conservation Corps, two New Deal initiatives to create employment for jobless workers. These work-relief programs bolstered the nation's infrastructure during the Great Depression, but more importantly, they gave people jobs and, with them, dignity.

All of the interventionist policies and programs I have just described, however, have their weaknesses. Unless countries can work together to prevent capital from fleeing to the least regulated and unionized nations, policies aimed at reducing overall inequality will be hard to implement effectively. And although significant minorities in both America and Canada favor the government creation of jobs for everyone who wants one, the prevailing view in mainstream economics is that this approach is inefficient and vulnerable to cronyism. Meanwhile, increasing the earned-income tax credit would mean even more government spending to subsidize the very businesses society could use less of: employers who cannot or will not pay a living wage.

Indeed, this is the crux of the problem. The toolbox of available policies to combat inequality is shrinking, owing not just to economic and technological changes but also to political and ideological ones. As the economic consensus has shifted to the right, policymakers have shied away from aggressive government intervention. They have fallen back on a social-safety-net approach that largely puts bandages on the wounds of discouraged workers and makes up for the shortcomings of corporations that pay low wages and benefits—the welfare state as a codependent of capitalism. As it is for my workers, this view is partly realistic. In an integrated global market, greater government intervention is punished in the capital markets and leads to diminished competitiveness. Perhaps in a world of uncontested European-style social democracies there would be more space for individual nations to build well-reinforced social safety nets, but in the world we have, the disruptive energies of capitalism in those parts of the world where it is unfettered can put unsustainable economic (and therefore political) pressures on strong welfare states, which must vie for jobs and growth.

At the same time, the political ideology makes the social policy more extreme, pushing its adherents toward a fixation on individual failings and skepticism with regard to robust efforts to ease suffering, however beneficial they may be—during the recession, for instance, economic stimulus and housing relief. And yet the "acceptable" policies nowadays are those that reinforce a meritocratic ideal that even by itself—in a perfect society or a perfect market economy, as I have argued—will perpetuate and exacerbate inequality. Indeed, it is noteworthy that over the decades the American public has largely moved away from any support of direct government intervention in the economy, instead preferring initiatives to expand educational opportunities—a sign in itself of the ways that both ideology and realism shape our policy choices.[22]

What should give hope to egalitarians is that in spite of the ideological cannonade raining down in recent years—on Americans in particular—public opinion remains mixed on these questions. With the right opening, strong social movements dedicated to fostering equality can win over the undecided. Beyond their work haggling with companies over wages and benefits, unions have long been involved in national and international efforts to push for big-picture policy changes and evangelize the egalitarian faith. But given that the climb back to labor glory will be long and tough, we also need to consider alternative forms of organizing against inequality. Scholars have written extensively about a very promising network of grass-roots activists, the Industrial Areas Foundation (IAF), which has established local and state-level operations to help working families throughout the country.[23] The IAF brings together people of faith and trains them to do methodical organizing around bread-and-butter issues of wages and community resources. Its hardnosed and unabashedly adversarial approach has led to numerous legislative victories, and in the process, it has swept a wide-ranging group of ordinary citizens into political activism and leadership. Beyond the IAF, a new generation of activists—working for groups like the Restaurant Opportunities Center and Justice for Janitors—have been thinking outside the (traditional union) box, finding ways to advocate for workers, many of them immigrants, even in sectors that have historically been difficult to organize. These worker centers and community organizations use a variety of methods—from savvy media campaigns to street protests, boycotts, and lawsuits—to influence government policies and corporate behavior.[24] More broadly, coalitions of these worker advocates along with traditional unions, faith groups, students, and others have rallied around a number of prominent campaigns in recent years—from globe-spanning strikes for higher wages in the fast-food industry, to demonstrations and lobbying for living-wage ordinances in many localities. Enterprising unions like the SEIU have taken a leadership role in these new struggles. The UAW, too, has focused more energy on building coalitions and championing social-justice issues in recent years.

The grass-roots organizing that began in 2011 with the Occupy Wall Street protests has been the most visible expression of anger against the growing class divide—in its activists' words, the rising fortunes of the "1 percent" at the expense of the "99 percent." Its much-publicized protests on Wall Street and elsewhere were modeled after past episodes of international activism over trade issues and other leftist causes, using a consensus-driven, "leaderless" style of organizing rooted in anarchist thought. Politicians such as Elizabeth Warren and Bill de Blasio later won office on similar anti-inequality platforms, and labor unions and advocacy groups adopted some of the same anti–"1 percent" rhetoric. Perhaps pushed along by this movement's momentum, Obama has addressed inequality in a number of major speeches.

Nevertheless, even these silver linings on the egalitarian horizon are flanked by clouds. Occupy has been much less successful than the American Tea Party in converting the energy of their street protests into the more pragmatic power of electoral politics. There are many reasons for this difference, and perhaps the most important is the funding that wealthy individuals and corporations have poured into certain Tea Party organizations.[25] But it may also hint at how the public's views on economic policy—again, over the long term—have shifted to the right. Indeed, more recent Occupy protests have gained little media attention, and a portion of the public has written off this kind of activism as fringe, according to polls.[26] Meanwhile, in his speeches on inequality, Obama has been careful to use less strident terms like "opportunity gap" and "broad-based growth." As I described in chapter 5, the faltering economic mobility he highlighted is still not as great a public worry as we might expect, given the meteoric rise in income inequality over the last few decades, and there is even less support for government intervention.

With the outsized influence that the wealthy generally have in politics, and the climate change–like hurdle of international cooperation needed to implement anti-inequality measures effectively, it is hard to see how any action will take place without a stronger popular movement clamoring for it. For that reason, too, it is troubling that labor unions have continued their decline in America, Canada, and elsewhere, with little hope as of now that public support for them will surge or that unions will roll back those losses anytime soon. The diverse groups fighting for workers' rights today cannot put nearly as many bodies on the streets or dollars in political war chests as unions used to do in their prime, and they have not been as adept in making the case for the "moral economy" in ways that connect with large swaths of the workforce. While Occupy may someday flourish into a more broad-based movement, its cause has a long way to go before it attains the mainstream appeal or electoral power of the civil rights and progressive movements of the twentieth century. Meanwhile, the pro-corporate movement has used its embarrassment of resources to conquer the ground ceded by unions, building an arsenal of think tanks, media outlets, lobbying groups, and grassroots organizations to advance its platforms of policy and ideology.

As the economic situation worsens for ordinary workers, of course, forceful government approaches may eventually win over the public and policymakers everywhere. But in the meantime, it is worth thinking about what we can do to speed up that process of cultural and political change and reduce some of the economic carnage along the way. Political leaders and organizers will need to build and strengthen movements that champion egalitarian goals, as I've discussed. But artists, intellectuals, and journalists also have an important, independent role. Their work can help counter the ideological arguments of those elites who defend today's stunted meritocracy. They can offer a compelling alternative understanding of a just economic system, one that dispels the meritocratic ideology's prevailing myths and opens up space for the kinds of policies that can deal with growing inequality and unemployment in a meaningful and enduring way. Right now, many of these efforts at cultural organizing and messaging are aimed at cultivating a sense of shared responsibility and common ground, justifying attempts to narrow the economic divide by drawing upon universal values like equal opportunity and fairness. I would like to encourage another strategy to complement this ongoing work: using the morality of grace to directly attack the pervasive culture of judgment.

MAKING PEACE WITH CLASS WARFARE

One difficulty that the Obama administration had in defending its economic stimulus legislation in 2009 was that it had to resort to a tepid sort of relative argument: without the stimulus, things would have been worse. Those who worry about inequality run into a similar problem when they argue, in this post–Berlin Wall era, for a more balanced economic approach—what can be characterized as "capitalism lite." In economics as in most areas of life, a happy medium is best. But it is not necessarily the best rallying cry for a popular movement. Not unlike how mainline Protestants, with their nuanced theologies and tolerant faith, have been outflanked by their fundamentalist rivals in the struggle over Christianity, advocates of efforts to temper capitalism's excesses have found themselves at a disadvantage in their ideological war with the free-market hard-liners on the other side.

Marxism had the dictatorship of the proletariat. Meritocratic morality has what amounts to the opposite ideal—a dictatorship of the productive. It has a straightforward and self-contained logic. As we can see in the views of my workers, even those who suffer within its economic system can see it as reasonable. Wealth needs to be created before it can be redistributed, the argument goes, and nothing succeeds better at creating wealth than the market. Its high rewards encourage high-risk ventures, which create new technologies and more efficient economies of scale, which bring greater material comfort to all. As a result, extraordinary pay for extraordinary talent is justified. Unemployment is a price of doing business in a dynamic economy—just another outbreak of creative destruction for realists to accept, and for go-getters to exploit. And unionism is an unethical form of advancing one's wages and benefits, bullying the employer into submission—that is, "mob rule" in the workplace—rather than gaining the skills, experience, or education that would give the individual an honorable means of leverage. For those who hold to these tenets of faith, the promised land is a libertarian meritocracy where talent is rewarded, responsibility demanded, and failure punished.

With the downfall of its own maximalist position—communism— the egalitarian ideology is left with an argument that is more timid and less coherent, even if it is ultimately more socially beneficial and sustainable. But beyond the half-hearted way it is often posed politically, the egalitarian argument has more fundamental difficulties dealing with the meritocratic critique. First, it does not get at one key part of the problem: meritocracy's focus on measurement and judgment.

To revise the biblical phrase, our love of measurement is a root of all kinds of evil. In the labor market, as I have argued, the drive to evaluate efficiency and effectiveness in all aspects of life creates new scarcities—new skills to acquire, new talents to master—and, in doing so, continually ratchets up the level of competition. It greatly expands the breadth and depth of the inequalities that exist, allowing some fortunate individuals to achieve ever-higher levels of success while reinforcing the overall disadvantage of those currently at the bottom of the labor market, who must now succeed across a growing set of criteria to compete. Muscular policies of taxation, regulation, and job creation are needed to deal with the consequences of this growing inequality, as I have argued. But such a steep degree of market intervention is vulnerable, in turn, to the moral arsenal of the meritocratic ideology, which dismisses redistribution as "unfair" and "unnatural," an outcome of envy and resentment, a cynical attempt to tear down our most fortunate citizens and engage in "class warfare."[27]

Egalitarian morality finds it difficult to overcome these objections, in part because it, like its meritocratic rival, has a fundamentally economic perspective as well. Sensitive to any inequalities that result, it measures and judges in the opposite direction—but it measures and judges nonetheless. The egalitarian perspective focuses on the material and quantifiable, and therefore even its adherents cannot help seeing the redistribution of their wealth as a sacrifice. Egalitarianism makes the case that this sacrifice serves a greater good that will either redound to their tangible benefit or fulfill their desires for social justice. But this is complicated by the fact that the people receiving the sacrifice may not be deserving of it—and here, too, an economic perspective demands the measurement of their deservingness. Racial, national, and other group biases make the people being evaluated appear less worthy of assistance, thereby etching further cracks into the egalitarian ideal of unity. Within today's increasingly diverse and globalized societies, fraternal partiality and meritocratic judgment in this way undermine efforts to coordinate an effective policy response to inequality. Meanwhile, to the extent that ordinary workers breathe in the cultural air of constant striving and achievement, the competition thrills, the dream beckons, and the high-stakes game goes on—with little concern for its dangers, and much contempt for responsible limits.

Grace morality is a direct assault on this ideal of deservingness and this idolization of success, both of which stand squarely in the way of a more equitable society. As I described in chapter 1, in its most inclusive and universalistic forms the essence of the doctrine is radical acceptance and a refusal to measure or judge. In this particular sense, it is the opposite of meritocratic morality—championing the virtue of equanimity over the virtue of excellence.[28] Like egalitarian morality, grace embodies an ethos of compassion and sacrifice, rather than competition and advancement. But it also can be distinguished from the egalitarian ideology in several key ways, which allow it to evade some of the criticisms that meritocratic morality throws at its egalitarian enemies. At the same time, it can serve the ends of egalitarianism, in a fashion not unlike how the morality of merit today serves the fraternal interests of privileged groups.

At its best, a morality of grace encourages us to downplay the importance of status, position, and material accumulation. It is not just that we should stop picking out the deserving from the undeserving. According to this viewpoint, the economic game itself, and its obsession with the acquisition of power and status, should not be the key source of meaning. Nor should the egalitarian pursuit of justice in the here and now, while important, become blinding. The world's major religious traditions, while diverse and contradictory, contain strands of this thinking. Love your enemies and turn the other cheek, say the Christians: God's kingdom is what truly matters. Reject the dualism of right and wrong, say the Buddhists, and abide in a spirit of compassion, reconciliation, and acceptance. Care little for worldly success or failure, admonishes the *Tao Te Ching*, and treat the good and bad with undiscriminating kindness. Ultimate reality is eternal and infinite, according to the Upanishads, and the individual self is one with it—and so on, across the various systems of spiritual thought, which may not use the term *grace* but offer examples of this concept in action.

In this sense, the cultural persuasion I advocate is about putting a spiritual heart into the hollow core of material strivings—pulling society back from its progression toward a future of, in Max Weber's words, "mechanized petrification," peopled by "specialists without spirit, sensualists without heart." Meritocratic morality maps onto the values that are essential to the market—industriousness, honesty, excellence, responsibility—but it winds up trapped in a materialist dead end.[29] On the other hand, the compassionate and all-encompassing perspective of grace, like the transcendent identity and community of fraternalism, grants us something more than the gains to be had in the day-to-day economic struggle.

Again, I need to emphasize that the particular religious traditions I have brought up so far are complex and cannot be placed within an ideological box of "grace" (or any single box, for that matter). More broadly, grace morality is not synonymous with religion. Many examples abound of the excessive moralizing of our modern-day Pharisees, in the pews and the markets alike, who judge other people zealously and expect purity and perfection in all areas. And yet throughout history there have been leaders and thinkers—saintly and secular—who have called for peace and redemption and an end to the constant competition of war, accumulation, and vengeance.

Indeed, while I have used the term *spiritual* to describe both fraternalism and grace, there are ways that secular and humanistic thought can tap into a similar perspective.[30] In our close friendships we see a model for the kind of nonjudgmental morality I have in mind. Initially, we may choose friends based on qualities we find interesting and praiseworthy, but over time, as relationships deepen, we care less about matters of merit and become more attached to the idiosyncrasies and uniqueness of that particular person—so that, as for the Velveteen Rabbit of the old childhood tale, even the shabbiness of age and decrepitude becomes a mark of beauty. In this sense, our failings and vulnerabilities make us lovable.

Likewise, a secular focus on the eternal and infinite universe puts human struggles in perspective. Astronomer Carl Sagan eloquently expressed this view in his book *Pale Blue Dot,* inspired by Voyager 1's photograph of Earth as a tiny speck against the vast blackness of space. Amid the competition and cruelty of human civilization, the image underscored the "folly of human conceits" and our responsibility to "deal more kindly with one another," Sagan wrote. "Our posturings, our imagined self-importance, the delusion that we have some privileged position in the universe, are challenged by this point of pale light."[31] In short, secular grace is about downplaying the importance of the struggles that tend to occupy humanity, and focusing instead on the exquisite nature of our ephemeral reality. Space, infinite, should remind us of life, finite; death, the great equalizer, is also a prophet of grace.

By tempering the judgments of meritocracy, grace morality can help bring us closer to a society of broadly shared prosperity. First, if the economic aspects of life are not so important, then the sacrifices required by redistribution do not weigh on us as heavily. The deservingness or otherwise of our peers does not matter as much, and the barriers of understanding between groups become less forbidding. Less focused on our accumulation and advancement across—in the broad scheme of things—meaninglessly finite metrics, we may be more willing to be charitable and conciliatory. Egalitarian policies that may have seemed anathema in a perspective of competition and scarcity can become less so in a perspective of compassion and abundance.

. . .

The morality of grace can also help achieve egalitarian outcomes by providing an overarching, oppositional ideology. As I noted earlier, egalitarianism has faced an ideological vacuum since the demise of communism and the discrediting of many Marxist doctrines. Grace morality offers another possible rallying point, which could conceivably win over some segments of the political Right. Fundamentally, it is about upholding a set of values not fixated on the material—building a society, perhaps, like the radical democracy that Karl Polanyi (a critic of Marxism) envisioned, one that looks to a horizon beyond the endless toil and quantified productivity of the market economy.

That said, grace morality is not intended to be a replacement for egalitarianism. It is not an opiate to help the disadvantaged forget their troubles in today's economy. In fact, the morality of grace perhaps has less to do with them, and more to do with those at the top—that is, changing the attitudes of elites toward those further down the labor market's totem pole.

As I noted earlier, surveys show that the American public has actually grown (at least in the past decade) somewhat *more* bothered by inequalities of pay—perhaps a sign of just how extreme income inequality has become. Do corporate executives have a different set of social norms today? Have they shifted away from the paternalistic mindset of earlier eras? Isolated within their gated communities and private jets, they may not feel as much pressure to keep their compensation to some reasonable multiple of how much they pay their workers, and they may see their stratospheric income as justified in an expansive global marketplace.[32] One recent survey of the attitudes of elites in the Chicago area (most of them among the nation's wealthiest 1 percent) does find that they, too, recognize that inequality is extreme and that executive pay is too high. However, they are much less likely to favor government action to address these concerns. (The survey did not ask many questions relating to meritocracy, but on one question, whether they support merit pay for teachers, elites overwhelmingly agreed, more so than the public as a whole.)[33] A separate body of research, meanwhile, finds that the more affluent tend to have less empathy for other people.[34] Much work could be done, then, to root out this dysfunctional "culture of prosperity" that prevails among elites, thereby improving the political chances of robust and sustained policies on behalf of the unemployed.

Political scientist Charles Murray has made the case for such a strategy, though his political objectives conflict with mine. For the sake of the common good, Murray argues, America's elites (he means here the well-educated professional population, rather than just the wealthy) must emerge from their stockades and lead the charge against a modern evil—namely, the cultural decline of the working class. He proposes a moral revolution—"a civic Great Awakening"—that would stir the new upper class from their complacent attitude of "ecumenical niceness" and inspire them to put forward their values, boldly and judgmentally so, as a standard that others can follow. Once society, led by the new upper class, places more pressure on the working class to shape up, they will stop behaving so badly. "To bring about this cultural change, we must change the language that we use whenever the topic of feckless men comes up," he writes. "Don't call them 'demoralized.' Call them whatever derogatory word you prefer. Equally important: Start treating the men who aren't feckless with respect."[35]

It is perhaps another indication of the growing strength of meritocratic morality that commentators like Murray find American civic culture remiss in its lack of judgmental thinking. If political correctness has made it more difficult to make distinctions based on gender, race, nationality, or sexual orientation, it has done little to squelch criticism in other areas. Indeed, today's labor market—shorn of the labor unions and government regulation that once provided a degree of restraint—judges with impunity, declaring some workers fit and others unfit. Such a perspective is a far cry from nonjudgmentalism; it is a form of ecumenical disdain.

If Murray calls for a Great Awakening on behalf of an even more purified morality of merit, I argue that what is needed is an opposing morality—one that balances the ideology of meritocracy, inequality, and judgment with an ethic of compassion, egalitarianism, and grace. Nevertheless, I believe Murray is right that more attention needs to be paid to elites—the well-educated, or the wealthy—and their role in creating a better society. As Murray observes, elites nowadays live walled off from the concerns of ordinary workers. Such isolation may feed the kinds of meritocratic zeal we find in the media—to take one particularly shrill example, the remarks by one venture capitalist that today's "rising tide of hatred of the successful one percent" is akin to Kristallnacht, the Nazi pogrom against Jews.[36]

Their social distance from the wealthy is not lost on my unemployed workers. "Rich people . . . only get richer, and . . . they don't see us— they don't see me down here," says John Hope, the fifty-five-year-old parts worker struggling to make ends meet in Detroit. "They don't see what's going on because they are living a good life. They don't know what you're going through. . . . You could try to tell them and they wouldn't even believe."

A RETURN TO BALANCE

How can society best deal with inequality, one of our generation's great moral challenges? Activists, artists, journalists, scholars, and other skilled communicators and organizers can help people come to a deeper understanding of society's widening divides through the various moral lenses I have described. In the mass media, they can appeal to the heart, weaving notions of grace into words and symbols that resonate with the public emotionally and spiritually. And on the ground, they can use this inclusive and energizing perspective to organize communities and lobby politicians on behalf of egalitarian policies. In short, grace can provide the messaging, fraternalism the organizing, and egalitarianism the policymaking.

As they did during the civil rights movement and countless others, clergy will have an important and natural role in this kind of activism. One pastor who has already taken up this banner is David Platt, a prominent evangelical Christian leader who heads a megachurch in Birmingham, Alabama. Platt has spoken out against the American Dream, arguing that the gospel as preached by Jesus is antithetical to a dogma of self-improvement and material acquisition. "It requires strong and steady resolve to live out the gospel in the middle of an American dream that identifies success as moving up the ladder, getting the bigger house, purchasing the nicer car, buying the better clothes, eating the finer food, and acquiring more things," Platt writes. In Platt's view, the law of God trumps the law of Caesar.[37] His activism on this issue reminds us that even the evangelical Christian movement, which has been so strongly identified with the American conservative base in the last several decades, does not march in lockstep with the meritocratic ideology.

More secular examples of activism along these lines include "voluntary downshifters," ordinary citizens who have chosen—to varying degrees—to consume and work less, place less importance on success and wealth, and focus more on personal happiness, simplicity, and fulfillment. In economically downtrodden Detroit, some community groups have taken up this approach with enthusiasm. Embracing the city's "postindustrial future," they grow crops and create artwork in razed lots and abandoned buildings. They deliberately reject economic advancement along conventional lines, moving away from "quantitative" approaches of monetary and material gain toward "qualitative" alternatives focused on cultural production—education and intellectual labor.[38]

Some of these countercultural movements are reminiscent of the subcultures of the sixties, and they, too, may remain marginal. Nevertheless, it appears that grace morality is already opening up more possibilities for unconventional political alliances on this issue of inequality, and with the right leadership, a broader movement could emerge. Even in mainstream circles, flashes of this kind of approach can be seen. In the news we occasionally hear of heroic individuals at the pinnacle of success—from corporate CEOs to university presidents—who show an uncommon grace (mixed, as often is the case, with egalitarian beliefs) in their roles as leaders of large organizations and holders of wealth and fame. They refuse the industry-standard compensation package, to set aside money for their workers and communities. They defy convention and shareholders to offer decent wages, benefits, and working conditions. They give away their wealth, not to stamp their name on buildings but to share hoards of treasure that they do not really need. In return they enjoy the intense loyalty of their workers and the admiration of the public, and also, perhaps, a sense of meaning that goes deeper than even personal legacy or social justice.

Some of the people I talked to in Detroit and Windsor spoke of their hopes for a future that was not just more equitable but also more meaningful. The constant competition is simply bad for society, they said. "You hear students—it's all right to cheat because in the end, it's worth it because I needed the A to get that job I need," says Ziggy Dordick, a forty-year-old former Ford worker now in school. Being successful in business, too, is about doing "whatever you can do for the bottom line," he adds. Managers promise stock market numbers they can't deliver because that's what they did last year—that's what they need to do to stay employed. Ziggy worries about how he's going to raise his kids to do right in such an unethical and uncaring system.

After witnessing the drama of the auto industry's near-collapse, a few of my workers also concluded that they do not need the highest wages to be happy. "I lived on both sides of the fence," says Alice Parrott, forty-three. Before she went to Ford, she worked a grueling job at a parts factory where she made half as much—for twice the work. "Everybody [should] make $20 or something," she says. "Then everybody would be happy." A local union official told me she questions the high incomes people receive, including the autoworkers she represents. We need to think about what we really need versus what we want, she says.

Capitalism, of course, continually blurs that boundary. Eight decades ago, John Maynard Keynes contemplated the day when "the economic problem will take the back seat where it belongs." At that point, he predicted, "man will be faced with his permanent problems—how to use his freedom from pressing economic cares, how to occupy the leisure, which science and compound interest will have won for him, to live wisely, and agreeably, and well."[39] Perhaps Keynes did not fully appreciate how science and market competition create ever-new demands to fulfill, constructing a Sisyphean economy that places the ideal life continually out of reach. No matter how great the wealth created, it is never enough. The hunger for more, reinforced by the self-justifications of meritocracy, drives countries ever onward. But if society could focus on goals other than material and reputational advancement, then the necessity of competition would be reduced.

Indeed, this state of grace was once, Jean-Jacques Rousseau argued, humanity's natural condition. With civilization's progress we were cut loose from that Eden, as an expanding society imposed the need for individuals to seek out the adulation of others, leading ultimately to envy and enmity and their endless conflicts.[40] It is important not to idealize the past, perhaps fictitious, envisioned here—Rousseau himself did not call for a radical return to a pre-social existence. And yet we do not have to embrace a romantic view of history to believe that in our twenty-first-century lives we can be less judgmental, and more compassionate—less materialistic, and more focused on the people and beauty around us—less enthralled by the game of advancement, and more content with what we are blessed to have.

It should be emphasized, nonetheless, that all of the competing moral views I have described have their shortcomings. Meritocracy leads to personal growth. But it also leads to inequality. Egalitarianism leads to shared prosperity. But it also discourages personal ambition. Fraternalism leads to a sense of community. But it also leads to cronyism and chauvinism. Grace leads to forgiveness and a focus on life's ultimate meanings. But it also leads to excessive leniency. How can we describe, then, what a balanced moral order would look like? One way is to refer, once again, to personal relationships. Love is the balance between competing goals in any relationship. When we admire someone based on their personal qualities, we value their merit. When we seek out shared bonds of experience, we desire fraternity. When we show mutual respect and a belief in our fundamentally equal status, we affirm egalitarianism. And when we marvel at the idiosyncrasy and serendipity of a relationship with one person out of billions, we know grace.

In arguing on behalf of egalitarianism and grace, I am calling for a return to balance. There is much to be said for meritocracy, which pushes us as individuals to do better and be better. There is much to be said for fraternalism, which provides a source of identity and meaning in an all-too-anonymous culture. But over the last few decades, the morality of meritocracy and the reality of fraternalism have come to dominate the market economy. The economy's winners use their power not to lift up entire communities but to sway politics and institutions in their own favor. Meanwhile, our ant-like obsession with efficiency at all costs and our unending jostling for status make a more compassionate politics impossible—even in societies, like ours, with sufficient affluence to provide amply for all.

As our society continues to polarize into separate camps of advantaged and disadvantaged workers, the higher stakes of the competition intensify its spitefulness and amplify levels of stress. The struggle becomes remorseless—not just in its ruthless sorting but also in the callous ways that we view the competition itself. It is unavoidable—we say—that more people today will move between jobs, sometimes voluntarily and sometimes not, as a matter of economic efficiency. Those who stay unemployed have only themselves to blame. In this way we justify unemployment, seeing it as just another rite of passage for modern workers, dismissing their suffering and the many scars it leaves behind—above all, a permanent loss in their sense of well-being, even after they find a new job.[41] Like many utopian proposals, meritocratic morality is disconnected from the reality of its actual consequences. It does not recognize that the anxiety and despair of being relegated to the bottom of society's pecking order is itself an impediment to personal virtue and civic engagement—as is perhaps most clearly seen in free-market America's, not socialist Europe's, urban ghettoes.

In a vicious circle of ideological politics and institutional failure, the meritocratic ideology leads to the further defunding of government and weakening of unions, worsening the quality of these institutions and spawning more public disgust with them—and more individualism in response. Therefore, to deal with society's growing divide, and the massive and enduring unemployment it threatens, exquisitely designed policies are not enough. A balanced strategy of reform is necessary, too. Policies need to be not only generous but also well-implemented. Unions need to be not only strong but also democratically and fairly governed. And politics needs to focus not just on winning elections and enacting policies, but also on working to change hearts and minds in ways that make a more just society possible and sustainable.

Grace would create space for a greater degree of equity and fairness in a society charging headlong in the other direction. Yet my view is that the best argument for grace is not its usefulness as a means to an egalitarian end. The best argument for grace is grace itself—its moral virtues of patient conciliation. If we truly believe in the dignity of our fellow human being, we have no choice but to curtail our instinctive appraisals and verdicts, purging our thoughts of disdain for those below—or jealousy of those above. By doing this, we can diminish the strife and cruelty of modern life. Grace is a forgiving god.

• • •

David Vihan has been avidly seeking a job in the two years since he finished school, but nothing so far has panned out. "With Ford on my résumé, it has really scared off potential employers," he writes in an email. "They all think that I will try to unionize their places of business." Fortunately, David continues to receive an income from the government for his permanent disability. He is grateful for that, and the security keeps him from worrying too much.

It also doesn't hurt that David has found love. His girlfriend, Jan, a social worker, works with children and people with disabilities. Meeting her, he says, has given him some perspective on what he went through to get to this point. "If it wasn't for all those experiences, maybe I wouldn't be where I am now. Maybe I wouldn't have met Jan."

Though the cancer is in remission, David's chronic conditions continue to hem in his daily activities. The intense pain of his chest injury never goes away: he pops three Oxycontin painkiller pills a day, with lower-strength Percosets between them to "bridge" the troughs in relief. And the long march of his chemotherapy treatment has left other, less obvious scars. His feet bleed from time to time because his skin is so delicate. In his lower extremities he has constant numbness and tingling. His father once chided him for having to take an hour's nap in the middle of the day. "What are you, an old man?" his old man asked. But it's true: often David feels as if he's lived ninety years in this frail, broken body of his.

But if the cancer taught him anything, he says, it's patience. "I mean, you're not going to be happy all the time . . . but I've learned you've got a lot of things to like." It is not that he doesn't have his regrets—especially about his failed marriage to Tracy. But nowadays, David tries not to worry anymore about measuring the trajectory of his life against the paths not taken, or the people doing better than him. "Certain age, you've got to let it slide," he says. "You'd be surprised how much little things irritate people."

A few years back he was driving for a nonprofit, shuttling cancer patients to far-off appointments at regional cancer centers. The patients were young and old, some of them terminal cases, many brutally scarred by their cancer. ("This one guy had no face," David says. "He loved me . . . because it doesn't bother me.") People opened up to David during the long drives, telling him stories from their youth, confessing—near the end of their lives—all the things they would miss. The volunteer gig brought back memories of the hospital. When David was going through chemotherapy, he would go through bouts of feeling sorry for himself. But then he would see children enduring the same treatment. They had hardly lived their lives yet, and yet they had few complaints, he says. "Here's a kid that's like five, and looks like a mess. But he's happy and tubes hanging out of his nose and mouth and everything else, and he don't know any different."

Shortly before he finished school, David came down with pneumonia. His doctor wanted him to have blood work done. The initial tests indicated a problem. For a few weeks, he worried that his cancer had returned. Jan took time off work to stay with him at home while he recovered. His family met to figure out a plan for caring for him, assuming another long foray into chemotherapy. Then the second round of tests came back. They were negative. It was just pneumonia.

Relieved, David could not help finding meaning in his latest health scare. It was "another wake-up call," he says, "to start appreciating again." David admits he has, at times, reverted to his old habits—

resenting a bad grade, letting the stress get to him. "I have kind of even fallen into a trap, where I forgot some of the things that I thought were special," he says. "Like we're almost getting back to normal. . . . I don't want to get back to normal."

He was once a perfectionist. Fixated on his appearance, his grades, his salary. Intent on being successful, buying a big house, living the dream. Planning out every aspect of his life. "I used to be so vain about so many things," David says. "I don't care about any of that now." Friends and family matter more to him. Material things matter less. "Had a great house before. It was a dream house, and yet the ten years I was there were the worst ten years of my life." For Christmas, Jan asked him what he wanted and he couldn't think of anything. There was nothing he really wanted, let alone needed, he says.

These days, he likes to take long jaunts to nowhere in his beaten-up 1999 Pontiac Grand Am. He finds it relaxing. "I see things through different eyes now," he says. "I'll look at trees, leaves, colors turning, where I wouldn't have given a care about that twenty years ago." He will remember when he was deathly ill, utterly exhausted by his chemotherapy treatments, and he and his friend took their road trip across the border. His friend let him get behind the wheel, and he drove straight on to Indiana. It was meditation, to a Metallica soundtrack.

He was, he says, changed by the suffering he went through—a suffering that his friends, family, and society relieved in crucial ways, but could not entirely keep from him. "It's taught me a lot, and in some ways I'm kind of grateful," David says. After coming so close to losing everything, he finds it easier to see the good in people, to understand what they're going through. Before, when he was a young jock drinking and dating random women and generally "screwing up" his life, there was a lot of anger inside him. "I used to never let nothing slide," he says. He was a worrier who drove himself into a nervous breakdown. He was a hothead who snapped at the smallest annoyance. Bird droppings on a just-washed car would send him howling in rage. Does it really matter? he asks himself now. "I lost everything," David says. "But I finally got peace."

Still, employment would be nice. "It would be good to even get a part-time job," he writes in his last email. "To feel like I'm contributing, you know what I mean?"

Appendix

Research Methods and Policy Details

PART I: RESEARCH METHODS

This study draws from the following data: interviews with seventy-one American and Canadian former autoworkers and observations within their households and in the Detroit and Windsor metropolitan areas (March 2009 to March 2010); interviews with thirty-six leaders and experts working for unions, businesses, nonprofits, government agencies, and other organizations; relevant company and union documents; U.S. Census Bureau (shortened to Census in the text) and Statistics Canada (StatCan) data; U.S. Bureau of Labor Statistics (BLS) data; and various social surveys and opinion polls, primarily the General Social Survey (GSS), International Social Survey Programme (ISSP), World Values Survey (WVS), Pew Research Center polling (Pew), and the Gallup Poll (Gallup). For the sake of brevity, I have described the survey data in prose; tables and figures can be found on my website, victortanchen.com.

My reliance on interviewing for this study raises questions about interviewer effects. I come from a different educational and ethnic background from the individuals I profile in this book. It is possible that they reacted to that social distance and the academic profession I represent by emphasizing the importance of educational achievement, a strong work ethic, and self-reliance. (On the other hand, they might have hidden their actual feelings of shame and self-blame as well.) As a solo researcher I could do little to deal with this problem, other than spending sufficient time with my respondents to encourage them to lower their defenses, examining relative cross-national differences in addition to the absolute intensities of stated beliefs, and using survey data to get a broader picture of trends in American and Canadian thought. I hope other researchers from different backgrounds can continue to shed light on the social and economic changes I explore here.

TABLE I. DEMOGRAPHICS OF DETROIT AND WINDSOR METRO AREAS, 2010

	Windsor census metropolitan area	Detroit-Warren-Livonia metropolitan statistical area
Population	331,600	4,296,250
Median family income (Canada)/ median household income (U.S.)	CAD 69,480 (USD 55,000)	USD 48,198
Unemployment rate	11.5%	13.9%
High school diploma or equivalent (Canada: ages 25–64; U.S.: ages 25+)	29.4%*	28.4%
Bachelor's degree or higher	23.4%*	27.3%
Immigrant (Canada) or foreign-born (U.S.)	22.3%*	8.6%
Visible minority (Canada) or racial/ethnic minority (U.S.)	17.2%* (3.4% black alone)	29.9% (22.8% black alone)

* 2011 census figures.

SOURCES: BLS, Census, StatCan.

The original aim of my research was to measure the effects of social policy on the unemployed. To do so, I used a cross-national comparative approach. Canada and the United States provide an ideal comparison because they have similar markets, workforces, and standards of living, as well as comparable experiences with deindustrialization, globalization, and skill-biased technological change.[1] Although Canada underwent a major retrenchment in social spending in the 1990s, it continues to offer a significantly stronger social safety net overall. This combination of cross-national similarity and small policy differences allowed me to link differences in outcomes to these policy differences more easily than would have been the case for countries with very disparate labor markets and social patterns.

Furthermore, like Dan Zuberi's study *Differences That Matter,* I take this comparative approach one step further by looking at communities just across the U.S.–Canadian border. I chose to study the Detroit and Windsor metropolitan areas because they both have strong auto industries, the same companies operate on both sides of their shared border, and the two cities are only minutes from each other by bridge or tunnel. By studying workers who used to do the same kinds of work in plants on either side of the Detroit River, I sought to control for firm, occupational, and demographic differences (table I).

Sample

I found most of the seventy-one workers I interviewed with the help of the UAW and CAW, which helped me establish trust early on. I found eleven additional respondents using snowball sampling. The sample is described in table 2.

For my Big Three sample, my Americans used to work at the Chrysler Mack Avenue Engine Complex in Detroit and the Chrysler Trenton Engine Plant, and

TABLE 2. DEMOGRAPHICS OF WORKER SAMPLE

	United States			Canada			All Big Three	All parts	Total
	Chrysler	Parts	All U.S.	Ford	Parts	All Canada			
Number of respondents	18	16	34	20	17	37	38	33	71
Unemployed[1]	8	14	22	3	10	13	11	24	35
Employed part-time[2]	1	0	1	2	4	6	3	4	7
Employed full-time[3]	2	1	3	1	0	1	3	1	4
Self-employed	2	0	2	0	0	0	2	0	2
Out of labor force: student	2	0	2	12	3	15	14	3	17
Out of labor force: other reason	3	1	4	2	0	2	5	1	6
Median length of unemployment (months)	10.5	7	8	21	13	14	13.5	13	13
Median age	43	46.5	45.5	45.5	38	42	44.5	42	43
Female	6	0	6	9	2	11	15	2	17
Black	12	13	25	1	1	2	13	14	27
Asian	0	2	2	1	2	3	1	4	5
Latino	0	0	0	0	2	2	0	2	2
Mixed	1	0	1	0	0	0	1	0	1
First-generation immigrant	0	2	2	1	7	8	1	9	10

[1]The category of "unemployed" here includes the marginally attached and is equivalent to the U5 measure of unemployment; "employed part-time" includes those working part-time for economic reasons and, combined with the previous group, is equivalent to the U6 measure (see the BLS website for definitions).

[2]Four of the seven workers employed part-time were working temporarily at the action centers.

[3]Two of the four workers employed full-time had temporary jobs.

my Canadians used to work at the Ford Essex Engine Plant and the Ford Windsor Engine Plant, both in Windsor. While they had worked under the same union contracts, some of the Canadians had last worked at the nearby Ford Foundry, also known as the Windsor Casting Plant, and the Nemak Essex Aluminum Plant and the Nemak Windsor Aluminum Plant (both formerly owned by Ford), which had drawn their workers from the same Ford union local. All of the Americans and seven of the twenty Canadians had taken buyouts. In terms of understanding unemployment trends, there are advantages and disadvantages to studying autoworkers who are on indefinite layoff versus those who took buyouts. Workers on layoff receive unemployment benefits and in this way are more comparable to the unemployed in general. However, in another sense buyout takers are more comparable because these individuals have truly cut their ties to the company—they will never be recalled to their factories.

For the parts sample, I focused on two parts suppliers that had been acquired by the same U.S. company, Flex-N-Gate. My Americans came from the Chrome Craft plant in Highland Park, Michigan (shut down in 2009), and my Canadians from two Chromeshield plants in Windsor (shut down in 2008). All three plants were dedicated to the chroming of bumpers for pickup trucks. None of these workers had the option of a buyout. One of the sixteen American parts workers was laid off from another company's plant; before I settled on Flex-N-Gate, I had been considering a focus on this other supplier.

I have used pseudonyms to hide the identities of my respondents, per the guidelines of Harvard University's institutional review board. The names of my expert respondents are real; their surnames are used on second reference, unlike for the workers.

Currency Conversion

I use Canadian dollar amounts exclusively when referencing Canadian policies or quoting Canadian respondents, except where noted in the text. Whenever comparisons are relevant, I convert Canadian dollars to U.S. dollars using the OECD's purchasing power parities for actual individual consumption.

Dan Zuberi argues that the proper conversion is closer to 1:1 at the Vancouver–Seattle border, based on his cross-border comparison of prices in supermarkets and other stores. If a similar situation holds in the Detroit-Windsor area, the amounts of the Canadian income supports would be considerably larger than what is listed below.[2]

PART 2: INCOME SUPPORTS

Tables 3–7 list the amounts of government benefits provided over a year in Michigan and Ontario for the types of households indicated. I use 2010 benefit levels in order to match the policy situation at the time of my fieldwork. The unemployed worker used as an example here receives the maximum amount of unemployment benefits possible, based on an annual income from the lost job of $40,000, which was the average for my parts workers. The replacement rates listed in the tables are the percentages of that income recovered. This hypothetical individual has ten years of seniority.

For further details, see the policy descriptions following the tables. The information provided here comes from the relevant federal and state or provincial agencies, except where noted.

Policy Details

Below I describe the policies and benefit levels available to the unemployed. Again, please note that I am describing the situation in 2010.

TABLE 3. BENEFITS FOR MARRIED COUPLE WITH TWO CHILDREN AND A SPOUSE
EARNING USD 40,000 (CAD 50,101), MICHIGAN AND ONTARIO, 2010

	Michigan	Ontario
Unemployment insurance and severance pay	Unemployment benefits USD 20,124 (52 weeks out of 99-week maximum, at USD 387 per week) **USD 20,124**	Unemployment benefits[1] USD 14,594 (CAD 18,280, 40 weeks out of 50-week maximum, at CAD 457 per week) Mandated severance, ten weeks USD 7,692 (CAD 9,634, 10 weeks) **USD 22,286 (CAD 27,914)**
Child benefits	Federal Child Tax Credit USD 2,000 Michigan Child Deduction[2] USD 52 (temporary policy)	Canada Child Tax Benefit USD 969 (CAD 1,214) Universal Child Care Benefit (if children are under six years of age; not included in tally below) USD 1,916 (CAD 2,400) **USD 969 (CAD 1,214)**
Other	Making Work Pay Credit USD 400 (temporary policy) Michigan Homestead Property Tax Credit[3] USD 177 **USD 577**	Ontario Sales Tax Transition Benefit USD 531 (CAD 665) (temporary policy) **USD 531 (CAD 665)**
Total assistance	**USD 22,753**	**USD 23,786 (CAD 29,793)**
Replacement rate	**56.9%**	**59.5%**
Difference		**+USD 1,033**

[1]The worker receives only forty weeks of unemployment benefits in the year because of the system's two-week waiting period before the first amount is paid, and also because of the payment of severance, which pushes back the start date by the number of weeks of severance pay received (here, ten weeks). Note that a pilot program allowed for the receipt of severance at the same time as unemployment benefits for long-tenured workers (see chapter 3).

[2]A family with two children would receive a deduction of USD 600 per child, amounting to a USD 52 benefit.

[3]Assuming a monthly rent of USD 1,000.

TABLE 4. BENEFITS FOR MARRIED COUPLE WITH TWO CHILDREN AND A SPOUSE
EARNING USD 20,000 (CAD 25,051), MICHIGAN AND ONTARIO, 2010

	Michigan	Ontario
Unemployment insurance and severance pay	Unemployment benefits USD 20,124 **USD 20,124**	Unemployment benefits USD 14,594 (CAD 18,280) Mandated severance USD 7,692 (CAD 9,634) **USD 22,286 (CAD 27,914)**
Child benefits	Federal Child Tax Credit USD 1,413 Federal Additional Child Tax Credit USD 587 Michigan Child Deduction USD 52 (temporary policy) **USD 2,052**	Canada Child Tax Benefit USD 1,769 (CAD 2,216) Universal Child Care Benefit (not included in tally below) USD 1,916 (CAD 2,400) **USD 1,769 (CAD 2,216)**
Other	Making Work Pay Credit USD 400 Federal Earned Income Tax Credit USD 1,100 Michigan Earned Income Tax Credit USD 220 Michigan Unemployment Compensation Deduction[1] USD 100 Michigan Homestead Property Tax Credit USD 597 **USD 2,417**	Ontario Sales Tax Transition Benefit USD 531 (CAD 665) Ontario Energy and Property Tax Credit[2] USD 8 (CAD 10) **USD 539 (CAD 675)**
Total assistance	**USD 24,593**	**USD 24,594**
Replacement rate	**61.5%**	**61.5%**
Difference		**+USD 1**

[1] A Michigan taxpayer whose unemployment compensation amounted to at least half of her adjusted gross income would receive a deduction of up to USD 2,300, amounting to a USD 100 benefit.
[2] Assuming a monthly rent of USD 1,000 (CAD 1,253).

TABLE 5. BENEFITS FOR MARRIED COUPLE WITH TWO CHILDREN AND A SPOUSE NOT EARNING WAGES, MICHIGAN AND ONTARIO, 2010

	Michigan	Ontario
Unemployment insurance and severance pay	Unemployment benefits USD 20,124 **USD 20,124**	Unemployment benefits USD 14,594 (CAD 18,280) Mandated severance USD 7,692 (CAD 9,634) **USD 22,286 (CAD 27,914)**
Child benefits	Michigan Child Deduction USD 52 (temporary policy) **USD 52**	Canada Child Tax Benefit USD 2,152 (CAD 2,696) National Child Benefit Supplement USD 2,397 (CAD 3,002) Ontario Child Benefit USD 1,251 (CAD 1,567) Universal Child Care Benefit (not included in tally below) USD 1,916 (CAD 2,400) **USD 5,800 (CAD 7,265)**
Other	Making Work Pay Credit USD 400 (temporary policy) Food stamps (SNAP)[1] USD 3,396 Michigan Unemployment Compensation Deduction USD 100 (temporary policy) Michigan Home Heating Tax Credit[2] USD 151 Michigan Homestead Property Tax Credit USD 1,017 **USD 5,064**	GST/HST Credit USD 608 (CAD 762) Ontario Sales Tax Credit USD 737 (CAD 923) Ontario Sales Tax Transition Benefit USD 531 (CAD 665) (temporary policy) Ontario Energy and Property Tax Credit USD 405 (CAD 507) **USD 2,281 (CAD 2,857)**
Total assistance	**USD 24,968**	**USD 30,367 (CAD 38,036)**
Replacement rate	**63.1%**	**75.9%**
Difference		**+USD 5,127**

[1] Assuming monthly shelter costs of USD 1,000 for the excess shelter deduction.

[2] The credit was increased for those receiving at least half of their household's income from unemployment benefits.

	Michigan	Ontario
Unemployment insurance and severance pay	Unemployment benefits USD 20,124 **USD 20,124**	Unemployment benefits USD 14,594 (CAD 18,280) Mandated severance USD 7,692 (CAD 9,634) **USD 22,286** (CAD 27,914)
Child benefits	Child Tax Credit USD 76 Michigan Child Deduction USD 52 (temporary policy) **USD 128**	Canada Child Tax Benefit USD 2,152 (CAD 2,696) National Child Benefit Supplement USD 2,397 (CAD 3,002) Ontario Child Benefit USD 1,251 (CAD 1,567) Universal Child Care Benefit (not included in tally below) USD 1,916 (CAD 2,400) Ontario Child Care Supplement for Working Families (if children are under seven years of age; not included in tally below) USD 335 (CAD 420) (temporary policy) **USD 5,800** (CAD 7,265)
Other	Food stamps (SNAP)[1] USD 1,260 Michigan Unemployment Compensation Deduction USD 100 (temporary policy) Michigan Home Heating Tax Credit USD 76 Michigan Homestead Property Tax Credit USD 699 **USD 2,135**	GST/HST Credit USD 608 (CAD 762) Ontario Sales Tax Credit USD 529 (CAD 663) Ontario Sales Tax Transition Benefit USD 531 (CAD 665) (temporary policy) Ontario Energy and Property Tax Credit USD 311 (CAD 389) **USD 1,979** (CAD 2,479)
Total assistance	**USD 22,387**	**USD 30,065** (CAD 37,658)
Replacement rate	56.0%	75.2%
Difference		**+USD 7,678**

[1]Following the CBPP's analysis of benefit levels for a three-person household, we assume a child care deduction of USD 77 and shelter costs of USD 779 for the excess shelter deduction. Center on Budget and Policy Priorities, *A Quick Guide to Food Stamp Eligibility and Benefits* (Washington, DC: CBPP, 2012).

TABLE 7. BENEFITS FOR SINGLE PERSON WITH NO DEPENDENTS, MICHIGAN AND ONTARIO, 2010

	Michigan	Ontario
Unemployment insurance and severance pay	Unemployment benefits USD 20,124 **USD 20,124**	Unemployment benefits USD 14,594 (CAD 18,280) Mandated severance USD 7,692 (CAD 9,634) **USD 22,286 (CAD 27,914)**
Other	Michigan Unemployment Compensation Deduction USD 100 (temporary policy) Michigan Homestead Property Tax Credit USD 699 **USD 799**	GST/HST Credit USD 304 (CAD 381) Ontario Sales Tax Transition Benefit USD 160 (CAD 200) (temporary policy) Ontario Energy and Property Tax Credit USD 270 (CAD 338) **USD 734 (CAD 919)**
Total assistance	**USD 20,923**	**USD 23,020 (CAD 28,833)**
Replacement rate	**52.3%**	**57.6%**
Difference		**+USD 2,097**

Child benefits

In the United States, the Child Tax Credit provides up to $1,000 for each child under the age of seventeen. Families that do not have tax liability can still receive the refundable Additional Child Tax Credit. The 2009 stimulus legislation lowered its minimum income threshold to $3,000, so that tax filers receive 15 percent of any earned income above the threshold, for a maximum of $1,000 per child. (Importantly, unemployment benefits are considered *unearned* income.) The federal Child and Dependent Care Credit covers up to 35 percent of expenses paid to a provider to care for children age twelve or younger, with a maximum credit of up to $1,050 (or $2,100 if the family has more than one child). However, the credit is not refundable, and the taxpayer (and their spouse) must be working or looking for work.

Michigan at the time of my research allowed a $600 tax *deduction* for each child eighteen and under, but in 2013 this was phased out.

The Canada Child Tax Benefit is provided to all families with children under eighteen. For the first two children, the tax-free grant per child is CAD 112 per month, less for higher-income households. The National Child Benefit Supplement provides low-income families with an additional CAD 174 per month for the first child and CAD 154 for the second. The benefit falls as income rises, disappearing altogether at CAD 40,970 for families with three or fewer children. If a Canadian parent has a child under the age of six, the household receives the taxable Universal Child Care Benefit of CAD 100 per month. Intended to offset child-care costs, it is paid regardless of whether the child goes to day care, and regardless of whether the household has any tax liability. (As a result, it is more effective than the nonrefundable U.S. Child and Dependent Care Credit at reaching families with unemployed workers.)

Lower-income residents are eligible for the Ontario Child Benefit, which provides a maximum benefit of CAD 92 per month per child. The benefit phases out at CAD 47,500 for a two-child family. During the time of my research, the Ontario Child Benefit was replacing the Ontario Child Care Supplement for Working Families, a tax-free monthly payment for low-to-moderate-income working families with children under seven years of age. Previously, under this program, single-parent families received $210 per child; its benefits were lower during the transition period.

Food assistance

Under the Supplemental Nutrition Assistance Program, American households with low incomes receive an allotment depending on the household's size, less 30 percent of the household's net income. The maximum allotment was $526 per month in 2010–11 for a household of three people.

Tax credits for workers

A temporary U.S. stimulus measure, the federal Making Work Pay Credit, was effective in 2009 and 2010. It was refundable but required earned income. It extended $400 to individuals (up to an income of $75,000) and $800 to couples (up to a joint income of $150,000), typically paid out as lower withholding in each paycheck. The 2009 legislation also removed the first $2,400 in unemployment compensation from the calculation of a household's taxable income, though this benefit was dropped in 2010, the year of my analysis.

American households with employed workers (in the cases described here, the unemployed worker's spouse) can receive the refundable Earned Income Tax Credit (EITC). In 2010, the maximum credit for workers without children was just $457, which diminishes with income and disappears altogether at $13,460. For families with children, the benefit goes up to $5,036 for a household with two or more children, with some benefit available up to the income limit of $43,352. Michigan had a state EITC as well (amounting to 20 percent of the federal credit in 2010), but the Republican-controlled legislature reduced it to 6 percent in the 2012 tax year. Likewise, a special deduction of $2,300 for households with unemployment compensation greater than half of their adjusted gross income was rolled back in the 2013 tax year.

The Canadian EITC is the Working Income Tax Benefit. For single workers without children in most provinces, including Ontario, the 2010 WITB benefit peaked at CAD 931, or $764, and fell to zero at an income of CAD 16,770, or $13,768. Families with children received a maximum of CAD 1,690, or $1,387, which became zero at CAD 25,854, or $21,226.

Sales-tax refunds

Canada and Ontario offer credits on amounts paid toward the combined federal and provincial sales tax, known as the Goods and Services Tax/Harmonized Sales Tax (GST/HST). The tax-free payments are made quarterly. The benefit amount depends on the number of children and net income of the household, with a maximum benefit level of CAD 762 per year for a family with two children, reduced by 5 percent of each additional dollar of income above CAD 32,506.

The Ontario Sales Tax Credit provides CAD 260 a year per adult or child, with a benefit drop-off set at 4 percent of any income above CAD 20,000 for single people and CAD 25,000 for couples and single parents. To help residents transition to the harmonized sales tax system effective in 2010, Ontario also provided three one-time payments in 2010–11 totaling CAD 1,000 for families and CAD 300 for single taxpayers (reduced for those with incomes greater than CAD 160,000 and CAD 80,000, respectively).

Housing assistance

Under the policies for subsidized housing on both sides of the border, low-income households are responsible for paying 30 percent of their monthly income on housing, though limitations are placed on where they can live. I do not consider this kind of more permanent housing assistance in the tables above because none of my long-term unemployed workers made use of them: on both sides of the border the programs have waits of several years.

The Michigan Homestead Property Tax Credit provides rent or property-tax relief for certain households—primarily senior citizens, people with disabilities, and surviving spouses of veterans, though other low-income households are also eligible.

The Michigan Home Heating Credit assists low-income households in paying the costs of heating homes they own or rent. The income cutoff is based on the number of tax exemptions being claimed, with an additional exemption if the household received 50 percent or more of its income from unemployment compensation. In 2010, the income ceiling was $28,387 for a household of four that was also eligible for the extra exemption.

The Ontario Energy and Property Tax Credit helps lower-income households (including renters) pay property taxes and the sales tax on their energy expenses.

Notes

CHAPTER I

1. Rather than Detroit Three, I use the more recognizable term Big Three to refer to U.S. automakers, even though Chrysler is no longer the third-largest domestic producer. According to data from the U.S. Bureau of Labor Statistics (BLS), auto employment shrank by a third (from 957,000 to 623,300) between the recession's official beginning in December 2007 and its end in June 2009. (All monthly figures used throughout this book are seasonally adjusted unless otherwise noted.) Applying a broader definition of parts suppliers than what the government uses, a 2010 report by an industry think tank estimated that original equipment vehicle manufacturers employed 313,449 and parts suppliers employed 685,892. Center for Automotive Research, *Contribution of the Automotive Industry to the Economies of All Fifty States and the United States*, Ann Arbor, MI, 2010.

2. October 2009 (United States), the highest since 1983; August 2009 (Canada), the highest since 1998. Michigan's unemployment rate was the country's highest in 2009. That year, Ontario's rate reached 9 percent, the highest among the large provinces. In 2011, 6 million Americans—43.8 percent of the unemployed—were out of work for 27 weeks or more; in 1983, the previous peak, the rate was 23.9 percent. BLS and Statistics Canada (StatCan) data.

3. Bruce Western, *Between Class and Market: Postwar Unionization in the Capitalist Democracies* (Princeton, NJ: Princeton University Press, 1997); Andrew Cherlin, *The Marriage-Go-Round: The State of Marriage and the Family in America Today* (New York: Knopf, 2009); Bruce Western, Deirdre Bloome, and Christine Percheski, "Inequality among American Families with Children, 1975 to 2005," *American Sociological Review* 73 (2008): 903–20.

4. According to U.S. tax data for 1917–2012 (arguably more reliable than census survey data), the income share of the top 10 percent in 2012 was 48.2

percent, compared to a peak in the last century of 46.3 percent in 1932. According to estate tax statistics, the wealthiest 10 percent had 71.5 percent of the country's wealth in 2010, its highest share since the Depression era (in 1930 it was 73.4 percent). Thomas Piketty and Emmanuel Saez, "Income Inequality in the United States, 1913–1998," *Quarterly Journal of Economics* 118 (2003): 1–39 (August 2013 update at http://elsa.berkeley.edu/~saez/TabFig2012prel. xls); Thomas Piketty, *Capital in the Twenty-First Century* (Cambridge, MA: Harvard University Press, 2014; online supplemental table at http://piketty.pse. ens.fr/files/capital21c/en/pdf/supp/TS10.1.pdf).

5. According to inflation-adjusted census data, U.S. median household income was $51,939 in 2013, 8.7 percent lower than in 1999 ($56,895), that measure's peak. According to OECD data for 1983–2012, the Gini index of inequality in disposable income rose from lows of 0.336 (United States, 1983) and 0.282 (Canada, 1989) to highs of 0.389 (United States, 2011) and 0.322 (Canada, 2004). In the United States, the CEO-to-worker compensation ratio—295.9 in 2013—peaked at 383.4 in 2000; it had never gone above the 20s in 1965–1978. In Canada in 2012, the 100 highest-paid CEOs made 171 times as much as Canadians earning the average wage; in 1998, the ratio was 105-to-1. In Canada, CEO compensation includes salary, annual bonus payments, grants of shares, stock options, and pension accrual, and is compared to a Canadian earning the average wage for working full-time during the full year. In the United States, "CEO annual compensation is computed using the 'options realized' compensation series, which includes salary, bonus, restricted stock grants, options exercised, and long-term incentive payouts for CEOs at the top 350 [publicly owned] U.S. firms ranked by sales," and is compared with the "annual compensation (wages and benefits of a full-time, full-year worker) of a private-sector production/nonsupervisory worker (a group covering more than 80 percent of payroll employment)." Hugh Mackenzie, *All in a Day's Work? CEO Pay in Canada* (Ottawa: Canadian Centre for Policy Alternatives, 2014); Lawrence Mishel and Alyssa Davis, "CEO Pay Continues to Rise as Typical Workers Are Paid Less," Issue Brief #380, Economic Policy Institute, Washington, DC, 2014.

6. Vicki Smith, *Crossing the Great Divide: Worker Risk and Opportunity in the New Economy* (Ithaca: ILR, 2001); Henry S. Farber, "Short(er) Shrift: The Decline in Worker-Firm Attachment in the United States," in *Laid Off, Laid Low: Political and Economic Consequences of Employment Insecurity,* ed. Katherine S. Newman (New York: Columbia University Press, 2008), 34n2; Jacob S. Hacker, *The Great Risk Shift: The New Economic Insecurity and the Decline of the American Dream* (New York: Oxford University Press, 2008); Arne L. Kalleberg, *Good Jobs, Bad Jobs: The Rise of Polarized and Precarious Employment Systems in the United States, 1970s to 2000s* (New York: Russell Sage, 2011).

7. Auto-industry employment partially recovered after the recession, reaching 906,300 in January 2015—significantly up from its trough during the recession (623,300 in June 2009) but still down from the start of the recession (957,000 in December 2007) and the industry's all-time peak (1,333,600 in June 2000). Overall manufacturing employment fell from 13,746,000 in December 2007 to a low of 11,453,000 in February 2010; in January 2015, the figure was 12,318,000 (BLS).

8. The U.S. annual unemployment rate peaked in 2010 at 9.6 percent (14.8 million jobless) and four years later had fallen to 6.2 percent (9.6 million). Canadian unemployment peaked in 2009 at 8.3 percent and four years later had dropped to 6.9 percent.

According to the World Bank, the labor-force participation rate (ages 15+) has consistently fallen in both countries between 2007 and 2013: in the United States from 64.9 to 62.5 percent, and in Canada from 67.1 to 66.2 percent.

At its peak in 2010, the number of long-term unemployed was 6.4 million—43.3 percent of the nation's unemployed—which fell to 3.2 million, or 33.5 percent, in 2014. The average unemployment duration was 33.7 weeks in 2014, down from 39.4 weeks in 2012. (Changes to the government's method of measuring unemployment duration mean that these averages cannot be compared to those from data collected before 2011.) In Canada the average duration was 20.2 weeks in 2012, slightly down from the peak of 21.1 a year earlier (BLS, StatCan).

9. More recently: Richard Sennett and Jonathan Cobb, *The Hidden Injuries of Class* (New York: Norton, 1972/1993); Lillian B. Rubin, *Worlds of Pain: Life in the Working-Class Family* (New York: Basic, 1976/1992); Katherine S. Newman, *Falling from Grace: The Experience of Downward Mobility in the American Middle Class* (New York: Free Press, 1988); David Halle, *America's Working Man: Work, Home, and Politics among Blue-Collar Property Owners* (Chicago, IL: University of Chicago Press, 1984); Kathryn Marie Dudley, *The End of the Line: Lost Jobs, New Lives in Postindustrial America* (Chicago, IL: University of Chicago Press, 1994); Thomas J. Sugrue, *The Origins of the Urban Crisis: Race and Inequality in Postwar Detroit* (Princeton: Princeton University Press, 1996); Ruth Milkman, *Farewell to the Factory: Auto Workers in the Late Twentieth Century* (Berkeley: University of California Press, 1997).

10. Harry J. Holzer, Julia I. Lane, David B. Rosenblum, and Fredrik Andersson, *Where Are All the Good Jobs Going? What National and Local Job Quality and Dynamics Mean for U.S. Workers* (New York: Russell Sage, 2011); Ofer Sharone, *Flawed System/Flawed Self: Job Searching and Unemployment Experiences* (Chicago, IL: University of Chicago Press, 2014).

11. My thanks to Bruce Western for suggesting the terms *stunted* and *deformed* to describe meritocracy. For diverse examples and reviews of more recent studies on rent-seeking and social closure, see Kim A. Weeden, "Why Do Some Occupations Pay More than Others? Social Closure and Earnings Inequality in the United States," *American Journal of Sociology* 108 (2002): 55–101; David B. Grusky, "The Past, Present, and Future of Social Inequality," in *Social Stratification: Class, Race, and Gender in Sociological Perspective*, 2nd edition, ed. David B. Grusky (Boulder: Westview, 2001); Neil Fligstein, *The Architecture of Markets: An Economic Sociology of Twenty-First-Century Capitalist Societies* (Princeton, NJ: Princeton University Press, 2001); Jacob S. Hacker and Paul Pierson, *Winner-Take-All Politics: How Washington Made the Rich Richer—and Turned Its Back on the Middle Class* (New York: Simon & Schuster, 2010).

12. For a more recent take on these cultural differences, see Michael Adams, *Fire and Ice: The United States, Canada and the Myth of Converging Values* (Toronto: Penguin, 2003).

13. Dan Zuberi, *Differences That Matter: Social Policy and the Working Poor in the United States and Canada* (Ithaca, NY: Cornell University Press, 2006). See also Gøsta Esping-Andersen, *The Three Worlds of Welfare Capitalism* (Princeton, NJ: Princeton University Press, 1990); Seymour Martin Lipset, *Continental Divide: The Values and Institutions of the United States and Canada* (New York: Routledge, 1990); Irene Bloemraad, *Becoming a Citizen: Incorporating Immigrants and Refugees in the United States and Canada* (Berkeley: University of California Press, 2006).

14. Katherine S. Newman and Victor Tan Chen, *The Missing Class: Portraits of the Near Poor in America* (Boston: Beacon, 2007), chapter 6.

15. For the short-term view, see the references to the economic crisis as a "mancession" in the next chapter; for the long-term, see Hanna Rosin, *The End of Men: And the Rise of Women* (New York: Riverhead, 2012).

16. Newman, *Falling from Grace*; Jennifer L. Hochschild, *Facing Up to the American Dream: Race, Class, and the Soul of the Nation* (Princeton, NJ: Princeton University Press, 1995); Michèle Lamont, *The Dignity of Working Men: Morality and the Boundaries of Race, Class, and Immigration* (New York: Russell Sage and Harvard University Press, 2000); Jay MacLeod, *Ain't No Makin' It: Aspirations and Attainment in a Low-Income Neighborhood* (Boulder: Westview, 2009); Carrie M. Lane, *A Company of One: Insecurity, Independence, and the New World of White-Collar Unemployment* (Ithaca: ILR, 2011).

17. Piketty (*Capital in the Twenty-First Century*, 416) has used the apt term *meritocratic extremism* to describe this more intense form of meritocratic morality.

18. My thanks to Howard Kimeldorf for suggesting a very useful reframing of the book's contributions as well as some of the language to describe it.

19. Dana Cloud, *We Are the Union: Democratic Unionism and Dissent at Boeing* (Urbana, IL: University of Illinois Press, 2011).

20. Bruce Western and Jake Rosenfeld, "Unions, Norms, and the Rise in US Wage Inequality," *American Sociological Review* 76 (2011): 517–18.

21. Sugrue, *Origins of the Urban Crisis*.

22. In 2007, 607,900 people (584,100 in December) worked in the motor vehicle parts sector; in 2009, 413,700 did (391,300 in June). The sector has recovered somewhat, with employment at 536,600 in 2014 (BLS).

23. Debbie Siegelbaum, "American Dream Breeds Shame and Blame for Job Seekers," *BBC News*, March 25, 2014.

24. Halle, *America's Working Man*.

25. See Kay Lehman Schlozman and Sidney Verba, *Injury to Insult: Unemployment, Class, and Political Response* (Cambridge, MA: Harvard University Press, 1979), for a discussion of how even in the 1970s blue-collar workers tended *not* to identify as working-class.

26. These figures include overtime.

Autoworkers fit this hybrid class particularly well. They have wages above the national mean, but autoworkers in less skilled occupations make more money than their counterparts in other industries. Jeffrey Holt, "Wages and Employment of Workers in Automobile Manufacturing," in *Occupational Employment and Wages, May 2005* (Washington, DC: U.S. Department of Labor, 2007).

27. In 2014, 42 percent of Americans over 25 had at least an associate's degree; 32 percent had at least a bachelor's degree. In 2014, 60 percent of Canadians over 25 had at least a postsecondary certificate or diploma; 26 percent had at least a university bachelor's degree. In 2012, blue-collar workers (in occupations categorized as natural resources, construction, maintenance, production, transportation, and material moving) accounted for 21 percent of the workforce. Of blue-collar workers, 16.4 percent were represented by unions; that was 3.5 percent of all employed Americans (Census, StatCan, BLS).

28. Work by Chinoy and Smith provides scholarly signposts for these two worlds of work, as once-sheltered workers have steadily gained the tools—and taken on the burdens—of individual autonomy and relentless skill development. Eli Chinoy, *Automobile Workers and the American Dream*, 2nd ed. (Urbana, IL: University of Illinois Press, 1992); Smith, *Crossing the Great Divide*.

29. Vicki Smith, "Enhancing Employability: Human, Cultural, and Social Capital in an Era of Turbulent Unpredictability," *Human Relations* 63 (2010): 279–303; Smith, *Crossing the Great Divide*; Lane, *A Company of One*.

30. Milkman (*Farewell to the Factory*) found that plant automation led to "more challenging and intellectually demanding" work for skilled-trades workers (which also implies that the bar of entry into those trades became higher), but jobs that were "simplified or further de-skilled" for production workers. See also Richard J. Murnane and Frank Levy, *Teaching the New Basic Skills: Principles for Educating Children to Thrive in a Changing Economy* (New York: Free Press, 1996).

31. Frank Levy and Peter Temin, "Inequality and Institutions in 20th Century America," Working Paper No. 13106, NBER, Cambridge, MA, 2007; Sanford M. Jacoby, *Modern Manors: Welfare Capitalism since the New Deal* (Princeton, NJ: Princeton University Press, 1997); Mark S. Mizruchi, *The Fracturing of the Corporate Elite* (Cambridge, MA: Harvard University Press, 2013).

32. Seymour Martin Lipset and Noah M. Meltz, *The Paradox of American Unionism: Why Americans Like Unions More Than Canadians Do but Join Much Less* (Ithaca: ILR, 2004); Piketty, *Capital in the Twenty-First Century*.

33. To avoid repetition, at times in this book I use the terms *educated* and *skilled* interchangeably. More precisely, *educated* refers to a high level of formal education—typically a college degree—acquired at degree-granting institutions. *Skilled* refers to a larger pool of workers, encompassing both those with higher education as well as those with competencies acquired through experience in the workplace or through licensing, apprenticeships, etc. My autoworkers were production workers who had not apprenticed to join the skilled trades; they might be termed "semi-skilled," given their factory experience, but it is questionable whether these skills (unlike formal education) would translate to other fields.

34. In this book I do not use the terms *neoliberalism* and *market fundamentalism*. I prefer terms that make an analytical distinction between (1) the meritocratic *ideology*, (2) the pro-corporate *political movement,* and (3) laissez-faire *economic policies,* which are three distinct phenomena, even if they reinforce one another. Gerald F. Davis, *Managed by the Markets: How Finance*

Re-Shaped America (New York: Oxford University Press, 2009); Fligstein, *Architecture of Markets*.

35. Block and Somers argue that "deregulation" as commonly understood is actually reregulation, given that it entails not removing government rules but rewriting them to favor certain elite interests. Fred Block and Margaret R. Somers, *The Power of Market Fundamentalism: Karl Polanyi's Critique* (Cambridge, MA: Harvard University Press, 2014).

36. As Goldin and Katz note, the polarization of the labor market since 1990 has hollowed out the middle of the labor market, which includes "high-end jobs taken by high school graduates and low-end jobs taken by those with any college." From a low of 1.7 percent in 2000, unemployment among college graduates rose to a peak of 3.1 percent in 2003 before falling—only to shoot up to 4.7 percent (2010) during the recession. Claudia Goldin and Lawrence F. Katz, *The Race between Education and Technology* (Cambridge, MA: Harvard University Press, 2008), 353, 432n21; see also David H. Autor, Lawrence F. Katz, and Melissa S. Kearney, "The Polarization of the US Labor Market," *American Economic Review* 96 (2006): 189–94.

37. "Careful studies of worker displacement show that when people are laid off from previously stable employment, they take a wage hit—if they are lucky enough to find work—of over 20 percent, and this gap persists for decades after the loss." Paul Osterman and Beth Shulman, *Good Jobs America: Making Work Better for Everyone* (New York: Russell Sage, 2011); John Maynard Keynes, *Essays in Persuasion* (New York: Classic House, 1931/2009).

38. For high school diploma holders in the U.S. in 2013, unemployment was 7.5 percent, long-term unemployment was 3.6 percent, and median weekly earnings were $651—compared to 3.7 percent unemployment (51 percent less), 1.7 percent long-term unemployment (53 percent less), and $1,108 in earnings (70 percent more) for bachelor's degree holders. In Canada in 2012, unemployment was 8.2 percent among high school graduates, compared to 5.0 percent among university graduates (39 percent lower). According to a Pew analysis of 2013 census data, millennial college graduates had an unemployment rate of 3.8 percent, compared to 12.2 percent for those with only high school diplomas. Heidi Shierholz, "Long-Term Unemployment Is Elevated across All Education, Age, Occupation, Industry, Gender, and Racial and Ethnic Groups," *Working Economics* (Economic Policy Institute blog), www.epi.org; Pew Research Center, *The Rising Cost of Not Going to College* (Washington, DC: Pew, 2014); BLS; StatCan.

39. The ratio of the unemployment rate of high-educated workers to that of low-educated workers plunged in the late 1970s (in the United States) and early 1980s (in Europe), before stabilizing over the next two decades at a lower level, and then increasing somewhat during the 2000s. Though it stabilized in the past decade, the pay gap between workers with more and less education had grown enormously over the prior four decades. Lourens Broersma, "Differences in Unemployment by Educational Attainment in the US and Europe: What Role for Skill-Bias Technological Change and Institutions," Working Paper No. 20, EU KLEMS, Groningen, Netherlands, 2008 (with author's update using data up to 2008); Gary S. Becker, "The Age of Human Capital," in *Education in the*

Twenty-first Century, ed. Edward P. Lazear (Stanford: Hoover Institution, 2002), 4–5; Holzer et al., *Where Are All the Good Jobs Going?*

40. When I call today's labor market meritocratic, I am talking about education and its importance for getting *employed* at jobs that pay *well.* Both employment and pay are crucial. If a few of the less educated have good jobs but most other workers with a similar educational profile find it impossible to get them, that is not a sign of an egalitarian labor market; and if many of the less educated can get jobs but those jobs don't pay well, that is not a sign, either.

41. Josh Mitchell, *Who Are the Long-Term Unemployed?* (Washington, DC: Urban Institute, 2013); David H. Autor and Mark G. Duggan, "The Rise in the Disability Rolls and the Decline in Unemployment," *Quarterly Journal of Economics* 118 (2003): 157–206. I did not study workers classified as permanently disabled, but two of my Canadian workers received workers' compensation.

42. Michael Young, *The Rise of the Meritocracy* (New Brunswick, NJ: Transaction, 1958/2011). Herrnstein argues that in a society with truly equal opportunity, inherited intelligence would become decisive; but given that, as Bell notes, "there is nearly as much inequality among men whose parents hold the same economic status as among men in general," it appears that there are elements of luck and other factors at work here, challenging the idea of a true meritocracy with respect to inherited talent even within the system that Herrnstein imagines. Richard Herrnstein, "I.Q.," *Atlantic Monthly,* September 1971; Daniel Bell, *The Coming of Post-Industrial Society: A Venture in Social Forecasting* (New York: Basic, 1973), 427.

43. "Not all societies invite invidious comparisons. The peasant did not compare his lot with the lord; he had his allotted place in the scheme of things and accepted it fatalistically" (Bell, *The Coming of Post-Industrial Society,* 436).

44. Piketty, *Capital in the Twenty-First Century.*

45. Bell, *Coming of Post-Industrial Society.*

46. See the distinction between "natural" and "developed" talents discussed in Harry Brighouse and Adam Swift, "Educational Equality versus Educational Adequacy: A Critique of Anderson and Satz," *Journal of Applied Philosophy* 26 (2009): 119. In my conception, a system of advancement whereby advancement depends on developed talents is meritocracy; a system whereby advancement depends on natural talents is a combination of meritocracy and equal opportunity.

47. William Julius Wilson, *When Work Disappears: The World of the New Urban Poor* (New York: Vintage, 1997), 129; William Julius Wilson, *More than Just Race: Being Black and Poor in the Inner City* (New York: Norton, 2009), 75.

48. Julia Isaacs, Isabel V. Sawhill, and Ron Haskins, *Getting Ahead or Losing Ground: Economic Mobility in America* (Washington, DC: Pew Economic Mobility Project, 2008).

49. See for example William H. Sewell and Vimal P. Shah, "Socioeconomic Status, Intelligence, and the Attainment of Higher Education," *Sociology of Education* 40 (1967): 1–23; William H. Sewell and Vimal P. Shah, "Parents' Education and Children's Educational Aspirations and Achievements," *American Sociological Review* 33 (1968): 191–209.

50. John Ermisch, Markus Jäntti, and Timothy Smeeding, eds., *From Parents to Children: The Intergenerational Transmission of Advantage* (New York: Russell Sage, 2012); James J. Heckman, "The American Family in Black and White: A Post-Racial Strategy for Improving Skills to Promote Equality," Discussion Paper No. 5495, Institute for the Study of Labor, Bonn, Germany, 2011; Flavio Cunha, James J. Heckman, Lance Lochner, and Dimitriy V. Masterov, "Interpreting the Evidence on Life Cycle Skill Formation," in *Handbook of the Economics of Education*, Vol. 1, ed. Eric A. Hanushek and Finis Welch (Amsterdam: North-Holland, 2006), 697–812.

51. Christopher Jencks et al., *Inequality: A Reassessment of the Effect of Family and Schooling in America* (New York: Basic, 1972); Dalton Conley, *The Pecking Order: Which Siblings Succeed and Why* (New York: Pantheon, 2004).

52. James S. Fishkin, *Justice, Equal Opportunity, and the Family* (New Haven, CT: Yale University Press, 1983), 5, 30–32. In a February 9, 2013, article, the *Economist* uses the phrase "paradox of virtuous meritocracy" to describe how meritocracy leads to unequal opportunity, as the "clever rich [turn] themselves into an entrenched elite." Following Fishkin, I would argue that meritocracy by its very nature—virtuous or not—leads to this outcome.

53. See the citations earlier in this chapter on rent-seeking and social closure.

54. The gains in productivity growth in recent years have gone disproportionately to America's top 1 percent of earners. Financial workers account for a growing portion of this group: 14 percent in 2005, compared to 8 percent in 1979. Nonfinance executives, managers, and supervisors account for 31 percent. Jon Bakija, Adam Cole, and Bradley T. Heim, "Jobs and Income Growth of Top Earners and the Causes of Changing Income Inequality: Evidence from US Tax Return Data," working paper, Economics Department, Williams College, Williamstown, MA, 2012; Neil Fligstein, *The Transformation of Corporate Control* (Cambridge, MA: Harvard University Press, 1990).

55. Dudley, *End of the Line*, 71, 74, 76–79.

56. Newman, *Falling from Grace*, 76, 268n64.

57. Elazar describes three political cultures visible, in various combinations, within the U.S. states: individualistic, moralistic, and traditional. The first favors minimal government and private gain; the second, the action of a responsive and reformed government on behalf of the common good; and the third, the power of a paternalistic elite preserving the status quo. This typology maps somewhat onto the meritocratic/egalitarian/fraternal dimensions I describe here, but in using just one nation's cultural legacy to encompass a broad range of viewpoints, it is too narrow: after all, there is no space here for the egalitarian extremes of socialism or communism. Daniel J. Elazar, *American Federalism: A View from the States* (New York: Harper & Row, 1984).

58. This idea of capitalism's legitimating ideology, of course, draws from the concept of "cultural hegemony" developed by the political theorist Antonio Gramsci. See also Hochschild, *Facing Up to the American Dream;* Lamont, *Dignity of Working Men.*

59. In fact, there is a case to be made that organized religion, as it consolidates and centralizes power, naturally moves in these two directions. In Christianity, this has ranged from the defense of hierarchy and the exercise of power

(epitomized in the Holy Roman Empire), to a focus on the deservingness of salvation and the justification of good works. Religious ritual and doctrine are used routinely to further material acquisition as well—from ideas that the faithful's virtue or "chosenness" will lead to material prosperity (e.g. in "prosperity theology"), to the mindfulness meditation now popular among deal-making corporate executives.

60. According to the Puritans, even the Protestant Church of England did not go far enough in renouncing practices that connected God's forgiveness with the merit of the supplicant. Yet this idealism soon stumbled upon the human need for the self-justification of merit. As Weber observed, church members wondered how they could know (and prove to others) that they were among the chosen. With time, the Puritans retreated somewhat from their focus on salvation by grace alone, most notably with the establishment of the Half-Way Covenant. The republicans who followed the early colonists steadily neglected their teachings on grace and embraced ever more blatant versions of a doctrine of works, paving the way for ultra-meritocrats like Benjamin Franklin and Horatio Alger. Alan Heimert and Andrew Delbanco, eds., *The Puritans in America: A Narrative Anthology* (Cambridge, MA: Harvard University Press, 1985); Max Weber, *The Protestant Ethic and the Spirit of Capitalism,* trans. Talcott Parsons (London: Routledge, 1904–05/1992).

61. Robert N. Bellah, Richard Madsen, William M. Sullivan, Ann Swidler, and Steven M. Tipton, *Habits of the Heart: Individualism and Commitment in American Life* (Berkeley: University of California Press, 1985).

62. Hochschild, *Facing Up to the American Dream,* 37.

63. This hedonic treadmill is similar to the meritocratic treadmill (the capital speedup) I describe in chapter 2. As Bok writes, "Any satisfaction people gain from a boost in their income tends to be eroded significantly if incomes all around them are rising just as fast." Society in this way improves in material affluence but not in overall subjective well-being, as the minimum of income needed to fulfill people's aspirations keeps rising. According to Adam Smith, as summarized by Bell (*The Coming of Post-Industrial Society*), "Men's primary motives are not economic, since most persons could live on a small amount, but sociological: the desire to be applauded and to be considered superior." See also Derek Bok, *The Politics of Happiness: What Government Can Learn from the New Research on Well-Being* (Princeton, NJ: Princeton University Press, 2010), 12–13.

64. Brighouse and Swift define positional goods as goods whose "absolute value" depends on their "possessors' place in the distribution of the good." Harry Brighouse and Adam Swift, "Equality, Priority, and Positional Goods," *Ethics* 116 (2006): 474. See also Michael Marmot, *The Status Syndrome: How Social Standing Affects Our Health and Longevity* (New York: Times Books, 2004); Robert Frank, *Falling Behind: How Rising Inequality Harms the Middle Class* (Berkeley: University of California Press, 2007); Fred Hirsch, *The Social Limits to Growth* (Cambridge, MA: Harvard University Press, 1976).

65. "A creditable day-labourer would be ashamed to appear in public without a linen shirt, the want of which would be supposed to denote that disgraceful degree of poverty which, it is presumed, nobody can well fall into without

extreme bad conduct." Adam Smith, *An Inquiry into the Nature and Causes of the Wealth of Nations* (Oxford: Clarendon, 1776/1976), 469–71.

66. If Darwinism entails the survival of the fittest, its social analogue is meritocracy: survival of the most praiseworthy.

67. According to the 2010 census, the city of Detroit is 82.7 percent black or African American (alone, not in combination), though in the larger Detroit-Warren-Livonia metropolitan statistical area the percentage is 22.8 percent (see the appendix).

68. Sugrue, *Origins of the Urban Crisis*.

69. For example, the white rate of nonmarital births is converging with the black rate, a trend that Furstenberg links to the growing class inequality in family structure. Frank F. Furstenberg, "If Moynihan Had Only Known: Race, Class, and Family Change in the Late Twentieth Century," *Annals of the American Academy of Political and Social Science* 621 (2009): 94–110. See also Charles Murray, *Coming Apart: The State of White America, 1960–2010* (New York: Crown Forum, 2012).

70. Lamont, *Dignity of Working Men*.

71. Milkman, *Farewell to the Factory*; Smith, *Crossing the Great Divide*.

72. David Schwartzman, *Black Unemployment: Part of Unskilled Unemployment* (Westport, CT: Greenwood, 1997); Sugrue, *Origins of the Urban Crisis*.

73. Murray, *Coming Apart*.

74. Karl Polanyi, *The Great Transformation: The Political and Economic Origins of Our Time* (Boston: Beacon, 1944/2001); see also Block and Somers, *Power of Market Fundamentalism*.

75. Kate Pickett and Richard Wilkinson, *The Spirit Level: Why Greater Equality Makes Societies Stronger* (New York: Bloomsbury, 2010); Ichiro Kawachi and Bruce P. Kennedy, *The Health of Nations: Why Inequality Is Harmful to Your Health* (New York: New Press, 2002); Brighouse and Swift, "Equality, Priority, and Positional Goods."

76. Louis Uchitelle, *The Disposable American: Layoffs and Their Consequences* (New York: Vintage, 2006/2007); Jonathan D. Ostry, Andrew Berg, and Charalambos G. Tsangarides, *Redistribution, Inequality, and Growth* (Washington: IMF, 2014); Holzer et al., *Where Are All the Good Jobs Going?*

77. Richard Sennett, *The Culture of the New Capitalism* (New Haven, CT: Yale University Press, 2006); Lane, *A Company of One*.

CHAPTER 2

1. Those low-wage service industries include, for example, accommodation and food services, retail trade, and temp services. Adam Hersh, "New Jobs Strain to Deliver Middle-Class Wages," MarketWatch.com, June 6, 2014.

2. For example, wind power holds the promise of more blue-collar employment, with 21 percent of its jobs in manufacturing and 11 percent in construction. However, many of these jobs are going to more educated personnel, such as wind turbine service technicians (hired through one- or two-year programs at community colleges and technical schools), engineers, scientists, land-

acquisition specialists, asset managers, and logisticians. In 2011, only 4.3 percent of U.S. manufacturing jobs related to the production of green goods and services (defined as "goods and services produced by an establishment that benefit the environment or conserve natural resources"), and manufacturing accounted for 15 percent of the 3.4 million green jobs. James Hamilton and Drew Liming, *Careers in Wind Energy* (Washington, DC: Bureau of Labor Statistics, 2010); BLS, "Employment in Green Goods and Services—2011," news release, March 19, 2013.

3. Amy Joyce, "New Engine Plant Marks a New Deal for Auto Industry," *Washington Post,* December 8, 2005.

4. Claudia Goldin and Lawrence F. Katz, *The Race between Education and Technology* (Cambridge, MA: Harvard University Press, 2008).

5. Holzer and his collaborators question whether "high road" companies like Kroger and Costco will continue to be able to compete with the Walmarts of the world or will eventually be forced to focus on "niche" products. Harry J. Holzer, Julia I. Lane, David B. Rosenblum, and Fredrik Andersson, *Where Are All the Good Jobs Going? What National and Local Job Quality and Dynamics Mean for U.S. Workers* (New York: Russell Sage, 2011); Harry J. Holzer, *What Employers Want: Job Prospects for Less-Educated Workers* (New York: Russell Sage, 1996); Fredrik Andersson, Harry J. Holzer, and Julia I. Lane, *Moving Up or Down: Who Advances in the Low-Wage Labor Market* (New York: Russell Sage, 2005).

6. In 2005, 46 percent of the children of Walmart's 1.33 million U.S. workers were uninsured or on Medicaid. Steven Greenhouse and Michael Barbaro, "Wal-Mart Memo Suggests Ways to Cut Employee Benefit Costs," *New York Times,* October 26, 2005;

7. Economist Jason Furman has argued that Walmart is a "progressive success story" because its low prices extend the poor's purchasing power. Unlike Henry Ford's workers, however, low-paid Walmart workers cannot afford to spend much money in the community, raising the prospect of a competitive cycle of low wages followed by lower prices followed by even lower wages. Osterman and Shulman note that this fundamental tension between the interests of consumers and workers is difficult to resolve, and requires not economic calculation but political compromise—one in which community, corporate, and labor interests are all represented. Lydia DePillis, "The Architect of Walmart's D.C. Defense: Obama's Chief Economist," *Washington Post,* August 19, 2013; Paul Osterman and Beth Shulman, *Good Jobs America: Making Work Better for Everyone* (New York: Russell Sage, 2011). The latter study also discusses the research on the labor-market mobility of low-wage workers.

8. Arne L. Kalleberg, *Good Jobs, Bad Jobs: The Rise of Polarized and Precarious Employment Systems in the United States, 1970s to 2000s* (New York: Russell Sage, 2011); Robert A. Moffitt and Peter Gottschalk, "Trends in the Transitory Variance of Male Earnings in the US, 1970–2004," Working Paper No. 16833, National Bureau of Economic Research, Cambridge, MA, 1999.

9. Eli Chinoy, *Automobile Workers and the American Dream,* 2nd ed. (Urbana, IL: University of Illinois Press, 1992), 83; Josh Mitchell, *Who Are the Long-Term Unemployed?* (Washington: Urban Institute, 2013), 3.

10. Ruth Milkman, *Farewell to the Factory: Auto Workers in the Late Twentieth Century* (Berkeley: University of California Press, 1997), 128–29.

11. For a review, see Jesse Rothstein, "The Labor Market Four Years into the Crisis: Assessing Structural Explanations," *ILR Review* 65 (2012): 467–500.

12. Credentials, Bell writes, "specify minimum achievement at best; they are an entry device into the system." Later achievement must justify the decision to hire someone. Daniel Bell, *The Coming of Post-Industrial Society: A Venture in Social Forecasting* (New York: Basic, 1973).

13. Richard Sennett, "What Do We Mean by Talent?" in *The Rise and Rise of Meritocracy,* ed. Geoff Dench (Malden, MA: Blackwell, 2006), 165.

14. Sennett, "What Do We Mean by Talent?" 167.

15. Chinoy, *Automobile Workers and the American Dream,* 7, 20–21.

16. Ofer Sharone, *Flawed System/Flawed Self: Job Searching and Unemployment Experiences* (Chicago, IL: University of Chicago Press, 2014).

17. In October 2009, when the gap reached its peak, it was 2.7 percent. (The gap in Michigan was the highest in the country.) The previous record was 1.6 percent, in October 1949 (BLS).

18. From the beginning of the Great Recession until 2013, 36 percent of those who were long-term unemployed in a given month had a job fifteen months later, and less than a third of those jobs were full-time for at least four consecutive months. Alan B. Krueger, Judd Cramer, and David Cho, "Are the Long-Term Unemployed on the Margins of the Labor Market?" conference paper, Brookings Panel on Economic Activity, Washington, DC, March 20–21, 2014.

19. For example, male registered nurses are 6 percent of RNs licensed before 2000, but 10 percent of those licensed in 2000 or later. Health Resources and Services Administration, *The Registered Nurse Population: Findings from the 2008 National Sample Survey of Registered Nurses* (Washington, DC: US Department of Health and Human Services, 2010). .

20. Launched in 2007, No Worker Left Behind was restricted to the unemployed and workers with a family income of $40,000 or less. The training had to lead to a degree or certificate in a "high-demand occupation or emerging industry, or in an entrepreneurship program." Funding came from the state as well as federal Workforce Investment Act funds. Chrysler covered the program's training costs for its buyout takers. By April 2010, No Worker Left Behind had enrolled 127,000 people.

21. Second Career was launched in 2008. Its assistance cap in 2009 dollars was USD 22,099 (CAD 28,000). The program also reimburses child-care costs and expenses for living away from home while studying, and covers up to one year of remedial instruction; these supports are not counted toward the cap. Even workers who can't receive unemployment benefits are eligible for Second Career, as are workers who took low-wage jobs to make ends meet but are still looking for better ones. The training must be strictly vocational and directed toward a higher-skill, high-demand occupation. Revisions to the program in 2009 imposed a cap on tuition at private career colleges and demanded some cost-sharing. As of 2013, Second Career had served more than 65,000 people.

In Canada, workers between the ages of 55 and 64 who live in areas of high unemployment with a population of 250,000 or less can also receive job-search and training assistance through the Targeted Initiative for Older Workers.

22. Workers can obtain funding for short-term training under the Workforce Investment Act. According to one state job center in Troy, Michigan, such funding cannot exceed $4,000.

23. Just 228,000 people nationwide were receiving benefits through TAA in 2010. In the past, Michigan has been willing to pay as much as $25,000 a year for TAA training, one union official told me. An additional six months of remedial training can also be covered, and small grants are available for job-search and relocation expenses.

24. In addition, unlike other manufacturing sectors devastated by the recession, the politically important auto industry was fortunate enough to receive a quick infusion of government funds through the auto bailouts.

25. To be covered by TAA, a group of three or more of the affected workers, the company, the union, or government officials on their behalf must submit a petition. The government then conducts a fact-finding investigation (which can take months) to determine whether imports "contributed importantly" to the job losses. A surge in petitions raised the average petition processing time to about 170 days by the end of March 2010; it dropped to about 110 days at the end of September 2010. Before 2009, the average wait was 36 days.

26. A second worker had enrolled in training and expected to receive TAA; another five planned to use the benefit in the near future.

27. Furthermore, workers complained that the program denied benefits to individuals who wanted to pursue their bachelor's degree and those who were already certified for a skilled trade but needed to refresh their knowledge.

28. Not including financial aid or tax rebates, the average Canadian undergraduate in 2009–10 paid CAD 5,598 (USD 4,461) in tuition and compulsory fees. In the United States that same year, average tuition and required fees across all institutions was USD 9,120. Looking at college financing from the other end, 53 percent of Canadian bachelor's degree recipients in the class of 2000 owed student debt, compared to 65 percent of their American counterparts. StatCan, National Center for Education Statistics data; Mary Allen and Chantal Vaillancourt, "Class of 2000: Profile of Postsecondary Graduates and Student Debt," research paper, Statistics Canada, Ottawa, 2004, table A-7.

29. According to the Organisation for Economic Co-operation and Development, U.S. expenditures on tertiary educational institutions were 3.1 percent of GDP in 2007, the highest of all OECD nations; Canada's expenditures were 2.6 percent, the second-highest. However, U.S. expenditures on public tertiary institutions were just 1.0 percent of GDP; Canada spent 1.5 percent. The Obama administration's proposal to address this imbalance and invest heavily in the system—the American Graduation Initiative, which would have provided $12 billion to community colleges over ten years—was ultimately dropped from the student aid legislation passed by Congress in 2010.

30. The typical outlay is CAD 500 (about USD 400) per jobless worker, though that funding varies according to a number of factors, including the skill level of the workforce (and thus their need for services).

31. Province officials routinely reach out to companies who terminate fifty or more workers in a thirty-day period, though sometimes smaller layoffs will prompt action. (Some employers routinely terminate workers in batches of forty-nine or fewer in order to get around the requirement to report layoffs, a government official told me.) Both the employer and employees can be involved in the adjustment process if they choose. They decide by consensus whether to set up an adjustment center, whether to hire peer helpers, and where to locate the center. The Ford and Chromeshield centers I got to know were located in strip malls not far from the union halls.

32. Sam Vrankulj, *CAW Worker Adjustment Tracking Project: Preliminary Findings* (Toronto: CAW, 2010).

33. For another example of centers that foster social capital—in this case, day care centers—see Mario Luis Small, *Unanticipated Gains: Origins of Network Inequality in Everyday Life* (New York: Oxford University Press, 2009).

34. A few other provinces have similar adjustment programs, though Ontario has been particularly aggressive in establishing action centers, typically funding them for one year and sometimes for more than three. Centre for Workplace Skills, *Worker Adjustment in Action: Policies, Practices and Programs* (Ottawa: CWS, 2011).

35. The UAW has set up peer-staffed job centers in the past—Dudley describes one established after the Chrysler plant closure in Kenosha—but no such arrangement existed for the workers I interviewed. Kathryn Marie Dudley, *The End of the Line: Lost Jobs, New Lives in Postindustrial America* (Chicago, IL: University of Chicago Press, 1994), 154.

36. According to a National Employment Law Project summary of a conference presentation by Man-Tra-Con, a regional TAA services contractor in Illinois, enrollment rates for dislocated worker activities "averaged 61 percent across seven dislocation events that took place between 2003 and 2006 in which peer networks were in place," compared to 13 percent at dislocation events without them. Andrew Stettner, Rick McHugh, Lynn Minick, and Mike Evangelist, *Rapid Response and Dislocated Worker Programs: What Should States Do? And What Are They Doing?* (New York: NELP, 2010).

37. In this Brampton, Ontario, study, almost all of the Chrysler workers returned to their plants after production picked up again, because they had not taken buyouts. Among the parts workers, two-thirds were working a few years after their layoffs. However, most of their new jobs were significantly worse in terms of pay, benefits, hours, and stability compared to their old jobs, especially for those workers who were production workers like mine. Sam Vrankulj, *Finding Their Way: Second Round Report of the CAW Worker Adjustment Tracking Project* (Toronto: CAW, 2012).

38. Amit Dar and Indermit S. Gill, "Evaluating Retraining Programs in OECD Countries: Lessons Learned," *World Bank Research Observer* 13 (1998): 79–101; Marcus Stanley, Lawrence Katz, and Alan Krueger, *Developing Skills: What We Know about the Impacts of American Employment and Training Programs on Employment, Earnings, and Educational Outcomes*, report for the G8 Economic Summit, Birmingham, UK, 1998; Thomas J. Kane and Cecilia Elena Rouse, "Comment on W. Norton Grubb, 'The Varied Economic Returns to

Postsecondary Education': New Evidence from the Class of 1972," *Journal of Human Resources* 30 (1995): 205–21; W. Norton Grubb, "The Returns to Education in the Sub-Baccalaureate Labor Market, 1984–1990," *Economics of Education Review* 16 (1997): 231–45.

39. At the time of the No Worker Left Behind survey in 2010–11, 47 percent had completed training, 46 percent were still enrolled, and 7 percent had left their programs. Carrie Floyd, Larry Good, Holly Parker, and Kathy Stocking, *Perspectives on No Worker Left Behind: Results from a Participant Survey* (Corporation for a Skilled Workforce, Ann Arbor, MI, undated); Ronald D'Amico and Peter Z. Schochet, *The Evaluation of the Trade Adjustment Assistance Program: A Synthesis of Major Findings* (Oakland, CA: Social Policy Research Associates and Mathematica Policy Research, 2012).

40. Osterman and Shulman, *Good Jobs America*, 44.

41. Holzer et al., *Where Are All the Good Jobs Going?*

42. Following Marxist theories of capital accumulation, we might ask whether the predicted concentration of capital in the hands of the few is mirrored within the consumer and labor markets. That is, do the winners—the few conglomerates that sell the largest portfolio of products, the few elites who offer the best portfolio of skills—take all? Do changing tastes reflect a top-down Sneetch effect?

43. Randall Collins, "The Dirty Little Secret of Credential Inflation," *Chronicle of Higher Education*, September 27, 2002; Randall Collins, *The Credential Society: An Historical Sociology of Education and Stratification* (New York: Academic, 1979).

44. Richard Arum and Josipa Roksa, *Academically Adrift: Limited Learning on College Campuses* (Chicago, IL: University of Chicago Press, 2011).

45. Dr. Seuss, *The Sneetches and Other Stories* (New York: Random House, 1961/1989). My thanks to Darius Mehri for suggesting this analogy pertaining to master's degree programs as postindustrial trade schools.

46. For a review, see Orley Ashenfelter and Cecilia Rouse, "Schooling, Intelligence, and Income in America: Cracks in the Bell Curve," Working Paper No. 6902, NBER, Cambridge, MA, 1999.

47. Leigh Van Valen, "A New Evolutionary Law," *Evolutionary Theory* 1 (1973): 1–30.

48. The mechanism by which the capital speedup operates—individuals adapting their behavior in response to changes in the labor market—is the same mechanism described by the Lucas critique, which argues that individuals may respond to changes in policies in ways that subvert the intended outcomes of those reforms. Robert Lucas Jr., "Econometric Policy Evaluation: A Critique," in *The Phillips Curve and Labor Markets*, ed. Karl Brunner and Allan H. Meltzer (New York: American Elsevier, 1976), 19–46.

49. These two effects can be seen in economic domains outside the labor market. In the housing market, bidding wars continually raise the prices of homes in exclusive neighborhoods with better schools, as more affluent families respond in star-bellied Sneetch fashion to the home purchases of less affluent families. In turn, recent work has applied the Red Queen theory to economic development, arguing that Chinese technology firms are constantly innovating only to stand in the same place within the global pecking order. Elizabeth

Warren and Amelia Warren Tyagi, *The Two-Income Trap: Why Middle-Class Mothers and Fathers Are Going Broke* (New York: Basic, 2003); Dan Breznitz and Michael Murphree, *Run of the Red Queen: Government, Innovation, Globalization, and Economic Growth in China* (New Haven, CT: Yale University Press, 2011).

50. Stephen V. Cameron and James J. Heckman, "The Nonequivalence of High School Equivalents," *Journal of Labor Economics* 11 (1993): 1–47; James J. Heckman and Paul A. LaFontaine, "Bias-Corrected Estimates of GED Returns," *Journal of Labor Economics* 24 (2006): 661–700.

51. Within-group wage inequality has also increased greatly over the past twenty-five years. A portion of that may be due to differences in the quality or prestige of the educational institutions that individuals attend, which prompt employers to treat workers with the same educational attainment differently. Goldin and Katz, for example, point out that demand for workers with BA degrees from "selective institutions" is "still soaring," whereas the demand for workers with BA degrees overall is "less strong." On the other hand, Gottschalk and Moffitt attribute a substantial portion of this within-group wage inequality to short-term, transitory increases or decreases in earnings. Goldin and Katz, *Race between Education and Technology,* 50, 302; Peter Gottschalk and Robert Moffitt, "The Growth of Earnings Instability in the US Labor Market," *Brookings Papers on Economic Activity* (1994): 217–72.

52. Sarah Lacy, "Peter Thiel: We're in a Bubble and It's Not the Internet. It's Higher Education," *TechCrunch,* April 10, 2011.

53. Stacy Berg Dale and Alan B. Krueger, "Estimating the Payoff to Attending a More Selective College: An Application of Selection on Observables and Unobservables," *Quarterly Journal of Economics* 117 (2002): 1491–1527; Dominic J. Brewer, Eric R. Eide, and Ronald G. Ehrenberg, "Does it Pay to Attend an Elite Private College? Cross-Cohort Evidence on the Effects of College Type on Earnings," *Journal of Human Resources* 34 (1999): 104–123.

54. On the other hand, Armstrong and Hamilton argue that colleges are differentially beneficial to students from poor and privileged backgrounds, giving privileged students more access to important job-market connections. Elizabeth A. Armstrong and Laura T. Hamilton, *Paying for the Party: How College Maintains Inequality* (Cambridge, MA: Harvard University Press, 2013).

55. At the extreme is Wall Street, which has a much-publicized fetish for Ivy League talent. Karen Ho, *Liquidated: An Ethnography of Wall Street* (Durham, NC: Duke University Press, 2009); Lauren A. Rivera, "Ivies, Extracurriculars, and Exclusion: Elite Employers' Use of Educational Credentials," *Research in Social Stratification and Mobility* 29 (2011): 71–90.

56. The for-profit sector went from enrolling 2 percent of U.S. students in 1995 to enrolling 10 percent in 2012. In 2013–14, its students received 20 percent of all Pell grants. Sandy Baum and Jennifer Ma, *Trends in College Pricing 2014* (New York: College Board, 2014), figure 23; Sandy Baum, Diane Cardenas Elliott, and Jennifer Ma, *Trends in Student Aid 2014* (New York: College Board, 2014), figure 9.

57. Vrankulj, *Finding Their Way.*

58. Neil Fligstein, *The Architecture of Markets: An Economic Sociology of Twenty-First-Century Capitalist Societies* (Princeton, NJ: Princeton University Press, 2001).

59. As Lane notes, for those higher up in the labor market—her tech workers—these new forms of merit in the job-search process include knowing how best to "strategically" change jobs. Carrie M. Lane, *A Company of One: Insecurity, Independence, and the New World of White-Collar Unemployment* (Ithaca, NY: ILR, 2011), 157.

60. Ofer Sharone, "Constructing Unemployed Job Seekers as Professional Workers: The Depoliticizing Work-Game of Job Searching," *Qualitative Sociology* 30 (2007): 403–16; Vicki Smith, "Enhancing Employability: Human, Cultural, and Social Capital in an Era of Turbulent Unpredictability," *Human Relations* 63 (2010): 279–303.

61. Pierre Bourdieu, "The Forms of Capital," in *Handbook of Theory and Research for the Sociology of Education*, ed. John G. Richardson (New York: Greenwood, 1986), 241–58; Sharone, *Flawed System/Flawed Self.*

62. Today's labor market, Goldin and Katz note, prizes "interpersonal skills, possibly garnered from being in diverse college peer groups and interacting with educated people." Goldin and Katz, *Race between Education and Technology,* 353, 432n21; Sharone, *Flawed System/Flawed Self.*

63. Sharone, *Flawed System/Flawed Self.*

64. Devah Pager, *Marked: Race, Crime, and Finding Work in an Era of Mass Incarceration* (Chicago, IL: University of Chicago Press, 2007); David Harding, "Jean Valjean's Dilemma: The Management of Ex-Convict Identity in the Search for Employment," *Deviant Behavior* 25 (1993): 571–95.

65. Along these lines, but in the very different domain of public health, Link and Phelan argue that creating policies and practices to address individual "risk factors" (for their population of interest, diet, exercise, etc.; for my population of interest, lack of education) may blind us to the broader problem of inequality that puts people "at risk of risks." From pursuing education to avoiding health "risk factors," more advantaged households have the initiative, knowledge, and resources to fare better, on average, regardless of how hard less advantaged groups try to catch up. Bruce G. Link and Jo Phelan, "Social Conditions as Fundamental Causes of Disease," *Journal of Health and Social Behavior* (1995): 80, 86–87.

66. Cited in Richard Sennett and Jonathan Cobb, *The Hidden Injuries of Class* (New York: Norton, 1972/1993), 67.

67. Louis Uchitelle, *The Disposable American: Layoffs and Their Consequences* (New York: Vintage, 2006/2007), x.

68. Erik Brynjolfsson and Andrew McAfee, *The Second Machine Age: Work, Progress, and Prosperity in a Time of Brilliant Technologies* (New York: Norton, 2014); Tyler Cowen, *Average Is Over: Powering America Beyond the Age of the Great Stagnation* (New York: Dutton, 2013).

CHAPTER 3

1. In 2013, forty-two million Americans, or 13.4 percent of the population, were uninsured for the entire year (Census).

2. Census; David Dooley, Jonathan Fielding, and Lennart Levi, "Health and Unemployment," *Annual Review of Public Health* 17 (1996): 449–65; Mel Bartley, "Unemployment and Ill Health: Understanding the Relationship," *Journal of Epidemiology and Community Health* 48 (1994): 333–37; Ulla Rantakeisu, Bengt Starrin, and Curt Hagquist, "Unemployment: A Double Burden and a Public Issue," *Social Justice Research* 10 (1997): 153–73.

3. Irma T. Elo, "Social Class Differentials in Health and Mortality: Patterns and Explanations in Comparative Perspective," *Annual Review of Sociology* 35 (2009): 553–72.

4. Starting in 2014, Obamacare extended Medicaid coverage to all adults under 65 with household incomes up to 133 percent of the poverty line. At the time of my research, Michigan's Adult Benefits Waiver provided limited coverage to adults whose incomes fell below 35 percent of the poverty line (45 percent if employed). Medicaid provided full coverage to adults with dependents if their incomes were below 37 percent of the poverty line (64 percent if employed); it covered pregnant women and infants up to age 1 with household incomes up to 185 percent (now 200 percent under Obamacare) and children 1–18 up to 150 percent (now 165 percent). MIChild, the Children's Health Insurance Program in Michigan, covered children under 19 with household incomes up to twice the poverty line (now 217 percent under Obamacare).

5. Those proportions were about the same in Michigan. Families USA, *Squeezed! Caught between Unemployment Benefits and Health Care Costs* (Washington, DC: Families USA, 2009).

6. The general subsidy, which expired in 2010, covered 65 percent of the premium for up to nine months, later extended to fifteen months. The other subsidy, provided during TAA retraining, had been 65 percent and was temporarily 80 percent in 2009–11.

7. Big Three workers who are laid off indefinitely (but do not take a buyout) receive company-paid extensions of their health care coverage. For workers with the highest seniority, Ford Canada extended insurance for up to three years. Dental coverage, however, ended the month after the layoff.

8. Katherine S. Newman and Victor Tan Chen, *The Missing Class: Portraits of the Near Poor in America* (Boston: Beacon, 2007), chapter 5.

9. According to Gallup surveys, the percentage of U.S. adults age eighteen and over who said they do not have health-insurance coverage fell from a peak of 18.0 percent in the third quarter of 2013 to 12.9 percent in the fourth quarter of 2014 (the Obamacare health-insurance exchanges launched in October 2013). A Centers for Disease Control and Prevention (CDC) report found that the percentage of Americans age 18–64 who were uninsured fell from 26.5 percent in 2013 to 20.9 percent in the first three months of 2014. Robin A. Cohen and Michael E. Martinez, *Health Insurance Coverage: Early Release of Estimates from the National Health Interview Survey, January–March 2014* (Washington, DC: CDC, 2014).

10. Military health care recipients were 4.5 percent of the population in 2013. Compared to a national sample, Veterans Health Administration patients received better care, one study found, because of technology and management innovations. Steven M. Asch, Elizabeth A. McGlynn, Mary M. Hogan, Rodney A. Hay-

ward, Paul Shekelle, Lisa Rubenstein, Joan Keesey, John Adams, and Eve A. Kerr, "Comparison of Quality of Care for Patients in the Veterans Health Administration and Patients in a National Sample," *Annals of Internal Medicine* 141 (2004): 938–45; Census.

11. Indeed, the U.S. military is one of the best examples of balancing meritocratic, egalitarian, and fraternal means and ends. It is merit-based to an extreme and manages to build solidarity in spite of racial and socioeconomic diversity. It aggressively cultivates social capital through fraternal bonds (with discrimination against women and gays being major blind spots) and takes an interventionist government approach to health care and other key sectors. In a sense, the military is the ideal social-justice institution—except for the killing part.

12. The wait for Americans is actually longer than in countries with socialized medicine, such as France and the United Kingdom. Cathy Schoen and collaborators, "How Health Insurance Design Affects Access to Care and Costs, by Income, in Eleven Countries," *Health Affairs* 29 (2010): 2323–34.

13. Marie Jahoda, *Employment and Unemployment: A Social-Psychological Analysis* (Cambridge: Cambridge University Press, 1982).

14. Ruth Milkman, *Farewell to the Factory: Auto Workers in the Late Twentieth Century* (Berkeley: University of California Press, 1997); Eli Chinoy, *Automobile Workers and the American Dream,* 2nd ed. (Urbana: University of Illinois Press, 1992).

15. In Isaksson's study of Stockholm welfare clients, individuals who worked—even in low-paying, casual jobs—were more active, more integrated, and psychologically healthier than the unemployed. Eero Lahelma, "Unemployment and Mental Well-Being: Elaboration of the Relationship," *International Journal of Health Services* 22 (1992): 261–74; Kerstin Isaksson, "Unemployment, Mental Health and the Psychological Functions of Work in Male Welfare Clients in Stockholm," *Scandinavian Journal of Public Health* 17 (1989): 165–69; Kay Lehman Schlozman and Sidney Verba, *Injury to Insult: Unemployment, Class, and Political Response* (Cambridge, MA: Harvard University Press, 1979), 347.

16. In 1971–96, the replacement rate fell from 66 percent to 50–55 percent; it is now 55 percent. Rodney Haddow, "Labour Market Income Transfers and Redistribution: National Themes and Provincial Variations," in *Inequality and the Fading of Redistributive Politics,* ed. Keith Banting and John Myles (Vancouver: UBC, 2013).

17. Given that the permanent joint federal–state Extended Benefits program provides between 13 and 20 weeks of additional unemployment benefits, in theory the longest a person can normally stay on unemployment benefits is 46 weeks. However, the EB program requires that current unemployment exceed that of past years, a threshold high enough that no states currently qualify, even though unemployment remains high in many parts of the country. In Canada, how long a worker receives unemployment benefits depends on the number of hours worked and the region's unemployment rate; some regions of the country currently qualify for the maximum limit, 45 weeks.

18. As part of its 2009 reforms, the Canadian government extended benefits by 20 weeks for long-tenured workers—those who paid 30 percent or more of

the maximum unemployment insurance premiums for seven out of ten years, and received no more than 35 weeks of benefits in the previous five years. For long-tenured workers going to school, a 2009–10 pilot program (which helped D. J. Packer, the worker profiled at the chapter's beginning) provided up to 104 weeks of benefits, plus 12 weeks following their coursework so that they could search for a job.

Under the 2009 emergency extensions, the maximum duration of unemployment benefits in the United States ranged from 60 weeks (in states with low unemployment rates) to 99 weeks (in hard-hit states), while in Canada it ranged from 41 to 50 weeks.

19. Trade Readjustment Allowances provide workers with additional unemployment benefits so long as they are in full-time training. This is the second phase of income support, called "additional TRA." (The first phase, "basic TRA," pays for a year of income support, but during the recession this benefit was moot because regular state unemployment benefits and federal extensions encompassed it.) A provision of the 2009 stimulus bill increased the maximum length of additional TRA temporarily from 52 to 78 weeks. In 2011, further changes to the program capped additional TRA at 65 weeks, with an additional 13 weeks possible to complete ongoing training ("completion TRA"). If a worker had been eligible for TRA during the recession, at most she would have received 99 weeks of state unemployment benefits and federal extensions, plus 78 weeks of additional TRA, for a total of 177 weeks. Today, the maximum duration is 52 weeks of basic TRA, plus 78 weeks of additional TRA and (possible) completion TRA, for a total of 130 weeks. Workers age fifty or older who have found a new job that pays $50,000 or less a year can receive a wage subsidy in lieu of trade-adjustment assistance. It amounts to 50 percent of the difference between their old and new wages, up to $10,000 over two years.

20. Effective in 2012, Michigan reduced the maximum length of state unemployment benefits from 26 weeks to 20.

21. Keith Banting, "Debating Employment Insurance," in *Making EI Work: Research from the Mowat Centre Employment Insurance Tasks Force* (Montreal: McGill-Queen's, 2012), 27–28.

22. Beginning in 2009, Michigan workers must have worked at least two quarters to qualify for unemployment benefits, and their cumulative wages must have hit a certain income threshold. In contrast, the "hours test" in Canada, Oregon, Washington, and New Jersey focuses on the number of hours worked, without regard to wage. In Canada, the threshold is lower for regions with high unemployment rates. In Windsor, 420 hours were required to be eligible in 2010. Andrew Stettner, Rebecca Smith, and Rick McHugh, *Changing Workforce, Changing Economy: State Unemployment Insurance Reforms for the 21st Century* (New York: NELP, 2004), 12–14.

The proportion of unemployed Americans filing for unemployment benefits was 40 percent in 2009, compared to 51 percent in Canada. In 1990, about 90 percent of unemployed Canadians received these benefits, a number which fell to just 50 percent in 1999 due to reforms. U.S. Department of Labor data; Andrew Jackson and Sylvain Schetagne, "Is EI Working for Canada's Unemployed? Analyzing the Great Recession," technical paper, Canadian Centre for Policy Alternatives, Ottawa, 2010; Haddow, "Labour Market," 384.

23. Michigan's maximum weekly benefit was $362 during the time of my research. In 2009–10, the federal government funded a $25 weekly increase in benefits. The Canadian Employment Insurance system has a replacement rate of 55 percent; in 2010, the benefit topped out at CAD 457 (USD 365) per week. For low-income families with children (annual net income of less than CAD 25,291), the EI Family Supplement ups the rate to 80 percent, topping out at the program's maximum. Ontario's Second Career program provides a living allowance equivalent to the province's minimum wage for a 40-hour week (in 2012, CAD 410), minus any unemployment benefits. Sam Vrankulj, *Finding Their Way: Second Round Report of the CAW Worker Adjustment Tracking Project* (Toronto: CAW, 2012), 49.

24. However, see the appendix for the argument that the conversion of Canadian dollars to U.S. dollars can be closer to 1:1 along the border. That would make the amount of the Canadian income supports larger.

25. In Ontario, the severance is equivalent to one week of pay for every year of seniority, up to twenty-six. Workers must have at least five years of seniority. Companies must pay severance if they have a payroll of at least CAD 2.5 million or laid off fifty or more employees within six months. Normally, severance delays unemployment benefits by the number of weeks of pay provided. However, a 2009–10 pilot program allowed long-tenured workers to receive both at the same time, so long as they used the severance to fund training. In Michigan, if a severance payment attributed to a week is 1.6 times the worker's weekly unemployment benefits, then the worker cannot receive benefits for that week.

26. The U.S. WARN Act covers terminations involving a hundred or more workers and requires sixty calendar days of advance notice—or equivalent severance, though notice and not severance was the norm for auto companies, according to UAW officials. (One union official pointed out that some companies stagger their layoffs so that each wave falls just under the hundred-person trigger.) In Ontario, the required notice is one week for every year of seniority the worker has at the firm, up to eight weeks.

27. During the time of my research, Ford Canada workers received a Supplemental Unemployment Benefit equivalent to 65 percent of gross pay for a forty-hour workweek, minus any unemployment benefits. After it ended, workers were covered by the Income Maintenance Benefit Plan, which paid 60 percent of gross pay. The duration of these benefits depended on seniority; those with ten years, for example, received three years of support in total.

For American Chrysler workers, sub-pay topped up unemployment compensation so that workers received three-quarters of their previous take-home pay. Under the 2007 contract, workers laid off for more than forty-eight weeks had gone into the Jobs Bank, under which the company, among other things, indefinitely provided those workers with most of their pay and benefits. However, contract amendments during the recession eliminated the Jobs Bank, replacing it with Transitional Assistance, which paid 50 percent of gross pay. A worker with ten years of seniority received a year and a half of income support in total.

28. The Canadian bankruptcy system requires individuals to devote their income beyond necessary living expenses to paying creditors until the discharge of debts is granted. The U.S. system has historically been more committed to a "fresh start" for debtors, but reforms in 2005 dramatically restricted the Chapter 7 bankruptcy option—among other things, by imposing a means test and tightening rules regarding what property is exempt from liquidation. Jacob S. Ziegel, "The Philosophy and Design of Contemporary Consumer Bankruptcy Systems: A Canada-United States Comparison," *Osgoode Hall Law Journal* 37, nos. 1 and 2 (1999); Iain Ramsay, "Models of Consumer Bankruptcy: Implications for Research and Policy," *Journal of Consumer Policy* 20 (1997): 269–87.

29. Examining the disability insurance programs in the two countries is beyond the scope of this book, but past research finds that Canadian disability insurance replaces substantially less income than the U.S. system does, though it redistributes that income in ways that better help the poor. Jonathan Gruber, "Disability Insurance Benefits and Labor Supply," Working Paper No. 5866, NBER, Cambridge, MA, 2010.

30. At the time of my research, the Home Affordable Modification Program allowed homeowners who were delinquent or at risk of default to lower their mortgage payments to 31 percent of their monthly income—first by reducing the interest rate, then by extending the loan term, and finally by deferring a portion of the principal or waiving interest. The unpaid principal balance had to be no greater than $72,750. HAMP was expected to help three to four million homeowners by 2012, but the program was only used by a few hundred thousand. In Michigan, the Unemployment Mortgage Subsidy Program paid up to half of mortgage payments—not to exceed $750 a month—for up to twelve months, and another program paid up to $3,000 in incentives to facilitate short sales. Edward N. Wolff, Lindsay A. Owens, and Esra Burak, "How Much Wealth Was Destroyed in the Great Recession?" in *The Great Recession,* ed. David B. Grusky, Bruce Western, and Christopher Wimer (New York: Russell Sage, 2011).

31. Deirdre A. Royster, *Race and the Invisible Hand: How White Networks Exclude Black Men from Blue-Collar Jobs* (Berkeley: University of California Press, 2003); Marianne Bertrand and Sendhil Mullainathan, "Are Emily and Greg More Employable than Lakisha and Jamal? A Field Experiment on Labor Market Discrimination," Working Paper No. 9873, NBER, Cambridge, MA, 2003; Sandra Susan Smith, *Lone Pursuit: Distrust and Defensive Individualism among the Black Poor* (New York: Russell Sage, 2007).

32. Thomas M. Shapiro, *The Hidden Cost of Being African American: How Wealth Perpetuates Inequality* (New York: Oxford University Press, 2004); Dalton Conley, *Being Black, Living in the Red: Race, Wealth, and Social Policy in America* (Berkeley: University of California Press, 1999); Melvin L. Oliver and Thomas M. Shapiro, *Black Wealth/White Wealth: A New Perspective on Racial Inequality* (New York: Routledge, 1997).

33. Rourke L. O'Brien, "Depleting Capital? Race, Wealth and Informal Financial Assistance," *Social Forces* 91, no. 2 (2012): 375–96.

34. Jim Stanford, "The Economic and Social Consequences of Fiscal Retrenchment in Canada in the 1990s," in *Review of Economic Performance*

and Social Progress—The Longest Decade: Canada in the 1990s, ed. Keith Banting, Andrew Sharpe, and France St-Hilaire (Montreal: McGill-Queen's University Press, 2001), 141–60.

35. To extend an idea put forward by Brown, *extended* families are "a mechanism for pooling resources," and strengthening them more broadly can to some extent make up for an individual family's lack of resources in "contacts, jobs and money." Belinda Brown, "Resolving the Conflict between the Family and Meritocracy," in *The Rise and Rise of Meritocracy,* ed. Geoff Dench (Malden, MA: Blackwell, 2006), 180.

36. In Canada, average unemployment duration rose from a low of 14.8 weeks in 2008 to a high of 21.1 weeks in 2011. In the United States, it was 16.8 weeks in 2007, its lowest point in the past decade, and 39.3 weeks in 2011. See chapter 1 for more recent figures. StatCan; BLS.

37. Jesse Rothstein and Robert G. Valletta, "Scraping By: Income and Program Participation after the Loss of Extended Unemployment Benefits," Working Paper No. 101–14, Institute for Research on Labor and Employment, University of California, Berkeley, 2014.

38. Martin Gilens, *Why Americans Hate Welfare: Race, Media, and the Politics of Antipoverty Policy* (Chicago, IL: University of Chicago Press, 1999).

CHAPTER 4

1. Paul Osterman and Beth Shulman, *Good Jobs America: Making Work Better for Everyone* (New York: Russell Sage, 2011).

2. Elizabeth Warren and Amelia Warren Tyagi, *The Two-Income Trap: Why Middle-Class Mothers and Fathers Are Going Broke* (New York: Basic, 2003).

3. Lillian B. Rubin, *Worlds of Pain: Life in the Working-Class Family* (New York: Basic, 1976/1992).

4. According to Brown, families provide resources for success as well as alternative values from those of the mainstream, and in these ways they can help even poor families overcome their "economic limitations," thereby leading to greater "equality and efficiency and merit" in the broader society. However, because family structures are so different among more and less advantaged households, and less advantaged families tend to have the most economically vulnerable structures, the power of this institution to help poor families, as a whole, catch up with the more affluent is questionable. Belinda Brown, "Resolving the Conflict between the Family and Meritocracy," in *The Rise and Rise of Meritocracy,* ed. Geoff Dench (Malden, MA: Blackwell, 2006), 178, 180.

5. Stephanie Coontz, "The New Instability," *New York Times,* July 26, 2014. See also David J. Harding, Christopher Jencks, Leonard M. Lopoo, and Susan E. Mayer, "The Changing Effect of Family Background on the Incomes of American Adults," in *Unequal Chances: Family Background and Economic Success,* ed. Samuel Bowles, Herbert Gintis, and Melissa Osborne Groves (New York: Russell Sage, 2005); Charles Murray, *Coming Apart: The State of White America, 1960–2010* (New York: Crown Forum, 2012); Susan L. Brown, "Family Structure and Child Well-Being: The Significance of Parental Cohabitation," *Journal of Marriage and the Family* 66 (May 2004): 351–67; Stacey R.

Aronson and Aletha C. Huston, "The Mother-Infant Relationship in Single, Cohabiting, and Married Families: A Case for Marriage?" *Journal of Family Psychology* 18 (2004): 5–18.

6. Coontz, "The New Instability."

7. David T. Ellwood and Christopher Jencks, "The Spread of Single-Parent Families in the United States Since 1960," in *The Future of the Family*, ed. Daniel P. Moynihan, Timothy M. Smeeding, and Lee Rainwater (New York: Russell Sage, 2004); Patrick Heuveline, Jeffrey M. Timberlake, and Frank F. Furstenberg, Jr., "Shifting Childrearing to Single Mothers: Results from 17 Western Countries," *Population and Development Review* 29 (2003): 47–71; Adam Thomas and Isabel Sawhill, "For Richer or Poorer: Marriage as an Antipoverty Strategy," *Journal of Policy Analysis and Management* 15 (2002), 589–99; Adam Thomas and Isabel Sawhill, "For Love *and* Money? The Impact of Family Structure on Family Income," *The Future of Children* 15 (2005): 57–74; Bruce Western, Deirdre Bloome, and Christine Percheski, "Inequality among American Families with Children, 1975 to 2005," *American Sociological Review* 73 (2008): 903–20.

8. Murray, *Coming Apart;* Coontz, "The New Instability." In 1970, men and women who only finished high school were slightly more likely to marry than their college-educated counterparts, Coontz notes. While marriage rates have plummeted among the former group, "high-earning women have actually increased their marriage rates"—from 58 percent in 1980 to 64 percent in 2010.

9. Another relevant trend is that the percentage of women who become lone mothers at some point during their prime childbearing years has stayed stable for decades among college-educated whites and blacks alike. Yet, for women who have less education, the rate has doubled since 1965. Ellwood and Jencks, "Spread of Single-Parent Families," figure 2.9; Joshua R. Goldstein and Catherine T. Kenney, "Marriage Delayed or Marriage Forgone? New Cohort Forecasts of First Marriage for US Women," *American Sociological Review* 66 (2001): 506–19; Andrew Cherlin, *The Marriage-Go-Round: The State of Marriage and the Family in America Today* (New York: Knopf, 2009), 167; Sheela Kennedy and Larry Bumpass, "Cohabitation and Children's Living Arrangements: New Estimates from the United States," *Demographic Research* 19 (2008): 1677; Lisa Mincieli, Jennifer Manlove, Molly McGarrett, Kristin Moore, and Suzanne Ryan, "The Relationship Context of Births outside of Marriage: The Rise of Cohabitation," Research Brief No. 2007–13, Child Trends, Washington, DC, 2007.

10. Cherlin, *Marriage-Go-Round,* 160; Andrew Cherlin, *Labor's Love Lost: The Rise and Fall of the Working-class Family in America* (New York: Russell Sage, 2014); Coontz, "The New Instability"; Kathryn Edin and Maria Kefalas, *Promises I Can Keep: Why Poor Women Put Motherhood before Marriage* (Berkeley: University of California Press, 2005); E. Mavis Hetherington and W. Glenn Clingempeel, *Coping with Marital Transitions: A Family Systems Perspective* (Chicago, IL: University of Chicago Press, 1992); Murray, *Coming Apart.*

11. Census data.

12. Here I am using the term "fragile families" in a different sense from, say, the way it is used in the Fragile Families and Child Wellbeing Study; I want to emphasize the *economic* fragility of these households.

13. Katherine S. Newman, *The Accordion Family: Boomerang Kids, Anxious Parents, and the Private Toll of Global Competition* (Boston: Beacon, 2012).

14. Viviana Zelizer, *Pricing the Priceless Child: The Changing Social Value of Children* (New York: Basic, 1985).

15. Jeffry H. Larson, Stephan M. Wilson, and Rochelle Beley, "The Impact of Job Insecurity on Marital and Family Relationships," *Family Relations* 43 (1994): 138–43; Lisa S. Matthews, Rand D. Conger, and K. A. S. Wickrama, "Work-Family Conflict and Marital Quality: Mediating Processes," *Social Psychology Quarterly* 59 (1996): 62–79.

16. Arthur Aron, Tracy McLaughlin-Volpe, Debra Mashek, Gary Lewandowski, Stephen C. Wright, and Elaine N. Aron, "Including Others in the Self," *European Review of Social Psychology* 15 (2004): 101–32.

17. For the highly educated, earning power can be trumped by other traits, as Sandberg notes—an ambitious woman needs to find a partner who fully supports her career, and shares responsibilities in the home—and yet the language of meritocracy (in cultural capital, if not human capital) remains central: "I truly believe that the single most important career decision that a woman makes is whether she will have a life partner and who that partner is." Sheryl Sandberg, *Lean In: Women, Work, and the Will to Lead* (New York: Knopf, 2013), 110; Cherlin, *Marriage-Go-Round;* Murray, *Coming Apart.*

18. Carrie M. Lane, *A Company of One: Insecurity, Independence, and the New World of White-Collar Unemployment* (Ithaca: ILR, 2011).

19. Here I do not intend to reduce blue-collar relationships to mere instrumentality; my point is that economic hardship pushes relationships in that direction (though policy may mediate that effect). Edin and Kefalas, *Promises I Can Keep;* Viviana A. Zelizer, *The Purchase of Intimacy* (Princeton, NJ: Princeton University Press, 2005); Allison J. Pugh, *The Tumbleweed Society: Working and Caring in an Age of Insecurity* (New York: Oxford University Press, 2015).

20. In using this term, I am not arguing on behalf of a normative view of marriage as the ideal. I am reflecting the ways that my respondents linked their unemployment to the failures of their relationships. William Julius Wilson, *The Truly Disadvantaged: The Inner City, the Underclass, and Public Policy* (Chicago, IL: University of Chicago Press, 1987).

21. William Julius Wilson, *More Than Just Race: Being Black and Poor in the Inner City* (New York: Norton, 2009), 131.

22. Cherlin, *Marriage-Go-Round.*

23. In Canada, the risk of divorce by the third decade of marriage for recently married couples is 38 percent, compared to 44 percent in America. Anne-Marie Ambert, *Divorce: Facts, Causes & Consequences* (Ottawa: Vanier Institute, 2009), 3, 5, 8; Cherlin, *Marriage-Go-Round.*

24. Data from the World Values Survey suggest that Americans on a whole do have a more materialist mindset than Canadians do, in that they prioritize personal safety and economic security (materialism) over freedom, self-expression,

and quality of life (postmaterialism): 11.1 percent of Americans surveyed in 2006 expressed support for such materialist values, whereas only 2.8 percent of Canadians did.

25. There are also fewer children in single-mother families in Canada—14 or 15 percent, compared to 21 percent in the United States. Lee Rainwater and Timothy M. Smeeding, "Single-Parent Poverty, Inequality, and the Welfare State," in *The Future of the Family*, ed. Daniel P. Moynihan, Timothy M. Smeeding, and Lee Rainwater (New York: Russell Sage, 2004), 97–98.

26. 2009 dollars. Alice receives a monthly living allowance of CAD 860, a monthly child benefit of CAD 160, and a quarterly sales-tax refund of CAD 189.

27. Frank F. Furstenberg, "If Moynihan Had Only Known: Race, Class, and Family Change in the Late Twentieth Century," *Annals of the American Academy of Political and Social Science* 621 (2009): 94–110; Murray, *Coming Apart*.

28. Schalet points out that the economic security provided by the Dutch welfare state has reduced the costs of teenage pregnancy there, helping allay parents' worries about their children's sexuality. In turn, cultural understandings have shaped the kinds of social policies adopted there. Amy T. Schalet, *Not under My Roof: Parents, Teens, and the Culture of Sex* (Chicago, IL: University of Chicago Press, 2011).

CHAPTER 5

1. Keith Banting and John Myles, eds., *Inequality and the Fading of Redistributive Politics* (Vancouver: UBC, 2013); Thomas Frank, *What's the Matter with Kansas?* (New York: Metropolitan, 2004).

2. The antipoverty policies that have been enacted in recent decades have mainly been targeted toward specific constituencies—the elderly and children above all. Meanwhile, the Federal Reserve has downplayed the goal of full employment codified in the Humphrey-Hawkins Act of 1978, focusing instead on inflation. Josh Bivens, *Failure by Design: The Story behind America's Broken Economy* (Ithaca, NY: ILR, 2011).

3. Public opinion regarding unions moved across similar trajectories in the two countries in those decades, but America's National Labor Relations Board and its labor laws both took a sharp rightward turn, making it harder to form unions. Martin Gilens and Benjamin I. Page, "Testing Theories of American Politics: Elites, Interest Groups, and Average Citizens," *Perspectives on Politics* (Fall 2014); Bivens, *Failure by Design*; Dan Zuberi, *Differences That Matter: Social Policy and the Working Poor in the United States and Canada* (Ithaca, NY: Cornell University Press, 2006), 52–54; Henry S. Farber and Bruce Western, "Accounting for the Decline of Unions in the Private Sector, 1973–1998," *Journal of Labor Research* 22 (2001): 459–85; Daniel Tope and David Jacobs, "The Politics of Union Decline: The Contingent Determinants of Union Recognition Elections and Victories," *American Sociological Review* 74 (2009): 842–64.

4. Frank, *What's the Matter with Kansas?*

5. Margaret R. Somers and Fred Block, "From Poverty to Perversity: Ideas, Markets, and Institutions over 200 Years of Welfare," *American Sociological*

Review 70 (2005): 260–87; Jonathan Rieder, *Canarsie: The Jews and Italians of Brooklyn against Liberalism* (Cambridge, MA: Harvard University Press, 1985).

6. Off-label uses of government policies are quite common, too—for example, Medicaid, which has become a supplemental form of insurance for (once) middle-class patients whose nursing-home stays are not covered by Medicare.

7. Jody Freeman and Martha Minow, *Government by Contract: Outsourcing and American Democracy* (Cambridge, MA: Harvard University Press, 2009); Suzanne Mettler, *Degrees of Inequality: How the Politics of Higher Education Sabotaged the American Dream* (New York: Basic, 2014).

8. Dana Cloud, *We Are the Union: Democratic Unionism and Dissent at Boeing* (Urbana: University of Illinois Press, 2011).

9. Kay Lehman Schlozman and Sidney Verba, *Injury to Insult: Unemployment, Class, and Political Response* (Cambridge, MA: Harvard University Press, 1979); Carrie M. Lane, *A Company of One: Insecurity, Independence, and the New World of White-Collar Unemployment* (Ithaca, NY: ILR, 2011).

10. In the past, political parties, like unions, offered a nonmeritocratic, fraternal alternative, through patronage jobs and clientelism more broadly.

11. Katherine S. Newman, *The Accordion Family: Boomerang Kids, Anxious Parents, and the Private Toll of Global Competition* (Boston: Beacon, 2012); Michael B. Katz, *In the Shadow of the Poorhouse: A Social History of Welfare in America* (New York: Basic, 1996).

12. Nan Lin, "Inequality in Social Capital," *Contemporary Sociology* 29 (November 2000): 785–95.

13. Victor Tan Chen and Katherine S. Newman, "Streetwise Economics," in *Chutes and Ladders: Navigating the Low-Wage Labor Market,* by Katherine S. Newman (New York: Russell Sage and Harvard University Press, 2006).

14. Lane, *A Company of One,* 39.

15. Rieder, *Canarsie.*

16. Jennifer L. Hochschild, *Facing Up to the American Dream: Race, Class, and the Soul of the Nation* (Princeton, NJ: Princeton University Press, 1995); James R. Kluegel and Eliot R. Smith, *Beliefs about Inequality: Americans' Views of What Is and What Ought to Be* (New York: Aldine de Gruyter, 1986), 37; Michèle Lamont, *The Dignity of Working Men: Morality and the Boundaries of Race, Class, and Immigration* (New York: Russell Sage and Harvard University Press, 2000); Jay MacLeod, *Ain't No Makin' It: Aspirations and Attainment in a Low-Income Neighborhood,* 3rd ed. (Boulder, CO: Westview, 2009).

17. Eli Chinoy, *Automobile Workers and the American Dream,* 2nd ed. (Urbana: University of Illinois Press, 1992); Richard Sennett and Jonathan Cobb, *The Hidden Injuries of Class* (New York: Norton, 1972/1993); Schlozman and Verba, *Injury to Insult.*

18. Robert E. Lane, *Political Ideology: Why the American Common Man Believes What He Does* (New York: Free Press, 1962), 66; David Halle, *America's Working Man: Work, Home, and Politics among Blue-Collar Property Owners* (Chicago, IL: University of Chicago Press, 1984), 61; Katherine S. Newman, *Falling from Grace: The Experience of Downward Mobility in the*

American Middle Class (New York: Free Press, 1988), 77; Kathryn Marie Dudley, *The End of the Line: Lost Jobs, New Lives in Postindustrial America* (Chicago, IL: University of Chicago Press, 1994).

19. Seymour Martin Lipset, *Continental Divide: The Values and Institutions of the United States and Canada* (New York: Routledge, 1990).

20. In a 2004 survey, Whyte finds that "Chinese respondents tend to stress individual merit rather than unfair external or structural explanations of why some people are rich and others are poor." With the partial exception of Japan, this tendency is stronger in China than in a host of capitalist societies—the United States included—and post-socialist transition societies. For the Chinese public, Whyte argues, greater inequality can actually be seen as more "equitable" when contrasted with the rigidities of the previous nonmeritocratic system. Martin King Whyte, *Myth of the Social Volcano: Perceptions of Inequality and Distributive Injustice in Contemporary China* (Stanford, CA: Stanford University Press, 2010).

21. For example, Dudley (*End of the Line*) uses the term *social Darwinism*; Lamont (*Dignity of Working Men*) uses *disciplined self* to describe the mindset of white working-class men, who value hard work and responsibility in the face of economic uncertainty. My emphasis, however, is on the ways that workers judge themselves and others according to (changing) notions of merit.

22. For tables and charts describing the survey data in this chapter, please go to my website, victortanchen.com. *First survey*: General Social Survey, 1973–2012. Americans' belief in hard work rose from a low of 61 percent in 1974 to 70 percent in 2012. In 1974, it was 60.7 percent among those with a high school degree or less education, and 59.9 percent among the more educated; in 2012, those figures were 73.0 percent and 64.3 percent, respectively. The unemployed and union members were less likely to believe that hard work leads to success.

Second survey: Pew Research Center for the People and the Press, *Trends in American Values, 1987–2012* (Washington, DC: Pew, 2012). Asked whether "success in life is pretty much determined by forces outside our control," 55 to 70 percent of Americans over the last three decades have said they *disagree*. The proportion of those disagreeing rose from a low of 56 percent in 1988 to a high of 67 percent in 1999 and 2003; in 2012, it was 63 percent.

Third survey: World Values Survey, 1990–2011. The question used a ten-point scale, with 1 representing agreement with the statement, "In the long run, hard work usually brings a better life," and 10 pegged to the statement, "Hard work doesn't generally bring success—it's more a matter of luck and connections." The percentage for answers 1 through 5 (belief in hard work) was 83.0 in 1990, 79.1 in 1995, 75.0 in 2006, and 74.3 percent in 2011—a steady decline. For answers 1 to 3 (strong belief in hard work), it was 60.1 in 1990, 56.5 in 1995, 47.0 in 2006, and 52.2 in 2011. In 2011, 71.4 percent of the less educated believed that hard work brings a better life, compared to 76.7 percent of the more educated.

23. Leslie McCall, *The Undeserving Rich: American Beliefs about Inequality, Opportunity, and Redistribution* (New York: Cambridge University Press, 2013), 225.

24. The percentage of Americans who said education was "essential" or "very important" in getting ahead was 84.0 in 1987, 87.1 in 1992, and 88.8 in 2009. Among those with a high school degree or less, the percentage rose from 81.1, to 85.0, to 87.7 over that period. There was no clear pattern among the unemployed or union members, though belief in education was weaker in those groups in two out of the three years of surveys. The percentage of Americans who said education should be "essential" or "very important" in deciding "how much people ought to earn" was 72.3 in 1992, 65.2 in 1999, and 62.7 in 2009. Among those with a high school degree or less, it rose from 72.9, to 64.6, to 64.4 over that period. The relationship between union membership and this belief was unclear; agreement appeared to be weaker among the unemployed, though again the relationship held up in only two out of three years. International Social Survey Programme (ISSP).

25. For the statement, "Differences in income in [the United States] are too large," the percentage who agreed or strongly agreed was 77.4 in 1992, 61.7 in 1996, and 64.6 in 2009. ISSP; McCall, *Undeserving Rich;* Katherine S. Newman and Elisabeth S. Jacobs, *Who Cares? Public Ambivalence and Government Activism from the New Deal to the Second Gilded Age* (Princeton, NJ: Princeton University Press, 2010).

26. When asked whether the government has a responsibility to reduce the income gap between "people with high incomes and those with low incomes," the percentage of Americans who agreed or strongly agreed was 39.2 in 1992, 32.6 in 1996, and 31.3 in 2009—a gradual decline. When asked about reducing the gap "between the rich and the poor," however, the percentage who said "definitely should be" or "probably should be" was 39.8 in 1985, 44.5 in 1990, 48.0 in 1996, and 51.0 in 2006—a gradual increase. Posed the question of whether government should provide a job for everyone who wants one, the percentage who said "definitely" or "probably should be" was 35.1 in 1985, 43.8 in 1990, 39.4 in 1996, and 39.7 in 2006. ISSP; Schlozman and Verba, *Injury to Insult,* 348.

27. According to the World Values Survey, the combined percentage of Canadians who believe that "hard work usually brings a better life"—specifically, those who gave answers 1 through 5 on the survey's ten-point scale—was 75.8 in 1990 and 73.9 in 2005, compared to U.S. percentages of 83.0 in 1990 and 75.0 in 2006, for gaps of 7.2 and 1.1, respectively. The other statistics come from the ISSP. In 1992, the percentages of the population who believe that education was "essential" or "very important" in getting ahead were 84.5 for Canadians and 87.1 for Americans. Between 1992 and 1999, the percentage who believed that education should affect pay fell from 56.7 to 53.4 in Canada, and from 72.3 to 65.2 in the United States; the gap fell from 15.6 points to 11.8 points. In Canada, the percentage saying that differences in income were too large was 71.1 in 1992 and 68.5 in 1999, compared to U.S. percentages of 77.4 in 1992 and 61.7 in 1996. The percentage of Canadians who agreed or agreed strongly that government should reduce income differences between rich and poor was 53.0 in 1996 and 66.4 in 2006—a substantial increase—while in the United States the proportion stayed fairly steady, at 48.0 percent in 1996 and 51.0 percent in 2006. In contrast, the percentage of Canadians who supported

government responsibility for reducing the gap between high and low incomes fell slightly: from 48.2 in 1992 to 45.6 in 1999, compared to U.S. percentages of 39.2 in 1992 and 32.6 in 1996. In 2006, 38.8 percent of Canadians felt that it "definitely" or "probably" should be government's responsibility to provide a job, compared to 39.7 percent of Americans.

28. McCall, *Undeserving Rich*, 225.

29. Karen Ho, *Liquidated: An Ethnography of Wall Street* (Durham, NC: Duke University Press, 2009); Robert N. Bellah, Richard Madsen, William M. Sullivan, Ann Swidler, and Steven M. Tipton, *Habits of the Heart: Individualism and Commitment in American Life* (Berkeley: University of California Press, 1985).

30. Lane's workers were less supportive of government solutions to the economy's problems than my workers. However, they criticized corporate executives and their high pay like my workers did. Lane, *A Company of One*, 152.

31. In other words, the hierarchy in society is largely justified, except when there are gross violations of the link between performance and reward. As research finds, arbitrary or unfair inequalities appearing at the level of one's reference group—the "lazy" workers that one worker rails against—are more heinous than inequalities resulting from high status "fairly earned" by elites. Daniel Bell, *The Coming of Post-Industrial Society: A Venture in Social Forecasting* (New York: Basic, 1973).

32. Chinoy, *Automobile Workers*, 129.

33. See MacLeod, *Ain't No Makin' It*, 219.

34. Between 2000 and 2014, union membership in America's private sector declined (from 9.0 to 6.6 percent), while public-sector membership was more stable (from 36.9 to 35.7 percent). Between 1999 and 2012, Canadian private-sector membership also fell (from 18.4 to 16.4 percent), while public-sector membership rose (from 70.8 to 71.4 percent). BLS, StatCan.

35. Asked whether they agreed more with the governors or unions on the question of curtailing collective-bargaining rights for state workers, 48 percent said the unions (Gallup Poll, March 25–27, 2011). Paul Egan, "Poll Finds Michigan Voters Divided on Right-to-Work Laws," *Detroit Free Press*, December 5, 2012.

36. Katz, *Undeserving Poor*, 138.

37. Lawrence Richards, *Union-Free America: Workers and Antiunion Culture* (Urbana: University of Illinois Press, 2008), 13.

38. Frank Levy and Peter Temin, "Inequality and Institutions in 20th Century America," Working Paper No. 13106, NBER, Cambridge, MA, 2007; Jake Rosenfeld, *What Unions No Longer Do* (Cambridge, MA: Harvard University Press, 2014).

39. Richard B. Freeman and Joel Rogers, *What Workers Want* (Ithaca: Cornell, 1999/2006); Seymour Martin Lipset and Noah M. Meltz, *The Paradox of American Unionism: Why Americans Like Unions More Than Canadians Do but Join Much Less* (Ithaca, NY: ILR, 2004).

40. In 1957, 75 percent of Americans told Gallup they approved of unions; 14 percent said they disapproved. Over the next three decades, approval fell and disapproval rose, with approval stabilizing in the high 50s and disapproval in the low 30s. When the economy tanked, so did the approval rate, which hit a

record low of 48 percent; disapproval soared to a record high of 45 percent. In 2014, 53 percent of Americans approved and 38 percent disapproved of unions.

In both countries, growing disapproval of unions may speak to a broader problem of political polarization, with conservatives in particular becoming more conservative and driving up overall rates of anti-union discontent. Jacob S. Hacker and Paul Pierson, *Winner-Take-All Politics: How Washington Made the Rich Richer—and Turned Its Back on the Middle Class* (New York: Simon & Schuster, 2010); Thomas E. Mann and Norman J. Ornstein, *It's Even Worse Than It Looks: How the American Constitutional System Collided with the New Politics of Extremism* (New York: Basic, 2012); Stuart Soroka, "Redistributive Preferences and Partisan Polarization: Canada in Comparative Perspective," presentation to the Canadian Studies Program and the Institute of Governmental Studies, University of California, Berkeley, May 9, 2014.

41. The problem with the Canadian data is that the questions and the polling firms vary across time. Gallup asked about union approval/disapproval in 1961–1975, but in other years it asked whether unions have been "a good thing or a bad thing for Canada." If we consider these to be the same question, the postwar years had the highest levels of approval, with a peak in 1956 (69 percent approval, 12 percent disapproval); approval largely stayed in the 50s in the decades that followed, while disapproval tripled by the 1970s and stayed largely in the 30s afterward. Gallup has not continued this line of questioning in more recent years, however, and to my knowledge no other national polls have asked comparable questions since a 2001 poll by Environics, which found that approval was 64 percent and disapproval 32 percent, compared to 57 percent and 39 percent in 1997. W. Craig Riddell, "Unionization in Canada and the United States," in *Small Differences That Matter: Labor Markets and Income Maintenance in Canada and the United States,* ed. David Card and Richard B. Freeman (Chicago, IL: University of Chicago Press, 1993), 139; Reginald W. Bibby, *Canadians and Unions: A National Reading at the Beginning of the New Century* (Mississauga, Ontario: Work Research Foundation, 2002).

The questions used in more recent years are significantly different in their wording and in their results. In 2007, Angus Reid asked Canadians whether they agreed that unions are "a necessary and important entity in our society"; 59 percent agreed, and 35 percent disagreed. In a 2013 Harris/Decima poll commissioned by the Canadian Association of University Teachers, a quarter of respondents said that unions were no longer needed; in contrast, polls commissioned by the employer-sponsored Canadian LabourWatch Association found in both 2011 and 2013 that four in ten Canadians believed unions were no longer necessary.

42. According to Lipset and Meltz's 1996 survey, agreement with the statement "there is too much corruption in unions here" was 64 percent in the United States and 54 percent in Canada, and the percentage agreeing that the "union movement is getting weaker" was 73 percent in the U.S. and 62 percent in Canada. In 2011–14, 49 to 55 percent of Americans told Gallup that in the future unions will become "weaker than they are today"; in the previous decade, support for that view registered on average in the low 40s. Lipset and Meltz, *Paradox of American Unionism,* 87, 89.

43. James B. Jacobs, *Mobsters, Unions, and Feds: The Mafia and the American Labor Movement* (New York: New York University, 2006), 260–61, xi.

44. Jay Rosen, "Public Journalism: The Case for Public Scholarship," *Change* 27 (1995): 38.

45. One example is the ways that meritocracy leads to inequality even in the absence of corrupt elites—though it certainly has them, too.

46. Thanks to Katherine Newman for suggesting this term.

47. Robert D. Putnam, "E Pluribus Unum: Diversity and Community in the Twenty-first Century," *Scandinavian Political Studies* 30 (2007): 137–74; Ted Miguel, "Ethnic Diversity, Mobility, and School Funding: Theory and Evidence from Kenya," Development Economics Discussion Paper No. 14, Suntory Centre, London School of Economics, 1999; Cybelle Fox, Irene Bloemraad, and Christel Kesler, "Immigration and Redistributive Social Policy," in *Immigration, Poverty, and Socioeconomic Inequality,* ed. David Card and Steven Raphael (New York: Russell Sage, 2013), 381–420; Martin Gilens, *Why Americans Hate Welfare: Race, Media, and the Politics of Antipoverty Policy* (Chicago, IL: University of Chicago Press, 1999).

48. Lipset and Meltz, *Paradox of American Unionism,* 87.

49. Richards, *Union-Free America,* 13; Dudley, *End of the Line,* 59.

50. Howard Kimeldorf, *Battling for American Labor: Wobblies, Craft Workers, and the Making of the Union Movement* (Berkeley: University of California Press, 1999).

51. For an alternative view, see Freeman and Rogers, *What Workers Want.*

52. In 2011, 61.4 percent of Canadians agreed that unions "have too much power for the good of the country." This amounts to a ten-point drop from two decades earlier, according to Environics surveys. Lipset and Meltz cite older Canadian surveys that show a steady rise in this view: from 32 percent in 1950 to 62 percent in 1968, staying in the 60s in the early 1980s; their 1996 survey, however, found 47 percent sharing this view. In 1971, Lipset and Meltz note, 55 percent of Americans thought unions were too powerful, a proportion that had fallen to 30 percent in 1996; Gallup found the percentage in 2011 to be 43 percent. According to Gallup, the percentage of Americans who believe that unions should have "less influence" was in the low 30s from 1999 until 2008. In 2009, it shot up to 42 percent. Public opinion stayed roughly in the same place until 2013, when support for the anti-union view fell slightly, to 38 percent; the following year it dropped precipitously, reaching 27 percent. Interestingly, in another 2014 Gallup poll, 71 percent of Americans said they would vote for right-to-work laws, 82 percent agreed that no worker should be required to join unions or other private organizations, and only 32 percent agreed that all workers should have to join and pay dues when they share in the gains won by a union. In contrast, Americans polled by Gallup in 1957 were more likely to take the unions' side in answering these same questions, with corresponding levels of agreement of 62 percent, 73 percent, and 44 percent, respectively. Environics Institute, *Focus Canada 2011* (Toronto: Environics, 2012); Lipset and Meltz, *Paradox of American Unionism;* Gallup.

53. The percentage of Americans belonging to unions was 31.8 in 1955, 28.9 in 1975, and 11.1 in 2014. The percentage in Canada fell from 37.5 in

1984 to 31.5 in 2012. BLS, StatCan; Riddell, "Unionization"; Bruce Western, *Between Class and Market: Postwar Unionization in the Capitalist Democracies* (Princeton, NJ: Princeton University Press, 1997), 195; Susan D. Phillips, "Restructuring Civil Society: Muting the Politics of Redistribution," in Banting and Myles, *Inequality and the Fading of Redistributive Politics*.

54. Schlozman and Verba, *Injury to Insult,* 349; Bruce Western and Jake Rosenfeld, "Unions, Norms, and the Rise in US Wage Inequality," *American Sociological Review* 76 (2011): 517–18.

55. Sandra Susan Smith, *Lone Pursuit: Distrust and Defensive Individualism among the Black Poor* (New York: Russell Sage, 2007).

56. Alford A. Young Jr., *The Minds of Marginalized Black Men: Making Sense of Mobility, Opportunity, and Future Life Chances* (Princeton, NJ: Princeton University Press, 2004); Hochschild, *Facing Up to the American Dream*; Lamont, *Dignity of Working Men.*

57. Daniel Bell, *The Cultural Contradictions of Capitalism* (New York: Basic, 1976/1996), 327.

CHAPTER 6

1. Richard Sennett and Jonathan Cobb, *The Hidden Injuries of Class* (New York: Norton, 1972/1993).

2. In other words, the outlook was a mix of fraternal and meritocratic principles: loyalty to the group based on the group's social and spiritual criteria of merit. Michael B. Katz, *The Undeserving Poor: From the War on Poverty to the War on Welfare* (New York: Pantheon, 1989). See also Herbert Gans, *The War against the Poor: The Underclass and Antipoverty Policy* (New York: Basic, 1995).

3. Geoff Dench, "Reviewing Meritocracy," in *The Rise and Rise of Meritocracy,* ed. Geoff Dench (Malden, MA: Blackwell, 2006), 9.

4. *Aretē* can be defined broadly as "any sort of excellence or distinctive power," Pakaluk writes. "In Aristotle's time, the term would be applied freely to instruments, natural substances, and domestic animals—not simply to human beings. . . . The term connoted strength and success." Michael Pakaluk, *Aristotle's Nicomachean Ethics: An Introduction* (Cambridge: Cambridge University Press, 2005), 5; Jean-Jacques Rousseau, *A Discourse on Inequality* (New York: Penguin, 1984).

5. In children, however, empathy is not yet "overlaid with learned ideas," the Dalai Lama argues; they feel it explicitly, unconsciously. Tenzin Gyatso, *Ethics for the New Millennium* (New York: Riverhead, 1999), 64, 69.

6. Rand Ghayad, "The Jobless Trap," presentation at the Institute for Career Transitions, MIT Sloan School of Management, May 6, 2014; Alan B. Krueger, Judd Cramer, and David Cho, "Are the Long-Term Unemployed on the Margins of the Labor Market?" conference paper, Brookings Panel on Economic Activity, Washington, DC, March 20–21, 2014.

7. Benedict makes a classic distinction between shame, which arises from the negative judgments of others, and guilt, which arises from one's own negative judgment of oneself. I use the term *self-blame* to counterpose it with the blame

of others discussed in the next section. Ruth Benedict, *The Chrysanthemum and the Sword: Patterns of Japanese Culture* (Boston: Houghton-Mifflin, 1946). See also Thomas J. Scheff, "Shame and Conformity: The Defense-Emotion System," *American Sociological Review* 53 (1988): 395–406.

8. Pierre Bourdieu and Jean-Claude Passeron, *Reproduction in Education, Society and Culture* (London: Sage, 1977/2000), 210; Ofer Sharone, *Flawed System/Flawed Self: Job Searching and Unemployment Experiences* (Chicago, IL: University of Chicago Press, 2013). As Young wrote, "If they think themselves inferior, if they think they deserve on merit to have less worldly good and less worldly power than a select minority, they can be damaged in their own self-esteem, and generally demoralized." Michael Young, "Meritocracy Revisited," *Society* 31 (1994): 87–89.

9. Carrie M. Lane, *A Company of One: Insecurity, Independence, and the New World of White-Collar Unemployment* (Ithaca, NY: ILR, 2011), 157; Richard Sennett, *The Culture of the New Capitalism* (New Haven, CT: Yale University Press, 2006).

10. Sharone, *Flawed System/Flawed Self.*

11. Eli Chinoy, *Automobile Workers and the American Dream,* 2nd ed. (Urbana: University of Illinois Press, 1992).

12. Michael Young, *The Rise of the Meritocracy* (New Brunswick, NJ: Transaction, 1958/2011).

13. Katherine S. Newman, *Falling from Grace: The Experience of Downward Mobility in the American Middle Class* (New York: Free Press, 1988), 154–55.

14. Michèle Lamont, *The Dignity of Working Men: Morality and the Boundaries of Race, Class, and Immigration* (New York: Russell Sage and Harvard University Press, 2000).

15. Interestingly, in the Lynds' classic study of Middletown, unemployed workers there expressed self-blame—and as happened to be the case, the union had been driven out by the city's elite. Robert S. Lynd and Helen Merrell Lynd, *Middletown: A Study in American Culture* (New York: Harcourt, Brace, 1959).

16. For example, a study of unemployment in Massachusetts around the turn of the twentieth century found that "unemployment was far too common an occurrence to have automatically induced feelings of guilt, self-blame, or individual inadequacy." During the Great Depression, Katz notes, "poverty lost much of its moral censure as unemployment reached catastrophic levels," yet the "the idea of relief remained pejorative and degrading." Alexander Keyssar, *Out of Work: The First Century of Unemployment in Massachusetts* (New York: Cambridge University Press, 1986), 167; Katz, *Undeserving Poor,* 15.

17. In his work on the auto industry and deindustrialization in Flint, Dandaneau makes a similar point when he calls what amounts to the realistic perspective I describe "enlightened false consciousness," a view by unions that they need to adapt pragmatically and defensively to changes in the market "in order to achieve immediate gains in security and power"—a stance he criticizes as an abandonment of efforts to rebel against the system. Steven P. Dandaneau, *A Town Abandoned: Flint, Michigan, Confronts Deindustrialization* (Albany: SUNY Press, 1996).

18. Barry Schwartz, *The Paradox of Choice: Why More Is Less* (New York: Ecco, 2004).

19. As Schulz and Robinson point out, the postwar period was an aberration for this reason, too. Jeremy Schulz and Laura Robinson, "Shifting Grounds and Evolving Battlegrounds: Evaluative Frameworks and Debates about Market Capitalism from the 1930s through the 1990s," *American Journal of Cultural Sociology* 1 (2013): 373–402.

20. Daniel Bell, *The Cultural Contradictions of Capitalism* (New York: Basic, 1976/1996), 293, 295.

21. For example, a study of college students finds that those whose families had less income had worse financial literacy. Haiyang Chen and Ronald P. Volpe, "An Analysis of Personal Financial Literacy among College Students," *Financial Services Review* 7 (1998): 107–128.

22. See Helaine Olen, *Pound Foolish: Exposing the Dark Side of the Personal Finance Industry* (New York: Portfolio, 2013), for a discussion of the personal-finance industry, which compounds this problem of inequality. See Marion Fourcade and Kieran Healy, "Classification Situations: Life-Chances in the Neoliberal Era," *Accounting, Organizations, and Society* 38 (2013): 559–72, for a discussion of the stratifying effects of credit scores.

23. Kathryn Marie Dudley, *Debt and Dispossession: Farm Loss in America's Heartland* (Chicago, IL: University of Chicago Press, 2000); David Halle, *America's Working Man: Work, Home, and Politics among Blue-Collar Property Owners* (Chicago, IL: University of Chicago Press, 1984), 203, 222.

24. Paul Krugman, "How the Case for Austerity Has Crumbled," *New York Review of Books,* June 6, 2013.

25. Katherine S. Newman, *Declining Fortunes: The Withering of the American Dream* (New York: Basic, 1993).

CHAPTER 7

1. Karl Polanyi, *The Great Transformation: The Political and Economic Origins of Our Time* (Boston: Beacon, 1944/2001); Fred Block and Margaret R. Somers, *The Power of Market Fundamentalism: Karl Polanyi's Critique* (Cambridge, MA: Harvard University Press, 2014).

2. Erik Brynjolfsson and Andrew McAfee, *The Second Machine Age: Work, Progress, and Prosperity in a Time of Brilliant Technologies* (New York: Norton, 2014); Tyler Cowen, *Average Is Over: Powering America beyond the Age of the Great Stagnation* (New York: Dutton, 2013).

3. This is a future that Young predicted in his epilogue, in which the narrator is killed in the eventual revolt of the talentless, immiserated masses. Michael Young, *The Rise of the Meritocracy* (New Brunswick, NJ: Transaction, 1958/2011).

4. Richard Sennett and Jonathan Cobb, *The Hidden Injuries of Class* (New York: Norton, 1972/1993).

5. To some extent, there is a chicken-and-egg problem here. The interventionist policies of the New Deal (along with the shocks of economic crisis and global war) undoubtedly helped shape the moral perspective of the time. Programs like Social Security and Medicare changed the American public's

attitudes about what was "normal" for the good society to provide its citizens. Nevertheless, my point is that these pieces of legislation were initially established against a backdrop of widespread populist movements, even if their existence later brought more people to the cause itself—as Obamacare, perhaps, will convince those who receive its benefits to believe in universal health care. Katherine S. Newman and Elisabeth S. Jacobs, *Who Cares? Public Ambivalence and Government Activism from the New Deal to the Second Gilded Age* (Princeton, NJ: Princeton University Press, 2010).

6. That is, social scientists like Karl Polanyi and religious prophets like Matthew (Matthew 12:25: "Every kingdom divided against itself is brought to desolation; and every city or house divided against itself shall not stand").

7. James S. Fishkin, *Justice, Equal Opportunity, and the Family* (New Haven: Yale University Press, 1983).

8. In 2013, Switzerland voters opposed, by a 2–1 margin, a measure that would have restricted executive salaries to twelve times that of the lowest-paid worker. However, earlier in the year voters passed a measure to ban bonuses and golden handshakes and to require companies to consult shareholders on executive compensation. Peter Stamm, "Why the Swiss Scorn the Superrich," *New York Times*, November 22, 2013.

9. Dana Cloud, *We Are the Union: Democratic Unionism and Dissent at Boeing* (Urbana: University of Illinois Press, 2011).

10. Matthew A. Crenson and Benjamin Ginsberg, *Downsizing Democracy: How America Sidelined Its Citizens and Privatized Its Public* (Baltimore, MD: Johns Hopkins Press, 2002).

11. Anthony H. Winefield, Marika Tiggeman, and Helen R. Winefield, "The Psychological Impact of Unemployment and Unsatisfactory Employment in Young Men and Women: Longitudinal and Cross-Sectional Data," *British Journal of Psychology* 82 (1991): 473–86; Jesse Rothstein, "Unemployment Insurance and Job Search in the Great Recession," *Brookings Papers on Economic Activity* (2011): 143–213; Rebecca Blank, "Does a Larger Social Safety Net Mean Less Economic Flexibility?" in *Working under Different Rules,* ed. Richard B. Freeman (New York: Russell Sage, 1994).

12. Jonathan D. Ostry, Andrew Berg, and Charalambos G. Tsangarides, *Redistribution, Inequality, and Growth* (Washington: IMF, 2014).

13. William Julius Wilson, "Race and Affirming Opportunity in the Barack Obama Era," *Du Bois Review* 9 (2012): 5–16. This approach of "affirmative opportunity" should be distinguished from multiplying the criteria that job seekers are *expected* to have, which I discussed in chapter 2. In the former, we are talking about allowing a person's strengths in key but less conventional measures of merit, such as leadership abilities, to compensate for her weaknesses in more conventional measures.

14. For example, in the initial stages of the hiring process employers could require résumés to be stripped of names (and instead coded to be identifiable later) or have workers input their information in standardized forms.

15. Ofer Sharone, *Flawed System/Flawed Self: Job Searching and Unemployment Experiences* (Chicago, IL: University of Chicago Press, 2013).

16. For a discussion of early childhood education, savings incentives, and other relevant social policies, see chapter 8 of Katherine S. Newman and Victor Tan Chen, *The Missing Class: Portraits of the Near Poor in America* (Boston: Beacon, 2007).

17. James J. Heckman, "Schools, Skills, and Synapses," *Economic Inquiry* 46 (2008): 289–324; Paul Attewell and David E. Lavin, with Thurston Domina and Tania Levey, *Passing the Torch: Does Higher Education for the Disadvantaged Pay Off across the Generations?* (New York: Russell Sage, 2007).

18. For example, charter schools are touted as a way of equalizing opportunities for low-income children, but because applying to these schools requires parental initiative they may end up maintaining the inequalities that exist between the children of more and less bureaucratically savvy (i.e., more and less educated) parents.

19. Along similar lines, Brighouse and Swift argue that "we cannot rely on growth—an increase in the total amount of the good available—to bring about a gradual improvement in the absolute position of the worse off." Harry Brighouse and Adam Swift, "Equality, Priority, and Positional Goods," *Ethics* 116 (2006): 475.

20. Paul Osterman and Beth Shulman, *Good Jobs America: Making Work Better for Everyone* (New York: Russell Sage, 2011); Christopher Jencks, *Inequality: A Reassessment of the Effect of Family and Schooling in America* (New York: Basic, 1972), 8–9.

21. More "market-friendly" government efforts to create jobs, such as incentives to attract private-sector jobs, frequently lead to bidding wars between localities and the waste of taxpayer dollars on businesses that would have done what they did regardless of any help.

22. Leslie McCall, *The Undeserving Rich: American Beliefs about Inequality, Opportunity, and Redistribution* (New York: Cambridge University Press, 2013).

23. Paul Osterman, *Gathering Power: The Future of Progressive Politics in America* (Boston: Beacon, 2002); Mark R. Warren, *Dry Bones Rattling: Community Building to Revitalize American Democracy* (Princeton, NJ: Princeton University Press, 2001).

24. However, these groups are often funded or even organized by unions, and their work often assumes the presence of a strong state to enforce regulations. Annette Bernhardt, "When Employers Go Rogue: Unregulated Work and Policies to Raise Standards in the US Labor Market," Institute for Research on Labor and Employment seminar, University of California, Berkeley, March 11, 2013; Janice Fine, *Worker Centers: Organizing Communities at the Edge of the Dream* (Ithaca, NY: Cornell University Press, 2006).

25. Another possible reason for its dearth of electoral achievements is Occupy's leaderless structure. While this movement of movements by definition defies easy categorization, the kinds of protests it organizes suggest that its activists are uncomfortable with a few people or groups speaking for the many, and more interested in changing the culture than in working within the system. That said, Tea Party groups have also played up their lack of hierarchy or prominent

leaders as a sign of their grass-roots authenticity, yet they have maintained an intense focus on getting their own candidates elected to public office.

26. According to several NBC/*Wall Street Journal* polls, the percentage of Americans who considered themselves to be supporters of the Occupy Wall Street Movement dropped from 29 percent in November 2011 to 16 percent in April 2012.

27. Nietzsche called this "ressentiment," or "envy, anger, or hatred toward those at top"; conservatives like Margaret Thatcher have called it "cutting down the tall poppies." Daniel Bell, *The Coming of Post-Industrial Society: A Venture in Social Forecasting* (New York: Basic, 1973).

28. While egalitarianism and fraternalism speak to opposite kinds of affinity (universal or particular), grace morality, like meritocratic morality, is concerned with evaluation—but in its case, a *non*judgmental orientation diametrically opposed to the harshly critical perspective of meritocratic extremism.

29. Max Weber, *The Protestant Ethic and the Spirit of Capitalism,* trans. Talcott Parsons (London: Routledge, 1904–05/1992); Robert N. Bellah, Richard Madsen, William M. Sullivan, Ann Swidler, and Steven M. Tipton, *Habits of the Heart: Individualism and Commitment in American Life* (Berkeley: University of California Press, 1985).

30. In a similar, secular-friendly vein, the Dalai Lama has called for a "spiritual revolution"—not something "religious" or "otherworldly" but "a call for a radical reorientation away from our habitual preoccupation with self." Tenzin Gyatso, *Ethics for the New Millennium* (New York: Riverhead, 1999), 23–24.

31. Carl Sagan, *Pale Blue Dot: A Vision of the Human Future in Space* (New York: Random House, 1994). Apollo 14 astronaut Edgar Mitchell put this sentiment in blunter terms: "You develop an instant global consciousness, a people orientation, an intense dissatisfaction with the state of the world, and a compulsion to do something about it. From out there on the moon, international politics looks so petty. You want to grab a politician by the scruff of the neck and drag him a quarter of a million miles out and say, 'Look at that, you son of a bitch.'"

32. CEO compensation is only weakly associated with the size or profitability of firms, challenging the notion that the truly talented are being fairly rewarded. Charles A. O'Reilly III, Brian G. Main, and Graef S. Crystal, "CEO Compensation as Tournament and Social Comparison: A Tale of Two Theories," *Administrative Science Quarterly* 33 (1988): 257–74.

33. In terms of merit pay for teachers, 93 percent of elites supported it, compared to 77 percent in the general population. Benjamin I. Page, Larry M. Bartels, and Jason Seawright, "Democracy and the Policy Preferences of Wealthy Americans," *Perspectives on Politics* 11 (2013): 51–73.

34. See for example Jennifer E. Stellar, Vida M. Manzo, Michael W Kraus, and Dacher Keltner, "Class and Compassion: Socioeconomic Factors Predict Responses to Suffering," *Emotion* 12 (2012): 449–59.

35. Charles Murray, *Coming Apart: The State of White America, 1960–2010* (New York: Crown Forum, 2012); Charles Murray, "Why Economics Can't Explain Our Cultural Divide," *Wall Street Journal,* March 16, 2012.

36. Journalist Christopher Hayes identifies this as another paradox of meritocracy: those at the top become so isolated from the rest of us that their social

distance leads to bad, uninformed decisions. Christopher Hayes, *Twilight of the Elites: America after Meritocracy* (New York: Crown, 2012); Tom Perkins, "Progressive Kristallnacht Coming?" *Wall Street Journal,* January 24, 2014.

37. Matthew 22:21: "Render unto Caesar the things which are Caesar's, and unto God the things that are God's" (King James version). While the meaning of this biblical passage is complex, in my adaptation it encapsulates the essential distinction between two sets of laws, one material and one spiritual. David Platt, *Radical: Taking Back Your Faith from the American Dream* (Colorado Springs, CO: Multnomah, 2010), 136.

38. Juliet B. Schor, *The Overspent American: Upscaling, Downshifting, and the New Consumer* (New York: Basic, 1998); Brian Milani, "From Opposition to Alternatives: Postindustrial Potentials and Transformative Learning," in *Expanding the Boundaries of Transformative Learning: Essays on Theory and Praxis,* ed. Edmund O'Sullivan, Amish Morrell, and Mary Ann O'Connor (New York: Palgrave, 2002).

39. John Maynard Keynes, *Essays in Persuasion* (New York: Classic House, 1931/2009), 198.

40. Jean-Jacques Rousseau, *A Discourse on Inequality* (New York: Penguin, 1984); "The Great Philosophers: Jean-Jacques Rousseau," *School of Life,* October 23, 2014, theschooloflife.com.

41. Michael Marmot, *The Status Syndrome: How Social Standing Affects Our Health and Longevity* (New York: Times Books, 2004); Cristobal Young, "Losing a Job: The Nonpecuniary Cost of Unemployment in the United States," *Social Forces* 91 (2012): 609–34; Richard E. Lucas, Andrew E. Clark, Yannis Georgellis, and Ed Diener, "Unemployment Alters the Set Point for Life Satisfaction," *Psychological Science* 15 (2004), 18; Derek Bok, *The Politics of Happiness: What Government Can Learn from the New Research on Well-Being* (Princeton, NJ: Princeton University Press, 2010), 21; Andrew E. Clark, Yannis Georgellis, and Peter Sanfey, "Scarring: The Psychological Impact of Past Unemployment," *Economica* 68 (2001): 221–41. For a discussion of unemployment's scar effects on later earnings (and ways to diminish those effects), see Markus Gangl, "Scar Effects of Unemployment: An Assessment of Institutional Complementarities," *American Sociological Review* 71 (2006): 986–1013.

APPENDIX

1. Dan Zuberi, *Differences That Matter: Social Policy and the Working Poor in the United States and Canada* (Ithaca, NY: Cornell University Press, 2006); Ronald Inglehart, Neil Nevitte, and Miguel Basañez, *The North American Trajectory: Cultural, Economic, and Political Ties between the United States, Canada, and Mexico* (New York: Aldine de Gruyter, 1996), 20.

2. Zuberi, *Differences That Matter,* 199n11.

Index

action centers, 60–62, 286n34; as
    employers, 79; funding levels, 285n30;
    and labor unions, 212; peer programs
    in, 61, 84–85, 97–98; and policy
    implementation, 164; and psychological
    effects of unemployment, 97–98; and
    social capital, 61–62; U.S.-Canadian
    comparisons, 30, 62
activist government policies: and merito-
    cratic morality, 247, 248, 253, 310n27;
    New Deal, 243, 307–8n5; as politically
    infeasible, 32, 154, 228, 229, 243–44,
    307–8n5; postwar period, 16, 152; and
    solutions, 228, 242, 243–44, 307–8n5
adjustment programs: and anti-union
    movement, 62; peer programs, 61–63,
    84–85, 97–99, 236–37, 238, 286n36.
    See also action centers; social safety nets
Affordable Care Act (Obamacare), 90, 92,
    238, 290n4, 308n5
Alger, Horatio, 281n60
American Dream ideology, 10, 168,
    170–71, 199, 234. *See also* meritocratic
    morality
American Graduation Initiative, 285n29
amour-propre, 203
anger, 87, 89, 206–7
anti-union movement, 62, 177–78, 235
aretē, 202–3, 305n4
Armstrong, Elizabeth A., 288n54
"at will" employment, 156–57

austerity policies, 152, 218, 226
auto industry: advantages in social-safety
    net, 58, 285nn23–25; bailouts, 2, 162,
    165, 174, 285n24; decline of, 2, 12–13,
    37, 161, 184; Great Recession effects
    on, 2–3, 13, 39, 273n1; and recovery,
    6, 274n7, 276n22; technological
    advances, 44
auto-parts workers: Great Recession effects
    on, 2–3, 13, 273n1, 276n22; self-blame,
    213; and social safety nets, 103–4; views
    on labor unions, 179; vulnerability of, 96
automation. *See* technological advances
autoworkers: as hybrid class, 13–14,
    276n26; past educational choices of, 33,
    35, 42–43, 44, 47–48, 53, 75, 116, 205,
    210; public resentment of, 22–23, 186;
    as study subjects, 12–15. *See also* auto
    industry

bankruptcy, 225, 294n28
Beerman, Mitch (case study), 48, 92–93,
    129–30, 175–77
Bell, Daniel, 193, 217, 279nn42,43,
    281n63, 284n12
Benedict, Ruth, 305–6n7
Bernanos, George, 223
Big Three automakers: Great Recession
    effects on, 2, 13, 273n1; and social
    safety nets, 102, 290n7, 293n27. *See*
    also auto industry

313

9 780520 283015